THE
FAR WESTERN FRONTIER

The

New American Nation Series

EDITED BY

HENRY STEELE COMMAGER

AND

RICHARD B. MORRIS

THE
FAR WESTERN
FRONTIER

1830 ★ 1860

By RAY ALLEN BILLINGTON

ILLUSTRATED

NEW YORK

HARPER & BROTHERS • PUBLISHERS

To Mabel

Contents

Illustrations

Maps

Editors' Introduction

WHEN John Quincy Adams was a boy of fifteen he saw his father negotiate the treaty that recognized the independence of the United States with boundaries west to the Mississippi River. Before he died he witnessed the annexation of Texas, the occupation of Oregon, the settlement of Utah, and the extension of the boundaries of the United States westward to the Pacific by the Treaty of Guadelupe Hidalgo. No other nation had ever expanded so rapidly, or expanded so far without putting an intolerable strain upon the existing political and economic fabric. To the parochial view the history of the American West from 1830 to 1860 was kaleidoscopic and turbulent. But compared with the expansion of older empires, from that of ancient Rome to that of modern Spain, or to the process of making and remaking nations in the Old World, what is most impressive about the American expansion is the ease, the simplicity, and the seeming inevitability of the whole process.

For if sections are to America what nations are to Europe, we have, in the years which Professor Billington here surveys, the emergence and early development of a series of great empires: Texas and New Mexico, Oregon, Utah, and California, each with its own geography and climate, its own prehistory—the native races—and its own history, and eventually with its own peculiar society and economy. Indeed the differences in origin and early history that distinguished these four or five American empires are comparable to those which distinguished the history of the early civilizations of the Near East or the early history of distinct nations such as Denmark, Norway, Sweden, Holland, and Belgium. Yet within a single generation all of the embryonic American empires had coalesced into a single nation, one which had already absorbed, in its swift and triumphant course, half a dozen potential nations, from Maine to Florida, from the Old Northwest to the Deep South.

The pioneers who went into these different Wests took with them not only the language and religion, politics and law of the older East, but the techniques and culture as well. These they had to adapt to a series of drastically new environments, and under emergency pressure. It is this process of the adaptation of old tools and techniques and the transplanting of old institutions of church and state and economy that gives a singular fascination to the story that Professor Billington has to tell. And it is this instinctive and speedy transplanting of institutions that goes far to explain not only the rapid progress from primitive to civilized communities but the triumph over all this vast area of the principle of political uniformity and unity.

The men and women responsible for this transformation occupy a twilight zone in our history, belonging in part to an almost legendary past, in part to our own time. Marcus Whitman and Jason Lee, Colonel Doniphan and General Kearny, Stephen Austin and Sam Houston, Josiah Gregg and Jedediah Smith, Captain Bonneville and Brigham Young—these are like the legendary heroes of ancient times, like Jason of the Golden Fleece and Ulysses, like Hengist and Horsa, or perhaps like those founders of modern states, Charlemagne and Barbarossa, Alfred and Valdemar Victorious. Yet in another sense they belong indubitably to the modern era. They opened up the last West, conquered the Indians, built the roads and the railroads, transformed trapping and mining into a business, laid the foundations of modern commonwealths. When they first loom up on the horizon of history much of the West was the Great American Desert; when we bid them farewell they have brought California and Oregon into the Union as states, and organized the rest of this vast area into Territories.

The history of this West is, peculiarly, the happy hunting ground of the romancers and the myth-makers who emphasize the episodic and the eccentric, the dramatic and the heroic. Professor Billington neglects neither drama nor heroism, but he brings to their interpretation scientific objectivity and critical acumen. He sees the barbarizing aspect of the frontier as well as the civilizing; he does not apologize for aggrandizement by calling it Manifest Destiny, and he is not readily taken in by the bombast of self-proclaimed conquerors, or their partisans today. Nor, for all his narrative skill, is he content with narrative merely, but insistently directs our attention to the emergence of those institutions and the establishment of those patterns of economy and society that were to characterize the West down to our own time.

Needless to say this volume does not tell the whole story of the West from 1830 to 1860. Professor Billington has not attempted, for example, a full account of American diplomacy in the forties, nor a history of the causes and conduct of the Mexican War, nor an analysis of the impact of Texas and California on American sectional politics. These and other relevant subjects will be adequately dealt with in other volumes of this series.

This volume is one of the New American Nation Series, a comprehensive, co-operative survey of the history of the area now embraced in the United States from the days of discovery to the mid-twentieth century. Since the publication by the House of Harper of the American Nation Series, over half a century ago, the scope of history has been immensely broadened, many new approaches explored, and some developed. The time has now come for a judicious reappraisal of the new history, a cautious application of the new techniques of investigation and presentation, and a large-scale effort to achieve a synthesis of new findings with the familiar facts, and to present the whole in attractive literary form.

To this task the New American Nation Series is dedicated. Each volume is part of a carefully planned whole and fitted to the other volumes in the series; at the same time each volume is designed to be complete in itself. From time to time, doubtless, the same series of events and the same actors will be presented from different points of view: thus other volumes will touch on the political, the constitutional, and the cultural history of the years embraced in this volume. That all this may result in some overlapping is inevitable, but it has seemed to the editors that repetition is less regrettable than omission, and that something is to be gained by looking at the same period and the same material from different and independent points of view.

HENRY STEELE COMMAGER
RICHARD BRANDON MORRIS

Preface

IN PREPARING this volume I have had a dual objective in mind. One was to describe, as thoroughly as space limitations permitted, both the movement of settlers into the Far West and the national or world events which directly influenced their migration. The reader will seek in vain for a full account of American territorial expansion and diplomacy in the 1840's, or for a comprehensive history of the causes and course of the Mexican War. He will find described instead only aspects of those topics which immediately affected the settlement process. For the complete story he is referred to other volumes in this series that have a national rather than a sectional focus.

No less important has been my second purpose: to advance evidence pertaining to the generations-old conflict over the so-called "frontier hypothesis." Since 1893, when Frederick Jackson Turner read his essay on "The Significance of the Frontier in American History" before the Chicago meeting of the American Historical Association, scholars have argued interminably over his thesis that man in America was as much a product of the continent's unique environment as of his European heritage. That this dispute will ever be resolved is too much to expect, but no historian of the frontier process can neglect making his minute contribution to its solution.

Professor Turner held that the most unique feature of the American environment was an area of cheap land which constantly drew men westward. As they moved from civilized communities into the virgin forests or boundless prairies, the cake of custom was broken; there occurred in every pioneer settlement a reversion toward the primitive as settlers discarded the complex social controls needed in areas where men lived elbow to elbow. Eventually each of these communities began the slow climb back toward civilization as population thickened, but in doing so customs and institutions that had been proven ill-suited to the environment were abandoned. The result was a gradual "Americanization" of both men and their customs. "The existence of an area of free land," Turner wrote, "its continuous recession, and the advance of American settlement westward, explain American development."

Few historians today would accept this statement literally; modern theories of multiple causation force them to recognize American civilization as the product of a variety of factors, including the European heritage, the continuing impact of the wider world, and the contributions of the many national and ethnic groups represented in its population. Yet the question still remains: Was the environment that Turner emphasized a primary factor in creating the distinctive institutions of the United States and the unique characteristics of its people? Or, as some would maintain, is American civilization only a transplanted European civilization, modified slightly by changing world conditions and the impact of alien groups?

The Far West in the years before the Civil War provides an admirable laboratory for the testing of these divergent theories. In that vast land the pioneer faced not one but a checkerboard of differing environments; the settler on the lush fields of eastern Texas lived in a different world from the Mormon zealot who sought to bring the deserts of Utah into bloom, just as the fifty-niner who dug Colorado's gold faced environmental problems that bore little relation to those of a farmer in Oregon's green Willamette Valley. I have sought, in this book, to examine the impact of each of these environments on those who settled under their influence. Did trappers who sought wealth along the swift-flowing beaver streams of the Rockies respond differently to their wilderness world than the miners who panned the gold-bearing creeks of California's Mother Lode country? Did the Mormons who tamed the arid lands south of Great Salt Lake devise the same institutions and utilize the same artifacts as the overland pioneers whose plows broke the sod of the Sacramento and Willamette valleys? If the record shows that each band of frontiersmen responded in its own way to the strange new world of the Far West, a fragment of evidence has been produced in support of the "frontier hypothesis."

The materials necessary for this task were gathered largely in two great libraries of western Americana. To Dr. Stanley Pargellis, the director of the Newberry Library of Chicago, and to Mrs. Ruth Lapham Butler, the custodian of its magnificent Edward E. Ayer Collection, I am especially indebted for countless courtesies and endless aid. My debt to Dr. John E. Pomfret, director of the Huntington Library and Art Gallery of San Marino, and to Miss Mary Isabel Fry, the registrar of that institution, is equally great. Both contributed generously toward making happy and profitable the eight months that I spent amidst the rich resources that they administer. Not only did the officials of the Newberry and Huntington libraries give me free access to their collections, but they allowed me to photograph a number of illustrations from rare volumes in their possession, to be used in this book. Unless otherwise indicated, all of the illustrative material on the following pages was obtained in this way. I have also made extensive use of the collections of the Deering Library of Northwestern University, and have probed less fully into the holdings of a dozen other institutions.

Grants from the Committee on Research of the Graduate School of Northwestern University have aided me immeasurably both in gathering materials for this book and arranging those materials for publication. I should also mention that a portion of Chapter 3 was used in the Inaugural Lecture which I delivered as Harold Vyvyan Harmsworth Professor of American History at the University of Oxford, and was published in 1954 by the Clarendon Press under the title *The American Frontiersman. A Case Study in Reversion to the Primitive*. Finally I am indebted to Mrs. Richard S. Barnes, who not only typed the final manuscript but saved me from many inglorious errors by her proofreading skills.

R. A. B.

Evanston, Illinois

THE
FAR WESTERN FRONTIER

CHAPTER 1

The Mexican Borderlands

THE CONQUEST of America's Far West during the three decades that followed Andrew Jackson's elevation to the Presidency was only accomplished by the expulsion of well-established European peoples: the English, whose Hudson's Bay Company ruled supreme in the vast empire of the Columbia River basin; and the Spanish-Mexicans, whose ranchos and presidios stretched in a giant arc from the fog-shrouded harbor at San Francisco to the fertile fields of eastern Texas. Their uprooting was a victory for the Anglo-American frontier technique. Developed over the course of centuries by cocksure pioneers, this emphasized the role of the individual in the subjugation of nature, giving him free rein to exploit the new land for his own benefit. The frontier philosophy of Spain, on the other hand, subordinated the individual to the state; the pioneer's principal function was not to enrich himself but to help create a strong nation and a powerful church. In the clash between these two techniques—these two differing ways of life—the outcome was never in doubt. The conflict ended with the triumphant American frontiersmen planting their flag—and their crops—on the blue Pacific's shores, the conquered continent behind them.

Spain's basic frontier philosophy was responsible for the very existence of its northernmost outposts. In the seventeenth and eighteenth centuries, Mexico was the heartland of the Spanish empire in the New World; through its ports passed gold and silver and spices from all of Central and South America as well as from the distant Philippines, to be carried to the mother country in deep-laden treasure galleons. To protect this land, buffer colonies were hurriedly established with each new threat from a foreign power. At the end of the sixteenth century, when England's bold sea dog, Francis Drake, sailed his *Golden Hind* into the Pacific, a colony was planted in present-day New Mexico to seek and close the Northwest Passage which the Spaniards were certain Drake had found. A century later France's occupation of the mouth of the Mississippi was answered when the first Spanish settlements were scattered over the vastness of Texas; at about the same time the venturesome Jesuit missionary, Eusebio Francisco Kino, began the conquest of Arizona's deserts with the building of the mission of San Xavier del Sac. Between 1769 and 1776 California was occupied to forestall Russian fur traders who were creeping southward along the Pacific's shores from their bases in Alaska and the Aleutian Islands. Thus were Spain's northern outposts established, with the needs of the nation taking precedence over the hopes of individual frontiersmen for gain.

In this northward advance of the Mexican frontier, Spain's principal tool was the mission station. Jesuits, Franciscans, or Dominicans, in pairs or in small groups, and with a handful of converted Indians as aids, were encouraged to begin the assault on each virgin region. Selecting a spot in a fertile river valley or on a mountain plateau, where the natives seemed ready to accept conversion, the missionaries would fashion a chapel and a few small shelters where instruction could begin. Over the course of years these rude buildings were expanded into an extensive station, complete with a church of plastered adobe garishly ornamented to please the Indians; workshops for blacksmiths, weavers, and other craftsmen; irrigated fields; extensive pastures; and homes for the converts. For the missionaries' purpose was not only to Christianize but to civilize the Indians, converting them into sedentary farmers or craftsmen who would be capable of guarding Spain's far-flung domains. About many mission stations clustered ranchos and haciendas as herdsmen or farmers from Mexico moved in to exploit the lands pioneered by the friars. With the civilized Indians, these pioneers were the principal guardians of the northern rim of Christendom.[1]

Although founded by the central government for its own ends, the ring of settlements that fringed Mexico had by the 1820's drifted far from the control of the mother country. For this two things were re-

[1] Herbert E. Bolton, "The Mission as a Frontier Institution in the Spanish-American Colonies," *American Historical Review*, XXIII (1917), 42–61.

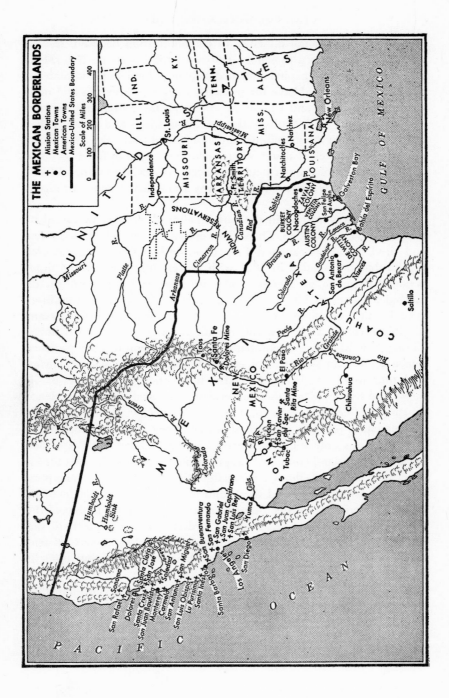

THE MEXICAN BORDERLANDS

+ Mission Stations
• Mexican Towns
o American Towns
— Mexico-United States Boundary

Scale of Miles
0 100 200 300 400

GULF OF MEXICO

New Orleans

Galveston Bay

Bahía del Espíritu

KY.

IND.

ILL.

TENN.

MISS.

LOUISIANA

St. Louis

MISSOURI

ARKANSAS

INDIAN TERRITORY

Fr. Smith

Natchitoches

Natchez

Sabine

Red

Nacogdoches

Independence

RESERVATIONS

Cimarron

Canadian

Red

BUKET COLONY

AUSTIN COLONY

DE WITT COLONY

San Felipe de Austin

Missouri

Platte

R.

Arkansas

R.

Brazos

Colorado

Guadalupe

San Antonio de Bexar

Nueces

R.

Saltillo

Santa Fe

Taos

Dolores Mine

Pecos

El Paso

Rio

Grande

Santa Rita Mine

Chihuahua

COAHUILA

Conchos

Rio

Green

R.

Colorado

NEW

MEXICO

RIO

SONORA

Tucson

San Xavier del Sac

Santa

Tubac

Yuma

Gila

Humboldt R.

Humboldt Sink

San Fernando

San Gabriel

San Juan Capistrano

San Luis Rey

San Diego

Los Angeles

San Buenaventura

Santa Barbara

Santa Inés

La Purísima

San Luis Obispo

San Miguel

San Antonio

Soledad

Carmel

Monterey

San Juan Bautista

Santa Clara

San José

Santa Cruz

Dolores

San Rafael

Sonoma

PACIFIC

OCEAN

UNITED STATES

sponsible. One was the difficulty of communication between Mexico City and the northern provinces. Between both Texas and New Mexico and the national capital stretched a thousand miles of arid plateau, much of it unpeopled save for scattered islands of Mexican and mestizo peons. Arizona and California were even more isolated. Sea voyages were made so difficult by the prevailing winds and currents that they were seldom attempted, while the only land trail—the Anza Road—traversed a parched desert where men and beasts suffered tortures. The inhabitants of the northern provinces, provincial as were all frontiersmen, naturally drifted rapidly away from their mother country's sway.

This drift was hurried in the early nineteenth century by turbulent conditions within Mexico. There the world-wide spirit of rebellion that had sired the American and French revolutions sparked a series of revolts that only ended in 1821 with the establishment of the independent Republic of Mexico under its popular leader, Agustín de Iturbide. These stirring events were watched with apathetic indifference by the inhabitants of the distant northern provinces. Texans placidly accepted their new role as citizens of the State of Coahuila-Texas; New Mexicans celebrated the transformation of their province into a republican state with a fiesta; Arizonians were scarcely aware that they were now living under the jurisdiction of the states of Sinaloa and Sonora. Only the Californians displayed any independence of spirit; after four years of misrule under Governor José María Echenadía, a juiceless cadaver of a man, they staged a rebellion in 1828 that was only suppressed after the rebel leader had "expended his ammunition and consumed his provisions."[2] During the next fifteen years nine more rebellions against the self-seeking incompetents sent north as governors revealed the Californians' lack of respect for their Mexican overlords. This constant turmoil, and the utter failure of the home government to provide either orderly rule or protection, did little to engender loyalty. More and more the settlers along Christendom's northern rim not only cared for their own affairs, but thought of themselves as virtually independent.

Thus isolated, they could develop the unique civilization that westward-thrusting American pioneers were soon to encounter—and engulf. Today's historian faces many problems as he tries to picture

[2] James Ohio Pattie, *The Personal Narrative of James O. Pattie of Kentucky* (Cincinnati, 1833), p. 293.

the pattern of life on this northernmost Mexican frontier. The Mexicans left few records of their daily affairs; newspapers were unknown among them and most were illiterate. Travelers who described their haciendas and villas were usually too prejudiced to leave an accurate record of what they saw. Nearly all were Americans, bred in a Puritanical atmosphere, who earnestly believed that any people who gambled constantly, preferred the riotous fandango to the stately waltz, and patronized cockfights on the Sabbath day had surely sold their souls to the devil; just as they sincerely felt that women who adorned themselves with barbaric jewelry, splashed color on their cheeks and lips, and smoked cigaritos incessantly were little better than strumpets, and deserved to be treated as such. Steeped in their own strict moral code, they failed to recognize that the mores of Mexican society were as ethically based as those of their own land. Their tendency was to condemn all that they saw or, in rare instances, to find life in the northern provinces unrealistically ideal. The truth lay somewhere between.

Yet even the most hostile Yankee critic yielded to the charms of life in Mexican California, where a bountiful nature, a genial climate, passive natives, and the home government's neglect allowed man to bask in an atmosphere reminiscent of the Garden before Adam's fall. The four thousand Mexicans who enjoyed this idyllic life occupied only a small portion of modern California, for the sun-dried San Joaquin and Sacramento valleys were largely unsettled. Instead population was concentrated along the narrow strip of coastland where streams cascading seaward from the mountains provided water for man and beast. There existed the three institutions that Spain had used in thrusting her frontier northward—the presidio, the pueblo, and the mission station.

The four presidios—at San Diego, Santa Barbara, Monterey, and San Francisco—were tiny forts of wood or mud where 307 soldiers and twenty-two officers lived their indolent lives. Each in time became the center of a cluster of homes, forming villages that rivaled the officially designated towns, or pueblos. San Diego, the southernmost of these settlements, was a tiny hamlet, its flat adobe houses straggling along the shores of an excellent harbor, and dominated by a towering mission station. Farther north, and clinging to the shores of a now-vanished river, stood the pueblo of Los Angeles, where fifteen hundred persons lived in the 1830's. Its flat-roofed houses overflowed the orig-

inal walled area in the town's center and straggled helter-skelter across
the flat lands beyond, all of them roofed with *brea* or tar from La Brea,
the pits on the village outskirts. In warm weather the tar dripped
stickily to the floors of homes, while travelers soon learned to follow
the practice of Los Angelenos and walk in the middle of dust-deep
streets to avoid the constant seepage. Still farther north the presidial
village of Santa Barbara nestled against the mountains, the twin towers
of its imposing mission reaching toward the sky. Beyond lay the unpre-
possessing provincial capital, Monterey, where twenty-two mud-walled
houses fringed the moon-shaped harbor, guarded by a presidio that
lay in partial ruin. Near the Santa Clara mission on the peninsula that
forms the southern half of San Francisco Bay was the pueblo of San
José, a village of one hundred houses that was noted for its riotous
inhabitants. The site of San Francisco was, in Mexican days, occupied
by a mission and presidio, but not until 1839 was the little town of El
Paraje de Yerba Buena (the place of the good herb) laid out on orders
from the governor. At the close of the Mexican era Yerba Buena, or
San Francisco as it was beginning to be called, boasted only twelve
houses and fifty inhabitants.[3]

More important than the pueblos or presidial towns in early California were the mission stations, for here life and economic activity
were centered. A chain of twenty-one of these imposing structures,
located fourteen leagues apart (that being a day's travel), stretched
from San Diego to the San Francisco peninsula. Their holdings were
astronomical, for at the height of their power they technically possessed all settled land in California, with the unsurveyed boundaries
of each overlapping with those to north and south. On these mission
lands lived thirty thousand Indians in 1830, all not only converted but
transformed into industrious farmers or herdsmen by the zealous Fran-
ciscan fathers. Farm produce and livestock were the principal products
of these neophytes, as fields were laboriously cleared and irrigation
ditches built. At the San José Mission a mile-square field produced so
much wheat that large quantities were exported each year, while
grapes grown in the mission vineyards were converted into a famous

[3] Excellent descriptions of the presidios and pueblos are in Alexander Forbes,
*California: A History of Upper and Lower California from Their First Discovery
to the Present Times* (London, 1839), pp. 199–228, and Eugene Duflot de
Mofrás, *Travels on the Pacific Coast* (2 vols., Santa Ana, Calif., 1937), I,
186–187.

aguardiente, or brandy, "as strong as the reverend fathers' faiths." [4] Livestock roamed the mission lands everywhere, until a French traveler could write that California was "but one continual pasture." [5] At the San Gabriel Mission the Indians cared for 150,000 cattle, 20,000 horses, and 40,000 sheep; while the holdings of all missions combined in 1834 amounted to 400,000 cattle, 60,000 horses, and 300,000 sheep and swine.[6] The Franciscans could look with pride on their accomplishments since 1769, when the first station was built by Father Junípero Serra.

The very prosperity of the missions led to their downfall. By the early 1830's influential Mexicans were demanding that their lands be secularized and the Indians allowed to care for themselves. Some unabashedly contended that the mission-controlled lands could better be used by others—meaning themselves; others argued that the natives were little better than slaves and that the dictates of humanity demanded their freedom; still more insisted that freedom from clerical control would benefit the Indians by forcing them to become self-sustaining citizens. These demands were realized in August, 1833, when the Mexican congress passed a Secularization Act, releasing the neophytes from all control and throwing the mission lands open to settlers. Governor José Figueroa of California pleaded in vain that the natives would squander everything on liquor and revert to a state of savagery. His protests were brushed aside; in 1834 the mission lands were opened to occupation.[7] As usual on frontiers, the land-hungry pioneers had triumphed over the forces of human decency.

The result was a wild carnival of looting. At mission after mission the freedom-crazed Indians slaughtered their herds in a carnage of sadistic glee; at the San Gabriel Mission alone thirty thousand animals were put to death for the mere joy of killing. For weeks thereafter the air around the stations was foul with the smell of decaying flesh, while over the next years settlers used the whitened bones to build miles of fences. In vain did the fathers plead with their charges that industry

[4] Guadalupe Vallejo, "Ranch and Mission Days in Alta California," *Century Magazine,* XLI (1890), 187.

[5] Charles F. Carter (ed.), "Duhaut-Cilly's Account of California in the Years 1827–28," *California Historical Society Quarterly,* VIII (1929), 149.

[6] Duflot de Mofrás, *Travels on the Pacific Coast,* I, 176–181.

[7] The decree ordering secularization is printed in Charles A. Englehardt, *The Missions and Missionaries of California* (4 vols., San Francisco, 1908–16), III, 523–530.

was still advisable even if no longer necessary; to a man they answered, "We are free. It is not our pleasure to obey. We do not choose to work." [8] Within a few weeks the Indians had returned to the hills and savagery from which they came, the patient labors of half a century wasted.

The secularization of the missions ushered in California's pastoral era. Land could be had now, almost for the asking, in grants of astronomical size. Under the Mexican Colonization Act of 1824, as amended by the *Reglamento* of 1828, any properly qualified person who could prove that he was a Mexican citizen, and had means to stock his holdings with cattle and horses, could apply to the governor for a rancho of from 4,428 acres (one league) to 48,708 acres (eleven leagues). In the next few years seven hundred rancho grants were made, most of them of eleven leagues or larger, as no restriction was placed on the size of family allotments. "It was," wrote an awed American observer, "a grand Mexican homestead law; and the chief complaint made about it was by the government, that the number of applicants for grants was not greater." [9]

During the remaining years of Mexican rule, the rancho was the principal economic unit, and the ranchero the all-powerful political figure. Each presided over a small principality to which he gave an appropriate name: Las Cienegas, Las Virgenes, La Brea, La Natividad. Each employed a *mayordomo,* who in turn supervised the labor of an army of semienslaved Indians who had been "persuaded" to do the actual work in return for food, cast-off clothing, and shelter in the *indiada,* a cluster of huts that closely resembled the slave quarters on southern plantations of that day. These workers performed a multitude of tasks. Most were *vaqueros,* or cowboys, who cared for the great herds of cattle and horses; others were farmers who produced the grain necessary to make the rancho self-sufficing; still others were house servants, blacksmiths, saddlemakers, tanners, leather workers, halter makers, tryers-out of tallow, and hewers of wood. All this cost the ranchero almost nothing, for the land was free, he paid his labor nothing, fencing and winter care were unheard of, and the cattle to

[8] Quoted in Theodore Hittell, *History of California* (4 vols., San Francisco, 1885–97), II, 190. An excellent contemporary account of these events is in Alfred Robinson, *Life in California; During a Residence of Several Years in That Territory* (New York, 1846), pp. 159–161.

[9] John S. Hittell, *The Resources of California* (San Francisco, 1863), p. 454.

stock his range could be borrowed from a neighboring rancho until he had bred his own herd.[10]

Society in this golden age of California's history remarkably resembled that in the ante-bellum South. In each case the pleasant lives of the upper classes depended on the labor of an inarticulate menial class, for there was little difference between the southern slaves and the California Indians. True, the Indians were free men technically, able to move from job to job if they wished, and entitled to compensation. Actually their liberty was nonexistent, for if they tried to run away they were hunted down and punished as the owner saw fit. Nor were they ever paid for their long hours of labor, save in the food and clothing that the ranchero allowed them. Working from dawn to dusk at the heavy tasks shunned by the Mexicans, living in squalid quarters with few physical comforts, and finding their only solace in cheap liquor, there is little wonder that the death rate among the Indians was twice that of southern slaves and four times that of the Californians themselves.[11] On them rested the burden of supporting a Mexican population that lived in indolence and luxury.

Certainly the rancheros' comforts were many. They lived in houses of adobe with plastered walls two or three feet thick and roof of tile. Among the wealthy the homes were luxurious imitations of Spanish country houses, with a central court bright with blooming flowers and cooled by a splashing fountain. By modern standards even these mansions were barren and uncomfortable, for furniture was plain and sparse in a land where sawmills were unknown, while heating of any sort was frowned upon as contrary to Spanish tradition and weakening for the body. Glass, like wood, was little used; a patch of rawhide covered the small windows and served as a door. Locks were unknown, for there were no thieves in this land of plenty.[12]

The food and clothes of the Californians were as primitive as their homes. Beef was their staff of life; no meal, from breakfast to supper, was complete without great strips of meat that had been roasted on spits over an open fire. *Frijoles,* or beans, were also eaten three times daily, while no meal was complete without a *tortilla*—a flat cake made

---

[10] Horace Bell, *Reminiscences of a Ranger, or Early Times in Southern California* (Los Angeles, 1881), p. 288.

[11] Robert W. Brackett, *A History of the Ranchos: the Spanish, Mexican and American Occupation of San Diego County and the Ownership of the Land Grants Therein* (San Diego, 1939), pp. 2–3.

[12] Nellie V. Sánchez, *Spanish Arcadia* (Los Angeles, 1929), pp. 88–93.

by mixing home-ground flour with water, then frying in cattle fat. This was simple fare, but appetites whetted by long hours in the open needed no stimulus. If the diet of the rancheros seemed mononotous, the clothes that they wore more than compensated, for their barbaric costumes rivaled the plumage of tropical birds. Short knee breeches were fashionable, ornamented with gold and silver buttons, and surmounting leggings of soft buckskin, dyed black or bright red, and elaborately embroidered. Shoes were always in contrasting colors, while a silk or velvet vest, garishly trimmed, was worn beneath a jacket of the same material. Over all was a broad-brimmed hat, held in place by a two-inch strap that was tied below the chin in the shape of a huge flower.[13]

For all their finery, the Californians lived simple lives that centered about their families. These were of gargantuan size, for children were no liability in a land of plenty; "the hen that has twenty chickens," they agreed, "scratches no harder than the hen that has one." [14] Each morning, when the twittering of birds signaled the coming of day, this brood was assembled with the house servants while the ranchero recited the *alba,* or prayer of the dawn, to thank the Lord for a night of peaceful repose. Then came a light breakfast—a *tortilla* and beef and chocolate perhaps—before the ranchero mounted his horse and rode away to supervise his estates, his *patrona* turned to the task of keeping the army of Indian servants busy, and the children scattered to play, for there were no schools in California to interfere with childish pleasures. With sundown the family assembled for the evening meal, then retired for the night, often as early as eight o'clock. Theirs was a healthy life. Long hours in the open, simple meals of meat and vegetables, no sweets, little alcohol save wine, and plenty of exercise meant that the rancheros and their wives remained robust until a ripe old age.

Self-centered as they were, the Californians still craved companionship that could not easily be provided on the widely separated ranchos; like the southern planters of that day, they tried to provide this by lavishing hospitality on all who knocked at their doors. No stranger

[13] Duflot de Mofrás, *Travels on the Pacific Coast,* II, 14–16; Robinson, *Life in California,* pp. 46–47; William H. Davis, *Seventy-five Years in California* (San Francisco, 1929), pp. 64–65; Richard H. Dana, Jr., *Two Years before the Mast; a Personal Narrative of Life at Sea* (New York, 1840), pp. 95–97.

[14] Walter Colton, *Three Years in California* (New York, 1850), p. 231.

suffered from want in that land. If he needed a new horse, he had only to rope one from the herd of the rancho he was passing, leaving his worn beast in exchange. If he needed food, he could kill a fat calf, for only the hide was valuable and the owner could retrieve that the next day. If he needed lodging, a knock on any door would bring the inevitable greeting: *"Pase, usted, la casa es suya"* (Enter, the house is yours). He could be sure, too, that his hosts would outdo themselves to provide him with the best of food and comfortable quarters, and as like as not send him on his way the next morning with a fresh horse and a basket bulging with a chicken or two, a loaf of bread, boiled eggs, and a bottle of wine or brandy. All that was asked in return was a word of thanks and a bit of gossip from the next community. Many a wanderer along the Camino Real, the trail that ran the length of California, lived like a king without a penny in his pocket. "Were the De'il himself to call for a night's lodging," one traveler wrote, "the Californian would hardly find it in his heart to bolt the door." [15]

So all-consuming was their love of companionship that even the distances in the sparsely settled rancho country could not keep them apart. With their horses, they bridged unbelievable miles in their endless search for amusement. For the horse was a part of their lives. Children learned to ride as soon as they could walk, and from that time on spent most of their waking hours in the saddle. Walking was unheard of; a Californian's first act in the morning was to saddle a horse which stood the day long at his front door, ready to be mounted even for a visit to a friend a few doors away. Everything was done on horseback; if a Mexican had to bring in firewood, he lassoed a bundle to drag to his door; if he was driven to murder (a rare occurrence), he shunned knife or gun but would rope his victim and drag him to his death. And what horsemen they were! They rode always at full gallop, no matter how short the distance, and if necessary could keep that speed up all day long. A Californian thought nothing of riding 150 miles in a day, pausing every few miles to catch a fresh mount in some neighbor's field, releasing his worn beast to find its way back to its owner. Gay young blades might ride all day at such a pace, dance all that night and day and through the next night, then ride home again at a furious gallop on the day following.[16]

[15] *Ibid.,* pp. 222–223; Sánchez, *Spanish Arcadia,* pp. 351–358.
[16] Duflot de Mofrás, *Travels on the Pacific Coast,* II, 11–13; Robinson, *Life in California,* pp. 93–94; Nicholas Dawson, *Narrative of Nicholas "Cheyenne"*

The mobility attained by such feats of endurance allowed a bustling social life to exist, for in that land of abundance pleasure was more eagerly sought than wealth. Wherever men gathered—at a rodeo or wedding or funeral—impromptu contests were devised, usually for horsemen. Perhaps a chicken would be buried with only its head projecting while riders swept down at full gallop and tried to snatch off the head. Perhaps a rawhide marker would be stretched across the ground, then horsemen approach at full gallop and stop their horses as soon as they touched the marker. Perhaps a hunt would be organized, with lasso and knife as the only weapons. To lasso a bear and drag the snarling beast through a town was the ambition of every sportsman, although chases after wild elk or horses or bulls were exciting enough to attract disciples. Horse racing, of course, was universal, while a unique form of bullfighting was also popular. This was performed on horseback, with each rider seeking to avoid the animal's furious charges by so narrow a margin that the horns actually grazed the horse's flesh. Fights between bulls and bears were common at all gatherings, often with one of the bull's forelegs strapped to a hind leg of the bear. Men, women, and children watched these savage encounters, bet enthusiastically, and argued for months afterward over the merits of the combatants. Betting, indeed, was usual at all contests, for the average Californian would bet on anything; travelers saw small children wagering the buttons on their clothes until they had none left to hold their shirts together.[17]

In few periods of history have men lived so well and with so few restraints upon them. Yet to a more progressive people, their happy existence was by no means perfect. In all their rich country there was no post office, no newspaper, no magazine, no theater, no art gallery, no school. Even the wealthiest rancheros signed their deeds with a cross; not one among them could enjoy escape into literature or experience the thrill of learning. True, the Californians were contented with their lot. Why, they asked, should we train lawyers when there is no litigation, engineers when there are no bridges to build, teachers when the children are happy without book learning? Ignorance might

---

Dawson: *Overland to California in '41 and '49, and Texas in '51* (San Francisco, 1933), p. 39.

[17] Colton, *Three Years in California*, pp. 92, 214–218; Carter (ed.), "Duhaut-Cilly's Account of California," pp. 152, 229–230; Robinson, *Life in California*, pp. 102–105.

be blissful, but man leads only half a life when he ignores the mind in his pursuit of bodily pleasures.

Even more dangerous was another fundamental weakness in the social structure. Life in pastoral California was *too* easy. Lulled into a sense of false security by the plenty that surrounded them, the rancheros became increasingly lazy, increasingly indolent, increasingly backward. Heroes or martyrs were not molded by such an existence. Yet the day was not far distant when heroes would be needed to turn back the hordes of aggressive Americans who came pressing in upon California from their eastern homes.

Nor was indolence confined to California alone, although in the other northern provinces of Mexico poverty rather than abundance bred laziness among the people. The deserts and mountains of Arizona provided a grim setting for one of the most backward regions. There good times had alternated with bad since the beginning of the eighteenth century, for each advance of the mining or agriculture frontier was soon pushed back by attacks from the fierce Yuma and Apache Indians. These reached a climax during the 1820's, when turbulent conditions within Mexico kept troops at home. One by one the Arizona missions were abandoned during those trying years, until by 1830 the only centers of population were at Tubac and Tucson, where adobe-walled presidios guarded the handful of brave souls who dared defy native wrath. The ranchos and mines near these outposts provided some wealth, but the lot of the pioneers contrasted sadly with those who lived from California's riches.[18]

New Mexico's golden age was also dying in the early nineteenth century. New Mexico was populous enough; her 44,000 inhabitants (in 1827) were ten times as many as those of California or Texas. But the nature of the economy dictated that most would live in poverty while a very few enjoyed great wealth. Sheep raising was the principal industry, with some four million woollies pasturing on the ranchos that stretched along the upper valley of the Rio Grande between El Paso and Taos. Most of these were owned by a few individuals who employed armies of herdsmen; the New Mexican who became governor in 1825 had herds of two million sheep tended by 2,700 workers, while his successor could boast of a mere million sheep divided into three hundred herds. Mining was scarcely less important. The Santa Rita Mines, on the site of present-day Silver City in southwestern New

18 Rufus K. Wyllys, *Arizona* (Phoenix, 1950), pp. 39–63.

Mexico, used a battalion of workers to produce a thousand tons of copper yearly. Almost as productive was the Real de Dolores Mine, discovered in 1827 in the Ortiz Mountains somewhat south of Santa Fe. Here almost pure gold was washed from the gravel, yielding the fortunate owners some $30,000 yearly.[19] Yet they, like the sheep rancheros and the operators of the irrigated haciendas that were scattered along the Rio Grande valley, shared little of this wealth with the mass of the people.

To make matters worse, New Mexico's economy was saddled with a government that was unblushingly corrupt and hopelessly archaic. Civil affairs were entrusted to a provincial governor who was usually chosen from among the great landowner class, and who looked upon his office as an open invitation to increase his own wealth at the expense of the poor. The little commercial activity that could endure under these conditions was rigidly controlled under an outworn system of mercantilism that dated from Spain's empire-founding days. Even without these restrictions, trade was difficult, for Mexico's nearest seaport was at Vera Cruz, reached over a tortuous mountain trail two thousand miles long. Little wonder that under these conditions New Mexico succumbed to a state of somnolent indifference to both progress and the outside world.

Yet the authorities of the Mexican Republic were wise enough to realize that a static society such as this could not long endure pressure from the dynamic United States. With a wisdom and foresight that is much to their credit, they began, as soon as independence was won, to revitalize their northern provinces. California they left alone; the Californians were too isolated and too smugly satisfied with their lot in life to accept change. The Arizona country they gave up as lost; why attempt to revive a region where every gain was wiped out by a new Indian attack? New Mexico, however, was worth saving. Clearly this could be accomplished by stimulating a commercial revival that would revitalize the region's economy. To this end, Mexico reversed the traditional Spanish policy and in 1822 threw open the doors of New Mexico to American trade, thus inaugurating that thriving commerce across the prairies that will be described later in this book. Texas was also worth saving, but here the problem required a different solution.

What Texas needed most of all was a larger population. In 1820

[19] Cleve Hallenbeck, *Land of the Conquistadores* (Caldwell, Ida., 1950), pp. 258–264.

only three tiny outposts stood guard over all that vast land: the presidial villa of San Antonio de Bexar, the presidio of Bahía del Espíritu Santo, and the pueblo of Nacogdoches. Of these the most important was the provincial capital, San Antonio, where lived the administrative agent for the government of Coahuila, of which Texas was a part, and where stood the leading presidio with its handful of half-starved soldiers. Both here and about the smaller towns of Nacogdoches and Bahía cattle raising was rapidly becoming the principal interest as enterprising Mexicans laid out ranchos and recruited *vaqueros* to watch their herds of rangy longhorns.[20] Most of the four thousand persons who lived in Texas in 1820 depended on cattle for their livelihood. Yet more settlers were needed if Texas was to prosper and play its role as a buffer against the aggressive United States.

The Mexican decision to open Texas to new settlers was no sudden whim, but the climax of a well-conceived policy that was taking shape even before the revolution of 1821. As early as 1801, when Napoleon's designs on Louisiana caused concern, plans for attracting immigrants were discussed, but nothing was done lest the newcomers be drawn entirely from the United States, rather than from all the world as Spain wished. These fears largely vanished with the establishment of the Mexican Republic. Relations with the United States were unusually cordial at that time, partly because the Mexicans were grateful for the aid given them in winning their independence, partly because they believed that a bond of union would perpetually exist between two republics dedicated to liberty, equality, and fraternity. They were aware, too, that the growing strength of their northern neighbor was due to the steady flow of immigrants from Europe, and were determined to follow a similar course.[21] A decision to open the gates of Texas to settlers from the United States was almost inevitable.

The decision was made easier by the few Americans who had already entered the province illegally. They began drifting across the Sabine River in 1815 and 1816 to settle on farms in the vicinity of Nacogdoches, paying as little attention to international boundaries as most frontiersmen. Another island of American settlement was formed

[20] Stephen F. Austin, "Journal of Stephen F. Austin on His First Trip to Texas, 1821," *Quarterly of the Texas State Historical Association*, VII (1904), 286–307.

[21] Mattie A. Hatcher, *The Opening of Texas to Foreign Settlement, 1801–1821* (Austin, 1927), pp. 286–292; Eugene C. Barker, *Mexico and Texas, 1821–1835* (Dallas, 1928), p. 10.

on the south bank of the Red River at about the same time when a
band of Missourians crossed from Arkansas to appropriate lands. Their
numbers were increased after 1825, when the country just north of the
Red River was allotted the Choctaw Indians as a reservation, forcing
squatters already there to cross to the Texas side.[22] A turbulent, unruly
crew, these pioneers of East Texas fitted in well with the half-wild
Mexicans of that distant frontier and helped convince the Mexican
government that Americans would be acceptable, if not exactly desirable, additions to the sparse Texan population.

So it was that when a request came to open the gates, an affirmative
decision was inevitable. This came from Moses Austin. Born in Con-
necticut in 1761, Austin had drifted westward to Spanish-owned Missouri in 1798 and there become a citizen. Aware that this would give
him a unique advantage in dealing with Mexican officials, he set out
for San Antonio in December, 1820, and there laid his plans before
the Texan governor. He wished, Austin told the governor, to renew his
allegiance to Mexico and to introduce a colony of three hundred
settlers into Texas, all of them pledged to become loyal Mexican citizens. Such a request was naturally welcomed, for this seemed a cheap
means of increasing the population just at a time when such a move
was being considered by the governmental leaders. The governor sent
the plan to his superiors with his blessing; sitting as a provincial depu-
tation in Monterrey on January 17, 1821, they quickly gave their
approval. Austin, elated with his success, started at once for Missouri
to recruit his colony, but on the way he sickened and died of exposure
and exhaustion.[23]

His death transferred the glory of founding the American settlements in Texas to his twenty-seven-year-old son, Stephen F. Austin.
By nature, if not by training, Stephen Austin hardly seemed destined
as a colony builder. Slight and lean of build, with the delicate features
and stately head of a scholar, he was sensitive to a fault and by habit
unduly introspective. His scholarly instincts had been sharpened by a
good education and by a training in music that left him an excellent
flute player. It is not surprising that he found few friends among the

[22] Hatcher, *The Opening of Texas,* pp. 332–333; Rex W. Strickland, "Miller
County, Arkansas Territory, the Frontier that Men Forgot," *Chronicles of
Oklahoma,* XVIII (1940), 12–34; XIX (1941), 37–54.

[23] Eugene C. Barker, *The Life of Stephen F. Austin, Founder of Texas, 1793–
1836* (Nashville, 1925), pp. 25–88.

rough frontiersmen that he was destined to lead, or that his life was to be a lonely one. Yet his sensitivities did not prevent him from becoming one of the most successful colonizers in American history. Charitable, tolerant, affectionate, and extremely loyal, he was a natural leader of men. All who knew him praised Austin for his fairness, his honesty, and his calm judgment; all recognized him as a statesman of proven ability and a diplomat of unsurpassed skill. Few men were as well fitted to lead turbulent pioneers to their new homes while keeping peace with unpredictable Mexican officials to whom distrust was second nature.[24]

As soon as he learned of his father's death, Austin hurried to Texas, where the governor received him kindly, assured him that the land grant was his, and authorized him to select a site for the proposed colony. After extensive explorations, he decided to locate his colonists in the valleys of the Colorado and Brazos rivers, where the soil was deep, the climate gentle, and rivers available to transport produce to the sea. This determined, Austin set out for New Orleans to recruit his first settlers. This proved easy; no sooner had he arrived than he was besieged by so many requests that he could, as he wrote, have taken fifteen hundred families rather than the three hundred authorized by his grant.[25] As many as possible were loaded aboard a sailing ship, the *Lively*, with orders to land at the mouth of the Colorado River, build a small fort, and plant a crop of corn. Austin himself journeyed northward to Natchitoches, where more applicants awaited him. With the cream of this group he started overland to the Colorado River, which was reached in December, 1821. To his disappointment he found no trace of the *Lively*; not until later did he learn that the ship had reached the mouth of the Brazos by mistake, and there disembarked its passengers.[26] Austin and his 150 followers faced the first winter in their new land without the corn they had counted on for food.

They survived those months and planted their crops that spring, but new troubles awaited their leader. In March, when he visited San

[24] *Ibid.,* pp. 523–524.

[25] *Ibid.,* p. 92.

[26] The reminiscences of a passenger on the *Lively* are in W. S. Lewis, "Adventures of the *Lively* Immigrants," *Quarterly of the Texas State Historical Association,* III (1899), 1–32, 81–107, and the ship's journey is described in Lester G. Bugbee, "What Became of the *Lively?*" *Quarterly of the Texas State Historical Association,* III (1899), 141–147.

Antonio, he learned that the letter from the Texan governor authorizing him to plant his colony had not been confirmed by the governor's superiors at Monterrey. A journey to Mexico City was the only answer. Although ill-equipped financially and fearful for the fate of his colonists, Austin started at once. Just as he reached the capital city, in August, 1822, a political controversy between Agustín de Iturbide, Mexico's liberator, and his numerous opponents flared into open conflict. For almost a year Austin waited while the antagonists debated in Congress or clashed in brief and bloodless revolutions; in the meantime he learned Spanish and showed his diplomatic skill by keeping on good terms with all the warring factions. At long last his patience was rewarded, for on April 14, 1823—almost a year after he reached Mexico City—his grant was finally confirmed. By its terms Austin was authorized to introduce three hundred families of good moral character who had agreed to accept the Roman Catholic faith. Each was to be given, without charge, one *labor* (177 acres) of land for farming and an additional seventy-four *labors* for stock raising, making a total of one *sitio,* or square league. Austin, in return for his services, was authorized to collect 12½ cents an acre from the settlers, and was promised a bonus of 65,000 acres for each two hundred families brought in.

His jubilant mood was dampened when he reached his colony again in August, 1823. Few newcomers had arrived, as uncertainty concerning land titles had discouraged immigration; a drought in the summer of 1822 ruined crops; and attacks from the fierce Karankawa Indians of the coast and the equally savage Tonkawa tribe of the interior had taken their toll. With his accustomed energy, Austin led two expeditions against the Indians, forcing them to agree not to come east of the Lavaca River, then turned his attention to recruiting new settlers. Advertisements in most of the western newspapers of the United States brought a steady stream of applicants, all of whom were carefully screened before admission. If a newcomer could prove that he was moral, industrious, and sober, and was willing to swear to support the constitution of Mexico, he was allowed to select the land that he wanted. This done, Austin supervised the surveys, accepting payment for his services in "horses, mules, cattle, hogs, peltry, furs, bees wax, home made cloth, dressed deer-skins," and even, on rare occasions, money.[27] "No one," he wrote at the time, "was turned away, or ever

27 Barker, *Life of Austin,* pp. 100–101.

waited for his title, because he was poor." [28] His care in selecting applicants and his constant supervision were destined to pay handsomely,
for few frontier settlements could match his in the industriousness and
morality of the settlers.

Gradually the colony took shape under his watchful eye. Its center
was the little village of San Felipe de Austin, laid out on the banks of
the Brazos River to serve as a seat for government and trade. About
this radiated the farms of the colonists, all of them nestled in the rich
bottom lands of the Brazos, Colorado, and Bernard rivers, with grazing land extending into the uplands on either side. By the end of the
summer of 1823 some three hundred families had been settled—the
"Old Three Hundred" as they are known in Texas history.[29] Their
success inspired a general influx during the following winter, until a
count in the spring of 1824 showed the colony's population to number
2,021. Their coming led Austin to petition the Mexican government
for an additional grant; this was allowed in February, 1825, when he
was authorized to bring in another five hundred families.[30]

Austin's success inspired imitators. Seemingly speculators had everything to gain and nothing to lose by securing Texas lands. Prospective
settlers swarmed throughout the Mississippi Valley. There the effects
of the Panic of 1819 still deadened commerce and depressed agriculture, turning the faces of the more aggressive westward. There land
prices were high, for the Land Act of 1820 required a cash payment
of $1.25 an acre. Why pay such prices when Austin's newspaper adver-
tisements promised them good land for the asking only a few miles
away? Texas, too, could be reached without an arduous journey.
Those who could not afford water travel could drive their wagons
over the rolling prairies without fear of bogging down in mudholes or
swamps. "The roads are all in a state of nature," one wrote, "yet so
smooth is the surface, and so gently undulating is the face of the
country, that in dry weather, better roads are not found anywhere." [31]

[28] *Ibid.*, p. 151.

[29] Eugene C. Barker, "Notes on the Colonization of Texas," *Southwestern
Historical Quarterly*, XXVII (1923), 108–119; Lester G. Bugbee, "The Old
Three Hundred," *Quarterly of the Texas State Historical Association*, I (1897),
108–117.

[30] Austin secured three additional contracts, one in 1827 authorizing him to
import one hundred families, one in 1828 for three hundred families, and one
in 1831 for eight hundred Mexican and European families. Barker, *Life of
Austin*, pp. 141–142.

[31] A. A. Parker, *Trip to the West and Texas* (Concord, N.H., 1835), p. 164.

Here, then, was the opportunity waiting land agents who cared to imitate Stephen Austin's example. Nor did they have to endure his difficulties in obtaining grants. On August 18, 1824, the Mexican Congress enacted a National Colonization Law which, in effect, turned over to the states the unoccupied lands within their borders, to be disposed of as they decreed, stipulating only that no foreigners be settled within twenty leagues of an international boundary or ten leagues of the coast, and that no person be given more than eleven leagues of land. Acting under this authority, the State of Coahuila-Texas, of which Texas was a district, adopted its land law on March 24, 1825. This opened the state to all Christians of good moral and personal habits who were willing to swear allegiance to Mexico, and exempted newcomers from taxes for ten years and from customs duties for seven years. Immigration was to be handled by land agents, or *empresarios,* who were promised a premium of five leagues (22,130 acres) of grazing land and five *labors* (885 acres) of farm land for each one hundred families they introduced. The *empresario* was authorized to give each family, free of charge, a league of land, including a *labor* of farm land. He could, under the law, introduce no more than eight hundred families, while his grant was to be forfeited if he did not settle at least one hundred families within six years.[32]

News of this law sent a swarm of speculators hurrying to Saltillo, the Coahuila-Texas capital. Nor were they disappointed, for in one day—April 25, 1825—the governor awarded *empresario* contracts for the settlement of 2,400 families, while additional contracts granted over the next four years provided for the introduction of seven thousand families. Many who received these plums were fly-by-night speculators whose only ambition was to sell their rights to others; still more lacked the skill or resources to live up to the agreed-upon terms. Even those with the will and means to bring in families faced almost insurmountable obstacles. Chief among these was the established success of the Austin colony; colonists preferred to seek land there, where they were assured of neighbors and Stephen Austin's skilled leadership, rather than on the lands of an unknown *empresario.*

Yet some did live up to their contracts, and nearly all helped stimulate migration into Texas. Of those who succeeded, the most prom-

[32] The national law of 1824 is printed in H. P. N. Gammel, *Laws of Texas* (Austin, 1898), I, 97–98, and the Coahuila-Texas law of 1825, *ibid.,* I, 99–106.

inent was Green DeWitt, whose grant lay southwest of Austin's on the Lavaca and Guadalupe rivers. There, about the town of Gonzales, he planted 161 families before his contract expired in 1831. Others who enjoyed some success were David C. Burnet, Joseph Vehlein, and Lorenzo de Zavala, whose lands lay in the Sabine and San Jacinto valleys of East Texas, where immigrants often preferred to stop rather than journey farther westward. Eventually they succeeded in settling enough families to live up to the terms of their contracts.[33] Nearly all of the other *empresarios* were forced to surrender their grants with nothing but empty pockets to show for their efforts.

Their sacrifices were not in vain, for their newspaper advertisements and personal appeals lured a steady stream of settlers to Texas between 1825 and 1830. Nearly all came from west of the Appalachians and south of the Ohio; Stephen Austin estimated that of the eight hundred families in his settlement in 1830, only one hundred were from the Atlantic seaboard states and of these only twenty from the Northeast.[34] But come they did, as the "Texas fever" raged in the lower Mississippi Valley. By 1830, 4,428 persons lived in Stephen Austin's colony, while the combined American population on the other *empresario* grants was almost as large. Mexico had succeeded in its avowed objective—revitalizing the Texan economy by building up population there—but Mexican officials were already wondering whether their action would not soon cost them dearly.

Well might they wonder, for by this time the American frontier was ready to engulf not only Texas but all the northern provinces that Mexico was guarding so jealously. By 1830 all the best lands east of the Mississippi River had been settled, save for islands in the south where Indians resisted expulsion and in the north where prairies provided an unfamiliar environment for the forest-adjusted pioneers. Moreover, two tongues of settlement were thrust west of the river, one in venerable Louisiana, which became a state in 1812; the other in Missouri, which followed in 1821. Arkansas, too, was receiving its first settlers, although statehood was not granted until 1836. There was still

[33] Mary V. Henderson, "Minor Empresario Grants for the Colonization of Texas, 1825–1834," *Southwestern Historical Quarterly*, XXXI (1928), 295–324; XXXII (1928), 1–28; Carl C. Rister, "The Rio Grande Colony," *Southwest Review*, XXV (1940), 429–441; Lois Garver, "Benjamin Rush Milam," *Southwestern Historical Quarterly*, XXXVIII (1934), 79–121; (1935), 177–202.

[34] Barker, *Life of Austin*, pp. 149–150.

good land to be had in the lower Mississippi Valley, of course, but that restless segment of frontier society that could never find contentment at home was already beginning to look ahead.

There they found not beckoning farm lands, but an insurmountable barrier. Along the western borders of Missouri and Arkansas lay the "Permanent Indian Frontier," established by Congress in 1825 as a haven for tribes that the government was then transplanting from the Old Northwest and from the Southeast. From the Big Bend of the Missouri to the Red River stretched a solid bank of reservations, all allotted perpetually to the red men, and all barred to immigrants. Even if this barrier could be surmounted, the Great Plains country beyond had been so often branded a "Great American Desert" by explorers that the pioneers had lost interest. As late as 1830 a government expedition reported that "the whole country is nothing but a barren waste, having no cultivable land, no game, no timber." [35]

Beyond the Indian barrier, beyond the Great American Desert, lay the rich lands of Mexico's northern provinces, weakly held by an "inferior" people. Beyond, too, lay the green valleys of the Oregon country, where land could be had for the asking. Once news of those riches reached the Mississippi Valley, there would be no holding back the pioneers. That news was carried to their doorsteps by traders, who were the first Americans to bridge the Great Plains and point the way west.

[35] Ralph C. Morris, "The Notion of a Great American Desert East of the Rockies," *Mississippi Valley Historical Review*, XIII (1926), 190–200.

CHAPTER 2

The Road to Santa Fe

SANTA FE, the sleepy little capital of provincial New Mexico, seemed an unlikely magnet to draw Americans westward into the Mexican borderlands. Long neglected by their rulers in distant Mexico City, its three thousand inhabitants lived their carefree lives with little concern for the rest of the world. Yet in Santa Fe were centered the commercial activities of some forty thousand New Mexicans, all of them starved for manufactured goods that their mother country could not provide. Why should they be denied cutlery and clothes and Yankee gimcracks, especially when they had gold and silver and furs aplenty for payment? So reasoned merchants of the Mississippi Valley in the 1820's. The inevitable result was the founding of the Santa Fe trade. For two decades great caravans of wagons, laden with goods of every description, regularly plied the thousand-mile-long trail between Missouri and New Mexico, bringing back good profits to enterprising merchants and revealing to all the United States the weakness of Mexico's hold upon its northern provinces. The trails blazed by the traders were soon to be followed by conquering armies.

Long before such a trade was feasible, the vision of commerce between Santa Fe and the Mississippi Valley had inspired venturesome pioneers. During the early years of the nineteenth century several bands of traders, undaunted by Spain's rigid exclusion of all foreign merchants from its territories, tried to reach Santa Fe, only to be turned back by Spanish troops. These efforts were renewed after 1810, when the short-lived Hidalgo Revolt inspired rumors that mercantile restrictions had been removed. One party of nine or ten men under Robert McKnight, James Baird, and Samuel Chambers reached the New Mexican capital in 1812, only to learn that Spanish officials were still in control and that they must repent their sins in a Chihuahua jail. Two St. Louis merchants, Auguste P. Chouteau and Julius De Munn, fared little better when they ventured too near the closed city in 1817. Arrested by a band of soldiers while camped on the upper Arkansas River, they were hustled off to Santa Fe, and only released after a trial that resulted in the confiscation of $30,000 worth of their furs and trading goods.[1] The Spaniards would go to any lengths to keep *Americanos* out.

So it was that when William Becknell, a merchant from the frontier hamlet of Franklin in Missouri, organized the expedition that won him the title of "father of the Santa Fe trade," he had no thoughts of invading Spanish soil; his advertisement for men in the Franklin *Missouri Intelligencer* mentioned only "trading for Horses and Mules, and catching Wild Animals of every description." With the twenty or thirty plainsmen who responded, Becknell started west about September 1, 1821. Threading their way through plains black with buffalo, they followed the left fork of the Arkansas River; then struggled upward over the tortuous Raton Pass, where they spent two days rolling rocks aside to get their horses through. There they stumbled on an encampment of Mexican soldiers. Becknell, aware of the fate of earlier American traders in that borderland, could hardly believe his ears when he was greeted "with hospitable disposition and friendly feelings."[2] Not until the troops told him that Mexican independence had been won did he realize the full extent of his good fortune. Now, with Spanish restrictions removed, American traders would be welcomed at Santa Fe.

Becknell started for the New Mexican capital at once. Trading his goods for great bags of Mexican silver dollars, he was ready to start for home in early December, bearing word from the governor that all American traders would be welcomed. On January 29, 1822, Becknell and one frostbitten companion rode into Franklin, having pioneered a

---

[1] Early attempts to reach Santa Fe are described in Alfred B. Thomas, "The First Santa Fe Expedition, 1792–93," *Chronicles of Oklahoma*, IX (1931), 195–208; Isaac J. Cox, "Opening the Santa Fe Trail," *Missouri Historical Review*, XXV (1930), 30–66; and Joseph J. Hill, "An Unknown Expedition to Santa Fe in 1807," *Mississippi Valley Historical Review*, VI (1920), 560–562. The journal of the De Munn party is in "The Journals of Jules De Mun [*sic*]," *Missouri Historical Society Collections*, V (1927–28), 167–208, 311–326.

[2] Becknell's journal is most conveniently available in Archer B. Hulbert (ed.), *Southwest on the Turquoise Trail; the First Diaries on the Road to Santa Fe* (Overland to the Pacific Series, II, Denver, 1933), pp. 56–68.

shorter route along the Cimarron River to avoid the snow-clogged Raton Mountains. Saddle-weary though they were, their hardships were forgotten as they dumped heaps of dollars on the sidewalks of Franklin, while all the populace gathered to watch in goggle-eyed wonder. No one knows Becknell's profits, but one of his townsmen realized a $900 return on a $60 investment in the enterprise.

If William Becknell had not blundered into his role as "father of the Santa Fe trade," the title would not have been vacant long, for two other parties of merchants were hard on his heels when he entered New Mexico. One, led by Thomas James, a St. Louis storekeeper laden with textiles that he had salvaged when the Panic of 1819 drove him into bankruptcy, reached Santa Fe on December 1, 1821, only two weeks after Becknell. There he remained until June, vainly trying to unload his somber fabrics on the color-loving Mexicans. Close behind James was a third party under Jacob Fowler and Hugh Glenn, both experienced plainsmen, whose twenty followers had intended to trade with the Indians of the southern Rockies. While camped at the site of Pueblo, Colorado, on December 30, 1821, they were visited by Mexican troops who informed them (as Fowler wrote in his inimitable language) "that the mackeson province Has de Clared Independence of the mother Cuntry and is desirous of a traid With the people of the united States." [3] Hurrying southward to Taos and Santa Fe, they plied a brisk trade until June, 1822, when they were ready to start homeward, well satisfied with their profits.

William Becknell, Thomas James, and the Glenn-Fowler party had opened the Santa Fe trail, but before trade assumed importance the traders must map a satisfactory road, improve transportation methods, and devise a profitable trading formula. In helping solve these problems, Becknell did much to justify his title as father of the trade. With twenty-one men and three heavily loaded wagons, he launched his second expedition from Franklin on May 22, 1822. Knowing the impossibility of pulling wagons up the steep trail to Raton Pass, Becknell led his caravan south and west after crossing the Arkansas River. This route took the party straight across the Cimarron Desert, a fifty-mile-wide waste where alkaline dust tortured the men and reduced the mules to near panic. For a time the traders resigned themselves to

[3] Elliott Coues (ed.), *The Journal of Jacob Fowler* (New York, 1898), p. 95. The James expedition is described in Thomas James, *Three Years Among the Indians and Mexicans* (St. Louis, 1916), pp. 94–135.

death in this desolation, but a stray buffalo that had just drunk deep in the Cimarron River crossed their path, and water drunk from the dead beast's stomach gave them strength to reach the river. Twenty-two days later they entered San Miguel, a Mexican settlement fifty miles from Santa Fe, where they paused to "salute the inhabitants with 3 rounds from our rifles, with which they appeared much pleased." [4] At Santa Fe trade was brisk, allowing the party to return to Franklin that fall with comfortable profits. More important was the fact that Becknell had not only pioneered the route used by future traders, but had demonstrated that wagon travel over the plains was feasible.

Only one problem remained to be solved: How could the traders protect themselves from marauding Indians, who molested the Becknell party in 1822, and who robbed of many of its animals the one party that ventured westward the year following? Their answer was to unite all traders in one party large enough to overawe the attackers. Word went out in the winter of 1823–24, urging all who intended to visit Santa Fe that summer to gather at the hamlet of Mt. Vernon, Missouri, in mid-May. The caravan that straggled out of that frontier outpost on May 25, 1824, contained twenty-five wagons carrying goods worth $30,000 and was guarded by eighty-one men. This time the journey was made without difficulty; Santa Fe was reached on July 28, and by September 24 the traders were back in Missouri with $180,000 in gold and silver and $10,000 worth of furs to reward their efforts.[5]

From this time on the trade followed a regular pattern, with one or two caravans from Missouri reaching Santa Fe each summer, and after 1826 similar Mexican caravans operating in the other direction. Each year the number participating in this commerce of the prairies increased, and each year the volume of goods involved mounted steadily. In 1830, 120 men made the journey in sixty wagons; in 1831, two hundred were involved, and the caravan of one hundred wagons carried goods worth $200,000.[6] William Becknell had launched a com-

    [4] Josiah Gregg, *Commerce of the Prairies* (2 vols., New York, 1844), I, 22–24.
    [5] The chronicler of this expedition was M. M. Marmaduke, whose "journal" is in Hulbert (ed.), *Southwest on the Turquoise Trail*, pp. 69–77.
    [6] Hiram M. Chittenden, *The American Fur Trade of the Far West* (3 vols., New York, 1902), II, 508–510, lists all expeditions during this period.

mercial enterprise that was daily bulking larger in the economic life of the West.

These developments did not long escape the attention of the region's leading political spokesman, Senator Thomas Hart Benton of Missouri, who was ever alert to the needs of his constituents. Visiting Missouri in the summer of 1824, he learned that the traders would welcome military protection as well as government help in improving their trail westward. When he returned to Washington that autumn he sponsored a bill that appropriated $20,000 to buy peace from the tribes along the trail, and an additional $10,000 to mark and improve the highway.[7] The three commissioners named to carry on negotiations reached Franklin early in 1825, where they hired thirty-three experienced frontiersmen after warning off all applicants who were "gentlemen coffee drinkers, and those unable to saddle a horse or cook their victuals." [8] On July 4, 1825, the little party left Franklin, accompanied by the cheers of the town's entire population.

The actual surveys began at Fort Osage, a government post in western Missouri; as they moved westward the commissioners sought the best fords over streams, leveled down the banks of canyons to make crossing easier, and threw up mounds of earth at regular intervals to mark the trail. Occasionally, too, they stopped to negotiate with the Osage and Kansa Indians, allotting goods and cash in return for promises that the traders would not be molested. Thus the party moved westward, out along the Arkansas River to Chouteau Island, southward to the Lower Spring of the Cimarron to avoid the Cimarron Desert, and on to the Mexican border, which was reached in early September. There the party stopped while one of the commissioners, George C. Sibley, pressed on to Santa Fe to seek permission to continue the surveys across Mexican territory. When this was granted in the summer of 1826 work was resumed, and was not concluded until well into 1827, when the final report was presented to the Secretary of War.[9] Glowingly as this described the work of the commissioners, little actually had been accomplished. The treaties with the

[7] *Register of Debates,* 18th Congress, 2nd Session, Appendix, p. 123. Petitions asking for such legislation are in 18th Congress, 2nd Session, *House Executive Document* No. 79, pp. 1–5.

[8] Frederick A. Culmer, "Marking the Santa Fé Trail," *New Mexico Historical Review,* IX (1934), 80.

[9] This report, together with diaries of the expedition and other materials, are in Kate L. Gregg (ed.), *The Road to Santa Fe* (Albuquerque, 1952).

Osage and Kansa Indians did stop some attacks, but the dread
Comanche and Pawnee tribes were still on the warpath. Nor did the
trail marked by the surveyors please the traders, for they preferred to
risk the horrors of the Cimarron Desert rather than follow the roundabout route to Chouteau Island.

Despite this failure, the Santa Fe trade was ready to enter its golden
era. Its "cradle" during these years was at first the Missouri town of
Independence, for the unpredictable Missouri washed Franklin away
in 1828, and after 1833 the village of Westport Landing, still farther
west on the banks of the Big Muddy. None of these hamlets delighted
the eye of travelers; Independence, for example, was a "much scattered town," perched crazily on the banks of the river, and containing
"five or six rough log-huts, two or three clap-board houses, two or
three so-called hotels, alias grogshops, a few stores, a bank, printing
office, and barn-looking church." [10] Yet in the spring of the year, as
the caravans prepared to depart, few cities in America could rival their
life and color. Singing roustabouts carrying crates and bales from rows
of steamships at the wharves, husky packers piling wagons high with
merchandise, armies of drivers training their animals for the trail
amidst torrents of profanity, all created an atmosphere of hustle and
excitement that both charmed and terrified travelers.

To the seasoned traders, there was method in all this, for no explorer in unknown lands prepared for a journey more carefully than
they. Upon the wagons that carried their merchandise and the animals
that pulled the wagons they lavished infinite attention. Most of the
vehicles used were "Murphy wagons," manufactured by a famous St.
Louis concern of that name. Great, cumbersome affairs they were,
three feet wide and up to sixteen feet long, with rear wheels that
stood five feet tall and were circled by iron tires four inches thick.
Over the blue-colored wagon boxes were stretched canvas covers of
white, to protect the three-ton load of goods. Each wagon was pulled
by ten or twelve mules, or by three or four yokes of oxen. The latter
could pull heavier loads, but they fared less well on the western
prairies where grass was scant, while their hoofs frequently gave out
on the rough trail, even when shod with moccasins of rawhide.
Within a few years after freighting began, the Santa Fe trail was lined
with their skeletons. The mules, on the other hand, thrived on the

[10] Charles J. Latrobe, *The Rambler in North America* (2 vols., London,
1836), I, 128.

sparse fare offered by buffalo grass and could stand any hardships, but their stubborn refusal to move unless the spirit willed exhausted the vocabularies of even the most gifted drivers.[11]

At last the loading was completed, the oxen and mules trained, and the traders ready to start westward, usually in mid-May when the prairie grass was turning green. As wagon after wagon rolled out of town the whole populace turned out to cheer, to shout, and to drink toast after toast to the traders' success in the fiery whisky of the frontier. "Even the mules," wrote an observer, "prick up their ears with a peculiarly conceited air." [12] There was no organization at this stage of the journey, for here there was no Indian danger and each trader made his way to Council Grove, 150 miles from Independence, by himself. Danger might be lacking, but troubles were not, for the spring rains usually turned the prairies into quagmires. Often the mud was so deep that wagons sank to their hubs while bullwhackers swore as they unhitched teams from two or three wagons and fastened them to one, in order to "double team" or "triple team" onto drier ground.

Ten days were usually required for the journey to Council Grove on the banks of the Neosho River. When the last wagon had lumbered in, the traders met together beneath the tall trees to organize for the journey westward; for like all frontiersmen beyond the pale of the law, they must weld themselves into a compact group that would assure protection for life and property. First a captain was elected after a round of speeches and campaigning that would do justice to a political campaign back in the "states." "Even in our little community," observed Josiah Gregg, the author of the classic description of life on the trail, "we had our 'office seekers' and their 'political adherents,' as earnest and as devoted as any of the modern school of politicians in the midst of civilization." [13] Usually common sense prevailed over political pressure, for most of the caravan captains elected were experienced plainsmen. Next four lieutenants were chosen to command the four columns into which the wagons were divided. Finally the men selected from four to eight "sergeants of the guard," on whom fell the unpleasant task of assigning and enforcing the nightly watches. By this thoroughly democratic process, each caravan was converted into an efficient unit, able to cope with the dangers that lay ahead.

[11] Gregg, *Commerce of the Prairies*, I, 35–36.
[12] Benjamin F. Taylor, *Short Ravelings from a Long Yarn, or Camp March Sketches of the Santa Fe Trail* (Chicago, 1847), pp. 3–4.
[13] Gregg, *Commerce of the Prairies*, I, 45.

The effectiveness of the organization varied from caravan to caravan. The frontiersmen, unaccustomed to social restraint, were seldom willing to accept orders from anyone, let alone an elected captain who had been one of the "boys" until his elevation. His orders, as Josiah Gregg observed, were "often obeyed or neglected at the caprice of the subordinates." [14] Only in time of danger did the caravan coalesce into an effective unit, and even then the captain was likely to be deposed at a moment's notice if he blundered. Under these circumstances his office was hardly one to be envied. Each day he had to direct the order of march, determine the route, choose the best crossings for streams, select the spots for "nooning" and the night's camp, and supervise the guards. Every decision that he made could be, and frequently was, disputed by his self-willed followers, while every error in judgment earned him a round of profane abuse. Nor could he remonstrate, for he was utterly without power to enforce his orders. Yet men were always eager for the post, for the democratizing influence of the frontier could not stifle the urge to command.

Thus organized the caravan plodded forward in a mile-long column, covering ten or twelve or even fifteen miles a day, as landmark after landmark was ticked off by the bullwhackers: Diamond Spring, where they usually stopped the first night out from Council Grove, Cottonwood Creek, Turkey Creek, the Little Arkansas River, Cow Creek. Gradually the face of the country changed as they left the tall grass of the prairies behind and emerged on the semiarid Great Plains. As they approached the Arkansas River they entered a belt of sand hills, corrugated by the wind to form "various and fanciful shapes"; just beyond they emerged at the Great Bend of the Arkansas, 270 miles from Independence. This was a welcome sight to the road-weary travelers, for they were in buffalo country now where their monotonous diet of sowbelly, tough bread, and lyelike coffee could be supplemented by juicy roasts of hump ribs. The great herds were everywhere; "every acre was covered, until in the dim distance the prairie became one black mass, from which there was no opening, and extending to the horizon." [15] Often the caravan camped for a day or so beside the majestic Arkansas, with its fringe of green cottonwoods, while the men

[14] *Ibid.*, I, 45.
[15] Jacob S. Robinson, "Sketches of the Great West. A Journal of the Santa-Fé Expedition in 1846," *Magazine of History,* Extra Numbers, XXXII (1927), 223.

gorged on fresh buffalo or "jerked" strips of the meat to carry with them.

Where buffalo lived, so did Comanche and Pawnee, and the traders carefully lived up to the injunction of one old trapper who told them to "keep your eyes skinned now." [16] If Indian "sign" was detected, the captain usually ordered a different order of march, with the caravan moving forward in four parallel columns, and with mounted scouts ranging ahead alert for danger. If hostile "redskins" were sighted the bullwhackers whipped up their animals and each column was wheeled about to form one side of a hollow square, a maneuver that took only a few minutes. With the animals within this enclosure and the wagons pushed together, the traders were safe in a fortress that could withstand any attack.[17] This method of travel was one of the significant contributions of the Santa Fe traders to the conquest of the Far West, for its adoption by the overland pioneers allowed thousands of persons to cross the plains in safety.

Marching in this fashion, the caravan moved westward along the north bank of the Arkansas, past a sandstone pinnacle known as Pawnee Rock, where the traders paused to carve their names, past stream after stream that coursed southward to join the Arkansas. These were difficult crossings, for the rivers had cut deep into the arid soil to form clifflike banks, some of them thirty feet high. At each, every wagon was lowered with hind wheels locked, a yoke or two of strong "wheelers" hitched to the rear axle, and all the men who could lay hold tugging frantically; but even with these precautions the descent was sometimes so rapid that teams tangled or oxen were run over. Not infrequently, too, wagons overturned as they were being pulled across the river beds, forcing the party to camp for a day or two while their contents were spread in the sun to dry. But on went the caravans, past "the Caches," mossy pits on the river banks where an earlier party had hidden its goods when caught in a snow storm, until at last they reached the Cimarron Crossing of the Arkansas, four hundred miles from Independence.[18]

[16] "Wetmore Diary" in Hulbert (ed.), *Southwest on the Turquoise Trail,* p. 187.
[17] Gregg, *Commerce of the Prairies,* I, 61, 101–102; Taylor, *Short Ravelings from a Long Yarn,* pp. 34–35.
[18] The exact route of the trail as surveyed by a commission in 1913 is described in Kansas State Historical Society, *Eighteenth Biennial Report of the Board of Directors* (Topeka, 1913), pp. 107–116.

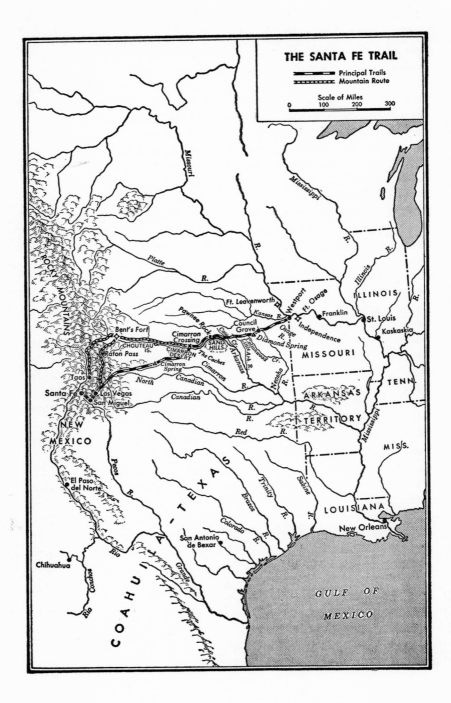

THE SANTA FE TRAIL

Principal Trails
Mountain Route

Scale of Miles
0   100   200   300

ROCKY MOUNTAINS

Missouri

Mississippi

Platte

R.

Illinois

ILLINOIS

R.

Pawnee Rock

Ft. Leavenworth

Kansas R.

Westport

Ft. Osage

Council
Grove

Franklin

St. Louis

Cimarron
Crossing

CHOUTEAU
IS.

SAND
HILLS

Diamond Spring

Independence

Kaskaskia

Bent's Fort

Raton Pass

CIMARRON
DESERT

The Caches

Cottonwood Cr.

Osage R.

Neosho R.

MISSOURI

Cimarron
Spring

Cimarron

Little Ark. R.

Arkansas

R.

ARKANSAS

TENN.

Taos

North

Canadian

R.

TERRITORY

Santa Fe

Las Vegas
San Miguel

Canadian

R.

Mississippi

MISS.

NEW

MEXICO

Pecos

Red

R.

R.

El Paso
del Norte

R.

T E X A S

Trinity

Sabine

LOUISIANA

Brazos

R.

R.

New Orleans

Chihuahua

Rio

Colorado

R.

San Antonio
de Bexar

C O A H U I L A

Rio

Grande

GULF   OF

Rio
Conchos

MEXICO

Here the trail turned abruptly southward to cross the river. This was always a trying experience, for the half-mile-wide Arkansas concealed treacherous beds of quicksand that shifted from year to year. These could only be avoided by following a twisting course, with sharp turns where wagons often overturned, especially as their boxes had been lifted to raise them above water level. "Double teaming" was always necessary; each wagon was pulled by twelve oxen goaded on by three or four drivers, and a file of men walked on each side ready to tug on mired wheels or hold the top-heavy vehicle upright if it started to tip. "A wagon," wrote one trader, "shakes and rattles by the sand washing from under the wheels as much as it would going over the worst cobblestone pavement." [19] Worse delays were encountered when the water was high; then one wagon box was calked and the goods of all the giant caravan floated across in this to keep them dry.

But still worse tribulations lay just ahead, for now the trail led across the fifty-mile-wide ocean of barren sand known as the Cimarron Desert, where there was "not a tree Bush or Hill of any kind to be Seen." [20] A day was spent preparing for this "water scrape"; draft animals were fed and watered, food was prepared, and every possible container was filled to the brim with water. The next morning the cry of "Catch up! Catch up!" rang out earlier than usual, and the dreaded march began. For the first five miles the wagons plowed through deep sand, then emerged on a flat plain where lizards scurried before them. Here the drifting sands covered all trail markers; until 1834, when a caravan crossed in such a heavy rain that its sun-baked ruts remained visible for years, captains steered by compass and frequently lost their way. Two or three days of this torture brought the traders near enough to the Cimarron River that their animals scented water. Then the thirst-crazed beasts often stampeded, overturning wagons and littering miles of the desert with precious merchandise.[21]

The worst was over when they reached the Cimarron, although many dreary miles lay ahead. For eighty-five miles the trail followed the river, then climbed for two hundred more through rock-strewn

[19] James J. Webb, *Adventures in the Santa Fé Trade, 1844–1847* (Glendale, Calif., 1931), pp. 55–56.

[20] Coues (ed.), *Journal of Jacob Fowler*, p. 151.

[21] Vivid descriptions of the desert crossing are in Gregg, *Commerce of the Prairies*, I, 71–74, and Hulbert (ed.), *Southwest on the Turquoise Trail*, pp. 72–73.

foothills where the dry air loosened the spokes and iron tires of the wagons, necessitating frequent stops as bullwhackers drove in white-oak wedges to hold the wheels together. Near the Red River crossing a band of merchants rode on ahead to purchase provisions, arrange warehouse storage, and "obtain an agreeable understanding with the officers of the customhouse." [22] As the caravan plodded on, the first signs of civilization were sighted: the little village of Las Vegas, where brown-skinned children skipped beside the wagons; the considerable settlement of San Miguel, perched on the banks of the silvery Pecos River. From San Miguel the trail climbed steeply to Glorieta Pass, but even the trials of double teaming were welcome now, for from the top of the pass the teamsters could look down on the town of Santa Fe, hugging against the Sangre de Cristo Mountains on the edge of a rolling plateau.

Hats flew, pistols sounded, and the bullwhackers' whips popped like gunfire at the first sight of their objective. "I doubt," wrote one traveler, ". . . whether the first sight of the walls of Jerusalem were beheld by the crusaders with much more tumultuous and soul-enrapturing joy." [23] The celebration was brief, however, for important preparations must be made. As the caravan waited the men washed their hands and faces, donned clean shirts, tied colorful handkerchiefs about their necks, and fixed new "crackers" to their whips. Then, when all was ready, the caravan wound its way down the six-mile-long hill that led into Santa Fe. All three thousand inhabitants of the city turned out to greet the traders with joyous shouts of *"Los Americanos!" "Los carros!" "La entrada de la caravana!"* How proudly the bullwhackers cracked their long whips as they guided their wagons through the throng with shouts of "gee-ho" and "ho-haw"; how eagerly they wound their way around the sun-baked plaza to La Fonda, the rambling inn where they could find cool shade, fiery Mexican beverages, and gambling tables to relieve them of the wages they were paid on arrival. [24]

While the wagoners gambled away their salaries or sported with the smiling *señoritas,* the proprietors busily disposed of their merchandise. This was a complex process, for something more than selling was in-

[22] Gregg, *Commerce of the Prairies,* I, 89; L. Bradford Prince, *Historical Sketches of New Mexico* (New York, 1883), p. 279.

[23] Gregg, *Commerce of the Prairies,* I, 110.

[24] *Ibid.,* I, 143–144; Taylor, *Short Ravelings from a Long Yarn,* pp. 144–147.

volved. The first task of each merchant was to reach an agreement on the customs duties he must pay. These varied from year to year according to the whim of the governor, and at times reached vast proportions. Traders might be asked to pay regular customs duties, a tax for each day they remained in Santa Fe, and a set sum for each wagon that they imported, as well as fines for bringing in goods that were specifically banned by Mexican law.[25] Nor did a merchant know until he arrived in Santa Fe whether the wagon tax that year would be $10 or $750. It is no wonder that customs collection degenerated into a game of wits between the traders and collectors in which honesty was as little heeded as the law.

Every merchant had two objectives: to smuggle as much as possible into Santa Fe without paying any duties, and to bribe officials into letting him import the remainder as economically as possible. Smuggling was accomplished by hiding contraband goods in wagons with false bottoms, or by loading the items on pack mules that were led into the city along unguarded mountain trails. Mexican officials made a pretense of stopping such practices by riding out to greet the caravan before it reached Santa Fe, but their coming was always anticipated. This practice, however, allowed them to ride with the traders for a day or two while bribes changed hands. Seldom, if ever, after such a journey was a full duty charged the importers. Nor did this practice of "making *diligencia*," as the Mexicans called it, prey on the consciences of the merchants. Why, one asked, should they surrender their profits "for the sole use and benefit of his obesity, the Governor?"[26]

These delicate matters settled—usually after a week of negotiations —the merchandise was released from the customs house and sales could begin. Each trader wanted to sell as much as possible at high retail prices; hence he rented a store or set up a booth on the plaza and for four or five weeks bartered continuously as he disposed of his stock of textiles, hardware, gimcracks, clothes, and other wonders from the Northeast's factories, receiving in return furs, mules, and gold or silver from the mines of New Mexico and Chihuahua.[27] If fortune smiled, a merchant watched his rainbow of bargains dwindle away rapidly; if not, he had to sell at wholesale to Mexican shopkeepers

[25] *Niles' Register*, XXXVI (July 25, 1829), 354.
[26] Taylor, *Short Ravelings from a Long Yarn*, p. 140.
[27] Merchandise used in the trade is described in 22nd Congress, 1st Session, *Senate Document* No. 90, pp. 8, 44, 53.

from nearby towns, or reload his wagon and move deeper into Mexico in search of a market. Most disposed of their goods by early autumn and were ready to start their return journey. The wagons were lighter now, with their loads of furs, blankets, and buckskin bags of gold or silver; hence travel was easier, allowing the caravans to reach Missouri well before snow fell.

There the merchants had only to reckon their profits to complete the year's work. During the early years of the trade this was a pleasant task, although returns later declined alarmingly. In 1824 the $35,000 worth of goods carried west sold for $190,000 in specie and furs, providing the traders with a profit of 300 per cent after transportation costs were deducted. In 1825 returns were almost as high. Thereafter they declined rapidly as competition for the limited Mexican market increased, averaging between 10 and 40 per cent, with occasional years of loss when Indian attacks or heavy customs duties increased expenses.[28] Nor did the traders themselves pocket all of these earnings. Most of them were small merchants or farmers who operated with little excess capital. Unable to arrange credit with the large wholesale houses of Philadelphia, they bought their supplies from storekeepers in Independence or St. Louis who specialized in goods "suitable for the Santa Fe trade," paying from 20 to 30 per cent above eastern prices. These merchants also advanced the traders credit, usually at 20 per cent or more yearly.[29] Few of those who made the arduous journey to Santa Fe grew rich under these arrangements.

This was especially the case as neither the precautions taken by the traders nor the 1825 treaties with the Osage and Kansa ended Indian attack on the caravans, always at heavy cost to the merchants. To the Pawnee of the Arkansas River country and the Comanche of the Cimarron valley, the long trains of wagons, following established routes at predictable times, were an irresistible temptation. Horse stealing, a profession of honor among Indians, was regularly practiced; often caravans were halted for days while merchants tracked down their stolen animals and bought them back at an outrageous price. More

[28] A statistical table showing the amount of merchandise carried west each year and the value of goods returned is in Gregg, *Commerce of the Prairies,* II, 160.

[29] Lewis E. Atherton, "Business Techniques in the Santa Fe Trade," *Missouri Historical Review,* XXXIV (1940), 335–341. The mechanics of the trade are illustrated in Ralph P. Bieber (ed.), "Letters of James and Robert Aull," *Missouri Historical Society Collections,* V (1927–28), 267–310.

serious was the loss of human life. The 1828 season was especially disastrous; forgetting their usual caution after a successful season, the merchants came straggling back that fall in a number of small parties, two of which were attacked by Comanche. Three traders were killed before the survivors straggled into Missouri with tales of hardships that sent a thrill of indignation coursing through the whole Mississippi Valley.[30]

From all the West rose a clamor for military protection; "savages," argued the Missouri legislature in a memorial to Congress, "are restrained by nothing but *force*." [31] The President responded by ordering Captain Bennet Riley, with 170 foot soldiers from newly established Fort Leavenworth, to accompany the 1829 caravan as far as the Mexican border. Riley's troops met the traders at Council Grove and for the next six weeks marched westward beside the slow-moving wagons. At the Arkansas River, the border between the United States and Mexico, there was grumbling among both troops and merchants when Riley gave the order to halt, for like all frontiersmen they paid scant heed to international boundaries. "This," one officer complained, "was like the establishment of a ferry to the mid-channel of a river." [32] These protests Captain Riley ignored as he watched the caravan cross the Arkansas and head away into the Cimarron Desert, then settled down with his soldiers to await the traders' return.

They were to taste excitement sooner than they knew. The train of thirty-eight wagons was only six miles from the Arkansas Crossing when it was attacked by fifty mounted Comanche. The traders managed to beat off the attack, with the loss of one man, but a rider was hurried back along the trail with the alarm. This time Captain Riley paid as little attention to the Mexican boundary as his most reckless follower; starting his troops forward on the double, he reached the camp at eleven that night, to find the traders tense with fear even though the Indians had fled after their first assault. The soldiers

[30] Narratives of survivors are in Henry Inman, *The Old Santa Fé Trail: The Story of a Great Highway* (New York, 1898), pp. 68–74, 77–85, and a list of all those killed or robbed on the trail between 1815 and 1822 is in 22nd Congress, 1st Session, *Senate Document* No. 90, pp. 81–86. The best modern account is in Otis E. Young, *The First Military Escort on the Santa Fe Trail, 1829; from the Journal and Reports of Major Bennet Riley and Lieutenant Philip St. George Cooke* (Glendale, Calif., 1952), pp. 15–29.

[31] 20th Congress, 2nd Session, *Senate Document* No. 52, pp. 1–3.

[32] Philip St. George Cooke, *Scenes and Adventures in the Army* (Philadelphia, 1859), p. 46.

marched with the caravan for two more days, then returned to the north bank of the Arkansas to await its return.[33]

Life in that encampment was anything but peaceful, for the Indians soon realized that they could attack the unmounted soldiers almost at will, then sweep away on their horses to avoid punishment. For two months Riley's men were under almost constant siege; during that time only two soldiers were killed, but they lost both horses and pride. "It was a humiliating condition," wrote one of the officers, "to be surrounded by these rascally Indians, who, by means of their horses, could tantalize us with the hopes of battle, and elude our efforts; who could annoy us by preventing all individual excursions for hunting, &c., and who could insult us with impunity." [34] Thus did the Army learn, at fearful price, that foot soldiers were useless in the Great Plains country. Little wonder the returning caravan was greeted with shouts of joy by the troops when it finally appeared on October 11, 1829, accompanied by five companies of Mexican cavalry who told of beating off one Comanche attack on the way. The return journey to the settlements was made without further adventures.

Despite its humiliating experiences, the Riley expedition accomplished much. Eastern opposition prevented the government from spending public funds to protect the traders during the next two years; but when two stragglers from the 1831 caravan were shot down by Pawnee and Comanche, the President hurried a report to Congress urging action.[35] The result was a measure, passed on October 15, 1832, authorizing the War Department to enlist a corps of mounted troops, or dragoons, for use on the western plains. A few of these rangers accompanied the 1833 caravan, and a larger number jogged westward with the one hundred wagons that made the journey in 1834. Captain Clifton Wharton, their commander, found to his surprise that his principal task was not to protect the traders but to guard peaceful Indians from bullwhackers who wanted to shoot down every red man on sight.[36]

The Santa Fe traders solved the Indian problem, partly through government help and partly by learning that they were safe only in

[33] Captain Riley's journal is in Fred S. Perrine, "Military Escorts on the Santa Fe Trail," *New Mexico Historical Review,* III (1928), 267–300.

[34] Cooke, *Scenes and Adventures in the Army,* p. 59.

[35] 22nd Congress, 1st Session, *Senate Document* No. 90, pp. 1–86.

[36] Wharton's report is in Fred S. Perrine, "Military Escorts on the Santa Fe Trail," *New Mexico Historical Review,* II (1927), 269–285.

well-organized caravans, but the task of continued peaceful dealing with the New Mexicans proved to be insurmountable. For this, turbulent conditions within Mexico and the increasingly strained relations between that country and the United States were responsible. As ill feeling mounted, between 1837 and 1845, restrictions on the trade multiplied so rapidly that it eventually died a natural death.

Trouble began in 1837, when changes in the governmental structure of the home country drove the New Mexicans to revolt. The revolution that followed was as complex and incomprehensible as many of those among Latin peoples—it eventually restored to power the same governor who had held office when it began—but it cost American traders heavily. Many were sent packing by one revolutionary faction or another before they had a chance to sell their goods. Again in 1841 they found themselves in disfavor when the ill-fated Santa Fe expedition of the Republic of Texas invaded New Mexico. Composed of both soldiers and merchants, this force was interested in trade rather than conquest, but the naturally suspicious Mexicans viewed it as a warlike move and hurried its members ingloriously off to the lockup. This was bad enough, for all Americans were thereafter looked upon with disfavor, but relations were further strained when a volunteer Texan army under Colonel Jacob Snively started north to avenge the capture of the Santa Fe expedition. In the sandhills just south of the Arkansas River this "gallant band of avengers" encountered and defeated a small Mexican force that was on its way to escort that year's caravan to Santa Fe, and then stayed there to wait for the Mexican trading caravan bound from Santa Fe to Missouri. Instead the American caravan appeared, with a sizable escort of dragoons under Captain Philip St. George Cooke, for the traders had been sufficiently alarmed by events along the borderland to demand military protection for the 1843 wagon train. Cooke's soldiers disarmed the Texans and sent them packing homeward, much to their disgust.[37]

These comic-opera conflicts were disastrous to the Santa Fe trade. The New Mexicans, with some reason, made no distinction between Texans and Americans; all were viewed now as open enemies of the

---

[37] Captain Cooke's journal of this expedition is in William E. Connelley (ed.), "Journal of the 1st Dragoon Escort of the Santa Fe Caravan, May 21 to July 21, 1843," *Mississippi Valley Historical Review*, XII (1925), 72–98, 235–249. Cooke's activities after the Snively party was dispersed are described in Otis E. Young, "Dragoons on the Santa Fe Trail in the Autumn of 1843," *Chronicles of Oklahoma*, XXXII (1954), 42–57.

state. In Taos, where many of the Mexican troops slain by Snively's attackers had lived, mobs attacked the hated *Americanos,* forcing them to flee for their lives. Amidst this tense atmosphere the governments of both Mexico and New Mexico hurriedly tightened trade restrictions. In April, 1842, a new tariff closed Mexico to more than fifty classes of articles and forbade the export of gold and silver bullion. This was followed by a presidential decree of August 7, 1843, closing the customs houses at Taos, El Paso del Norte, Presidio del Norte, and Chihuahua to all foreign commerce, thus restricting the market for American goods to Santa Fe. A week later the importation of another two hundred classes of items was forbidden. On September 23, 1843, foreigners were denied the right to engage in retail trade; three days later a tax of 6 per cent was levied on all gold and silver coins exported from the country.[38] Further trade under these repressive measures was virtually impossible. The few small caravans that defied Mexican restrictions and ignored the coming war between Mexico and the United States during the next few years were but travesties of the giant wagon trains that crossed the prairies in the golden era of the Santa Fe trade.

The traders of that happier day had earned their place in history. They had laid the basis for later overland migrations by demonstrating the feasibility of wagon travel across the plains and by perfecting the techniques that made such journeys reasonably safe from Indian attack. They had spread through the Mississippi Valley word of the weakness of Mexico's hold on its northern provinces and of the disloyalty of the New Mexicans. They had helped plant the impression in the minds of all frontiersmen that "greasers" were a lazy, indolent breed who had no right to the rich lands they occupied. When their work was done, everyone in the West who knew of the Santa Fe trade (and who did not?) firmly believed that the eventual conquest of the provinces of northern Mexico by enterprising Yankees was as inevitable as the sequence of day and night.

[38] These laws are described in the introduction by Ralph P. Bieber to Webb, *Adventures in the Santa Fé Trade,* pp. 24–25, and Lewis Atherton, "Disorganizing Effects of the Mexican War on the Santa Fé Trade," *Kansas Historical Quarterly,* VI (May, 1937), 115–119.

CHAPTER 3

The Era of the Mountain Men

WHILE Texan pioneers and Santa Fe traders were beginning their assault on the Mexican borderlands, another band of frontiersmen—the fur traders—were blazing their trails into the heartland of the Far West. Their hour of glory was brief; the trade flourished only between the mid-1820's and the early 1840's. But during those years the fur trappers played a heroic role in opening the land to more permanent settlers. Theirs was the task of spying out fertile valleys that needed only man's touch to yield bountiful harvests, of spreading word of the West's riches throughout the Mississippi Valley, of pioneering routes through mountain barriers, and of breaking down the self-sufficiency of the Indians by accustoming them to the firearms and firewater of civilization. When their day was done all the Far West was readied for the coming of the pioneer farmers.

Trappers used three jumping-off points when they began their invasion of the beaver country in the 1820's. One was the northern New Mexican outpost of Taos, an isolated village seldom visited by Mexican officials, who had a troublesome habit of insisting that hunters be licensed. From there they ran their trails eastward along the Pecos and westward across the Gila River valley; over these plodded bands of Mexican and American hunters led by such masters of their craft as Ewing Young, Céran St. Vrain, and George C. Yount, and immortalized by James Ohio Pattie, who recorded their adventures in a volume that mixed fact and fancy to become a classic of frontier literature. Skimming off modest fortunes in peltry as they moved, they penetrated as far as southern California by the end of the 1820's, leaving behind them a land so ruthlessly overtrapped that beaver were virtually exterminated.[1] As the hunters disappeared from the scene, victims of their own greed, their place was taken by Mexican traders. In 1829 a party of thirty-one men under Antonio Armíjo pioneered a path between Santa Fe and Los Angeles, swinging northward to avoid southern deserts and the uncrossable Grand Canyon country. Over this "Old Spanish Trail" moved regular caravans during the next fifteen years, carrying blankets and silver, and returning with horses and mules. By 1833 the trade was so extensive that California acted to prevent traders from "borrowing" mules and horses from the ranchos they passed.[2]

A second pathway into the beaver country began at Fort Vancouver, nestling against the banks of the broad Columbia River in the far Northwest. Built in 1824 by the venerable Hudson's Bay Company of England, this strategic outpost was under the command of Dr. John McLoughlin, a rawboned giant of a man with piercing eyes that gleamed from beneath a disordered patch of prematurely white hair, and "a beard that would do honor to the chin of a Grizzly." Genius of the trade that he was, Dr. McLoughlin helped devise the "brigade system" that allowed his "Honourable Company" to dominate the beaver streams of the Northwest. Every autumn, during the golden era of trapping, several giant processions wound their way out of Fort Vancouver, each containing dozens of trappers with their Indian wives, and each led by a "partisan" who proclaimed his exalted position by wearing a broadcloth suit, white shirt, high collar, and tall beaver hat. Some moved southward into the Sacramento and San Joaquin valleys of California; others tramped eastward along the Snake River to trap beaver in the heart of the northern Rocky Mountains. At the end of the 1820's, when competition with American trappers was reducing profits in the Rockies, Dr. McLoughlin began concentrating his brigades on the Pacific slope, but this withdrawal was only temporary. During the next decade the Americans were to

[1] James Ohio Pattie, *The Personal Narrative of James Ohio Pattie of Kentucky* (Cincinnati, 1831), *passim*. A critical study by Joseph J. Hill, "New Light on Pattie and the Southwestern Fur Trade," *Southwestern Historical Quarterly*, XXVI (1923), 241–254, demonstrates that many of Pattie's statements are not to be taken literally. The best study of the trade in the Southwest is Robert G. Cleland, *This Reckless Breed of Men: The Trappers and Fur Traders of the Southwest* (New York, 1950), *passim*.

[2] Armíjo's brief journal, together with other documents on this trade, are collected in LeRoy R. Hafen and Ann W. Hafen, *Old Spanish Trail: Santa Fé to Los Angeles* (Glendale, Calif., 1954), pp. 131–165.

find to their sorrow that the Hudson's Bay Company was still one of their most formidable foes in the battle for control of the West.[3]

These Americans reached the trapping country from the third jumping-off spot, St. Louis. From the day Lewis and Clark returned with tales of teeming beaver streams in the northern Rockies, traders had made their way up the Missouri to that hunting ground; but the trade did not come of age until the middle 1820's, when William Henry Ashley entered its ranks. A Missourian experienced in business and politics, Ashley sought to recuperate a fortune shattered by the Panic of 1819, first by sending trading parties to the upper Missouri and then, when Indian hostility made these unprofitable, by blazing a new trail to the central Rockies. The little band of pioneers under Jedediah Strong Smith that he sent westward in 1823 was the first to cross the Rockies in a westerly direction through South Pass, a broad highway through the mountain barrier that was to become the pathway of countless overland pioneers. More important from Ashley's point of view, Smith's party found the southward-flowing Green River, just beyond the mountains, to be rich in beaver. News of their find sent Ashley himself hurrying westward early in 1825. That year he devised the "rendezvous system" that was to dominate the fur trade during its heyday: trappers were sent out in small bands to trap the beaver streams, and then gathered at an agreed-upon spot each summer to trade their year's catch for trading goods sent westward by pack-horse caravan.[4]

From that day the rendezvous was a regular feature of the trade. Ashley brought out the trading goods in the 1826 caravan, returning with 123 packs of furs, worth enough to allow him to retire from the mountains forever. Before he left he sold his interests to three former employees headed by Jedediah Smith; during the next few years these partners sent trappers over the whole Rocky Mountain country in their quest for pelts. Forever seeking new beaver streams, Jed Smith led two remarkable expeditions westward, exploring the Colorado and

[3] The best study of the Hudson's Bay Company's strategy on the Pacific coast is in the introduction of Frederick Merk (ed.), *Fur Trade and Empire, George Simpson's Journal* (Cambridge, Mass., 1931). Important documents on the brigade system are in Alice B. Maloney (ed.), *Fur Brigade to the Bonaventura. John Work's California Expedition, 1832–1833, for the Hudson's Bay Company* (San Francisco, 1945), and E. E. Rich (ed.), *Peter Skene Ogden's Snake Country Journals, 1824–25 and 1825–26* (London, 1950).

[4] Harrison C. Dale, *The Ashley-Smith Explorations and the Discovery of a Central Route to the Pacific, 1822–1829* (Cleveland, 1918), pp. 85–90.

Gila rivers, trafficking with Mexicans in the interior valleys of California, and pushing northward as far as Fort Vancouver before rejoining his partners at the rendezvous in 1829. He could report few prospects for trade in the lands that he had seen, but he had gained a place in immortality as the most venturesome of all American explorers. A year later he and his partners were ready to retire from the West with fortunes that assured them lives of indolent luxury. At the 1830 rendezvous they sold their interests to a group of traders under Thomas Fitzpatrick, James Bridger, and Milton Sublette, organized as the Rocky Mountain Fur Company. Well was their retirement earned, for they, with Ashley, had devised the techniques that allowed the fur trade to enter its palmiest days.[5]

They had, moreover, conjured into existence a reckless new breed of men: the "free trappers," or "Mountain Men," as they loved to call themselves. These aristocrats of the wilderness spent their entire lives in the mountains, renewing contact with civilization only once each year when they visited the rendezvous to sell their furs and buy the few necessities that the forest could not provide. Calling no man master, and free to move where or when they wished, these Mountain Men contributed more than any other group to the exploration of the West. Their significance in the history of the frontier, however, extended beyond the service they performed as pathfinders or trail blazers. The lives that they led, and the characteristics that those lives forced upon them, illustrated in exaggerated form the corrosive effect of a wilderness environment on transplanted Easterners. On all frontiers, pioneers grappling with the untamed forces of nature cast off the artifacts and institutions and habits of civilization; the Mountain Men, divorced entirely from traditional patterns of civilized life, reverted more completely toward the primitive than any other pioneers. Their pattern of existence illustrated, even in caricature, the extent to which environment transcended hereditary factors in molding the lives of frontiersmen.

This varied little from year to year, but was never monotonous. The year's activities began in the spring when the warming sun thawed the valley streams; alone with their Indian wives, or in small groups, the trappers then began their endless search for beaver "sign." When this was found they set their traps with a skill that Indians might envy,

[5] The most thorough history of this phase of the trade is in Dale L. Morgan, *Jedediah Smith and the Opening of the West* (Indianapolis, 1953), *passim*.

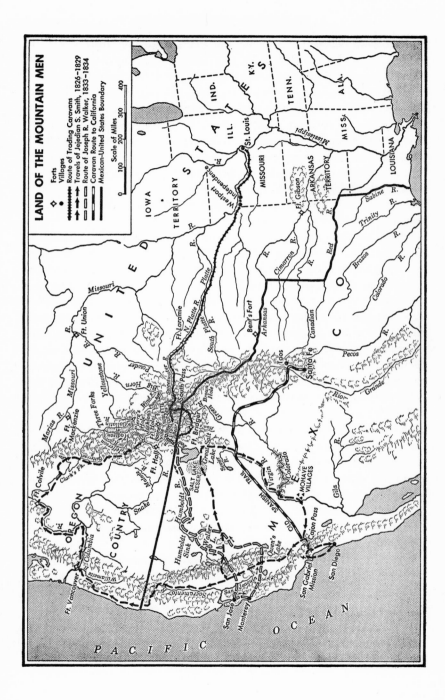

LAND OF THE MOUNTAIN MEN

Forts
Villages
Route of Trading Caravans
Travels of Jejedian S. Smith, 1826–1829
Route of Joseph R. Walker, 1833–1834
Caravan Route to California
Mexican-United States Boundary

Scale of Miles
0   100 200 300 400

gradually working their way up the rivers until late June when the animals started shedding and ended the "spring hunt." Then, from all the West, the Mountain Men turned their steps toward the site of the annual rendezvous. This had been selected a year in advance by the company sending out its pack train of goods: sometimes beneath the red sandstone cliffs of the Wind River Mountains, where the valleys of the Popo Agie or Wind rivers were bright with flaming wild flowers; sometimes along the shores of the meandering Bear River, where the grass was lush and tall; sometimes in Jackson's Hole or Pierre's Hole, where calm lakes reflected the naked peaks of America's most majestic mountains, the snow-dappled Grand Tetons. To this spot came flocking trappers from all the West: bearded Mountain Men with their fur-laden pack mules, brigades of "company men" who worked for one of the trading companies that invaded the Rockies in the 1830's, dark-skinned Mexicans from Taos or Santa Fe, French-Canadian deserters from the Hudson's Bay Company, and whole villages of friendly Indians who pitched their skin lodges and settled down to watch the fun. Often more than six hundred trappers and as many Indians met together at the annual "Rocky Mountain Fair."

Shortly after the first of July the caravan of trading goods arrived from St. Louis, equipped by merchants willing to endure the dangers of wilderness travel for profits that sometimes touched 2,000 per cent. The trappers asked eagerly for year-old news first, then watched as the merchandise was displayed: powder from the du Pont works in Delaware, lead from the Galena mines of Illinois, stubby rifles from the shops of Missouri gunsmiths, knives and beaver traps from England's distant factories, beads and trinkets from Italy, coffee and sugar from South America, blankets from New England's textile mills, hanks of tobacco from Kentucky, fiery whisky from Taos, and cask after cask of raw alcohol from the distilleries of Cincinnati. Trading came first as the Mountain Men cheerfully surrendered their "hairy bank notes," the beaver skins, for needed items or scarce-remembered luxuries or gaudy fineries for the squaws. It did not matter that prices were astronomical; why quibble over blankets at twenty dollars, tobacco at three dollars a pound, sugar and coffee at two dollars, and alcohol at five dollars a pint when beaver pelts could be had for the taking and were worth from three to six dollars each? [6]

[6] Osburne Russell, *Journal of a Trapper, or Nine Years in the Rocky Mountains, 1834–1843* (Boise, Ida., 1921), pp. 62–63; Joseph Williams, *Narrative of*

Even at these prices the Mountain Man used only a portion of his year's catch to buy what he needed; the merchants secured the rest after they opened the flat casks of raw alcohol that were universally used in the trade. As kettles of this lethal fluid were passed about, day after day, night after night, the rendezvous was transformed into a scene of roaring debauchery. Some staged races on foot or horseback; some wrestled and fought; some gambled recklessly at cards or the Indian game of "hand" until they had squandered away in a few hours their entire year's earnings, their rifles, their horses, their wives, and in a few cases their own scalps. Neither misers nor repentants could be found among men who risked their lives daily; a trapper who had lost his all would only shrug away his disappointment with a "There goes ha'r and beaver" and take solace in more alcohol. Others stamped through Indian dances amidst barbaric yells of

Hi-Hi-Hi-Hi! Hi-i—Hi-i—Hi-i—Hi-i!
Hi-ya—Hi-ya—Hi-ya—Hi-ya
Hi-ya—Hi-ya—Hi-ya—Hi-ya

or indulged in sexual orgies with passively indifferent Indian maidens. Occasionally, as drunkenness mounted, duels were fought, usually with rifles at twenty paces, with one or both participants sure to be killed, or acts of sadistic cruelty performed. A drunken trapper might, as happened once, douse the hair of a sleeping companion with alcohol, then turn his victim into a human torch with a brand from the campfire.[7]

Eventually both the alcohol and the Mountain Men were exhausted. Those who had gambled away their guns and horses pledged their next year's catch for new supplies, and all stumbled away into the wilderness, their year's earnings squandered in a few days of barbaric dissipation. For a few weeks they rested to recover from the effects of the rendezvous; but as the cold nights of approaching autumn restored the quality of the beaver pelts, the "fall hunt" began. Starting high in the mountains, they trapped their way down the rivers until the last

---

a Tour from the State of Indiana to the Oregon Territory in the Years 1841–2 (Cincinnati, 1843), p. 14.

[7] For these episodes see Russell, Journal of a Trapper, p. 62; George F. Ruxton, Adventures in Mexico and the Rocky Mountains (London, 1849), pp. 245–246; and Frances F. Victor, River of the West (Hartford, 1870), pp. 110–111. The best modern study of the rendezvous is Carl P. Russell, "Wilderness Rendezvous Period of the American Fur Trade," Oregon Historical Quarterly, XLII (1941), 1–47.

was frozen and the animals hibernating. Then the Mountain Men
scattered to their "winter camps." Some joined their wives' tribes to
live as the Indians lived; others banded together in some sheltered
valley such as Brown's Hole of the Green River or along the banks of
the Big Horn, where towering peaks protected them from winter's
blasts; still more established lonely camps on mountain streams, where
they lived cozily with their squaws in skin lodges, venturing out only
to bring in the game needed for food. With the first sign of spring they
scattered again to resume the quest for beaver that was their sole aim
in life.

To follow this routine year after year—and stay alive—the Mountain Men must adjust themselves completely to the wilderness world
about them. Enemies were everywhere. Some were Indians; the Blackfeet and their cousins, the Piegan, Bloods, and Grosventres, were sworn
enemies of all whites, while even such friendly tribesmen as the Crows
could not resist stealing a carelessly watched horse or pouncing on an
unwary trapper. Others were wild animals. Grizzly bears—great savage beasts as tall as a man and with raking claws that cut to the bone
with every sweep—roamed the Rockies in such numbers that one
Mountain Man counted 220 in one day, while fifty or sixty were commonly sighted. Constant vigilance was needed just to stay alive in such
a land. Wrote one who knew them well: "Habitual watchfulness de-
stroys every frivolity of mind and action. They seldom smile: the
expression of their countenances is watchful, solemn, and determined.
They ride and walk like men whose breasts have so long been exposed
to the bullet and the arrow, that fear finds within them no resting
place." [8]

To exist in this savage environment, the Mountain Men must slip
backward in the scale of civilization until their wilderness skills
matched those of their red-skinned opponents. Some, in this reversion
toward the primitive, descended to a level of savagery below that of
their foes. Edward Rose was such a man; a morose, moody misfit of
mixed blood and lawless disposition, he eventually joined the Crow
tribe and abandoned civilization entirely. A fellow trapper saw Rose
lead his tribesmen to victory against a Blackfoot war party in 1834,
then whip his followers into a bloody frenzy as they hacked off the

[8] Thomas J. Farnham, *Travels in the Great Western Prairies, the Anahuack
and Rocky Mountains, and in the Oregon Territory* (2 vols., London, 1843),
I, 293.

hands of the wounded enemy warriors, pierced their bodies with pointed sticks, and plucked out their eyes.[9] Equally touched by the wand of savagery was Charles Gardner, who borrowed the nickname of "Phil" from his native Philadelphia. Sent on a journey with a lone Indian companion, he was given up for lost after a howling winter gale swept the countryside. To his friends' surprise, Phil reappeared after several days, but without the Indian. As he unpacked his mule they saw him pull out a shriveled human leg, which he threw to the ground with: "There, damn you, I won't have to gnaw on you any more." "Cannibal Phil," as he was known thereafter, added to his unenviable reputation a little later when, marooned in the mountains by a snow storm, he subsisted comfortably on the flesh of his current squaw.[10]

Few among the Mountain Men reverted to such complete savagery, but all slipped far backward from a state of civilization. Certainly in their appearance there was little to distinguish them from the Indians. Gaunt and spare, with skin tanned the color of the red men's by life in the open, they let their unkempt hair hang to shoulder length while their faces were hidden beneath beards that "would scarcely disgrace a Bedouin of the desert." They wore buckskin hunting shirts, ornamented at every seam with colored porcupine quills or leather fringes, and pulled in at the waist by a broad belt. In this was thrust a pistol and tomahawk; from it dangled a scalping knife in a leather sheath and a whetstone in a buckskin case. Their pantaloons were similarly of leather and as carefully ornamented, while their moccasins showed the skillful beadwork of their squaws. On their heads they wore a cap of skins, decorated with animals' tails or braided horsehair. About their necks hung a "possibles sack" containing pipe, tobacco, awl, bullet mold, and other necessities; over their shoulders was slung a bullet pouch and powder horn, while a stubby "Hawkins rifle" dangled from the crook of their arms. Romantic as these clothes were, they could best be appreciated at a distance, for they were never removed from the time they were put on until they were discarded, except, perhaps, when their owner laid them across an ant hill for those busy insects to eat some of the lice.[11]

[9] Zenas Leonard, *Adventures of Zenas Leonard, Fur Trader and Trapper, 1831–1836* (Cleveland, 1904), pp. 262–270.

[10] LeRoy R. Hafen, "Mountain Men: Big Phil the Cannibal," *Colorado Magazine,* XIII (1936), 53–58.

[11] Of the many travelers who described the dress of the Mountain Men, the

Thus clothed and equipped, the Mountain Men were ready to cope with the wilderness about them. Of their sworn enemies, the Indians, they asked no more quarter than they gave. What superb fighters they were! They fought as did their foes, taking advantage of brush and rock cover as they moved toward their enemies, shooting with unerring accuracy. After one battle a group of trappers fell to arguing over who had killed one gaudily dressed chief. One insisted they would find his bullet in the chief's left eye; when the body was pulled from the creek where it had fallen, the bullet was exactly in the spot prophesied. Like the red men they ended all battles in hand-to-hand combat, where they used their knives and tomahawks with deadly skill; like the red men they scalped their victims when the fight was over. Taking firm hold of the scalp with the left hand, they made two semicircular incisions with and against the sun, loosened the skin with the point of a knife, and pulled with their feet against the dead man's shoulders until the scalp came loose with a characteristic "flop." [12]

If their fighting methods were those of the Indians, so were their eating habits. They seldom knew where their next meal would come from, for planning was a virtue as unknown among the Mountain Men as among the red men. When caught by winter blizzards or while on unexpectedly long desert marches, many a trapper escaped starvation only by bleeding his horse and drinking the blood, cutting off and eating the ears of his mules, or choking down the leather thongs of his moccasins after they had been boiled until soft. One old Mountain Man recalled: "I have held my hands in an ant-hill until they were covered with ants, then greedily licked them off. I have taken the soles of my moccasins, crisped them in the fire, and eaten them. In our extremity the large black crickets which are found in the country were considered fair game. We used to take a kettle of hot water, catch the crickets and throw them in, and when they stopped kicking, eat them." [13] In both their primitive belief that nature would always provide and their willingness to consume anything that walked, swam, wriggled, or crawled, the trappers were strikingly akin to Indians.

---

most accurate was Ruxton, *Adventures in Mexico and the Rocky Mountains,* p. 243. An excellent modern account is in Frederic E. Voelker, "The Mountain Men and Their Part in the Opening of the West," *Bulletin of the Missouri Historical Society,* III (1947), 155.

[12] Nolie Mumey, *The Life of Jim Baker, 1818–1898* (Denver, 1931), pp. 32–33; Richard F. Burton, *The City of the Saints* (London, 1861), p. 138.

[13] Victor, *River of the West,* p. 120.

Like the red men, too, they grew accustomed to alternate periods of feast and famine. During the winter months when the buffalo left the mountains, the mountaineers grew thin and gaunt; in the spring when the herds returned they grew fat and sleek once more. For when the first fat cow was killed in the spring they were assured a feast fit for a king—a savage king, that is. About a fire of buffalo chips—which they preferred to wood because of the peppery flavor imparted to the meat —they propped row on row of choice "hump ribs." While these sizzled temptingly the Mountain Men often began their repast by drinking some of the blood, which reminded them of warm milk. Then the liver was eaten raw, flavored with the contents of the gall bladder. If the cow buffalo was pregnant they savored one of the trappers' most exotic luxuries: the raw legs of unborn calves. These appetizers were sometimes followed by a soup made by mixing blood with the rich marrow extracted from the leg bones. The thick mixture resulting turned the stomachs of Easterners, but made the faces of Mountain Men "shine with grease and gladness." [14]

After these delicacies, the trappers were ready for their feast. This always included the hump ribs, which were pulled away by hand and the fat meat gulped down, while grease dripped over the face and clothing. These might be alternated with strips of the tenderloin, partially roasted or boiled, or by chunks of the tongue. Another prized portion was the "fleece," the inch-thick layer of fat that lay just beneath the buffalo hide. Scarcely less tempting were the intestines, or *boudins,* which were roasted in the fire until puffed with heat and fat, then coiled on a blanket and gulped down without chewing. On such an occasion two trappers would start on the opposite ends of a pile of intestines and work their way toward the middle, each eating faster and faster to get his share, and shouting to the other to "feed fair." [15]

How the Mountain Men did eat when such a feast was ready and the cook sang out: "Hyar's the doins; freeze into it, boys." Eight or nine pounds of meat a day was normal consumption when hunting was good. For, like the Indians, the mountaineers never knew when the next meal was coming—if ever. "When we have a plenty," one wrote, "we eat the best pieces first, for fear of being killed by some

[14] Farnham, *Travels in the Great Western Prairies,* I, 236.

[15] *Ibid.,* I, 237–238; F. Adolphus Wislizenus, *A Journey to the Rocky Mountains in the Year 1839* (St. Louis, 1912), pp. 51–52; Ruxton, *Adventures in Mexico and the Rocky Mountains,* pp. 267–268; Lewis H. Garrard, *Wah-to-Yah, and the Taos Trail* (Cincinnati, 1850), p. 26.

brat of an Indian before we have enjoyed them." [16] And, like the Indians, they were content with buffalo meat alone. Occasionally they added a roasted beaver tail to their menu; now and then they feasted on lynx or puppy-dog meat; sometimes in the spring they nibbled on such roots as *pomme blanche* or *commote* or ate handfuls of fresh berries. But these refinements were by no means necessary. Buffalo was all they needed. "We live upon it solely," one wrote, "without bread or vegetables of any kind," while another lyrically agreed that "if a man could always live on such 'didins,' he would *never die*." [17]

The Mountain Men borrowed not only their eating habits but their language from the Indians. Their voices were usually high-pitched, with a strong nasal twang, and they emphasized each syllable carefully as did the red men. They gestured frequently and meaningfully as they spoke, for they were adept in the sign language that was the Indians' means of intertribal communication. From the Indians, too, they borrowed a colorful imagery that added spice to their speech. A man was a "child" or a "hoss" or a "coon" or a "nigger." A hungry person was "wolfish" and needed to fill his "meatbag" with "buffler meat" or "cow meat"; one who was thirsty drank to satisfy his "dry." To scalp an Indian was to "lift his ha'r," or "tickle his fleece"; one who had been killed had been "rubbed out" or had "gone under." Phrases such as "hyar's a nigger lifted ha'r that spree," were sprinkled through their conversation. Winter to the Mountain Men was "robe season," or "freezin' time." Said one who rose early on a winter morning: "This hoss is no ba'r to stick his nose under cover all robe season." A celebration was a "big dance"; to run was to "make tracks"; to get something free was to "have it on the prairie." "How are ye off for cow meat?" one trapper asked another when they met in the Rockies one winter. "Hell," said the other, "cow meat *this* freezin' time? You've been down to Santa Fee too long. Why, poor bull is hard to get. . . . Howsomever, if you want to chaw on lean buffler dryed, you can have it on the prairie." [18] Nor could the Mountain Men utter

[16] Farnham, *Travels in the Great Western Prairies*, I, 235.

[17] Warren A. Ferris, *Life in the Rocky Mountains, 1830–1835* (Salt Lake City, 1940), p. 39; Rufus B. Sage, *Rocky Mountain Life; or, Startling Scenes and Perilous Adventures in the Far West* (Boston, 1859), pp. 69, 71.

[18] Garrard, *Wah-to-Yah, and the Taos Trail,* p. 185. This work contains some of the best examples of the speech of the Mountain Men; equally valuable is the novel from the pen of an English observer who lived for some time in the Rockies: George F. Ruxton, *Life in the Far West* (Norman, Okla., 1951), pp. 7–8, 14, 40, 144.

more than a few words without injecting the "Wah" or "Ugh" or "Heap" of the red men.

If the speech of the Mountain Men showed the corrosive influence of their environment, so did their mental attitudes reveal their reversion toward savagery. Their philosophy of life was based on the uncertainty of survival; men could live in the wilderness only by inuring themselves completely to hardship and misfortune. "They become," wrote one who had lived among them, "callous to any feeling of danger, and destroy human and animal life with as little scruple and as freely as they expose their own." [19] Death was so commonplace in a land where danger lurked at every turn that there was no mourning for the dead in the mountains; when a trapper heard that a friend had been killed he would only shrug his shoulders and say, "Poor fellow! Out of luck." Joe Meek, a famous mountaineer, was hunting buffalo when one of the party was thrown from his horse amidst the trampling herd. Joe was told to ride to his friend's rescue.

"What'll I do with him if he is dead?" he asked.

"Can't you pack him to camp?"

"Pack hell," Joe objected. "I should rather pack a load of meat." There was nothing disrespectful in that remark. Joe only reflected an attitude normal among men who lived constantly under the shadow of death. "Live men war what we wanted," he explained to a friend later; "dead ones war of no account." [20]

The Mountain Men had even less respect for the lives of their foes; not even the savages of the forest could rival their cold-blooded cruelty and their callous indifference to the value of human life. To them any red-skinned stranger was an enemy, to be killed first and questioned later. Thus on one occasion a band of trappers were working their way along the Snake when the alarm of "Injuns!" was sounded. All grabbed their rifles, while a hurried cry of "Shoot! Shoot!" rang out. The leader checked this "precipitation" as the red men approached, to reveal themselves as friendly Crows who only wanted to trade for some tobacco. [21] On another occasion a few Blackfeet caught stealing horses were chased into a tinder-dry thicket. This was heartlessly fired, while the trappers settled down to shoot those trying to escape and watch the rest burn to death. One disappointed white man wrote

[19] Ruxton, *Adventures in Mexico and the Rocky Mountains*, pp. 241–242.
[20] Victor, *River of the West*, pp. 249–250.
[21] *Ibid.*, p. 80.

later: "As they were all more or less roasted, we took no scalps." [22]
Even when Mountain Men did exhibit any humanity their motives
were hardly laudable. In one brush with the Blackfeet, all but one of
the natives was killed. A young trapper was about to pick him off
when a grizzled old mountaineer knocked the gun aside, saying: "Ef
ye kill that Injun, ye'll do it over my carcase. I want that red varmint
to live so's he kin drag into his village an' tell the rest o' them skunks
jes' who 'twas rubbed out their war party. Otherwise they might never
know. They gotta larn t' respec' decent Christians." [23]

Yet the savage cruelty of the Mountain Men concealed the fact that
the ties that bound them to the past—and to civilization—were badly
strained, but never broken. Often their thoughts turned toward home.
James Clyman recorded such a moment. Alone in the mountains, he
rode into a grove of cottonwoods where birds sang merrily. "I laied
down in the shade and enjoyed their twittering for some hours," he
wrote in his diary that night. "It reminded me of home & civilisa-
tion." [24] The hold of their heritage was even better shown when they
assembled in winter camps, there to waste away the hours in recapturing moments from a long-dead past. "Some of the better educated
men," one trapper recalled, "who had once known and loved books
. . . recalled their favorite authors, and recited passages once treas-
ured, now growing unfamiliar." Another confessed that he had
learned much "from the frequent arguments and debates held in what
we termed 'Rocky Mountain College.' " On such occasions well-worn
books were sometimes produced from trappers' packs, to be read and
read again. At one winter camp a mountaineer remembered reading
from Byron, Shakespeare, and Scott, in addition to the Bible and
Clark's commentary on the Scriptures, as well as "other small works
in Geology, chemistry and philosophy." [25] Even those who could not
read loved nothing better than to listen. Thus Jim Bridger was never
happier than when hearing the classics. On all he expressed strong
opinions. The murder of the two princes in the tower aroused him to
violent abuse of Shakespeare, who must, he declared, "have had a bad

[22] James P. Beckwourth, *The Life and Adventures of James P. Beckwourth*
(New York, 1856), p. 80.
[23] Quoted in Voelker, "Mountain Men," pp. 157–158.
[24] Charles L. Camp (ed.), *James Clyman, American Frontiersman, 1792–
1881* (San Francisco, 1928), p. 35.
[25] Victor, *River of the West,* pp. 83–84; Russell, *Journal of a Trapper,* pp.
55, 109.

heart and been as devilish mean as a Sioux, to have written such scoundrelism as that." [26]

Half-civilized, half-savage, these were the men of brave and reckless breed who brought the western fur trade to its height—and decline —during the 1830's. Few eras have produced beings as free as they, for neither society nor their consciences imposed restraints upon them. "They had," wrote one who knew them, "little fear of God and none at all of the devil." [27] Utterly the masters of their own lives, they could trap or hunt, sleep or wake, wander or camp, kill or forgive, as the whim of the moment dictated. Yet they had scarcely entered upon the scene when forces began to take shape that would soon degrade them to mere pawns in the hands of men whose might was based on wealth rather than brawn. For the early profits of the trade inevitably attracted to the Far West great capitalists from the East, each anxious to monopolize the traffic in furs and each determined to do so by fair means or foul.

The day of eastern domination seemed far away in 1830, when Thomas Fitzpatrick and his partners formed the Rocky Mountain Fur Company. They had secured not only trading goods and good will, but the services of most of the seasoned trappers in the mountains; surely no outsider could wrest the trade from such herculean defenders. Nor did the record of the new company in its first two years indicate anything but success for its future. The partners led several brigades out of the rendezvous that summer to hunt the southern and northern Rockies; that enjoying the greatest success was commanded by Thomas Fitzpatrick, Jim Bridger, and Milton Sublette and contained two hundred men. So formidable was this company that it could defy the long-hostile Blackfeet in the little-trapped Three Forks country where beaver were abundant. The next year, 1831, was less rewarding, largely because Fitzpatrick sought to economize by buying goods for the rendezvous at Santa Fe rather than St. Louis, then missed his way on the return and did not reach the Green River country until the men had scattered for the fall hunt.[28] This was bad enough, but a worse blow was soon to fall. For as Jim Bridger and Milton Sublette led the prin-

[26] Margaret I. Carrington, *Ab Sa-Ra-Ka, Land of Massacre* (Philadelphia, 1868), p. 114.

[27] William E. Connelley, *Doniphan's Expedition and the Conquest of New Mexico and California* (Topeka, 1907), p. 5.

[28] J. Cecil Alter, *James Bridger, Trapper, Frontiersman, Scout and Guide* (Salt Lake City, 1925), pp. 113–119.

cipal Rocky Mountain Fur Company brigade into the Powder River valley to prepare for winter camp, they stumbled on a large party of trappers flying the banner of a rival concern, the American Fur Company.

This eastern corporation, formed in 1808 and nurtured by the business genius of John Jacob Astor, had been slowly creeping westward for two decades, crushing or absorbing rivals as it moved. By 1822 it dominated the trade of the Great Lakes country; in that year the invasion of the lower Missouri began when the company established a Western Department with headquarters at St. Louis. The next move —to the upper Missouri—came in 1827, when Astor bought out the Columbia Fur Company, a small but ably manned concern that had been one of his rivals for the trade of the lower river. Its principal owner, Kenneth McKenzie, a trader of such exceptional abilities that he was soon to be known as "King of the Upper Missouri," was placed in charge of a new branch of the company, the Upper Missouri Outfit, with instructions to use any means to monopolize the trade of the upper river. His first step, in 1828, was to build Fort Union at the mouth of the Yellowstone as a center of operations. Just beyond, Mc-Kenzie knew, lay the forbidden land of the Blackfeet, the last great virgin beaver country in the West. What a feather in his cap if he could open this to the American Fur Company!

His chance came in 1830 when an old trapper named Berger, a deserter from the Hudson's Bay Company, appeared at Fort Union with tales of experience among the Blackfeet while stationed at a post near the borders of their country. Only McKenzie's eloquence was needed to persuade Berger and twelve other trappers to undertake a dangerous mission into the Blackfoot domain to seek their trade. They started with little hope, fearing that they would be shot down before they could explain their purpose, but such was their wilderness skill that they managed to approach a large Blackfoot village without being sighted. Berger and one trembling companion, carrying the American flag, rode ahead now. As warriors came riding out to meet them Berger shouted his name in their own tongue. Fortunately some of his friends were in that village; he was greeted as a long-lost brother and easily persuaded forty of the leading braves to accompany him back to Fort Union. There they fixed their marks to an agreement in which they promised "hereafter and for ever to live as brethren of one large united happy family; and may the Great Spirit, who watcheth over us all, approve our conduct and teach us to love each other." [29] McKenzie acted at once to turn these pious sentiments into profits. A party sent into the Blackfoot country in the summer of 1831 spent the winter trading, and returned with more than four thousand beaver pelts. That summer a new fort, Fort McKenzie, was built on the Marias River in the heart of the Blackfoot hunting grounds. That summer, too, the first snorting steamboat reached Fort Union, so overawing the natives that they were mightily impressed with the power of the American Fur Company.

These steps were all important, but in McKenzie's eyes they were only preliminary to his main task: wresting the trade of the central Rockies from the Rocky Mountain Fur Company. For this something more than power or wealth was necessary. Thomas Fitzpatrick and his partners commanded the services of virtually every trapper who had sufficient knowledge of the country to locate profitable beaver streams. Why not, McKenzie reasoned, turn the experience of his rivals to his own advantage? Why not use the Rocky Mountain Fur Company's brigades as guides to the hunting grounds? This was in his mind in the autumn of 1831, when he sent out three parties under the command of the company's ablest partisans: Lucien Fontenelle, Andrew Drips, and William H. Vanderburgh. Each was instructed to look for trappers from the rival concern who could lead them to beaver streams. Fontenelle failed to run down his quarry, but Vanderburgh and Drips were more successful. In the Powder River valley they stumbled on the main Rocky Mountain Fur Company brigade under Jim Bridger and Milton Sublette and promptly went into winter camp nearby.

Thus was the stage set for a comic game of chase that began with the spring hunt in 1832. The disgusted Rocky Mountain Company traders had slipped away during the winter, hoping to avoid pursuit, but their trail was easy to follow and in the Bear River valley they found Vanderburgh and Drips awaiting them. Doggedly the pursuit went on until the spring hunt came to a close; when they turned their steps toward Pierre's Hole for the 1832 rendezvous, their rivals were at their heels. There even more disheartening news awaited them: the

[29] This is printed in Prince Maximilian, *Travels in the Interior of North America, in the Years 1832, 1833, and 1834* (Reuben G. Thwaites, ed., *Early Western Travels, 1748–1846*, Cleveland, 1906), II, 317. Events leading up to the agreement are described in Kenneth W. Porter, *John Jacob Astor, Business Man* (2 vols., Cambridge, Mass., 1931), II, 737–750.

American Fur Company was sending two caravans of goods to the rendezvous, one from Fort Union and one from the East. This was alarming indeed, for if either reached Pierre's Hole before the Rocky Mountain Fur Company caravan, the several hundred free trappers would sell their season's furs to Astor's outfit. Thomas Fitzpatrick was hurried eastward to urge its leader, Milton Sublette, to hurry; he accomplished his purpose so successfully that Sublette arrived on July 8, 1832, with the American Fur Company caravans still not heard from, and departed when trade was over with 168 packs of skins worth $85,000.[30]

The partners of the Rocky Mountain Fur Company could take little solace in their victory, for the race between the rival caravans symbolized a new era of bitter competition in the trade. They had only to look about them at that Pierre's Hole rendezvous to realize this. Among the trappers riotously carousing there were not only their own men and American Fur Company employees, but followers of other smaller companies that had been lured into the mountains by the hope of sharing in the rich profits. In one corner of the camp grounds were the lodges of a party commanded by a wealthy Boston merchant named Nathaniel J. Wyeth; in another, members of a brigade sent by the St. Louis firm of Gantt and Blackwell; in another, those of a small band of Arkansas trappers whose leader was the experienced Alexander Sinclair; in still another lived eighty seasoned Mountain Men from Taos with two old trappers, John Harris and Bill Williams, in nominal control.[31] Not far away, they learned from the Indians, was still another large party under an Army officer from the East, Captain Benjamin L. E. Bonneville. Rumors reached them, too, that the Hudson's Bay Company had changed its policies, and was moving into the Rocky Mountain country from the northwest once more. Gone was the day when the West was the domain of a few free-roving trappers; a new era of bitter competition was at hand. The Secretary of War spoke wisely when he declared in his annual report that year: "This

[30] These events are described by a participant in Ferris, *Life in the Rocky Mountains,* pp. 65–67.

[31] Contemporary accounts of these expeditions are in Frank G. Young (ed.), *The Correspondence and Journals of Captain Nathaniel J. Wyeth, 1831–1836* (Eugene, Ore., 1899), pp. 155–219; William H. Ellison (ed.), *The Life and Adventure of George Nidever, 1802–1883* (Berkeley, 1937), *passim;* and Albert Pike, *Prose Sketches and Poems* (Boston, 1834), pp. 37–80.

state of things will, before many years, lead to the entire destruction of the beaver." [32]

He might well have added that men as well as beaver would be destroyed, for such a mass invasion of their country would never be accepted peacefully by the Indians. The future was prophesied with the breakup of the 1832 rendezvous on July 17. That afternoon one of the Rocky Mountain Fur Company brigades under Milton Sublette, accompanied by Nathaniel Wyeth and his thirteen followers, started westward. The next morning, while they were encamped only eight miles from Pierre's Hole, a band of Blackfoot Indians approached. Hostile at first, the red men showed signs of friendship when they saw that the American party numbered 150 men, and signaled that they wanted a parley. Sublette foolishly delegated two stanch enemies of the Blackfeet to carry on these talks; instead of negotiating they cold-bloodedly shot down one of the chiefs just as they were shaking hands. With this declaration of war the Indians took refuge in a clump of timber while the traders scattered to find cover. Word was hurried to the rendezvous site, bringing all of the trappers who remained there out on the gallop. All that day the Battle of Pierre's Hole went on as the Mountain Men vainly tried to dislodge the Blackfeet from their position. It only ended when one of the besieged Indians shouted that eight hundred of their tribesmen were approaching. The trappers, fearing that this was not just a ruse and that their unprotected supplies at the rendezvous site might be stolen, hurried back to Pierre's Hole, allowing the Blackfeet to slip away. Five trappers and seven friendly Indians were killed in this useless battle, while two others were killed later as they left the rendezvous on their way east.[33]

Nor did the chain of disaster end there. When the principal Rocky Mountain Fur Company Brigade, led by Thomas Fitzpatrick and Jim Bridger, drifted northward from Pierre's Hole, the American Fur Company trappers were no longer dogging their footsteps, but only because their supplies were depleted by the failure of their company's caravans to reach the rendezvous. Hurrying eastward, Vanderburgh and Drips, with their followers, met the caravan from Fort Union in

[32] 22nd Congress, 1st Session, *Senate Document* No. 90, p. 3.
[33] Many of the trappers participating left full accounts of the Battle of Pierre's Hole. Among the best are Young (ed.), *Corr. and Journals of Wyeth,* pp. 159–160; Victor, *River of the West,* pp. 112–118; and Leonard, *Adventures of Zenas Leonard,* pp. 112–116. A lively history of the affair is in Washington Irving, *Adventures of Captain Bonneville, U.S.A.* (New York, 1850), pp. 73–80.

early August, took on fresh supplies, and started at once after the Fitz-patrick-Bridger party. By September 10, 1832, they had run their quarry down in the Jefferson River valley. For a time the usual game of hide-and-seek went on, in and out of the mountains and plains of the Three Forks country, but this time the American Fur Company trappers could not be shaken. Not until mid-October, when Vander-burgh's followers stopped to trap on the upper Madison and Jefferson rivers, did the Rocky Mountain Company trappers slip away, leaving their inexperienced rivals in the heart of a dangerous Indian country. There they were lured into an ambush by Blackfoot Indians seeking revenge for the Battle of Pierre's Hole. Vanderburgh's bullet-ridden body and that of one of his companions were left on the battlefield, while the rest fled southward. Fitzpatrick and Bridger narrowly escaped the same fate themselves when they tangled with Indians on an open plain a short distance away; Jim Bridger carried a barbed iron arrowhead in his back for the next three years as a memento of that affair.[34]

Competition for the fur trade between these rival giants had cost heavily in human life; the cost in profits was to be just as great. This became clear as the numerous brigades and trapping parties then in the mountains began their spring hunt in 1833. In the Three Forks country bands of American Fur Company and Rocky Mountain Fur Company men roamed ceaselessly in their constant effort to elude each other and at the same time find streams not already trapped out. In the southern Rockies seventy employees of the Gantt and Blackwell Company competed bitterly with about one hundred trappers from Taos for the little fur still available. Farther to the west a Rocky Mountain Company brigade under Milton G. Sublette suffered im-possible hardships as it sought to reach the Malade River and other streams in the Snake River country reportedly still teeming with beaver. Vying with them for these prizes were the trappers com-manded by Captain Bonneville, until an estimated four hundred were trapping there. Even in this long-neglected land they were doomed to disappointment. For, starting in 1830, the Hudson's Bay Company had reversed its former policy of concentrating on the Pacific slope and sent its annual brigades eastward. John Work, the leader of this Snake Country expedition, led forty men through the region in 1830 and

---

[34] Hiram M. Chittenden, *The American Fur Trade of the Far West* (3 vols., New York, 1902), II, 664–672; Ferris, *Life in the Rocky Mountains,* pp. 140–142. Ferris was with Vanderburgh but escaped.

sixty a year later, penetrating as far eastward as the Blackfoot hunting ground near the headwaters of the Missouri. American traders could not face such competition. "Wherever they are," wrote Dr. John McLoughlin triumphantly, "we should have a party to oppose them even at a loss." [35] In the Snake Country, as throughout the West, the chance for large profits was waning.

The results appeared when the trappers assembled at Horse Creek in the Green River valley for the 1833 rendezvous. Never in the memory of the oldest trappers had the trade been so poor. Captain Bonneville had only twenty-three packs of beaver to show for his year of trapping—less than twenty skins for each of his men. Fitzpatrick and Milton Sublette departed for St. Louis with only fifty-five packs, taking with them the Boston merchant, Nathaniel J. Wyeth, who had visited the rendezvous on his way east from a disastrous attempt to challenge the Hudson's Bay Company in the Columbia basin. Before they parted Wyeth, who still had trading ambitions, agreed to supply the Rocky Mountain Fur Company with $3,000 worth of goods for the 1834 rendezvous. These scant profits indicated that the fur trade could survive only by finding virgin beaver country or by effecting consolidations that would end the bitter competition. Both expedients were to be tried in the next year.

Veteran Mountain Men were sure that the search for untrapped streams was futile; they had explored the entire Far West so thoroughly that they knew none could be found. But no such doubts harassed the newest of the traders, Captain Benjamin L. E. Bonneville. A West Point graduate who had become infected with the frontier fever, Bonneville had secured the financial backing of a wealthy New Yorker and had come west in 1832 with 110 men. His experiences since that time had hardly been of the sort to delight his patron; the elaborately planned Fort Bonneville that he built in the Green River valley was abandoned almost as soon as completed, while his brigades had been so handicapped by his inexperienced leadership that their catch in furs was small. Still clinging to hopes of a fortune, he ordered one of his bands of mountaineers westward at the close of the 1833 rendezvous, with instructions to search the barren lands beyond the Great Salt Lake for likely hunting grounds. This was the expedition

[35] E. E. Rich (ed.), *The Letters of John McLoughlin from Fort Vancouver to the Governor and Committee. Third Series, 1844–46* (Toronto, 1944), p. 127.

that gave its leader, Joseph Reddeford Walker, an opportunity to earn his niche among the pathfinders of the American West.

With forty followers, including some of the most skilled Mountain Men of the Rockies, Walker skirted the north shore of the Great Salt Lake, found his way through the wild land of rocks and sand that lay beyond, followed the well-trapped Humboldt River to the Sierra Nevada Mountains, and crossed this awesome barrier where swirling snow and icy winds reduced even his seasoned hunters to near desperation, to emerge at last amidst the warmth of the San Joaquin valley of California.[36] Pushing on to San Francisco, the party turned southward along the coast to Monterey, where they spent the winter of 1833–34. In mid-February Walker took the trail once more, moving south along the San Joaquin valley to the Kern River, which was followed eastward into the low defile since known as Walker Pass. There the hunters turned northward to skirt the Sierras as they marched through Owens Valley and across parched deserts where they nearly died of thirst. In June they picked up their own trail, which led them back along the Humboldt in time to reach the 1834 rendezvous at Ham's Fork of the Green River.

Walker's report of the country he had seen—with stream after stream so well trapped that not a beaver remained—only confirmed the belief of old Mountain Men that new hunting grounds could never be found. With this hope dying, they realized that the trade could be saved only by checking the bitter competition among rival companies. The evil effects of this conflict were everywhere apparent at that 1834 rendezvous. They were revealed by the pitifully small catch; the Rocky Mountain Fur Company had only forty packs of furs to show for its year's work, the American Fur Company a slightly smaller number, and Captain Bonneville's outfit only twelve or fourteen packs. They were revealed, too, by the treatment afforded Nathaniel Wyeth. This merchant, armed with his previous year's agreement to supply the Rocky Mountain Fur Company with $3,000 in trading goods, had reached the 1834 rendezvous with a pack train of laden mules and golden dreams of the profits he would make. To his shocked horror he found that the Rocky Mountain Company partners, aware of their small year's catch and reluctant to share any of their returns with an

---

[36] Trappers who accompanied Walker describe their adventures in Leonard, *Adventures of Zenas Leonard,* pp. 146–187; Ellison (ed.), *Life and Adventures of Nidever,* pp. 32–34; and Stephen H. Meek, *The Autobiography of a Mountain Man, 1805–1889* (Pasadena, 1948), pp. 5–6.

outsider, had hurriedly dispatched their own caravan westward under William L. Sublette. Slipping past Wyeth's party by using a short cut since known as Sublette's Cutoff, the company caravan reached the rendezvous three days before Wyeth's. When he arrived "those honorable gentlemen" simply informed him that they could use none of his goods.[37]

This dishonorable procedure not only revealed the depths to which competition could drive normally honest men, but led directly to two important changes in the nature of the fur trade. For one the indignant Nathaniel Wyeth was responsible. No Yankee of his shrewdness would stand quietly aside while a contract was violated in this inexcusable manner. "Gentlemen," he was reported to have told the Rocky Mountain Fur Company partners, "I will roll a stone into your garden that you will never be able to get out." [38] In this angry mood he decided to build a fort on the Snake River, where he could sell the goods left on his hands; such a fort, he reasoned, would not only turn a certain loss into a probable profit, but would allow him to skim away some of the trade that might otherwise go to his rivals. Acting at once, he led his 126 pack horses northward and, on a grassy plain bordering the Snake, set his men building a stoutly palisaded enclosure that was called Fort Hall. No sooner was work completed on August 4, 1834, than Wyeth sent out two brigades to scour the country for beaver. Little matter that one was attacked by Blackfeet with the loss of most of its supplies, and that the other was turned back from the lower Snake River country by the polite but ruthless underbidding of Hudson's Bay Company men. Still a new rival had invaded the mountains to increase the already bitter competition.

It was also clear at the 1834 rendezvous that the Rocky Mountain Fur Company and the American Fur Company were ready to come to terms, convinced that the overtrapped Rockies could never produce enough furs to support both. The widely flung activities of the latter, however, made withdrawal impossible; if it abandoned its mountain trade its prestige among Indians in more profitable areas would suffer. Hence before the year was out it had reached an agreement to buy out the good will and assets of the Rocky Mountain Fur Company, and to employ both the former partners and their trappers. Thus did competition ring down the curtain on the company which, under var-

[37] Young (ed.) *Corr. and Journals of Wyeth,* p. 225.
[38] Victor, *River of the West,* p. 164.

ious names, had not only pioneered the beaver streams of the Far West, but in twelve years had shipped out more than one thousand packs of furs valued at nearly $500,000. Only Captain Bonneville remained as a competitor of the American Fur Company now. For another year he kept up the unequal struggle, then, after the 1835 rendezvous, started east, never to return. "The mountains," in the thankful words of an American Fur Company leader, "were clear of him." [39]

The next few years were relatively peaceful and mildly profitable for this concern. The 1835 rendezvous yielded 150 packs of skins; changing conditions were mirrored when these were carried east by pack animals only as far as Fort Laramie, a newly established company post on the upper Platte River, then shipped to St. Louis by steamboat. Again, in 1836, the rendezvous at Horse Creek was marked by the usual carefree debauchery, especially when Edward Rose claimed a $300 prize offered by the company for the greatest number of skins, and invested his earnings in five gallons of alcohol at $32 a gallon to treat his friends. Yet for those who could see, signs of decay were everywhere. The 120 trappers who attended the 1836 rendezvous represented only a fraction of the numbers present in former days, while Thomas Fitzpatrick, a giant of the trade since its origin, announced his retirement before the gathering broke up.

Worse was to come, for during the winter and spring of 1836–37 the trade staggered under two more blows. One was dealt by the exceptional cold of that winter; for months on end the snow lay seven feet deep in the mountains while the thermometer skidded far below the zero mark. Death by freezing took a frightful toll from the few animals that had managed to escape the hunters' traps. The second blow fell in the spring when the American Fur Company's annual steamboat reached Fort Union with smallpox on board. Within a few days friendly Indians at the fort were dying like flies; others who fled to escape carried the virus with them to spread it through native village after native village. No one will ever know how many hundreds— or thousands—of red men died before that epidemic ran its course. Those left alive were bitterly hostile, blaming the whites for deliberately killing off their brothers. "All that you hold dear," one warrior told his inflamed followers, "are all Dead, or Dying, with their faces all rotten, caused by those dogs the whites. . . . Rise all together, and

[39] Leonard, *Adventures of Zenas Leonard,* p. 281.

Not leave one of them alive." [40] Seldom had the Rockies been so dangerous for trappers as in those next months.

Given time, the American Fur Company might have recovered from these disasters, but that was a commodity that was running out. For moving relentlessly in from the west was a rival that could never be absorbed: the Hudson's Bay Company. In 1837 this concern bought Fort Hall from Nathaniel J. Wyeth, thus placing its eastern headquarters in the middle Snake River country, where its well-organized brigades could move easily over the whole Rocky Mountain hunting ground. Nor could the Americans compete with its efficient methods. Able to purchase the British goods that were always demanded by the trade without paying duties on them, and using the Columbia and Lewis rivers to provide cheap transportation, the Hudson's Bay Company caravans could outbid their rivals for the few furs left in the West. From 1837 on the American Fur Company was fighting a losing battle whose outcome was inevitable.

Certainly the pall of impending disaster hung over the rendezvous in 1838 and 1839. Gone were the drunken shouts of the alcohol-befuddled traders, their wild revels with Indian maidens, their reckless games where a year's profits might be lost with the turn of a card. Men thought twice about risking everything when there were no beaver to replace their squandered earnings. Instead, at the 1839 rendezvous, the well-mannered trappers gathered to listen to a sermon preached by a missionary on his way west to Christianize the tribesmen of the Oregon country. "He had," wrote an observer, "quite a number of white men and more Indians to hear him. After meeting many got drunk." [41] At both the 1838 and 1839 rendezvous the air of restraint was encouraged by rumors that the American Fur Company would no longer send caravans into the wilderness. When the 1840 caravan reached the rendezvous site at Horse Creek of the Green River, these rumors were confirmed. When it departed eastward that July its leaders announced that no more would be sent into the mountains. The rendezvous era of the fur trade had ended.

Yet the fur trade lived on for one brief but romantic interval. Its center, after 1840, was no longer the heart of the Rockies, but in a number of trading posts that were built along the fringes of the moun-

[40] Annie H. Abel (ed.), *Chardon's Journal at Fort Clark, 1834–1839* (Pierre, S.D., 1932), pp. 124–125.

[41] Asahel Munger, "Diary of Asahel Munger and Wife," *Oregon Historical Quarterly*, VIII (1907), 395.

tain country. Strategically located at points where they could be supplied with goods from the East by wagon trains and with furs from the West by the few Mountain Men and the larger number of Indians who continued trapping, they were able to thrive on smaller profits than those needed to sustain the rendezvous system. In such posts, moreover, the trade could continue all year rather than for a few days each summer, while the traders were protected from hostile Indians by stout walls—something that was important when overtrapping and white intrusion left the red men restless and unpredictable.

Of the 150 posts that were operating or had been recently abandoned in 1843, three played an especially important role in the later history of the trade. One was Fort Hall, which, as the Hudson's Bay Company's principal eastern outpost, dominated the traffic in furs in the western Rocky Mountain country. Another was Fort Laramie on the upper Platte River. Built in 1834 as a way station for caravans by the Rocky Mountain Fur Company, and later used for the same purpose by the American Fur Company, this stoutly built fort for many years controlled the trade of the central Rockies. To the south lay the third outpost, Bent's Fort, which was completed in 1833 near the junction of the Arkansas and Purgatory rivers by the brothers William and Charles Bent and their partner, Céran St. Vrain. The most elaborate of all the posts, Bent's Fort was surrounded by adobe walls fifteen feet high and seven thick at the base, enclosing an oblong court 100 by 180 feet, and surmounted by bastions thirty feet tall. Within the court were trading rooms, warehouses, homes for the officers, and a two-story recreation center containing a billiard room and bar; nearby was a corral enclosed by adobe walls that were planted on the top with cacti to prevent scaling, and an icehouse that was filled from the frozen river each winter.[42]

Few of the forts were as sumptuous as that of the Bent brothers, but all preserved a touch of the romance that the fur trappers had brought to the frontier. During the fall and spring especially all was life and bustle within their walls. Then the supply train arrived from the East, filled with luxuries almost forgotten and bringing news of events that were nonetheless exciting because they were a year old. Then bands of free trappers came storming in from the mountains, ready to exchange their packs of furs for a few necessities and large quantities of

[42] David Lavender, *Bent's Fort* (Garden City, N.Y., 1954), *passim*, is a thorough history of this phase of the fur trade.

alcohol. Then caravans sent out by the post itself came clattering back from distant Indian villages with tales of adventure and pack animals loaded with pelts. Then, too, travelers stopped to rest a few days, or to replenish their supplies before continuing their journey. Each night, during these seasons, the forts hummed with activity as grizzled old trappers swung their squaw partners through stomping dances or gulped "trapper whisky" until they were roaring drunk. As summer heat ended trapping or winter cold stopped travel, peace descended on the forts once more. Travelers saw only "clerks and traders, seated in the shade of the piazza, smoking the long native pipe, passing it from one to another, drawing the precious smoke into the lungs by short hysterical sucks till filled, and then ejecting it through the nostrils . . . old trappers withered with exposure to the rending elements, the half-tamed Indian . . . seated on the ground around a large tin pan of dry meat, and a tankard of water." [43]

Colorful as they were, these forts could only sweep the crumbs from a table that had once groaned under riches. Their owners could live comfortably if not luxuriously by trading liquor for pelts—despite laws that made this practice illegal—but they could never restore the glories of the era of the rendezvous. The trappers had helped to eliminate themselves by their ruthless extermination of fur-bearing animals. By 1840 the Rocky Mountain country was so completely trapped out that, as one complained, "lizards grow poor, and wolves lean against the sand banks to howl." [44] Another, with tears in his eyes, bemoaned the fate of his kind: "Now, the mountains are so poor that one would stand a right good chance of starving, if he were obliged to hang up here for seven days. The game is all driven out. No place here for a white man now. Too poor, too poor. What little we get, you see, is bull beef. Formerly, we ate nothing but cows, fat and young. More danger then, to be sure; but more beaver too; and plenty of grease about the buffalo ribs. Ah! those were good times; but a white man has now no more business here." [45]

So the fur trade died, as the old Mountain Men passed from the pages of history. They had played their role in opening the Far West to more stable pioneers. They had weakened the Indians by debauching the red men with liquor, infecting them with venereal diseases and

---

[43] Farnham, *Travels in the Great Western Prairies,* I, 189–190.
[44] *Ibid.,* II, 5.
[45] *Ibid.,* I, 283.

smallpox, and robbing them of their self-sufficiency. They had explored every nook and cranny of that giant country, and carried eastward news of the opportunities that awaited farmer and herdsman. Wrote one who knew and admired them: "Not a hole or corner . . . but has been ransacked by these hardy men. From the Mississippi to the mouth of the Colorado of the West, from the frozen regions of the North to the Gila in Mexico, the beaver-hunter has set his traps in every creek and stream. All this vast country, but for the daring and enterprise of these men, would be even now a *terra incognita* to geographers." [46] Over the trails that they blazed and through the passes that they discovered were to come the long wagon trains of the pioneers, to fill the valleys that once rang with the shouts of drunken trappers with fertile farms, and to transform their isolated trading posts into bustling villages that symbolized the conquest of the Far West.

[46] Ruxton, *Adventures in Mexico and the Rocky Mountains,* p. 234.

CHAPTER 4

The Coming of the Pioneers

M OUNTAIN MEN had marked the trails that led to the Far West, but something more was needed to set the tide of population rolling toward the Pacific. Throughout the history of the American frontier, mass migrations occurred only when attracting and expelling forces operated in conjunction; not until people were unhappy at home and assured of greater prosperity ahead were they willing to risk the uncertainties of a new land. By the end of the 1830's such a combination of pressures was beginning to operate. In the Mississippi Valley hard times that followed the Panic of 1837 left men dissatisfied and restlessly eager to seek opportunity elsewhere. At the same time they heard tales of the riches that awaited them in the distant West. In the level valleys of California's Sacramento and San Joaquin rivers, they were told, ranches the size of kingdoms and farms as large as principalities could be had for the asking; in Oregon's lush Willamette Valley lands rivaling those of Eden were being parceled into 640 acre lots for all comers. Those who spread these tales were the first American pioneers on the Pacific slope—merchants, explorers, missionaries, and visionary empire builders—and their propaganda inspired the overland migrations of the 1840's.

Not unnaturally, the first voices to urge the occupation of the Far West were those of eastern visionaries rather than western frontiersmen; not unnaturally, too, they counseled the overrunning of the Oregon Country rather than of California. California, after all, was indisputably a part of Mexico, and national arrogance had not yet reached the point where men could recommend grabbing a neighbor's lands. No such restraints applied to the Oregon Country. Claimed originally by England, Spain, Russia, and the United States on the basis of discovery and exploration, this tempting region had become, by the middle 1820's, an important object of contention between the American and British governments. By this time, too, the disputed area had been defined geographically; when Spain withdrew from the controversy in 1821, it ceded to the United States its claims north of the forty-second parallel; when Russia followed in 1824 and 1825, it surrendered to the other contestants its rights south of the line of 54° 40'. Neither England nor the United States was ready for the show-down; hence they agreed on a treaty of joint occupation that allowed the nationals of both to trade or settle "on the North West Coast of America, Westward of the Stony Mountains." [1] To the nation that succeeded in occupying the country, the prize would fall.

This was the situation that inspired the first Oregon propagandist, Dr. John Floyd, a congressman from Virginia. As early as December, 1820, he moved that Congress name a select committee to "inquire into the situation of the settlements upon the Pacific Ocean and the expediency of occupying the Columbia River." His colleagues responded by naming him chairman of this committee, giving him an opportunity to belabor them with a series of fiery speeches urging the immediate occupation of the entire Columbia basin. His listeners failed to catch his enthusiasm; they argued that populations east and west of the Rockies would have a "permanent separation of interests" as one looked to Europe, the other to the Orient, for trade, and they insisted that any settlements founded on the "bleak and inhospitable" Pacific coast would soon separate from the Union anyway. In the end pessimism prevailed as Dr. Floyd's bill was thumpingly defeated.[2]

His mantle as a western prophet descended to a visionary New Englander named Hall Jackson Kelley. Harvard educated, a writer of schoolbooks, and a surveyor, Kelley had been avidly, almost fanatically, interested in the Pacific coast since reading the reports of the Lewis and Clark expedition. Having devoured every possible work on

[1] The Treaty of Joint Occupation was signed in 1818 for a ten-year period and renewed indefinitely in 1827, with the stipulation that it could be terminated by either party on six months' notice.

[2] Floyd's contributions are best described in Charles H. Ambler, "The Oregon Country, 1810–1830: A Chapter in Territorial Expansion," *Mississippi Valley Historical Review*, XXX (1943), 3–24, and his speeches and resolutions are conveniently assembled in Archer B. Hulbert (ed.), *Where Rolls the Oregon: Prophet and Pessimist Look Northwest* (Overland to the Pacific Series, III, Denver, 1933), pp. 39–102.

his subject, he was ready, in February, 1828, to prepare a "Memorial of Citizens of the United States, praying for a grant of land, and the aid of Government in forming a colony on the Northwest coast of the United States," which was presented to Congress and widely publicized. This was only the first of a flood of propaganda works from his fevered pen. A bulky pamphlet, *A Geographical Sketch of that Part of North America called Oregon,* followed in 1830, while letters to newspapers and other pamphlet publications appeared regularly during the next two years. In all he played the same tune. In Oregon, he told his readers, they would find a beautiful valley, cut off from the winds of the Pacific by mountains, well watered, "nourished by a rich soil, and warmed by a congenial heat," and "exactly accommodated to the interests of its future cultivators." [3]

Kelley, however, was something more than a propagandist. His dream was to lead a band of settlers to his self-discovered paradise. With this in mind he organized in the spring of 1831 the American Society for Encouraging the Settlement of the Oregon Territory, then issued *A General Circular to All Persons of Good Character, who Wish to Emigrate to the Oregon Territory,* in which he told of his plans in detail. All willing to accompany him, he wrote, should assemble at St. Louis in the spring of 1832; they would journey overland with all of their expenses paid by the government. This grandiose scheme collapsed when Congress showed something less than enthusiasm at the prospect of shouldering the costs, but Kelley started west himself that autumn, traveling by way of New Orleans and Mexico. At San Diego he met the trader, Ewing Young, and with him pushed on to Oregon where he was received with unusual coldness by the Hudson's Bay Company's Dr. John McLoughlin. "Kelley," wrote one who was there, "is not received at the Fort . . . as a gentleman a house is given him and food sent him from the Gov. Table but he is not suffered to mess here." [4] Four months of this frigid treatment started Kelley home again. That his efforts had aroused no wild interest was certain; he

[3] Fred W. Powell (ed.), *Hall J. Kelley on Oregon; a Collection of Five of His Published Works and a Number of Hitherto Unpublished Letters* (Princeton, 1932), p. 22. Most of Kelley's important works are in this volume, and other letters that he wrote are in Archer B. Hulbert (ed.), *The Call of the Columbia: Iron Men and Saints Take the Oregon Trail* (Overland to the Pacific Series, IV, Denver, 1934), pp. 14–66.

[4] Frank G. Young (ed.), *The Correspondence and Journals of Captain Nathaniel J. Wyeth, 1831–1836* (Eugene, Ore., 1899), p. 250.

had, however, planted a seed that would soon flourish beyond his own hopes.

Kelley's futile efforts had shown that the time was not ripe for a colony in the Oregon Country; there remained, however, the question of whether a commercial enterprise could flourish there. The ill-fated individual who decided to test this possibility—and to serve as the next publicist for Oregon in doing so—was a twenty-nine-year-old businessman from Cambridge named Nathaniel J. Wyeth. His imagination fired by Kelley's works, Wyeth organized a joint-stock company to engage in the fur trade and salmon fishing along the Columbia River. His advertisement in the Boston papers for "industrious and temperate men, and of good constitutions and peacible [sic] dispositions" attracted thirty-one recruits who spent the spring rehearsing wild-west tactics on an island in Boston harbor, clothed in their "showy and attractive uniform suits" of "coarse woolen jacket and pantaloons, a striped cotton shirt and cowhide boots." [5] Then, having sent a supply ship, the *Sultana,* around the Horn, Wyeth and his oddly assorted followers began their overland trek in the spring of 1832. Traveling westward from St. Louis with a caravan of the Rocky Mountain Fur Company, they spent some time at the 1832 rendezvous before they reached the Hudson's Bay Company post, Fort Vancouver, in November. There Wyeth learned that the *Sultana* had been wrecked in the Society Islands and reluctantly started home again, his hopes of trade gone glimmering.

Bowed but not broken by these disasters, Wyeth spent the winter of 1833–34 organizing the Columbia River Fishing and Trading Company and securing backing from Boston capitalists. Once more, in the spring of 1834, he sent a ship, the *May Dacre,* around the Horn, and once more he started overland himself. Pausing to build Fort Hall as a trading post on the Snake River, he reached the coast on September 14, 1834, just one day ahead of the *May Dacre.* For a time fortune seemed to smile. The Hudson's Bay Company allowed him to fish and trade so long as he did not engage in the fur trade, and to construct a small post, Fort William, on an island at the mouth of the Willamette River under the very shadow of Fort Vancouver.[6] There Wyeth re-

[5] John B. Wyeth, *Oregon; or A Short History of a Long Journey* (Cambridge, Mass., 1833), p. 12. Wyeth's journal of the expedition is in Young (ed.), *Corr. and Journals of Wyeth,* pp. 112–153.

[6] A full journal by a member of the party is John K. Townsend, *Narrative*

mained through the winter as farms were laid out and salmon fishing began. But as the months passed, misfortunes multiplied. His men succumbed, one by one, to the damp climate; his salmon fishing proved so disappointing that the *May Dacre* sailed for home in the summer of 1835 with her hold half full; his farms produced little. For, all unknown to Wyeth, he was being politely but firmly frustrated at every step by the Hudson's Bay Company. "We opposed him," Dr. McLoughlin wrote his employers, "as much as was Necessary." [7] By the end of that summer Wyeth was ready to sell his interests to the company and retire from the West. His well-publicized efforts were not completely in vain, for he had interested a small but influential group of Easterners in the Oregon Country.

Nathaniel Wyeth's role as propagandist for the West was more than matched by another group of New England traders who were even then operating along a distant portion of the coast. Lured to the Pacific shores first in the late eighteenth century by the profitable trade in sea-otter skins, they had been temporarily expelled by traders of the Russian-American Fur Company who pushed relentlessly southward from Alaska. In 1811, when the Russians capitalized on Spain's weakness by founding Fort Ross not far above San Francisco, the American merchants seemed doomed to lose their foothold in the Pacific. Such might have been the case had not Mexico won its independence in 1821. This meant that California's long-closed ports were opened to any shipowners who believed they could make a profit there. Canny merchants in both Britain and America, who, as one writer has put it, would gladly carry coals to Newcastle if Newcastle wanted them, were quick to seize the opportunity. The missions and ranchos of California, they had heard, produced thousands of hides and tons of beef tallow each year. They knew, too, that tallow was in demand in South America, where candles were needed for workers in silver mines, and that leather would fetch a high price from shoe manufacturers in either Old or New England. At the same time the Californians were so starved for manufactured goods that they would gladly welcome merchants. These were the circumstances that gave rise to the "hide and tallow trade."

For a time British vessels dominated this trade, but in 1827 the

---

of a Journey Across the Rocky Mountains, to the Columbia River (Philadelphia, 1839), pp. 27–169.

[7] E. E. Rich (ed.), *The Letters of John McLoughlin from Fort Vancouver to the Governor and Committee. First Series, 1825–38* (Toronto, 1941), p. 177.

monopolistic agreement they had wrung from the Mexicans expired and the traffic was open to all. Ships came in droves now, most of them from New England, for if anyone in that day could scent profits halfway around the world, it was a Yankee trader. Some were sent by the Boston firm of Bryant, Sturgis & Company, which in twenty years of the trade exported half a million hides,[8] but more were owned by small merchants anxious to share in profits which on some voyages reached 300 per cent. Until the middle 1840's this trade went on, with each returning ship making Easterners more and more aware of California's potentialities.

The nature of the trade made this possible. Ships destined for the Pacific loaded in Boston or Salem or New York with a cargo of "everything under the sun" that would appeal to the Californians. "We had," wrote one trader, "spirits of all kinds, (sold by the cask,) teas, coffee, sugars, spices, raisins, molasses, hard-ware, crockery-ware, tin-ware, cutlery, clothing of all kinds, boots and shoes from Lynn, calocoes and cottons from Lowell, crapes, silks; also shawls, scarfs, necklaces, jewelry, and combs for the ladies; furniture; and in fact, everything that can be imagined, from Chinese fire-works to English cart-wheels." [9] Thus stocked, the vessel beat its way around the Horn and up the coast to the California capital of Monterey, where the captain haggled with customs officials until a "reasonable" duty was agreed upon. While this was going on he sent his supercargo overland on horseback to spread the word among rancheros and missionaries that the ship would soon arrive. All was hurry and confusion in the wake of this agent; cattle were slaughtered by the thousands and their hides pegged in the sun to dry, bags were filled with hot tallow, and Californians and Indians alike took stock of their needs as they decided what to buy from the wonder house of merchandise that would soon be available.

Just before the ship arrived the stiffened hides and great leather *botas* of tallow were loaded on solid-wheeled carts that went creaking and screeching to the shore amidst the shouts of the Indian driver

[8] The early British trade is described in Adele Ogden, "Hides and Tallow; McCulloch, Hartnell and Company, 1822–1828," *California Historical Society Quarterly*, VI (1927), 254–264. The same author's "Boston Droghers Along California Shores," *California Historical Society Quarterly*, VIII (1929), 289–305, is a scholarly history of the firm of Bryant, Sturgis & Company.

[9] Richard Henry Dana, Jr., *Two Years before the Mast; a Personal Narrative of Life at Sea* (New York, 1840), p. 94.

and the yelping of an army of dogs. There the hides were piled, to be watched by an Indian or two until the white-crested vessel sailed slowly into the harbor and cast its anchor slightly offshore. From all the country round came friars and rancheros and natives, to be rowed to the ship in small boats manned by the crew. What marvels awaited them there! The main deck was fitted out like a store, with cases of goods temptingly displayed and freshly scrubbed clerks standing about waiting to bargain. "For a week or ten days," one observer of such a scene wrote, "all was life on board. The people came off to look and to buy—men, women, and children; and we were continually going in the boats, carrying goods and passengers,—for they have no boats of their own. Everything must dress itself and come aboard and see the new vessel, if it were only to buy a paper of pins." [10]

Even the crew enjoyed these gala days, despite the hard work. As each purchase was completed, the sailors rowed the happy buyer ashore with his goods, then carried back the number of hides needed for payment. These were loaded, one or two at a time, on the heads of woolen-capped sailors, who, precariously balancing, waded through heavy sand or across kelp-slippery rocks to the waiting boat. When the hides reached the ships they were hoisted aboard, salted, and carefully stowed away in the hold. As the ship moved down the coast, stopping to trade at each harbor or inlet, the hold grew fuller and fuller until only a few feet remained below the beams. Then "steeving" began; "books" or bundles of twenty-five hides were pulled into the narrow space with ropes and pulleys until it was so tightly filled that not even the rough seas of the Horn could shift the cargo. Only then, usually after a year or eighteen months along the coast, was the vessel ready to begin its return voyage. [11]

These trading methods gave the crews of the "hide and tallow" vessels a thorough knowledge of the California coast, but a shift in techniques during the 1830's led to even more intimate contacts. So long as traders dealt with mission fathers they could extend credit almost indefinitely without risk; with the secularization of the missions after 1834 the situation changed. Trusting merchants who sold freely on credit to a ranchero in the hope of securing his future business soon

[10] *Ibid.*, p. 94.

[11] A typical voyage along the coast is described by the supercargo in Alfred Robinson, *Life in California: During a Residence of Several Years in That Territory* (New York, 1846), pp. 7–38.

found that he was likely to sell his hides to another trader rather than try to pay his debts. To meet this situation, shippers began establishing agents to buy hides in small quantities, then store them in warehouses until called for by a company vessel. Thus were the first permanent American residents of California scattered along the coast.

They were not numerous, these alien interlopers in Mexico's domain, but their energy gave them remarkable influence. Of such a stripe were Alfred Robinson, who used his post as agent for Bryant, Sturgis & Company as a springboard into marriage with a Santa Barbara beauty and a prosperous business career for himself; Abel Stearns, who became the wealthiest rancher in southern California; William Heath Davis, whose friendly charm won him a prominent role in commercial affairs; J. J. Warner, whose ranch near San Diego was to become a haven for later American arrivals; John Marsh, whose Los Medanos rancho earned him a modest fortune; and Thomas O. Larkin, who was destined to a leading role as businessman and politician in the 1840's.[12] Nearly all adopted Mexican wives and ways, even sharing with their new countrymen the belief that there was *poco tiempo*— too little time—to do anything today that could be done tomorrow. Yet they never forgot the land of their birth; their letters home advertised California everywhere in the United States, while their ability to profit mightily in that land of sunshine helped convince other Americans that the move west would not be in vain.

In still another way these first permanent American settlers on the Pacific slope paved the way for later migrations. They, or others like them, were to provide havens for the weary "emigrants" who had trekked across the plains and mountains to seek opportunity in that newer land. Businessmen such as Alfred Robinson and Thomas O. Larkin could not play this role; the migrants of the 1840's were farmers who were not attracted by the coastal towns where they lived. Instead the newcomers were drawn to the lower Sacramento Valley in California, where, waiting to receive them, were two hospitable ranchers who, by providing a definite objective for the overland pioneers, did yeoman service in encouraging the American occupation of the coast.

One was John Marsh, a Harvard-educated adventurer who had drifted into Los Angeles in 1836 with the works of Tom Paine, Johnson's *Lives of the Poets,* a hymnal, and a Bible in his saddlebags. On

[12] Nellie V. Sánchez, *Spanish Arcadia* (Los Angeles, 1929), pp. 132–142.

learning that there was not a single doctor in the pueblo, he proclaimed himself a physician, exhibiting his Harvard diploma as proof. For a time he practiced this profession, performing operations from amputations to deliveries with such success that the shelter where he stored the hides received in payment resembled a warehouse. Then, carrying his profits, he drifted northward to the lower San Joaquin Valley, where, at the foot of Mount Diablo, he purchased a rancho that he soon transformed into a minor principality. His fifty thousand acres, stocked with thousands of cattle and horses, earned Marsh a fortune within a few years, but he was still not contented. Cautious and miserly by nature, he developed the obsession that his giant holdings would become really valuable only if American settlers crowded in around them, and really safe only if the United States acquired California. To this end he wrote endless letters to friends and newspapers in the East, all praising the riches of California, urging the people to migrate there, and describing the routes they should follow.[13] His infectious enthusiasm, and his promise to provide work and food for all who came, played their part in stimulating migration.

Even more influential was another rancher, whose holdings dwarfed those of John Marsh. John A. Sutter was a rotund little man who mixed bluff, deceit, and ability to a remarkable degree. When he fled his native Switzerland to escape a bankruptcy warrant in 1834, his pockets were empty but his head was jammed with grandiose plans. In New York his glib tongue won him the friendship of numerous prominent persons who were too impressed with his tales of a noble background to inquire into his antecedents; from them he obtained letters of introduction that assured him an unquestioning welcome in mercantile circles wherever he went. These magic talismans he used to obtain service first on a Santa Fe caravan, then as a means of joining an American Fur Company outfit that deposited him at Fort Vancouver in 1838. They carried him to the Hawaiian Islands next, where he charmed leading merchants into advancing him money to buy a small ship. On this he reached California in July, 1839, carrying a cargo that he sold at a good profit.[14]

Money, however, was only one of John Sutter's objectives in life;

[13] George D. Lyman, *John Marsh, Pioneer* (New York, 1930), pp. 192–215, 237–240.

[14] James P. Zollinger, "John Augustus Sutter's European Backround," *California Historical Society Quarterly*, XIV (1935), 28–46.

most of all he wanted power. Where could he find this more easily than as master of a colony in the unpeopled valleys of interior California? To secure the land was easy for one with his gifted tongue; using the twenty letters of introduction to the governor that he had collected in his travels, he talked himself into a giant grant in the lower Sacramento Valley. Then, sending his ship back to be sold, he chartered a small schooner, filled it with a few crewmen picked up in San Francisco and with eight Kanakas who had come with him from Hawaii, and sailed up the Sacramento to his new home. At the head of navigation on the American River, a tributary of the Sacramento, he ordered his men to land. With eight Kanakas, three whites, and one friendly Indian he began building his empire.

During the next months the abilities of this strange little man were amply demonstrated. When Indians proved troublesome, he led his army of six men against them with such effect that they not only promised not to molest him but many enlisted as his servants. When his workers needed materials, he hypnotized Californians into loaning him seed for planting and livestock to start his herd. During all this time he drove his growing army of workers as they labored to build a great adobe fort, with walls eighteen feet high and two feet thick, surrounding a courtyard large enough to hold an army of one thousand men. When Fort Sutter was completed by the summer of 1843 it was an imposing sight indeed, with its towering bastions and cannon-studded walls enclosing a whole village of warehouses, homes, mills, and shops for gunsmiths, blacksmiths, flour millers, bakers, carpenters, and blanket makers. Over all Sutter ruled like a king. "I was everything," he wrote at the time, "—patriarch, priest, father, and judge." [15]

Comic-opera figure though he seemed—and was—Sutter played an important part in the migrations of the 1840's. Sutter's Fort, conveniently located at the end of the most commonly traveled trail across the Sierras, provided the pioneers with an objective for their journey, and both food and shelter at its end. To all who came he gave employment at respectable wages, even though he was in no need of labor. "All of them," he wrote in his diary, "was allways hospitably received under my roof and all those who could or would not be employed,

---

[15] Erwin G. Gudde, *Sutter's Own Story* (New York, 1936), pp. 66–67. These events are described in James P. Zollinger, *Sutter: The Man and His Empire* (New York, 1939), pp. 17–48.

could stay with me as long as they liked, and when leaving, I gave them Passports which was everywhere respected." [16]

Sutter's role as succorer of "emigrants" was duplicated in the Oregon Country by missionaries. Moved by a pious desire that the natives "should hear the Gospel before they are prejudiced against it by the fraud, injustice, and dissolute lives" of inevitable immigrants,[17] these earnest souls began interesting themselves in the Columbia Valley in the late 1820's, when the American Board of Commissioners for Foreign Missions sent an agent to investigate the possibility of founding stations there. Before this emissary's "chill report" had completely dampened enthusiasm, an unbelievable conjunction of impossible circumstances forced a renewal of interest. In October, 1831, four Indians from the Oregon Country—three Nez Percés and one Flathead—reached St. Louis with a band of trappers, having made the journey to satisfy their curiosity concerning the white man's way of life. While they were still in St. Louis, William Walker, an educated Wyandot Indian from the East, arrived to arrange the migration of his tribe westward. There he heard of the western tribesmen, but did not actually see them.[18]

Fourteen months later, in January, 1833, Walker wrote a completely distorted account of the visit to a friend; the natives, he said, had made the wearisome journey to ask that the white man's "Book of Heaven" be sent to them and that ministers show them the path to Heaven. Seldom had a letter created such a sensation when it was published in the March 1, 1833, issue of the *Christian Advocate and*

[16] John A. Sutter, *The Diary of Johann Augustus Sutter* (San Francisco, 1932), p. 19.

[17] Jonathan S. Green, *Journal of a Tour on the North West Coast of America in the Year 1829* (New York, 1915), p. 18.

[18] Most of the documents on the disputed question of these Indians' interest in religion are in Archer B. Hulbert and D. P. Hulbert (eds.), *The Oregon Crusade. Across Land and Sea to Oregon* (Overland to the Pacific Series, V, Denver, 1935), pp. 85–131. The best discussion of the evidence is in Clifford M. Drury, *Henry Harmon Spaulding: Pioneer of Old Oregon* (Caldwell, Ida., 1936), pp. 72–90. Two careful studies show that the Indians did have some knowledge of religion: T. C. Elliott, "Religion Among the Flatheads," *Oregon Historical Quarterly*, XXXVII (1936), 1–8, and Clifford M. Drury, "The Nez Percé 'Delegation' of 1831," *Oregon Historical Quarterly*, XL (1939), 283–287. J. Orin Oliphant, "Francis Haines and William Walker: A Critique," *Pacific Historical Review*, XIV (1945), 211–216, demonstrates that the Indians were still in St. Louis when Walker arrived there, while Francis Haines, "The Nez Percé Delegation to St. Louis in 1831," *Pacific Historical Review*, VI (1937), 71–78, shows that Walker never actually met the visitors.

Journal, a Methodist publication. Overnight the "plea" of these be-nighted heathen for the word of God became the concern of every religious person in America; not a pulpit in the land but echoed their request, or a church editor who could refrain from pathetic discourse on the "Wise Men from the West" who had tramped two thousand miles to ask for the Bible. A single letter from an imaginative Indian had done more to stimulate interest in the Oregon Country than the efforts of a generation of propagandists.[19]

The Methodists were galvanized into action first. As contributions poured into the offices of the *Christian Advocate and Journal,* the Methodist Missionary Society hurriedly voted to establish a mission among the Flatheads. On July 17, 1833, the Reverend Jason Lee was named its head. This thirty-year-old stripling hardly seemed equal to the task that lay before him. Tall and slightly stooped, with fair com-plexion and mild blue eyes, Lee was meek, warmhearted, and affable, but there was little of the blood of martyrs in his veins.[20] Time was to show that the very qualities that lessened his effectiveness as a mission-ary—his easy-going nature, his lack of fanatical zeal, his elevation of the practical above the ideal—were to make him one of the most suc-cessful colonizers in the history of the Far West.

Accompanied by his nephew, Daniel Lee, an assistant, and two helpers, Jason Lee started west in the spring of 1834, traveling from Independence with Nathaniel Wyeth's party of that year. At Fort Hall he preached the first sermon heard west of the mountains to a stoic audience of trappers and Indians "who sat upon the ground like statues." [21] The party reached Fort Vancouver on September 16, 1834, to find the whole population out on the riverbank to welcome them, with Dr. McLoughlin towering above the rest as he waved his cane in greeting.

A few conversations with this canny Hudson's Bay Company official were enough to convince Jason Lee that he should not establish his mission among the Flatheads as his instructions decreed. Dr. Mc-Loughlin had no objection to missionaries; indeed he welcomed them

[19] Drury, *Henry Harmon Spaulding,* pp. 91–92, proves that the Walker letter aroused interest because it stressed the Indians' alleged concern with religion, and not because it described the cruel devices used by the Flatheads to distort the shape of their children's heads, as historians formerly believed.

[20] William H. Gray, *A History of Oregon, 1792–1849. Drawn from Personal Observation and Authentic Information* (Portland, Ore., 1870), p. 107. Gray was a friend of Jason Lee.

[21] Townsend, *Narrative of a Journey,* p. 107.

as a force for order among his trappers. He was determined, however, to keep them out of the Indian country, where they might interfere with trade, and near Fort Vancouver, where they could be carefully controlled. Hence he suggested the Willamette Valley as an ideal mission field. There they would not only be dependent on the company for supplies and protection, but would be south of the Columbia River in a region that England did not covet. Using all his eloquence, the wily doctor dwelt at length on the fertility and safety of the Willamette country, in contrast to the danger of life among the Flatheads, where Blackfoot raids meant almost certain death. His arguments carried the day. After "much prayer for direction as to a place for present location," Lee decided to build his station in a grove of fir and oak trees on the southern fringe of French Prairie, a grassy meadow on the east bank of the Willamette River. "A larger field of usefulness," wrote Daniel Lee, "was contemplated as the object of the mission than the benefiting of a single tribe. The wants of the whole country, present and prospective . . . were taken into the account." [22]

With his decision thus rationalized, and with supplies and animals loaned by Dr. McLoughlin, Jason Lee and his followers fell to building a log house and chapel near a settlement of twenty retired French-Canadian trappers. To these indifferent subjects they directed their missionary zeal; indeed there were no other prospects, for an epidemic of a few years before had wiped out all Indians of the Willamette Valley save a few specimens so degraded they could arouse little enthusiasm in the most fanatical man of God. A branch mission established by the Methodists at The Dalles did become a religious center of some importance, but Lee's station through its history proved more useful in luring new souls to the Oregon Country than in saving those already there. Gradually settlers drifted in—deserters from the Wyeth party, old Mountain Men, retired Hudson's Bay Company trappers—until by 1836 Americans outnumbered the English in the growing settlement.

The success of the Methodists—in founding a mission if not in saving souls—sent other denominations scurrying into action. The Presbyterians made their bid for a share of the field in the spring of 1835 when they sent two missionaries—the Reverend Samuel Parker and the Reverend Marcus Whitman—westward with the American

[22] Daniel Lee and J. H. Frost, *Ten Years in Oregon* (New York, 1844), p. 127.

Fur Company caravan. At the rendezvous they learned from visiting Snake, Flathead, and Nez Percé Indians something of the difficulties that lay ahead; hence Whitman returned to the East to raise more funds while Parker went ahead to select sites for the stations they would found. Both performed their tasks admirably. Parker decided that their missions would be located at Waiilatpu among the Cayuse, at Lapwai in the Nez Percé country, and in the Spokane region, then returned to the East by ship; Whitman secured needed funds, a wife, and a handful of assistants before he started for Oregon again in the spring of 1836. This time the journey offered problems, for the wives of two of the missionaries were along, and the American Fur Company leaders were afraid that white women in the mountains would offer too many temptations to the Indians and Mountain Men. Hence the caravan slipped away without the missionaries. Marcus Whitman, whose determination was unsurpassed, led his followers in a series of forced marches that allowed them to join the traders before dangerous Indian country was reached. The whole party arrived safely at Fort Vancouver on September 12, 1836.[23]

Whitman was no one to be lulled into planting a mission under the protection—and restraint—of the Hudson's Bay Company; hence he ignored Dr. McLoughlin's pleas and established two stations, one at Waiilatpu with himself in charge and the other at Lapwai under his assistant, the Reverend Henry H. Spaulding. Dr. McLoughlin, generous as always, provided every help. Even with this the task proved difficult. The Cayuse and Nez Percé Indians were nomads accustomed to following the buffalo herds and salmon streams; sedentary life about a mission station held little appeal to them. Whitman and Spaulding gradually won some support from a handful of the natives who consented to alter their way of life in the hope of salvation, but even these soon showed signs of insolence and rebellion. "Really," wrote Spaulding in despair, "I fear that they will all prove to be a selfish, deceptive race of beings." [24]

[23] Whitman's journal is in F. G. Young (ed.), "Journal of Report of Dr. Marcus Whitman of His Tour of Exploration with Rev. Samuel Parker in 1835 beyond the Rocky Mountains," *Oregon Historical Quarterly*, XXVIII (1927), 239–257, and Parker's in Samuel Parker, *Journal of an Exploring Tour beyond the Rocky Mountains* (Ithaca, N.Y., 1838). Letters and other documents are in Archer B. Hulbert and D. P. Hulbert (eds.), *Marcus Whitman, Crusader* (Overland to the Pacific Series, VI-VIII, Denver, 1936–41).

[24] Quoted in Melvin C. Jacobs, *Winning Oregon* (Caldwell, Ida., 1938), p. 26.

The failure of these earnest Presbyterians to win converts indicated, far more than did the record of the indifferent Jason Lee, the ineffectiveness of missionaries as savers of souls in the Oregon Country. Yet their contribution to history was significant, not as apostles of Christianity, but as promoters of migration. More than any other group they kept alive the spark of interest in Oregon and hurried the westward surge of population into the Willamette Valley.

Their efforts in this direction bore tangible fruit in 1836, when President Andrew Jackson sent an official agent west to investigate their progress and the country they occupied. William A. Slacum, who was selected for the task, spent the winter of 1836–37 in Oregon. The missions, Slacum soon realized, must be more firmly rooted economically if they were to serve as magnets for later migrants. He saw, too, that both their economy and their independence would be bolstered if they had cattle of their own rather than using those borrowed from the Hudson's Bay Company herds. Hence he helped the settlers organize the Willamette Cattle Company, raise money, and send ten men under Ewing Young into California to purchase several hundred head. The enterprise was a hazardous one, for Mexican law forbade the export of cattle and the drive back over parched plains or mountains piled on mountains would have tried the patience of a saint. "Nearly every inch of progress has been gained by the use of clubs, sticks, stones, and bawling," wrote a member of that party.[25] But at last the 630 cattle that survived were safe in the Willamette Valley. "We will have plenty of butter and milk in future I expect," Mrs. Jason Lee wrote happily.[26]

Slacum's efforts had helped lay the basis for future settlements, but his contribution was even greater than this. The publication of his report, in December, 1837, with its enthusiastic description of the Oregon countryside, not only aroused interest in the East but brought into the arena a new congressional champion. Senator Lewis F. Linn of Missouri lost no time in introducing a Senate bill to create an "Oregon Territory" where settlers would be welcomed and protected by the

[25] Philip L. Edwards, *The Diary of Philip Leget Edwards; the Great Cattle Drive from California to Oregon in 1837* (San Francisco, 1932), p. 35. Slacum's own account is in "Memorial of William A. Slacum, Praying Compensation for his Services in obtaining Information in Relation to the Settlements on the Oregon River, December 18, 1837," 25th Congress, 2nd Session, *Senate Executive Document* No. 24, pp. 12–13.

[26] Theressa Gay, *Life and Letters of Mrs. Jason Lee, First Wife of Rev. Jason Lee of the Oregon Mission* (Portland, Ore., 1936), p. 163.

American Army. This was necessary, he told his colleagues, to prevent the whole region falling into Britain's hands. As usual Congress was not ready to take such a belligerent step, but it did name Linn chairman of a special committee to study the situation. The resulting report was an enthusiastic paean of praise for Oregon and an unabashed invitation to Americans to migrate there as rapidly as possible.[27] Widely circulated, it did much to prepare the way for later migrations.

Nor did Slacum's influence end there, for he left the settlers in the Willamette Valley seething with dissatisfaction at their own government's neglect. Jason Lee, who was increasingly seeking compensation for his failure as a missionary by assuming the role of civil leader, capitalized on this sentiment by calling the Americans together on March 16, 1838, to draw up a "Settlers' Petition" to Congress. Bearing this document, which demanded an immediate extension of the laws of the United States over Oregon, Lee started east a few weeks later. During the next months he traveled widely throughout the northern United States, lecturing to thousands on the richness and beauty of the Willamette Valley. In all he collected $40,000 for his mission, as well as planting the germ of the Oregon fever in hundreds of listeners. He also found time to deliver his petition to Senator Linn, who presented it to Congress in January, 1839.[28] Once more congressmen turned a deaf ear to the request of the settlers, but the era of indifference was drawing to a close. The time was not far distant when the American population in the Oregon Country would be so large that its demands could no longer be ignored.

The missionaries saw to that, for during the late 1830's their constant pleas for support drew a steady trickle of population westward. The Methodists sent twenty helpers to Lee's mission during 1837, including Dr. Elijah White, who was to become an active champion of migration, while the Presbyterians that year dispatched three missionaries and their helpers to found stations on the Clearwater River and among the Spokane Indians. A larger migration arrived in the fall of 1839, when Jason Lee returned, leading a "Great Reinforcement" of fifty-one new settlers. As these newcomers laid out their farms, built their sawmill at the Willamette Falls, and opened a store nearby, the Willamette Valley began to take on the appearance of a thriving frontier community. Others drifted in over the next months, many of them

[27] 25th Congress, 2nd Session, *Senate Document* No. 470, pp. 1–23.
[28] 25th Congress, 3rd Session, *House Report* No. 101, pp. 3–6.

old Mountain Men who were leaving the Rockies as trapping declined. These untamed spirits provided problems for the missionaries —one told a minister when asked to pray: "that's your business, not mine"—but each strengthened the nucleus of settlement there. By 1840 a traveler found 120 farms in the valley, operated by five hundred whites and one thousand Indian servants, and boasting 3,000 cattle, 2,500 horses, and "an infinite multitude of hogs." [29]

The missionaries, like the hide-and-tallow traders of California, played a significant role in the drama of westward migration. Their glowing reports, widely reprinted in religious journals, awakened thousands to an interest in the Oregon Country, while thousands more were stirred by the enthusiastic speeches of Jason Lee or Marcus Whitman. Their prospering farms in the Willamette Valley served as a tempting example of the profits waiting husbandmen at the end of the long trail west, as well as havens where newcomers could find shelter and friendly companionship until they established themselves. Lee's mission in Oregon and Sutter's Fort in California were literally the meccas of all whose trains of covered wagons plodded toward the Pacific during the 1840's.

In still another way these precursors of the pioneers helped set in motion the tide of immigration: they publicized their adopted lands so effectively that by 1840 not a farmer or shopkeeper in the Mississippi Valley but carried in his mind a golden—and largely false—picture of the Willamette and Sacramento valleys. Virtually every form of communication was employed by these propagandists. Some wrote books; Richard Henry Dana's account of his adventures in the hide-and-tallow trade, *Two Years before the Mast*, was recognized as a classic from the day of its appearance in 1840. Some gave speeches; a boy whose parents later moved to Oregon remembered hearing a soapbox orator in Platte City, Missouri, describing that land as "a pioneer's paradise" where "the pigs are running about under the great acorn trees, round and fat, and already cooked, with knives and forks sticking in them so that you can cut off a slice whenever you are hungry." [30] Some wrote letters to newspapers, either with the avowed purpose of attracting immigrants or simply because they were so contented with their new homes that they wanted to share their good for-

[29] George Simpson, *An Overland Journey Round the World, During the Years 1841 and 1842* (2 vols., London, 1847), I, 249–250.
[30] Edward H. Lenox, *Overland to Oregon in the Tracks of Lewis and Clarke. History of the first Migration to Oregon in 1843* (Oakland, Calif., 1904), p. 13.

tune. These were widely printed in such expansionistic eastern newspapers as the New York *Sun,* the New York *Herald,* and the *Journal of Commerce,* and in all western papers; a St. Louis editor noted that one Oregon letter had appeared in thirty of his exchanges. Even private letters were passed from hand to hand, or read to eager listeners in churches and schoolhouses.

The content of this propaganda was as uniform as the methods of diffusion were varied. All pictured the western valleys as modern (but somewhat more perfect) replicas of the Garden of Eden, where land in fabulous quantities could be had for the asking. All described soil of such fertility and climate of such perfection that crops surpassed any grown in the East. All spoke of available markets where every farmer's surplus would be sold at consistently high prices. All dwelt on the healthy atmosphere and the lack of disease in those valley paradises. And all expressed confidence that only a few American settlers were needed to drive out foreign interlopers and make those coveted lands a part of the United States. One prospective immigrant, after being subjected to this barrage, felt that the Far West offered "such fascinations as almost to call the angels and saints from their blissful garden and diamond temples in the heavens." [31]

That farms as large as kingdoms could be had for the taking was constantly emphasized. In California, they pointed out, the smallest amount granted by the government was one league, or six square miles, while eleven-league grants were more commonly given to anyone who cared to become a citizen. So long as Oregon remained in dispute between England and the United States pioneers could appropriate an estate of any size they chose. After the United States took over the region (as everyone knew it would), Senator Linn would take care of the pioneers. Not one of them but knew he already had a bill before Congress to give every Oregon settler 640 acres of land, plus another 160 acres for his wife and each of his children. A man with a dozen children could secure a handsome estate under those conditions, then sell off his surplus to the later comers who would soon be crowding in. A Missouri farmer who heard such talk called his family together and spoke in this fashion: "Out in Oregon I can get me a square mile of land. And a quarter section for each of you all. Dad burn me, I am done with this country. Winters it's frost and snow to freeze a body; summers the overflow from Old Muddy drowns half my acres; taxes

[31] Edwin Bryant, *What I Saw in California* (New York, 1848), p. 16.

take the yield of them that's left. What say, Maw, it's God's country." [32]

And what yields these giant farms would produce—according to the propagandists. In that frost-free land, it was pointed out, wheat could be planted in January and corn and beans in April, thus assuring a newcomer a first year's crop and an established farmer two or three crops a year. That rain seldom fell was a blessing rather than a curse, for constantly sunny skies kept vegetation growing while heavy nightly dews provided all moisture necessary. Amidst these conditions, and with soil so rich and fruitful that not even the delta of the Nile could match it, wheat grew as tall as a man with each stalk sprouting seven kernels, oats reared eight feet high with stalks half an inch thick, clover shot upward to a height of five feet and was massed so tightly that a man could scarcely force his way through a field, and beets were harvested when three feet in circumference and turnips when five feet!

Moreover, the publicists insisted, markets waited all foodstuffs that could be produced. In the Oregon country the Hudson's Bay Company stood ready to purchase any quantities and pay "the very highest prices, even at the doors of the farmers," while in California visiting ship owners were so desperate for supplies that price was no object with them. Within a short time even greater markets would be opened, for beyond lay the teeming millions of India and China "with nothing intervening but the blue and stormless Pacific." [33] It is not surprising that wheat in the West sold for from fifty cents to one dollar a bushel, flour at five dollars a barrel, potatoes at fifty cents a bushel, and beef or pork at eight or ten cents a pound. Yet commodities needed by the farmer cost no more than in the Mississippi Valley.

Prospects such as these stirred many a Middle Western farmer in the depression years after 1837, but no less tempting were the propagandists' wide-eyed accounts of the good health enjoyed by all Westerners. To men who spent every summer shaking with malaria, and each winter racked with "congestive fever," news of a land where these illnesses were unknown was worth hearing. Oregon was healthy enough, if its publicists could be believed, but California was the land that then, as now, inspired writers to heights of lyricism. "If a man

[32] Quoted in Verne Bright, "The Folklore and History of the 'Oregon Fever,'" *Oregon Historical Quarterly*, XII (1951), 252.

[33] Overton Johnson and W. H. Winter, *Route Across the Rocky Mountains, With a Description of Oregon and California* (Lafayette, Ind., 1946), p. 62. Most of the guidebooks of the period contained similar statements.

were to ask of God a climate," wrote one enthusiast as he described the "perpetual spring" there, "he would ask just such an one as that of California." [34] There disease of any kind was unknown. Missourians heard an old trapper grow indignant when they asked him if the "ague" was troublesome along the Sacramento. "There was," he said, "but one man in California that ever had a chill there, and that was a matter of so much wonderment . . . that they went eighteen miles into the country to see him shake." [35] Indeed, the Californians' only problem was dying, for the climate was so healthy that they lived forever. A traveler in Missouri told of one man who, tired of life at the age of 250 years, finally made his will and moved to another spot, requesting only that he be brought back for burial. That was a mistake, for no sooner was he safely in his grave in that health-giving land than "the energies of life were immediately restored to his inanimate corpse! Herculean strength was imparted to his frame, and, bursting the prison-walls of death, he appeared . . . reinvested with all the vigor and beauty of early manhood." [36]

Tales such as these, even if slightly exaggerated, were certain to interest Middle Westerners, but migrations have never been impelled by economic forces alone, and those of the 1840's were no exception. The West in that decade promised men not only riches but, in the words of Senator Linn, the opportunity of "finding and founding empires for us." [37] Those who journeyed to Oregon would drive back the hated Hudson's Bay Company and win that disputed region for their beloved United States. Those who made California their objective would eventually wrest that garden spot from the indolent Mexicans, adding another rich prize to their nation's territories. Those who accomplished such wonders were more than mere seekers after wealth; they were, as one of them solemnly believed, "the benefactors of their race—the founders of a new, enlightened and powerful state." [38]

That migration would win both Oregon and California was never questioned. Every one knew that possession was nine points of the law; all that Americans needed to win the Oregon country was to

[34] Waddy Thompson, *Recollections of Mexico* (New York, 1846), p. 233.

[35] John Bidwell, *Echoes of the Past* (Chico, Calif., n.d.), p. 6.

[36] Bryant, *What I Saw in California,* pp. 16–17.

[37] *Congressional Globe,* 27th Congress, 3rd Session, Appendix, p. 152.

[38] P. L. Edwards, *Sketch of the Oregon Territory: or, Emigrants' Guide* (Liberty, Mo., 1842), p. 20.

move there in sufficient numbers that the British would be displaced. California would fall to the United States just as easily, for the Californians were an indolent, shiftless people so dedicated to the pursuit of pleasure that they would never bother to defend their land. People so lackadaisical that they spent their time selecting "shade trees, under which they shall spend the day in sloth, or in stealing a bullock's hide on which to throw their lazy carcasses at night" [39] were hardly to be feared. Even if the Mexicans wanted to protect themselves they could not, for they could muster an army of no more than "ten or eleven hundred men—in efficiency nearly equal to a party of one hundred and fifty well-armed Americans." [40] Pioneers moving to such a land could add a rich prize to their country's possessions by scarcely lifting a finger.

Even Americans sensible enough not to believe these sanguine estimates knew there was some truth in all the propagandists said. California was ripe for the plucking in the 1840's. By this time Mexican authority had virtually vanished. With the death of the able governor, José Figueroa, in 1835, began a "Decade of Revolution" in which corrupt officials sent from the mother country vied with equally corrupt native Californians for the right to rule. During those years the governorship changed hands with kaleidoscopic frequency; in one thirteen-month period no less than four men held the office. Matters reached a climax in 1844, when General Manuel Micheltorena arrived from the mother country to assume the governorship, leading three hundred unruly ex-convicts who paraded as his soldiers. After only a few weeks the native Californians sent him back; when he sailed for home the last vestige of Mexican control vanished. To make matters worse, his victors could not agree among themselves. Pío Pico, who "commanded" the revolutionists in the south, was soon at sword's points with José Castro, who was in "control" in the San Francisco area. Here was a situation handmade for American intervention. There was scarcely an influential native Californian who would not welcome rule by the United States as the only means of restoring order and protecting property rights.

Seldom in the history of the frontier had a new land offered such

[39] Thomas J. Farnham, *Travels in California, and Scenes in the Pacific Ocean* (New York, 1844), pp. 356–357.

[40] Rufus B. Sage, *Rocky Mountain Life; or, Startling Scenes and Perilous Adventures in the Far West* (Philadelphia, 1846), p. 249.

tempting possibilities as did the Pacific slope at the beginning of the 1840's. It did not matter that this area of opportunity lay two thousand miles away. The end was worth any means, especially for a people so ridden by debt and depression as the inhabitants of the Mississippi Valley as the Panic of 1837 ran its course. Why stay at home when wheat sold for ten cents a bushel, corn had to be given away, and bacon was so cheap that steamboats used it for fuel? Why not let the mortgage holder have what was left and begin life anew in the golden West? Here were the ingredients that sent the "Oregon fever" and the "California fever" sweeping across the Middle West in the decade of the 1840's.

CHAPTER 5

The Overland Trails

PAST generations of historians conjured up a variety of reasons to explain the great migrations of the 1830's and 1840's. Men went west, they said, to plant the institution of slavery, or to win distant territories for freedom, or because land speculators had aroused their avaricious desires. Perhaps some Southerners did hope to perpetuate slavery in the Southwest; perhaps some Northerners did believe that the abolitionist crusade would gain by their sacrifices. But their numbers were few; the westward movement during these years would have followed the same course if the slavery conflict had not arisen and if speculation was an unknown art. One motive alone underlay the great migrations, and that was land hunger. So long as good lands lay ahead, nothing could hold back the American frontiersmen, whether distance or hardship or international boundaries. If anything in history approached an irresistible force, it was the pioneer who had learned that fertile fields to the west awaited his plow.

Always a chronic disease among those who lived on the fringes of settlement, this land fever at times became acute. This was the case by the late 1830's, when the call of the Willamette and the Sacramento was heard in the Mississippi Valley. Everywhere letters from those beckoning lands were passed from hand to hand until tattered, or were read to intent gatherings by ministers and schoolmasters. Everywhere newspapers were eagerly scanned for the latest dispatches from Oregon or California; editors gave over more and more space to these items as they sensed mounting public interest. And in town after town "Oregon Societies" or "California Societies" were formed to collect information on trails, publish reports, and secure pledges from those willing to promise that they would migrate. By 1839 at least ten of these societies were operating, with more organizing constantly.[1]

That spring the first little band of thirteen men—from Peoria, Illinois, and guided by Thomas J. Farnham—made their way west to the Willamette Valley with a train of pack horses, but not until 1841 did the first sizable party take to the trail. The ambition of a twenty-five-year-old named John Bidwell was responsible. A recent arrival in Missouri from Ohio, Bidwell had been left penniless when gunmen wrested his farm from him just at the time he first heard of California's riches through a letter of John Marsh. Falling victim to the fever at once, he spent the winter of 1840–41 enlisting members in the Western Emigration Society, which he formed; by early spring he had promises from five hundred persons to journey westward. Before the time for their departure the number declined sharply, partly because shopkeepers started an anti-California campaign to keep their customers at home, but more because Thomas Farnham returned from his journey with the "Peoria Band" to report that the trail was difficult and the country not the Eden it had been pictured. Only sixty-nine men, women, and children finally reached the rendezvous point at Sapling Grove.

One could have searched the West in vain for a less likely-appearing group of pioneers. Not a single member of the party had the slightest experience with life beyond the settlements, nor did any of them have more than the haziest notion of either their objective or the route there. "We knew only that California lay to the west," Bidwell wrote.[2] All, moreover, were poverty-stricken, with the total cash assets of the entire band totalling less than $100, and with one of the emigrants, "Cheyenne" Dawson, owning only seventy-five cents after he paid for his mule and provisions. Their equipment reflected their humble stations: "some had wagons drawn by oxen; others wagons drawn by horses; a few had hacks . . . many were to make the journey on horseback; and a few brought nothing but themselves." [3]

[1] A contemporary description of the "Oregon fever" is in David H. Coyner, *The Lost Trappers* (Cincinnati, 1847), pp. 248–249, and a modern appraisal in Verne Bright, "The Folklore and History of the 'Oregon Fever,'" *Oregon Historical Quarterly,* LII (1951), 241–253. The operations of the societies are described in Harrison C. Dale, "The Organization of the Oregon Emigrating Companies," *Oregon Historical Quarterly,* XVI (1915), 205–227.

[2] John Bidwell, *Echoes of the Past* (Chico, Calif., n.d.), p. 20.

[3] Nicholas Dawson, *Narrative of Nicholas "Cheyenne" Dawson Overland to California in '41 and '49, and Texas in '51* (San Francisco, 1933), p. 9.

Before they left they suffered two strokes of fortune, one bad when they passed over John Bidwell to choose the harsh-tempered John Bartleson their captain, and one good when they were joined by a party of experienced Mountain Men under Thomas Fitzpatrick on their way west. With these guides in the lead, the little party pulled away on May 19, 1841. When they had been on the trail less than a week they were overtaken by an eccentric clergyman, the Reverend Joseph Williams, who felt so impelled to bring the Gospel to the Indians that he had started west on horseback without a gun or weapon, "depending wholly on Providence for protection and support." Williams was welcomed, for even a sixty-four-year-old minister would strengthen the group, but his open disapproval of Bartleson as a "backslider" and of Fitzpatrick as a "wicked worldly man" did not make for harmony.[4]

Thus constituted, the little party reached the Platte River on June 1, followed its south bank westward, and by Independence Day was climbing upward toward South Pass over an open plain covered with tall sagebrush "through which the wagons forced their way raking and scraping." Beyond the Green River they turned northward and westward through a country so hilly that they kept the wagons upright "only by having fastened to the top of our loads ropes to which men clung."[5] At the Bear River the party divided, with the trappers and about half the emigrants turning northward toward Fort Hall, and with the rest—thirty-two men, one woman, and one child—continuing westward to California. The first group reached the Willamette Valley safely after abandoning their wagons at the fort,[6] but the second was destined to suffer unbelievable hardship before the sight of the San Joaquin Valley greeted their travel-weary eyes.

They had precious little information to guide them. From the Great Salt Lake, they had learned, they must strike west to the Humboldt River; if they veered too far to the south they would find themselves in a desert wasteland where they would die of thirst; if they wandered to the north they would lose themselves in a broken land of canyons and precipices. Guided only by these meager directions, the

[4] Joseph Williams, *Narrative of a Tour from the State of Indiana to the Oregon Territory in the Years 1841–2* (Cincinnati, 1843), pp. 3, 9.

[5] Dawson, *Narrative*, p. 14.

[6] An account of this party's journey is in H. E. Tobie, "From the Missouri to the Columbia, 1841," *Oregon Historical Quarterly*, XXXVIII (1937), pp. 135–159.

emigrants reached the northern end of the Great Salt Lake in early September, then plodded westward through arid plains "glimmering with heat and salt" and across deserts where the wagons sank so deeply in drifting sand that they could scarcely be pulled. As exhaustion beset men and animals alike they decided to abandon their wagons and pack their most essential belongings on the horses and oxen—no easy task for farmers unversed in that fine art; they agreed, too, that they were too far south and must turn northward. Eventually they found the Humboldt, which was followed westward to the base of the towering Sierras, then southward until they reached the swift-flowing Walker River where it gushed from the mountains. Beyond this barrier, they knew, lay California.

But that beckoning land was still far away. For a time they debated whether to risk freezing while crossing the mountains or starving while returning to their homes, then voted almost unanimously to move on. On October 18 all started up the north bank of the Walker River among "naked mountains whose summits still retained the snows perhaps of a thousand years." [7] A passing Indian consented to serve as their guide, but he led them along paths so narrow that "frequently a pack would strike against . . . rocks and over the precipice would go pack and animal," [8] until he finally abandoned them in a walled canyon. They hoisted their mules up the near-perpendicular sides, with four men pulling and four pushing, then wandered on, eating the flesh of their pack animals "half roasted, dripping with blood," or nothing at all. At last they stumbled on a westward-flowing stream, the Stanislaus, which they followed along twisting canyons as the threat of snow grew more ominous. On October 29 they reached an open spot and saw a sight that sent their hearts sinking: range on range of mountains stretching ahead as far as their eyes could see. Almost without hope now, they struggled on for three miles when suddenly a wide valley opened before them. Unknowingly they had looked across the San Joaquin Valley to the Coast Ranges beyond. Their journey was over.

Once they reached the valley floor they stopped to kill and dry deer meat before an Indian appeared to tell them that John Marsh's rancho was only two days' travel away. On November 4, 1841, they reached their destination at last. The disappointments of the journey were as

[7] John Bidwell, *A Journey to California* (San Francisco, 1937), pp. 24–25.
[8] Dawson, *Narrative*, p. 23.

nothing to their heartsick sensations as they saw for the first time the sun-withered fields and adobe buildings of the "paradise" that Marsh had pictured in his letters. "We had expected to find civilization," wrote one, "with big fields, fine houses, churches, schools, etc. Instead, we found houses resembling unburnt brick kilns, with no floors, no chimneys, and with the openings for doors and windows closed by shutters instead of glass." [9] Nor did the reception that Marsh provided restore their sunken spirits. He entertained them well that night—with a cask of mellow *aguardiente,* beef *tortillas,* and fat pork—but he charged them five dollars each for passports that had cost him nothing. Grumbling over this excessive board bill, the members of the party scattered to seek work. Their sufferings had brought them the distinction of being the first major emigrant party to reach the Far West.[10]

Although California was the objective of the Bidwell-Bartleson party, Oregon proved a stronger magnet when the immigrant tide began to roll again in 1842. For this shift in interest Dr. Elijah White was responsible. Having learned something of the Willamette Valley while serving at Jason Lee's mission, White visited the Missouri country in the early spring of 1842 and was immensely impressed with the extent of the "Oregon fever" there. He was going west himself to become Indian agent; why not take a party of settlers with him? No sooner had he reached this decision than White began seeking recruits. Although five hundred agreed to go, only 112 appeared at Independence, Missouri, at the time named, largely because time was so short that few could sell their farms. These elected Dr. White their leader and drafted a code of laws which ruled there should be "no profane swearing, no obscene conversation, or immoral conduct, allowed in the company," then adjourned "to meet again at Fort Vancouver, on the Columbia River, on the first day of October next, the powers of Heaven willing." [11]

Ineffectual leadership plagued the party from the beginning to the end of its journey. Scarcely had the sixteen wagons rumbled out of Independence on May 16, 1842, than the "American character"

[9] *Ibid.,* pp. 29–30.

[10] Rockwell D. Hunt, *John Bidwell, a Prince of California Pioneers* (Caldwell, Ida., 1942), pp. 15–95. A second party of twenty-five Americans under William Workman and John Rowland reached Los Angeles from Santa Fe in 1841. Hubert H. Bancroft, *History of California* (7 vols., San Francisco, 1884–1890), IV, 276–278.

[11] Elijah White, *Ten Years in Oregon* (Ithaca, N.Y., 1848), p. 146.

asserted itself with all "determined to govern, but not to be governed." Dispute followed dispute from that time on—over the code of laws that had been drafted, over the route to be followed, over each night's camp site—until matters reached a climax in a near-war between dog owners and non-dog owners. The latter, claiming that the dogs were frightening away game and attracting Indians, took matters into their own hands and killed a few of the animals before the owners armed themselves with threats of executing the executioners. Before blood was shed an election displaced Dr. White and elevated Lansford W. Hastings to the captaincy, but not until one faction had broken from the main company.[12] The new leader proved so energetic that both men and beasts suffered; "cattle's feet verry sore," wrote one member, "traviled slow." [13] But progress was sure now, especially after Thomas Fitzpatrick was secured as a guide at Fort Laramie, and in September all reached Fort Vancouver, having carried their goods on pack horses beyond Fort Hall. There they were hospitably received by Dr. John McLoughlin, the Hudson's Bay Company commander, who gave some work while others found jobs at the missions.

The two small parties that journeyed westward in 1841 and 1842 added little to the population of California and Oregon, but their sacrifices paved the way for the mass migration of 1843. For the next years the tide rolled on, until trappers bound for the mountains with their caravans complained of delays because "the road was much Cut up by Waggons" and Plains Indians planned, as they watched the never-ending procession, on moving to the eastern United States, which must now be vacant as "the whole white village" was moving beyond the Rockies.

Three parties reached California in 1843, one from Oregon, another by way of the San Joaquin Valley, and the third through the northern Sacramento Valley. The first, that from Oregon, was led by Lansford Hastings when the Willamette Valley proved not to his liking. Recruiting fifty-three other malcontents, he started south in May, 1843. Deep in the mountains the Hastings' company met a smaller group of Americans who had decided to abandon California's arid valleys for Oregon's lush fields. For a time the two parties argued, with the mem-

[12] Lansford W. Hastings, *The Emigrants' Guide to Oregon and California* (Cincinnati, 1845), pp. 6–9.
[13] Medorem Crawford, *Journal of Medorem Crawford* (Eugene, Ore., 1897), p. 10.

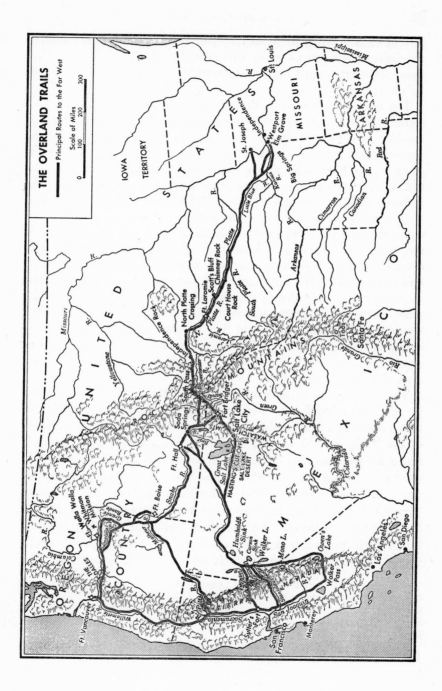

THE OVERLAND TRAILS

Principal Routes to the Far West

Scale of Miles

0   100   200   300

bers of each berating the land they had abandoned. In this exchange the Californians proved more persuasive, for about one third of Hastings' followers started back with them. The remainder reached Sutter's Fort in July.[14]

The other two companies that invaded California that year started together from Independence with equipment which included not only furniture and farm machinery but parts for a saw mill, and with two experienced frontiersmen, Joseph B. Chiles and Joseph R. Walker, as captains. At Fort Boise they divided, with one hundred men under Chiles entering the upper Sacramento Valley over a new route that followed the Malheur and Pitt rivers. The remainder, with Walker at their head, reached the Sierras over the usual trail along the Humboldt, then turned southward past Mono Lake into Owen's Valley. As they marched the towering mountains on their right grew gradually less awesome, until Walker could turn westward into the pass that he had discovered a few years before and that today bears his name. The men blessed their leader as they scaled the Sierras over easy grades where snow and frost were unknown, but their praises turned to curses when they emerged on the arid San Joaquin Valley. For miles they struggled through choking alkaline wastes before Sutter's Fort was reached at last. There they scattered to find work, as had others who arrived before them.[15]

The trickle of emigrants into California during 1843 was dwarfed by the mass migration to Oregon during that eventful year. By this time prosperity was returning to the Mississippi Valley as the influence of the Panic of 1837 waned; men could get a decent price for their farms for the first time in five years and could invest the profits in good wagons and proper outfits to make life on the long trail less irksome. So they listened to the enthusiastic speakers who addressed "Oregon Conventions" in town after town throughout the Middle West, and were infected with the "fever" by what they heard. Many began their preparations long before spring, buying specially built wagons, rounding up oxen for draft animals and fat young cows that

[14] Hastings, *Emigrants' Guide*, pp. 64–69. A year later another group of thirty-seven Americans reached California from Oregon. Their journey is described by a member of the party in Overton Johnson and W. H. Winter, *Route Across the Rocky Mountains, With a Description of Oregon and California* (Lafayette, Ind., 1846), pp. 70–77.

[15] Douglas S. Watson, *West Wind. The Life Story of Joseph Reddeford Walker* (Los Angeles, 1934), pp. 86–97.

could be sold in the Willamette Valley, packing bacon in strong bags, and storing flour and sugar in double sacks to keep out moisture. Each step was taken only after weighty consultation with others making similar preparations, or after thumbing through the pages of one of the hastily compiled guidebooks then being rushed from the presses. For every guidebook warned that loads of more than one ton could not be taken across the mountains, at the same time cautioning travelers against buying supplies in the West, where flour sold at twenty-five cents a pint, and sugar or coffee at twice that sum.

With preparations completed, the emigrants came straggling into Independence from all the Middle West during April and early May. There they made their last purchases, then alone or in small groups moved on to Elm Grove—thirty-three miles away—where the company was to rendezvous. Some of the farmers from the wooded Mississippi Valley were shocked to find only two elm trees marking this spot: "I have learned for the first time," one wrote, "that two trees could compose a grove." [16] As the first arrivals waited there, wagon after wagon arrived, until nearly one thousand emigrants and more than 1,800 cattle and oxen were gathered on the open prairie. For a time they gossiped about the camp fires or shattered the still night with the song of their violins and the happy shouts of dancers. But on May 22, 1843, the first wagon pulled away, and the others soon followed. They went as they willed here, for this was lush prairie and there was no Indian danger. Eight miles from Elm Grove a lone sign erected on the treeless plain pointed the way along the "Road to Oregon"; following this they reached their next rendezvous point at Big Springs on the rich bottom lands of the Wakarusa River. Here, where the trail divided to lead to two fords over the Kansas River, they stopped to organize their caravan.

This was a universal practice in the overland migrations. Realizing that they were passing beyond the pale of the law, and aware that the tedious journey and the constant tensions of the trail brought out the worst in human character, the pioneers, of this and every subsequent caravan, created their own law-making and law-enforcing machinery before they started. Assembling together under a temporary chairman, the men of that 1843 company listened first to orators who proposed adopting the constitutions of either Missouri or Tennessee as a govern-

[16] Peter H. Burnett, "Letters of Peter H. Burnett," *Oregon Historical Quarterly*, III (1902), 405–406.

ing code, then sensibly brushed these suggestions aside to draw up a
simpler body of laws suited to their primitive social group. "Whereas,"
this began, "we deem it necessary for the government of all societies,
either civil or military, to adopt certain rules and regulations for their
government, for the purpose of keeping good order and promoting
civil and military discipline," certain rules and regulations were necessary. These were listed: every male over sixteen could vote; a captain
and orderly sergeant were to be elected by popular ballot; a Council
of Ten was to be chosen to settle disputes and try offenders for any
acts that were "subversive of good order and military discipline"; new
officers could be chosen if those first elected proved unsatisfactory.[17]

The election of leaders came next, after tempers had cooled with
another day's march. Peter H. Burnett, a Missouri farmer, was named
captain and J. W. Nesmith orderly sergeant. Then candidates for the
Council of Ten were nominated and asked to form a line somewhat in
advance of the mass meeting. At a signal each nominee started forward, while those who favored his election fell in behind to form a
long "tail" where they could be counted. "It was really very funny,"
wrote an observer, "to see the candidates for the solemn council . . .
run several hundred yards away, to show off the length of their tails,
and then cut a half circle, so as to turn and admire their longitudinal
popularity *in extenso* themselves." [18] Ludicrous as this "running for
office" might be, the Council chosen was a serious and essential body.
During the weeks ahead it ruled firmly over the traveling commonwealth, enacting rules, changing those proven unsatisfactory, settling
disputes, trying offenders, enforcing laws, and generally providing for
the peace and security of the company. Its most important decision
was made shortly after it was constituted. When some of the men
complained that others with large herds of cattle were slowing down
the march, the Council wisely decided to cut the party in two. One
group moved ahead rapidly without cattle; the other, the "cow column," progressed more slowly under a new captain, Jesse Applegate.[19]

Thus organized, the two columns settled down to life on the trail.
For a time they marched across a fertile prairie where soft breezes set
the glistening grass dancing, "seeming to spread a stream of light along

[17] *Ibid.,* pp. 406–407, prints the compact in full.
[18] Letter in New Orleans *Picayune,* November 21, 1843, reprinted in *Oregon
Historical Quarterly,* I (1900), 400.
[19] Jesse Applegate, *A Day with the Cow Column in 1843* (Chicago, 1934),
pp. 4–5.

the surface of the wave-like expanse," [20] then over low sand dunes where a close watch was kept against thieving Pawnee Indians, to emerge finally at the Platte River, 316 miles from Independence. This absurd stream inspired every traveler to his worst humor; it was, they insisted, a mile wide and six inches deep, filled with water too thick to drink and too thin to plow, and impossible to cross because quicksand prevented fording while the water was too shallow to float a boat. The trail ran along the south bank for more than one hundred miles, climbing steadily the while, over level plains where the tall prairie grass gave way to shorter grasses that alone could live in the arid country. On they plodded, day after day, covering sometimes ten, sometimes fifteen, occasionally even twenty miles between sunrise and sunset.

As they moved the routine of trail life gradually became second nature to men and beasts alike. The day began when the sun's rays reddened the night sky; then shouts of the night guards brought sleepy-eyed men and women pouring from tents and wagons, some to bring in the pasturing animals, others to build fires of buffalo chips and prepare a hot breakfast. Then tents were struck, blankets tucked away, oxen yoked, and amidst Babel-like confusion the column formed. At seven o'clock the clear notes of a bugle signaled the start, sending the creaking wagons into motion. As they moved, the "pilot," a trained Mountain Man hired as a guide, ranged far ahead, followed by the mile-long train. This was divided into four platoons that changed places each day, so that no one would always have the dust-choking rear position. The wagoners walked beside their teams, flicking their whips, while their wives and children scattered to either side to pick wild flowers or simply romp away some of the animal spirits bred by that healthy life. At the rear a herd of spare horses trotted along, so broken to the trail that they scarcely needed watching, and behind them the loose cattle with their sweating herdsmen.

So they marched, crossing each stream where flags planted by the pilot indicated the best spot for fording, and stopping at a spring or creek when he gave the signal for "nooning." The animals were left in their yokes while a light meal was eaten, then the columns moved on at the blast of a bugle. All were tired now; women or children crawled into wagons to sleep, drivers nodded as they walked, and even

[20] Frank S. Edwards, *A Campaign in New Mexico with Colonel Doniphan* (Philadelphia, 1847), p. 24.

the oxen seemed to doze as they plodded along. As night began to fall they reached the spot where the pilot had marked out a large circle on the ground. Each driver guided his team along these marks, to form a circular barricade of wagons that was safe from Indian attack. For a time all was bustle as teamsters drove their animals out to graze, children gathered buffalo chips, and housewives set about preparing the evening meal of salt meat, fresh-baked bread, and black coffee. Comfortably filled, the men settled back to spin yarns about the camp-fires, children romped, and young couples courted furtively. The Council of Ten usually met at this interval, for rare was the day when no business was to be transacted. But as darkness settled the tired travelers crawled into their blankets, the guards took their posts, and the quiet of the black prairie night descended over all.

This was the routine followed for monotonous day after monotonous day, with occasional variations. Now and then the women cajoled the pilot into allowing the caravan to stop for a day or two while they did the washing—always a difficult task, for old Mountain Men despised cleanliness as much as godliness. Then the men spent their time hunting, or drying meat, while the children splashed away the grime of the trail in a clear stream. Occasionally, too, the march was halted under less pleasant circumstances. Thunder storms might burst upon them with such fury that tents were blown away, wagons overturned, and the trail vanished under "water Shoe mouth deep." Or the caravan might be stopped by a stampeding buffalo herd which swept down with all the fury of an avalanche. Captains sighting the wildly running beasts as they approached sometimes set the prairie grass on fire to turn them from a wagon train, or called out hunters to shoot the lead animals until the rest were divided by the pile of carcasses. At times the travelers' own animals might stampede at the slightest excuse, rushing madly across the plains in all directions while their drivers did their best to stay with their wagons until the beasts were exhausted. Life along the trail was not all monotony.

There were sights to be seen, as well, as the caravans made their way along the Platte. One by one the pioneers ticked off the landmarks: the crossing of the South Platte, the masonry-like formation of Court House Rock, the forty-foot spire of Chimney Rock rising abruptly from the flat plain, the "lofty spires, towering edifices, and spacious domes" of the eroded rock formation known as Scott's Bluffs. The Laramie River was so high that one of the party had to swim the raging torrent with a rope in his teeth; then the wagons were hauled across like so many ferry boats. Just beyond they could see the fifteen-foot adobe walls of Fort Laramie, where the travelers stopped for several days while the women washed and the men swapped yarns with the traders gathered there. One night a dance was held within the fort, "where some of the company got gay." [21] The trail, as they started once more, joined the North Platte, then climbed upward along that stream into the foothills of the Rockies. Crossing the North Platte by pulling the wagons with ropes once more, the caravans plodded through a desolate country where the few waterholes were so tainted with salt that even the animals would not drink.

The mountains were in clear view now as the trail climbed steeply along the rushing Sweetwater River toward Independence Rock, 838 miles from Independence. Here the pioneers followed the usual custom of writing their names in the soft stone, and of clambering to the top to survey the countryside. Just beyond, still climbing steeply, they followed the Sweetwater through a narrow canyon, Devil's Gate, where the walls rose perpendicularly for three hundred feet. Knowing that the buffalo had been exterminated west of the mountains, they paused for a few days to dry meat before moving on over South Pass. This broad highway was always a disappointment: "If you dident now it was the mountain you woldent now it from aney outher plane," one traveler noted disgustedly.[22] Not until they reached Pacific Springs, and saw water trickling toward the west, did they know they had crossed the backbone of the continent. "HAIL, HAIL OREGON," one wrote in his journal that night.[23]

The trail ran downhill now, but their hardships were far from over. For twenty miles the caravans plodded across a desolate, waterless waste, traveling at night to escape the sun's glaring rays, until they reached the Little Sandy River. This, and the Big Sandy, led them to the Green River, which was forded with great difficulty. Earlier parties had turned north there, but the 1843 emigrants wanted to visit the fort that Jim Bridger had established nearby, so they followed a south-

[21] John Boardman, "The Journal of John Boardman. An Overland Journey from Kansas to Oregon in 1843," *Utah Historical Quarterly*, II (1929), 103.

[22] Harry N. M. Winton (ed.), "William T. Newby's Diary of the Emigration of 1843," *Oregon Historical Quarterly*, XL (1939), 229.

[23] Joel Palmer, *Journal of Travels over the Rocky Mountains to the Mouth of the Columbia River; Made During the Years 1845 and 1846* (Cincinnati, 1847), p. 33.

westerly course to blaze a new section of the Oregon Trail. Fort Bridger was hardly worth the effort; Jim was away on one of his periodic hunting trips, leaving the few ramshackle cabins that he had built to the care of "three little, starved dogs." Pausing only briefly, the emigrants swung northward to the Bear River, where grass and water were plentiful. They marveled, as did all travelers, at the bubbling pools of water known as Soda Springs, where the hiss of escaping gas could be heard for some distance; half a mile farther on they marveled anew at the sight of Steamboat Spring, where hot water spurted from a conical rock every fifteen seconds. But a more welcome sight was Fort Hall, 1288 miles from Independence, nestled against the Snake River in a grassy valley. They were nearing their journey's end.

At the fort, however, disquieting news was heard. The trail ahead, the Hudson's Bay Company officials told them, was so rough that no wagons could get through. For a time dismay swept the party as some talked of turning back rather than leave their belongings behind. Marcus Whitman, who was traveling with the caravan, soon dispelled their gloom by assuring them that he would guarantee to lead their wagons into Oregon. With this missionary leading the way in a light wagon, the train rumbled out of Fort Hall along the south bank of the Snake, through a "wild, rocky, barren wilderness, of wrecked and ruined Nature; a vast field of volcanic desolation." [24] At times they jolted over rocks that cut the oxen's feet until the trail was splashed with blood; at others they twisted along mountainsides so steep that files of men marched beside each wagon to keep it from overturning; at still others wheels sank in hub-deep sand until double teaming was necessary. So they labored on, covering only a few miles each day, while a burning sun sapped the energy of men and beasts alike. Until at last they saw, many hundreds of feet below them, the green surface of the Grand Ronde, an idyllic valley six miles wide and surrounded by snow-clad peaks.

The descent, over a trail that was "very sidling and uncomfortable rocky," was pure torture, but what luxuries were theirs when they reached the valley floor. For a time the caravan rested there, as the animals fed on abundant grass, women washed travel-stained clothes, and men lolled in unaccustomed shade as they listened to the scarce-remembered song of the meadow lark. Then, well refreshed, they

[24] Johnson and Winter, *Route Across the Rocky Mountains,* p. 31.

assaulted the last barrier, the Blue Mountains, whose "lofty peaks seemed a resting place for the clouds." [25] Struggling upward along a rocky canyon over a "road two bad to discribe, crawsing the creek 10 or 15 times, passing through tremendious high mountains, dubel teaming," [26] the emigrants emerged on a plateau that sloped gradually downward to the arid plains of eastern Oregon. At The Dalles, a narrow defile where the water of the Columbia River boiled and foamed as it cut through the Cascade Mountains, the wagons were rebuilt into boats which floated the travelers to Fort Vancouver, while youths drove the stock overland along mountain trails. The journey was over; before the trail-weary travelers lay the Willamette Valley, which they found to their liking. As they marked out their farms or took jobs with Americans already there, one closed his diary with these words:

"Friday, October 27.—Arrived at Oregon City at the falls of the Willamette.

"Saturday, October 28.—Went to work." [27]

News of this first successful mass migration set the Oregon and California fevers raging again in the Mississippi Valley. Once more the farming frontier bustled with preparations during the winter of 1843–44, and once more as spring approached families from all the West started their loaded wagons toward Independence. In all, five companies of emigrants made the journey during 1844, all of them traveling closely enough together that they could unite in case of danger. Yet the numbers migrating were disappointing, for less than one thousand persons reached the Far West that summer.

Three of the companies reached their destinations without incident, but the remaining two pioneered important new portions of the western trails. The larger of these, a party of five hundred emigrants with Nathaniel Ford as their captain and Moses ("Black") Harris as their pilot, suffered interminably during the first weeks on the trail, for rain fell steadily that spring, turning the roads into quagmires where double teaming was constantly necessary and reducing life to a dismal routine of wet blankets, cold food, and ankle-deep mud. Beyond the Rockies the rains ceased, as "Black" Harris guided his followers along the usual route past Fort Bridger and Fort Hall to the Grand Ronde. From there

[25] Crawford, *Journal of Medorem Crawford,* pp. 18–19.

[26] Winton (ed.), "Newby's Diary," p. 235.

[27] James Nesmith, "Diary of the Emigration of 1843," *Oregon Historical Quarterly,* VII (1906), 359.

the pilot led his caravan in a northwesterly direction across the Blue Mountains to the Umatilla River, which was followed to the Columbia. From that time on this route was used by Oregon-bound wagon trains.

The second 1844 company to pioneer a new trail was the Stevens-Murphy party under the guidance of an old Mountain Man named Elisha Stephens. Following the usual route to Fort Hall, some turned off there to Oregon, but most swung southward along the road marked by the Bidwell-Bartleson party of 1841 as far as Humboldt Sink, the swampy marsh that had formed where the Humboldt River lost itself in the sand. Instead of turning south there, the emigrants began a frontal assault on the mountains, with an Indian whom they nicknamed "Truckee" as their guide. The path that he discovered—up the canyon of a cascading river, across the rocky summit, and down along the bed of Bear Creek—was no easy highway, but it was more passable than any route used before. The Stevens-Murphy party could not only send back word that it had been the first to take wagons across the Sierras, but could advise later comers to follow the Truckee River valley and the Truckee Pass. From 1844 on this was the usual emigrant route into California.[28]

These easier trails, and knowledge that all five parties in 1844 had reached the West without undue hardship, brought migration to a new peak in the next years. By this time, too, those already settled in the Willamette and Sacramento valleys were writing glowing accounts of their success to friends in the East, for they were anxious to lure newcomers to buy their surplus produce and their excess land holdings. Magazines such as *Niles' Register*, the *North American Review*, and *Hunt's Merchants' Magazine* filled their columns with unadulterated praise of the West, while even eastern newspapers published every scrap of information they could gather on California and Oregon. Their most active correspondent was Thomas O. Larkin, a prosperous American merchant in California who was named consul to Monterey in 1843. Filled with practical advice on reaching the frontier as well as unblushing praise for California, Larkin's dispatches appeared regularly in such important New York papers as the *Herald* and the *Sun*, and were reprinted everywhere. With such signs of interest, it is

[28] The reminiscences of a member of the party, Moses Schallenberger, are in H. S. Foote (ed.), *Pen Sketches from the Garden of the World, or Santa Clara County, California* (Chicago, 1888), pp. 38–53.

not surprising that prophets predicted that from 7,000 to 100,000 persons would migrate westward.

Even though these estimates proved optimistic, the trails were crowded that summer. Independence was still the favorite jumping-off point, although some caravans started from Westport and others from the newer port of St. Joseph, which was fifty miles farther up the Missouri River. There was a tendency, too, for the emigrants to travel in smaller parties, as they learned that large herds exhausted the scant pasturage on the western portions of the trail, that delays caused by the breakdown of one wagon could prove costly to a large company, and that discipline was easier to maintain among a handful of men than among an army of self-willed frontiersmen. Where the average party in 1843 or 1844 had contained from twenty to thirty wagons, in 1845 and later years no more than eight or ten traveled together.

Five companies reached California in 1845, one arriving from Oregon and the other four from the Mississippi Valley. The largest of these, the Grigsby-Ide party, was late in making the assault on the Sierras, and when threatened by snow lost all semblance of discipline. Its one hundred members, abandoning wagons and goods, struck out for themselves in all directions and came scrambling into the Sacramento Valley in late October. In marked contrast was the record of the last company to arrive. Led by the Mountain Man Lansford W. Hastings, and made up of twenty vigorous young men, this left Independence in late August, yet moved so efficiently that it managed to cross the Sierras just a few days before the passes were blocked by snow. Hastings attracted less attention when he marched his followers into Sutter's Fort on Christmas day, 1845, than did a member of his party, Dr. Robert Semple. Standing six feet eight inches high, and with legs so long that he wore spurs strapped to his calves rather than his ankles, Dr. Semple was to become the editor of California's first newspaper.[29]

Oregon attracted three thousand emigrants during 1845, most of them in small parties that reached the Willamette Valley without undue hardship. One company that started with 145 wagons left a different record. Torn by dissension from the outset, this soon broke into a

[29] Simin Ide, *A Biographical Sketch of the Life of William B. Ide* (n.p., 1880), pp. 28–50. The other three parties to arrive that year were forty-three persons under James Clyman who made the journey from Oregon, the Swasey-Todd party of thirteen men from the East, and a company of fifteen from St. Louis led by the Sublette brothers.

·number of smaller units that agreed to stay close enough together to offer protection in case of danger. All went well until they had passed Fort Hall. Then their pilot, a former trapper named Stephen Meek, told them that he would lead them directly to the Willamette Valley through the Cascade Mountains. Leaving the main trail near the Hudson's Bay Company post at Fort Boise, the emigrants became hopelessly lost in the mountains and only reached The Dalles after untold suffering—and repeated threats to lynch Meek. So incensed were the farmers of the Willamette Valley when they heard this tale that they spent the winter of 1845–46 building two roads across the mountains. The Barlow Road and the Old South Road, as they were christened, were used by about 150 wagons in 1846, yet despite these improvements the migration of that year—only 1,350 emigrants—was disappointing.[30]

California also proved less attractive in 1846, luring only three hundred settlers, but the new arrivals more than made up in drama what they lacked in numbers. Lansford W. Hastings was responsible. Ever since he first visited California in 1843 Hastings had been pursued by one ambition: he would wrest that garden spot from Mexico and establish it as an independent republic with himself as head. For this settlers were necessary, and Hastings dedicated himself to attracting them there. One step was taken in 1845, when he visited the East long enough to publish a remarkable guidebook, *Emigrants' Guide to Oregon and California*, which damned Oregon by faint praise but painted the Sacramento Valley as the Eden of the West. More than this was needed, for emigrants still preferred the shorter trail to Oregon; the only answer, Hastings decided, was to popularize a cutoff that would lessen the distance to his chosen land. Carefully studying the reports of explorers—for he knew precious little of western geography himself—he concluded that he could reduce the time to 120 days and the distance to 2,100 miles by advising wagon trains to leave the regular trail at Fort Bridger, "thence bearing west southwest, to the Salt Lake; and thence continuing down to the Bay of St. Francisco." [31] Thus did Lansford Hastings wave away burning deserts and towering mountains, and with a stroke of the pen create the "Hastings Cutoff."

Boundlessly optimistic though he was, he still recognized that these

---

[30] Mary S. Barlow, "History of the Barlow Road," *Oregon Historical Quarterly*, III (1902), 72–79.

[31] Hastings, *Emigrants' Guide*, pp. 137–138.

directions were a bit too vague to serve as a guide for California-bound emigrants. Hence he started east in the spring of 1846 to wait along the trail and offer more explicit advice. Fortunately he had as companions two old Mountain Men, James Clyman and Caleb Greenwood; if he had not the route that he had described so airily might have proven too much for Hastings himself. Following the regular California trail in reverse along the Humboldt, the little band branched off to cross the dread Great Salt Lake Desert—eighty miles of choking alkali dust with no water and not a living thing in sight save lizards and snakes and scorpions—then to make their way south of Great Salt Lake, through the Wasatch Mountains, and to Fort Bridger.[32] Clyman had had enough; he moved on up the trail to warn emigrants to stick to the regular roads, but Hastings and "Old Greenwood" settled down to wait their victims.

These were not long in coming. The first party to arrive was led by W. H. Russell, and was made up of a mixed group bound for both Oregon and California. Hastings happened to be away from Fort Bridger at the time, but one of his lieutenants, a trapper named James M. Hudspeth, explained the virtues of the cutoff and offered to serve as guide. Most refused to listen, but eventually Russell and eight others agreed to make the try. Trading their wagons for mules, they packed their belongings carefully and set out. Hudspeth led them through the rocky canyons of the Wasatch range and across the barren reaches that bordered the Great Salt Lake until they camped on the eastern edge of the Great Salt Lake Desert. Then, pointing out a hill known as Pilot Peak on the far side as their objective, and telling them to "ride like hell," he left them. Two days of terror lay ahead for the Russell party as they plodded through knee-deep alkaline dust without food or water, and with Pilot Peak so obscured by smoke that they frequently lost their way. All were near exhaustion when they reached the opposite side, but experienced little difficulty from then on as they found their way to the Humboldt and entered California over the Truckee Pass.[33]

To follow the Hastings Cutoff with pack animals was one thing; to get wagons through was quite another. This was discovered by a company under George W. Harlan and Samuel C. Young which reached Fort Bridger shortly after the Russell party left there. Lansford Has-

[32] Charles L. Camp (ed.), *James Clyman, American Frontiersman, 1792–1881* (San Francisco, 1928), pp. 217–220, 229.

[33] Edwin Bryant, *What I Saw in California* (New York, 1848), pp. 114–130, is a description of the cutoff by a member of the Russell party.

tings awaited them, bubbling with eager advice and with an offer to serve as their guide if they would follow his route. The first difficulties were encountered in Echo Canyon, a rocky defile skirting the eastern edge of the Wasatch Mountains, but no real hardships were experienced until they turned westward into Weber Canyon, which, Hastings said, would lead them through the range. Boulders that had to be rolled or blasted away clogged this narrow passage; three times they had to use a windlass to pull their wagons up the face of cliffs. Inching forward at the rate of only a mile or two a day, the emigrants finally emerged on the desolate valley of the Great Salt Lake. That night, as they camped on the shores of the River Jordan, music sounded about the camp fires for the first time in weeks.[34]

Yet still more trying experiences lay ahead. Before Hastings left them he marked out their route, explaining that the Great Salt Lake Desert was only forty miles wide. When they reached its eastern edge the emigrants filled their wagons with enough hay and water to last them the day and night needed for such a distance and boldly started across, just as night was falling. All that night they trudged along, and all the next day under a burning sun. By sunset they had expected to be safely across; instead the alkaline sand glimmered in the distance for as far as eye could see. By the morning of the next day, after another night of travel, the draft animals were dropping one after another, or were so crazed with thirst that they were uncontrollable. Not until that noon did they reach the end, after a march of eighty-two terrifying miles. Even then their trials were not over, for water and grass had to be hauled thirty miles into the desert to rescue the animals and wagons abandoned along the way. The Harlan-Young party experienced no further difficulties as they followed the usual route into California, but some say that the blue haze noted on Utah's hills since that day is the last remnant of the curses against Hastings that they scattered along the trail.

Their sufferings were as nothing, however, when compared with those of the next company to follow the cutoff, the famous Donner party.[35] Organized in central Illinois by two well-to-do brothers, Jacob

[34] The only first-hand account of the Harlan-Young party is a diary printed in William W. Allen and R. B. Avery, *California Gold Book. First Nugget. Its Discovery and Discoverers* (San Francisco, 1893), pp. 57–67.

[35] The fullest contemporary accounts of the Donner party are in Charles F. McGlashan, *History of the Donner Party; a Tragedy of the Sierra* (Truckee,

and George Donner, and elaborately supplied with both goods and money, the members from the first decided to follow the route described by Hastings in his *Emigrants' Guide*. At Fort Laramie they met James Clyman, who urged them to stick to the well-known trails, but they refused to listen. "There is a nigher route," one stoutly maintained, "and it is of no use to take so much of a roundabout course." [36] A few of a cautious turn of mind left the main company at the Big Sandy to journey to Fort Hall and reach California safely over the usual trail, but the eighty-nine members of the Donner party hurried on to Fort Bridger. There they learned that Hastings was leading the Harlan-Young party westward, but had left word that he would mark the trail.

Thus assured, they started at once, only to meet their first setback at the head of Weber Canyon. Stuck into a forked stick was a note from Hastings asking them to wait until he could show them a better route through the Wasatch Mountains. For eight days they camped— the first of many delays that brought them disaster—then sent a messenger to seek him. The messenger returned without Hastings, but with instructions to follow another trail. This proved almost impassable; for days the toiling emigrants pushed aside boulders, or guided their cattle along twisting paths with giddy depths below, before they emerged in the valley south of Great Salt Lake. Thirty days had been required for a journey that should have taken twelve. They hurried on, with food supplies running low, until they stood on the edge of the desert on September 9. For sixty-four hours they plodded across this grim expanse toward Pilot Peak; then at the far side they had to waste more precious days while men returned to search for lost draft animals.

When they paused to take council they realized for the first time the direness of their straits. Supplies were virtually exhausted with much of their journey remaining; just how much no one knew, for all had lost faith in everything Hastings told them. The season, too, was well advanced; September was passing rapidly, and with it the hope of crossing the Sierras before snow began to fall. Should they press on, or try to return to Fort Bridger? Memories of their recent suffering provided the answer: "feeble and dispirited . . . they slowly resumed their journey," [37] after sending two mounted men ahead to

---

Calif., 1879), and J. Quinn Thornton, *Oregon and California in 1848* (2 vols., New York, 1849), II.

[36] Camp (ed.), *James Clyman*, p. 229.

[37] Thornton, *Oregon and California in 1848,* II, 104–105.

bring back food from California. Those were trying days, for hardship and despair had exhausted the emigrants emotionally as well as physically. Quarrels were commonplace as tempers flared; in one a man was murdered, necessitating another delay as the whole company halted to judge and banish the murderer. Indians also proved troublesome, for the travelers were too exhausted to protect their stock. Hopes revived somewhat on October 19, 1846, when one of the men sent ahead returned with five pack mules loaded with food and with two Indian guides. When, on the morning of October 23, the company left the grassy meadows along the Truckee River and started into the Sierras, they believed they had nothing more to fear. Heavy snows did not begin falling in the mountains until mid-November, and they would be safely at Sutter's Fort by then.

The climb up the narrow canyon of the Truckee was cruelly difficult, but five days later the first pioneers camped on the shores of a calm lake high in the mountains, where they could look ahead to the steep granite ridge of the summit two thousand feet above them. At Prosser Creek, six miles behind, the rest of the party had stopped to repair a broken wagon. Another day or two would see all safely across. But that night the first storm of the winter came whistling in from the north, a month early. By daylight six inches of snow covered the ground, while the passes ahead were blocked with drifts from three to five feet deep. In a flurry of panic they forgot all discipline and rushed blindly toward the rocky crest, but as reason returned discipline was re-established. Now they packed their supplies on their animals' backs and started ahead, only to be driven back by sleet that coated the rocks with slippery ice. The next day, they planned, they would try again on foot, but that night a new storm roared in. When it subsided several days later their animals were gone, and all the mountains were buried under three feet of snow.

There was no question now; they were snowbound in the High Sierras. Frantically they turned to building crude shelters at both Donner Lake and Prosser Creek: tents from the canvas of their wagons, huts of brush and snow. In these the eighty-one survivors huddled day after day as the snow deepened and the numbing cold grew more intense. "No liveing thing without wings can get about," wrote a diarist on November 28.[38] With each day the scant food supply dwindled,

---

[38] Patrick Breen, "Diary of Patrick Breen, One of the Donner Party," *Academy of Pacific Coast History Publications,* I (1910), 274.

until by mid-December they were eating anything they could chew: hides boiled to the consistency of glue, bones crisped until powdery, twigs and the bark of trees. Four men had died and one was insane by then; clearly something must be done or all would perish. So fifteen of the bravest—eight men, five women, and the two Indian guides from California—volunteered to scale the summit in the hope that one or two might get through to summon help. This little band—the "Forlorn Hope"—started on December 16, carrying starvation rations designed to last six days. Thirty-two days were to pass before they saw the first signs of civilization.

Few parties in history have endured such terrors as the Forlorn Hope—and lived to tell the tale. By December 25, when they had been without food for four days, they reached the inevitable conclusion that one must die that the others might live. Huddled together, they drew lots, but when one held up the shortest stick none of the remainder had the heart to kill him. Nor was that necessary, for nature was a more ruthless executioner. That night a new storm blew in; for two days and nights the little group huddled under blankets as the snow piled deep upon them. When, at noon on the 27th, the wind and snow ceased, four of the party were dead. The survivors stripped the flesh from their bones, "roasted and ate it, averting their faces from each other, and weeping." For two more days they stayed in this "Camp of Death" regaining their strength, then packed the last flesh and started on again—carefully labeling each piece so that no one would eat his own kindred. This was soon exhausted; strings of moccasins and snow shoes were boiled and consumed, a stray deer was killed, and eventually the two Indians, who refused to touch human flesh, were themselves shot and eaten after they had collapsed on the trail. All this time the seven survivors were struggling through waist-deep snow as they moved down the west slope of the mountains. At last, on January 10, 1847, they reached an Indian village, so exhausted that they reeled and staggered like drunken men.

The first of several relief parties that hurriedly organized reached the Donner Lake camp on February 19, and others followed until all survivors were brought down the mountains. Their tale of suffering rivaled that of the Forlorn Hope. For two months they had lived on nothing but boiled hides and charred bones; there too death had been a frequent visitor, and cannibalism was practiced as a last resort. Of the eighty-nine emigrants who had set out so bravely from Fort Bridger, only forty-five survived this ordeal by hunger.

The sufferings of the Donner party added a new epic to the annals of the American frontier, but they also prepared the way for momentous events in the nation's history. Long before the close of 1846 these pioneers had helped precipitate the series of crises that eventually added California and Oregon to the United States. For no sooner were the emigrants safe in their new homes than they began to demand the protection of the United States. Concentrated as they were about Sutter's Fort in California or in the Willamette Valley of Oregon, they were in a position to stage meetings, circulate petitions, draft resolutions, and plot incidents that were deliberately designed to force the distant government in Washington to intervene in their behalf. The pattern that evolved in the Oregon Country was typical. There efforts on the part of the American settlers to form even a local government were frustrated by the Hudson's Bay Company until after the arrival of the first large emigrant party in 1842. Definitely in the majority now, Americans converted the Pioneer Lyceum and Literary Club into a political forum as they spent the winter debating the manner of government most to their liking. By the spring of 1843 they were ready to act; in a series of "Wolf Meetings" called to discuss means of protecting livestock from wild animals, they named a committee to consider "the propriety of taking steps for the civil and military protection of the colony." [39]

When this reported to a meeting held at Champoeg on May 2, 1843, the Hudson's Bay Company faction was out in force, but its members were outvoted and left in disgust. The Americans remaining named a committee to draw up a frame of government. The resulting "First Organic Law," adopted on July 5, 1843, provided for simple governmental machinery to function in the "Oregon Territory" until "such time as the United States of America extend their jurisdiction over us." This early "constitution" was altered somewhat a year later to conform to the wishes of newer settlers who arrived in the "Great Migration" of 1843, and in this form served as the instrument of government over the next years. [40]

[39] The minutes of the "Wolf Meetings" are printed in William H. Gray, *A History of Oregon, 1792–1849, Drawn from Personal Observation and Authentic Information* (Portland, Ore., 1870), pp. 261–267.

[40] Russell B. Thomas, "Truth and Fiction of the Champoeg Meeting,"

Both the Oregon pioneers and the people of the United States knew that these arrangements were mere stopgaps. By migrating into Oregon—and into California and Texas—the emigrants had created a situation where the flag must follow. Neither they nor their fellow countrymen at home could breathe easily until the British were driven from the Oregon Country, and the Mexicans from California and Texas. From their insistent demands rose the diplomatic settlements that carried the boundaries of the United States to the Pacific, with Texas the first plum to fall.

Oregon Historical Quarterly, XXX (1929), 218–237; J. Neilson Barry, "The Champoeg Meeting of March 4, 1844," *Oregon Historical Quarterly*, XXXVIII (1937), 425–432.

CHAPTER 6

Texas: Revolution and Republic

T HE pattern of conquest which eventually added all the Far West to the United States was perfected in Texas. Americans had been crowding into that Mexican province since 1821, when Stephen Austin's grant opened the gates; a decade later they vastly outnumbered their rulers and their numbers were growing yearly. Most were sober and law-abiding; most, too, were devotedly loyal to the Mexican government. Yet no amount of good will could forestall conflicts between them and Mexico or prevent those conflicts from increasing in intensity until revolution and Texan independence followed as naturally as day follows night. Peoples of such divergent cultural backgrounds could no more maintain harmony under conditions that existed in Texas than could lions and lambs when penned together.

Friction began to mount even in the 1820's, with the religious and slavery questions touching off the conflict. The religious issue concerned the right of the American colonists, who were overwhelmingly Protestant in belief, to worship as they chose in a land that was unswervingly Roman Catholic. Their rulers did not force them to attend Catholic churches, but they did forbid public worship for any other sect, and this was sorely resented. So, too, was the constant effort of the Mexican government to free their slaves. Nine tenths of the Americans came from southern states and confidently expected to use slave labor as soon as circumstances permitted. Hence they were horrified when the constitution adopted for the state of Coahuila-Texas in 1827 provided for the gradual emancipation of all bond servants; then were shocked still more two years later by a presidential decree abolishing slavery everywhere in Mexico. Pressure from Americans forced officials to modify both of these rulings; the Texas-Coahuila legislature decided that labor contracts made outside the state were perpetually binding, while the President in a decree of December 2, 1829, specifically exempted Texas from his earlier ruling.[1] On this issue the colonists triumphed, but the bad blood resulting meant that each party would view the other with suspicion from this time on.

Ill feeling was heightened by clashes between Mexicans and Americans in Texas. One occurred in the fall of 1826, when a conflict over land claims by two *empresarios,* Green DeWitt and Martin DeLeon, led to a brief armed clash between their settlers. More serious was the outbreak that followed the high-handed action of another *empresario,* Haden Edwards, in attempting to remove American and Mexican squatters from his grant in East Texas. These "old settlers" protested so lustily that the authorities at the state capital, Saltillo, ordered his contract annulled and Edwards himself expelled from the country. His brother, Benjamin Edwards, responded by gathering a handful of ragged followers and riding into Nacogdoches on December 16, 1826, there to proclaim himself ruler of the Republic of Fredonia, which stretched "from the Sabine to the Rio Grande." The Fredonian Revolt ended abruptly when Stephen Austin raised a small army to march against the rebels, but the harm was done. Americans forgot that Haden Edwards was a greedy land speculator and remembered only that a tyrannical Mexican government had canceled his contract without a word of warning. Mexicans forgot that the uprising had been put down by Stephen Austin; instead they saw in the Fredonian Revolt a sure sign that bloodthirsty Americans intended to wrest away their northern provinces by force. From that day on each side viewed the other with mounting distrust.

To make matters worse, the United States chose this unfortunate time to open negotiations designed to secure Texas by diplomatic means. Since 1819, when the Adams-Onís treaty with Spain set the eastern boundary of Texas at the Sabine River, all the West and most of the East had clamored for the return of all or part of that land. John Quincy Adams, who became President in 1825, sought to rectify his earlier error by instructing his minister to Mexico, Joel R. Poinsett, to negotiate a more acceptable boundary. Poinsett offered the Mexican government $1,000,000 for all of Texas, but was politely refused.

[1] Eugene C. Barker, "The Influence of Slavery in the Colonialization of Texas," *Mississippi Valley Historical Review,* XI (1924), 5–28.

Andrew Jackson upped the offer to $5,000,000, and when this was again declined, ordered Poinsett back to Washington to be replaced by the less savory Anthony Butler. This shady negotiator resorted to a variety of devices, each more disgraceful than the one before; he sought to bribe Mexican officials into selling, tried to force an unpayable loan upon them with Texas as security, and urged the President to seize the region as far west as the Neches River by force. Fortunately the full details of these schemes were not known to the rulers of Mexico, but they were aware that Butler had orders to secure Texas at any cost.[2]

These blundering diplomatic moves, coming at a time when the American press was clamoring for Texas and the Texans were showing their disloyalty by staging the Fredonian Revolt, convinced Mexico to review its entire policy. With this in view an able student of Texan affairs, General Manuel de Mier y Terán, was hurried northward to survey the situation. His three reports, the last issued in January, 1830, were alarming. In the country east of San Antonio, he wrote, North Americans were not only dominant, but were increasing in numbers steadily while Mexican strength slowly dwindled. "Either the government occupies Texas *now,*" he warned, "or it is lost forever." This could be accomplished, Terán believed, by a fourfold program: Mexicans should be sent north as colonists, immigration from Switzerland and Germany encouraged, a coastal trade between Mexico and Texas built up, and garrisons established among the Texans to keep them under control.[3]

These sensible suggestions were incorporated in an important measure passed by the Mexican Congress on April 6, 1830. This not only sought to stimulate migration from Europe and provide for stronger economic ties between the mother country and Texas, but ordered the size and numbers of garrisons increased and ruled that "citizens of foreign countries lying adjacent to the Mexican territory are prohib-

[2] Eugene C. Barker, *Mexico and Texas, 1821–1835* (Dallas, 1928), pp. 32–42. A hostile interpretation of the Butler mission is in Eugene C. Barker, "President Jackson and the Texas Revolution," *American Historical Review,* XII (1907), 788–809; one more favorable to Butler is in Richard R. Stenberg (ed.), "President Jackson and Anthony Butler," *Southwest Review,* XXII (1937), 391–404.

[3] Terán's reports are printed in Alleine Howren, "Causes and Origin of the Decree of April 6, 1830," *Southwestern Historical Quarterly,* XVI (1913), 395–413. His mission is described in Ohland Morton, *Terán and Texas: A Chapter in Texas-Mexican Relations* (Austin, 1948), pp. 42–82.

ited from settling as colonists in the states or territories of the Republic adjoining such countries." [4] If enforced, this law would have ended all migration from the United States; in practice *empresarios* whose colonies were "well advanced" were allowed to bring in further settlers until their quotas were filled. The population in Austin's colony increased from 4,248 just before the law was passed to 5,665 a year later, while Green DeWitt's gained proportionately. In all probability still more entered illegally, for the Texan border was too long to be policed and newcomers were always welcomed by Americans. Thus the effect of the law was to bar sober migrants who had been carefully selected by a responsible *empresario* while opening the gates to lawless elements. Nor did the hoped-for immigration from Europe materialize; the few Mexican *empresarios* who took over the canceled grants waited in vain for settlers. Realizing how badly it had blundered, the Congress of the Republic in November, 1833, ruled that after six months immigrants from the United States would again be welcomed.

The result was a new flood of settlers as the "Texas fever" swept through the Mississippi Valley. In the first two months of 1835 no less than two thousand homeseekers landed at the mouth of the Brazos River; before the year was out Anglo-American population was close to thirty thousand souls and vastly outnumbered the 3,500 Mexicans.[5] To make matters worse for Mexico, nearly all were from the southern and western United States, although a handful of Germans found homes in Austin's colony and two shiploads of Irish peasants established themselves in the coastal region between the Lavaca and Nueces rivers. No second visit from General Terán was needed to show that Americans were rapidly dominating this northern province. Any traveler could read the signs: the decline of the old Mexican stronghold at San Antonio into sleepy indolence, the rise of bustling new commercial centers—San Felipe de Austin, Brazoria, Matagordo, Nacogdoches —where shopkeepers showed amazement at the sound of soft Spanish accents. Texas was being Americanized; the time was drawing near when the cocky new arrivals would translate their numerical superiority into political action.

[4] The act is printed in John Sayles and Henry Sayles (comps.), *Early Laws of Texas* (3 vols., St. Louis, 1888), I, 55–57.

[5] These figures are based on estimates by Henry Morfit, who visited Texas in 1836 as an agent of President Andrew Jackson. His report is in 24th Congress, 2nd Session, *Senate Document* No. 20, pp. 13–14.

This was inevitable, not because the Mexican government was guilty of tyrannical acts, but because of two basic cultural conflicts between the American newcomers and their rulers. One stemmed from the sense of racial superiority common to Americans of that day, the other from differing concepts of the role of government in the life of the people.

Certainly the Americans felt themselves vastly superior to the "backward" peons whose subjects they had become. This feeling was based on fundamental cultural differences. Spanish, and hence Mexican, civilization stemmed from that of ancient Rome, and had developed over the course of centuries its unique languages, customs, religion, laws, and institutions. Anglo-American culture, on the other hand, was rooted in northern Europe, where it had fathered the liberal doctrines of Protestantism and political democracy. Mexicans accepted as their duty blind obedience to state and church. Americans believed in their natural right to govern themselves and to enjoy the blessings of religious and political freedom. Between these two civilizations—one stressing the authority of rulers and the other the authority of individuals—there was no compromise.

This was bad enough, but the situation was complicated by the group attitude that persisted among the Americans. Intruders in a foreign land, they felt a strong compulsion to unite in the face of a common enemy. This, in turn, magnified their natural ethnocentric conception of their own superiority. The United States became, in their eyes, the world's mightiest nation; this pre-eminence was based on the excellence of its customs, the truth of its religious teachings, and the extent of freedom it allowed individuals. Because Mexican institutions were different they were, by definition, inferior. This inferiority, Americans believed, stemmed from the degraded nature of the Mexican people. All were cowards; Texas repeatedly stated that "five Indians will chase twenty Mexicans, but five Anglo-Americans will chase twenty Indians." All were treacherous and untrustworthy. All were selfish and completely lacking in gratitude. All were so lazy they preferred indolence to work.[6] Yet fate had placed these slovenly,

[6] Mary A. Holley, *Texas* (Baltimore, 1833), pp. 128, 149–150. An excellent discussion of these cultural conflicts is in Samuel H. Lowrie, *Culture Conflict in Texas, 1821–1835* (New York, 1932), pp. 58–68, 73–92; equally challenging is the thesis of Gerald Ashford, "Jacksonian Liberalism and Spanish Law in Early Texas," *Southwestern Historical Quarterly*, LVII (1953), 1–37.

dirty, slothful, inefficient, backward misfits in temporary control of Americans! Surely the Divine Plan intended something different.

As basic to Texan discontent as group consciousness was Mexico's failure to grant them self-rule. The state of Coahuila-Texas, of which Texas was a minor part, was dominated by Mexicans, who made up nine tenths of its population; the capital at Saltillo was seven hundred miles away, while the one-house legislature of twelve members admitted only one (and later two) Texan representatives and the governor was chosen by a complex process in which Texans had little voice. These arrangements fairly represented the population differences between Coahuila and Texas, but they deprived Americans of any control over their own affairs. Even more objectionable was the judicial system. Under this the alcalde, or magistrate, in each community listened to pleas in civil and criminal cases, then sent the trial record to an *asesor general* at Saltillo who handed down a ruling, or *dictamen*. The long delays resulting proved irksome, but worse to Americans was a legal system where juries were unknown, the judge never faced the accused, and decisions were rendered on the basis of written testimony rather than experience in court. They were sure that the method had been devised to deny them justice.

Actually Mexico's governmental procedures were a product of Spanish cultural tradition, and alien in both theory and practice to those of Anglo-American civilization. In England and the United States legal power derived from the people, while the function of government was to protect the rights of individuals through written constitutions, the interaction of state and nation, and a division of powers. In Spain and Mexico authority stemmed from the right or power of rulers, and the government's purpose was to exact unquestioning obedience from its subjects. This tradition had been modified when Mexico established a federal system and adopted a written constitution, but these novelties had not become part of the culture pattern. Instead the habit of absolutism was so strong that Mexican leaders moved constantly toward a centralized government less responsible to the people. This Americans could understand, for history taught them that all rulers were tyrants, but they could never realize why Mexicans accepted these oppressions without protest. With this lack of understanding went lack of respect.

These cultural conflicts allowed Americans to translate every innocent measure of the Mexican government into an act of tyranny. The law of 1830 ending further colonization from the United States was viewed as a deliberate attempt to snatch land from *empresarios* who had entered into contracts in good faith; no property could be safe under such a government. Similarly the persistent attacks on slavery were seen as blows at private property. These reached a climax in 1832, when the Coahuila-Texas legislature limited all labor contracts to ten years, thus ending the system of indentured servitude that allowed planters to keep their slaves. Outraged Americans muttered that nothing they owned would be safe under the tyrants who ruled Mexico.

The land and slavery questions were irritating enough, but far more inflammatory was the Mexican decision to plant garrisons among the Texans. These were recommended in General Terán's report and authorized in the law of 1830; during the next year the posts at San Antonio, Goliad, and Nacogdoches were strengthened and new garrisons established at Anahuac on Galveston Bay, at the mouths of the Brazos and Nueces rivers, and at a principal crossing on the Brazos. Resentment flamed at once, for not only did Americans note that the new posts were strategically placed to guard all approaches to their settlements, but they bristled at the thought of military rule. A bad situation was made worse when commanders arrived to take over the garrisons; most were renegade Americans who showed less compassion to their countrymen than the Mexicans themselves. Conflict between these worthies and the Texans was inevitable.

It began early in 1831 when the government sent an agent to issue land titles to squatters living east of the San Jacinto River. The commander of the post at Anahuac was Colonel John Davis Bradburn, a cruel and stubborn man, who ruled that further grants were forbidden and sent the agent away, much to the disgust of settlers who had waited overlong for titles. During the next months Bradburn increased his unpopularity by pressing supplies from the people, forcing slaves to work on the fort without compensation, encouraging slaves to escape, and refusing to punish solders guilty of offenses. Matters reached a climax when two Americans who had protested these highhanded actions were jailed in an old brick kiln without trial. The brother of one of the prisoners raised a force of 160 men at San Felipe de Austin, marched on Anahuac, and on June 10, 1832, laid siege to the fort there. Fortunately calmer spirits on both sides persuaded the impromptu attackers to disband, but this did not forestall bloodshed. A small American force which had been sent to Brazoria for a cannon was stopped on its way to Anahuac by the Mexican garrison at Velasco. The bloody engagement that followed ended with the surrender of the fort.[7]

The fat was in the fire now, even though Americans in Texas were almost unanimous in deploring the attack and protesting their loyalty to Mexico. This was rebellion, and retaliation seemed certain. Yet surprising enough, the crisis passed with no further loss of life. Partly responsible were the peace efforts of Stephen Austin, who worked feverishly to soothe angry feelings on both sides; equally important was the cautious nature of Mexican officials, who had so little stomach for war that they hurriedly withdrew the garrisons from Anahuac, Velasco, and the post on the upper Brazos. Despite these efforts, troubles might have multiplied had not the situation within Mexico played into the hands of the American rebels. The "Anahuac Disturbances" coincided with one of the periodic Mexican revolutions and the American insurgents were lucky enough to cast their lot with the winner. While waiting before Anahuac they adopted the "Turtle Bayou Resolutions," pledging their support for the revolutionary leader, General Antonio López de Santa Anna. By the time the smoke of battle had cleared Santa Anna was in control of all Mexico, and the Americans were so much in his favor that retaliation was unthinkable.

Clearly the time was ripe to press for the settlement of grievances. On August 22, 1832, a call was circulated to all American communities, asking them to send delegates to a convention at San Felipe de Austin on October 1. The fifty-five Texans who attended outdid themselves in professing loyalty to both General Santa Anna and Mexico, but unhesitatingly expressed their demands that land titles in eastern Texas be secured, defense against Indians improved, customs duties suspended for three years, provisions prohibiting further immigration be repealed, and—most important of all—Texas be separated from Coahuila and made into a separate state.[8] Then, before adjourning, they urged each community to set up a "Committee of Safety" to rally support for their program. Perhaps the parallel between these com-

[7] Edna Rowe, "The Disturbances at Anahuac in 1832," *Quarterly of the Texas State Historical Association,* VI (1903), 265–299.

[8] The journal of the convention is in H. P. N. Gammel, *Laws of Texas* (2 vols. Austin, 1898), I, 475–503.

mittees and the "Committees of Correspondence" that operated so successfully before the American Revolution did not escape the Mexican officials; certainly word reached Texas in December, 1832, ordering them to disband. Before doing so they issued a call for a second convention, to meet at San Felipe de Austin on April 1, 1833.

The "Convention of 1833" reflected the increasing impatience of the insurgent American group with Mexico's failure to grant their reforms. Its demands varied little from those of the year before, but now the members went ahead to draft a constitution for the new state of Texas they hoped to create. This, with the usual petition, was entrusted to Stephen Austin for delivery to General Santa Anna in Mexico City. Austin began to sense the magnitude of his task as soon as he reached the Mexican capital in July, 1833; for months on end he met only casual indifference or open hostility from the cordon of officials who surrounded the President. When, on November 5, 1833, he was finally granted an audience, he found Santa Anna in a genial mood and willing to grant all of the Texan demands save separate statehood. Well satisfied, Austin started home, only to be arrested at Saltillo and hurried back to Mexico City under heavy guard. There he learned that a letter to one of his friends, written in anger during the height of his quarrel with the Mexican officials and urging the Texans to form a state government, had fallen into the hands of the police. For this indiscretion he cooled his heels in the Prison of the Inquisition until July, 1835, when he finally returned to Texas.[9]

He found the situation radically altered there, and for the worse. For a time after his departure relations were surprisingly cordial; crops were good in 1833 and 1834, a cholera epidemic distracted attention from problems of statehood, business was booming. Amidst this peaceful atmosphere Texas was visited in the summer of 1834 by an official observer, Colonel Juan N. Almonte, who expected to find the revolutionary spirit flaming. Instead all was peace and harmony; so convinced was he of Texan loyalty that he wrote a glowing report approving nearly all their requested reforms.[10] Swept along on this tide of

[9] Eugene C. Barker, *The Life of Stephen F. Austin, Founder of Texas, 1793–1836* (Nashville, 1925), pp. 417–455.

[10] Portions of Almonte's report are printed in Carlos E. Castañeda (ed.), "Statistical Report on Texas. By Juan N. Almonte," *Southwestern Historical Quarterly*, XXVIII (1925), 177–222; his mission is described in Helen W. Harris, "Almonte's Inspection of Texas in 1834," *Southwestern Historical Quarterly*, XLI (1938), 195–211.

good feeling, the Coahuila-Texas legislature granted a number of concessions: a law restricting retail merchandising to Mexicans was repealed, the court system was reformed to lessen delays and grant jury
trial, and Texan representation in the legislature was increased from
two to three members. By the beginning of 1835 the revolutionary
party had been reduced to a handful of malcontents who labored in
vain amidst an atmosphere of harmonious peace.

This honeymoon era might have continued for some time but for
the ambitions of General Santa Anna. Having proclaimed himself a
liberal to secure control in 1832, Santa Anna halfheartedly attempted
a few democratic reforms, but when these brought down the ire of the
clergy and landed classes on his head he gratefully reverted to a more
natural role. In April, 1834, he repudiated his reform program and
dissolved Congress; in October he wiped out the entire federal system,
abolished state governments, and proclaimed himself dictator of a
centralized state. Rumors of these changes reached Texas late in 1834,
when word spread that Santa Anna intended to disenfranchise all
Americans, abolish local governments, and eventually drive all intruders back to the United States. Nor did they have to wait long to
learn that these were not idle words. In January, 1835, garrisons were
re-established at Anahuac and the mouth of the Brazos River to enforce customs collections. Texans were perfectly willing to pay legit-
imate duties, but when the agents demanded bribes and exorbitant
fees, clashes between merchants and troops multiplied. News of this
trouble was hurried to Santa Anna, who dispatched a courier northward with word that reinforcements were on the way. On June 21,
1835, this messenger was halted at San Felipe de Austin while his
cases were opened and the dispatches read. Realizing that they must
strike before fresh troops arrived, a group of some forty hotheads
under W. B. Travis marched away to Anahuac, and on June 30, 1835,
forced the surrender of the garrison there without a shot being fired.[11]

Moderation on the part of the Mexican government would have
nipped the revolutionary movement in the bud, for the vast majority
of Texans condemned the Anahuac radicals and were outspokenly
loyal to Mexico. Instead orders were rushed northward for the arrest
of the four leading offenders: W. B. Travis, Samuel Williams, F. W.
Johnson, and "Three-Legged Willie" Williamson. Once more indig-

[11] Eugene C. Barker, "Difficulties of a Mexican Revenue Officer in Texas,"
Quarterly of the Texas State Historical Association, IV (1901), 190–202.

nation flamed; once more "Committees of Safety and Correspondence" sprang up in every community to exchange information and fan the flames of revolt. Just at this time Stephen Austin returned from Mexico, seething with resentment after his long imprisonment, and convinced that independence was the only answer. As Texans listened to his fiery sentiments, more and more agreed that they could never know security under such a dictator as Santa Anna. The tide of revolution was running strong; only the spilling of blood was needed to produce a full-scale revolt.

Nor was this long in coming. Santa Anna was leading an army northward at this time, partly to quell the Texans but more to put down rebellions among his own people. Hearing exaggerated reports of events beyond the Rio Grande, he sent a cavalry detachment on ahead. When this reached the town of Gonzales and demanded the surrender of a cannon there, Americans from all the countryside rallied as an army of resistance. On the morning of October 2, 1835, they crossed the Guadalupe River and attacked so fiercely that the Mexicans went scurrying southward. Then, with Stephen Austin in command, the American force of five hundred men moved to San Antonio where most of the remaining Mexican troops had taken refuge. After a siege of six weeks the attackers swarmed into the city, forcing the defenders to surrender. The revolution had begun; the Texans had committed themselves to independence or death.[12]

Yet even now some hesitated to make the decision. Before fighting began a call had been issued for a "consultation" to create some type of government; this met at San Felipe de Austin on November 3, 1835, with representatives of all twelve American communities present.[13] Three days of bitter debate between radicals wanting immediate independence and moderates wishing a return to constitutional government under Mexico ended with the members voting 33 to 15 against independence. Instead they drafted a "Declaration of Causes" impelling them to take up arms that was carefully designed to appeal to Mexican liberals without displaying any weakness on the part of the

[12] The battle is described by a participant in Joseph E. Field, *Three Years in Texas* (Boston, 1836), pp. 17–23.

[13] Until the Consultation of 1835 met, Texas was governed by a "Permanent Council" made up of the San Felipe de Austin Committee of Safety augmented by delegates from two other communities. Eugene C. Barker (ed.), "The Journal of the Permanent Council (October 11–27, 1835)," *Quarterly of the Texas State Historical Association*, VII (1904), 252–278.

Texans; it recited the evils of Santa Anna's dictatorship, pledged defense of the "republican principles of the federal constitution of Mexico," and promised continued loyalty to the Mexican government "so long as that nation is governed by the constitution and laws." [14] This done, the consultation named Sam Houston as commander of the army and provided for a provisional governor and council of twelve, to be chosen from the membership of the consultation. Just before adjournment on November 14, 1835, Henry Smith was elected governor and entrusted with control of the somewhat rocky ship of state.

The new government did little during the trying winter of 1835-36; the duties of both governor and council were so poorly defined that they spent their time quarreling over power rather than tending to business. By spring the need for better organization was so obvious that the Provisional Government itself issued a call for a new consultation to meet on March 1, 1836. When the fifty-nine delegates gathered at the little village of Washington the air had marvelously cleared. Santa Anna, at the head of an army of conquest, was almost at hand, scattering threats as he moved. In face of this danger there was no room for division or debate; Texans could survive only by declaring their independence and winning the battles that would follow. So the grim-faced delegates wasted no time on oratory when they crowded around the long wooden table in the drafty shed set aside for them. As curious townspeople peeked over their shoulders, and as the blasts of an icy "norther" sent the room temperature tumbling to the freezing point, they set to work on a declaration of independence.[15]

The document adopted on March 2 was modeled closely on the American Declaration of Independence,[16] but a constitution for the Republic of Texas proved more difficult. Blending phrases from the federal Constitution and from those of several American states, it provided for a President who would serve three years and not be eligible for re-election, an elected congress, and a judicial system similar

[14] Eugene C. Barker (ed.), "The Texan Declaration of Causes for Taking Up Arms against Mexico," *Quarterly of the Texas State Historical Association*, XV (1912), 182-183.

[15] William F. Gray, *From Virginia to Texas, 1835* (Houston, 1909), p. 121. The proceedings of the General Council are in Texas Republic, *Journal of the Proceedings of the General Council of the Republic of Texas, held at San Felipe de Austin, November 14, 1835* (Houston, 1839), pp. 1-363.

[16] James K. Greer, "The Committee on the Texas Declaration of Independence," *Southwestern Historical Quarterly*, XXX (1927), 239-251; XXXI (1927), 130-149.

to that of the United States. Congress was forbidden to interfere with slavery, while every head of family then in Texas was assured a league and a *labor* of land.[17] Until this document could be ratified, the Consultation of 1836 set up an interim government, and also reaffirmed Sam Houston as commander in chief of the armed forces. Thus was the Republic of Texas born of free Americans who refused to bow before the dictatorship of General Santa Anna.

To declare independence was one thing; to win it was quite another. So the Texans discovered in the next troubled months. The first blow fell at San Antonio, where a small garrison barred the path of Santa Anna as his army of revenge moved toward eastern Texas. By February 25, 1836, the Mexican force, four thousand strong, was camped before the gates of the city, ready for the attack. The defenders, who numbered less than 200, realized they could never triumph over such numbers, but were resolved, in the words of Colonel William B. Travis, their commander, to make "victory worse to the enemy than a defeat." Hence they took refuge behind the adobe walls of an abandoned mission, the Alamo, and prepared to sell their lives as dearly as possible. For ten days the Mexicans made thrust after thrust, only to be beaten back with frightful losses. Then, in the grey dawn of March 6, the whole enemy force surged forward, shouting as they came. Twice they were beaten back, but on the third assault they came swarming over the walls like sheep. Gradually the Texans fell back, fighting with rifle butts and knives, until by noon the last survivor was dead.

Victory had been won, but at a terrifying cost. All of the 187 Texans then in the Alamo were killed, including such frontier heroes as Davy Crockett, William B. Travis, and Jim Bowie, but Mexican losses reached the staggering total of 1,544 men killed.[18] This was bad enough for Santa Anna, but worse was the effect of his victory on the surviving Texans. Not only had he been delayed long enough for them to form an army, but he had inspired them with a thirst for revenge that gave them superhuman strength. "Remember the Alamo" became a rallying cry that would stir the blood of the most sluggish Texan— from that day to this. Santa Anna was certain to meet fanatical resistance as he continued his conquest.

[17] Rupert N. Richardson, "Framing the Constitution of the Republic of Texas," *Southwestern Historical Quarterly*, XXXI (1928), 191–220.

[18] The most reliable study of the battle is Amelia Williams, "A Critical Study of the Siege of the Alamo and of the Personnel of Its Defenders," *Southwestern Historical Quarterly*, XXXVI (1933), 251–287; XXXVII (1934), 237–312.

This resistance was made even more fanatical by the next setback. Far to the south was another detachment of the Texan army, a force of 350 men under James W. Fannin, Jr., that had marched against Matamoros, the Rio Grande city which guarded one approach to Texas. Failing to reach their objective, they began falling back on March 19, 1836, with the intention of joining the principal army that General Sam Houston was welding together. That noon they camped on an open plain just beyond the San Antonio River, despite word that a large enemy force was nearby. While they were in this defenseless position they were surprised by a major Mexican army. The men coolly formed a hollow square and primed their guns for the attack, but Fannin knew that his outnumbered troops would be slaughtered or starved into submission, and accepted honorable terms of surrender. All were marched to nearby Goliad, where, on the morning of Sunday, March 27, they were routed from their blankets and formed into three columns, supposedly to forage for wood. Instead all were marched a short distance from the town and cold bloodedly shot down. Santa Anna himself, it was believed, was responsible for this massacre.[19]

The slaughter of Texans at the Alamo and Goliad marvelously united opinion throughout the Republic. This was exactly what Sam Houston needed for victory, for like all frontiersmen his countrymen were too self-centered to accept orders except in dire emergency. Now volunteers came flocking into his army, muttering curses at Santa Anna as they did so. Just as important was the effect on the Republic's leaders. Realizing that they would all hang unless they stopped their petty squabbling, they hurriedly entrusted Houston with sole responsibility for a plan of campaign. Nor were these responsibilities ill placed. Houston was a giant of a man, standing six feet two inches tall, whose leopard-skin vests, fur hats, and eccentric devotion to whittling could not hide his abilities as a leader. With supreme self-confidence, he personally shouldered the fate of the new Republic. "Had I consulted the wishes of all," he wrote, "I should have been like the ass between two stacks of hay. . . . I consulted none—I held no councils of war. If I err, the blame is mine." [20]

[19] Harbert Davenport, "The Men of Goliad," *Southwestern Historical Quarterly,* XLII (1939), 1–41, is the best account. A colorful description by a doctor who escaped execution that he might minister to the sick is in Joseph H. Barnard, *Dr. J. H. Barnard's Journal* (n.p., 1950), pp. 16–36.

[20] Amelia W. Williams and Eugene C. Barker (eds.), *The Writings of Sam Houston 1813–1863* (8 vols., Austin, 1938–1943), I, 384–385.

Sam Houston did not err. Taking command of the feeble Texan force at Gonzales in mid-March, just as news arrived of the defeats at the Alamo and Goliad, he saw at once that in numbers, equipment, or morale his men were not ready to make a stand against Santa Anna's well-supplied troops. His was the task of welding an army together as it retreated before the enemy. So Houston led his soldiers eastward— to the Colorado River, to the Brazos, to San Felipe de Austin, which was burned to the ground—accustoming the men to discipline and picking up recruits along the way. Behind him he left his countrymen in a state of panic. The Mexican barbarians would kill them all unless they escaped! So the rumor spread as men and women and children fled eastward in the wake of the Texan army, leaving behind their houses and goods and even their children. "The roads," wrote an observer of this "runaway scrape," "were literally crowded with wagons, men, women, and children, hurrying on with the greatest speed to a place of safety." [21] The government fled with the people, to Washington, to Harrisburg, to Galveston Island, pleading constantly with Houston to stop and fight before all was lost.

The wily commander was too canny to listen to this advice until he had some hope of winning a decisive battle. By April 20 he was ready to make his stand. His army had been swelled to 783 men, many of them recruits who had flocked in from the United States. All had been hardened and accustomed to a modicum of discipline. Santa Anna's force, which had been constantly at his heels, was camped that day on the open prairie just west of the San Jacinto River, and had dwindled away to only seven hundred men. The hour of decision was at hand. Houston ordered his men southward along the banks of the San Jacinto, across Buffalo Bayou, and to a spot just beyond. A mile away, and separated only by rolling prairie broken here and there by clumps of trees, was the Mexican encampment.

Had Houston attacked at once his force would have outnumbered Santa Anna's, but just before dawn on April 21 five hundred Mexican reinforcements arrived. That was the day chosen for the assault. All that morning the Texans made final preparations, while their commander rode among them, telling them: "Victory is certain. Trust in God and fear not!" At noon they started forward, just as the Mexicans were settling down to their usual siesta. Moving in three columns, they were not sighted until they had deployed into a long line

[21] W. B. Dewees, *Letters from an Early Settler of Texas* (Louisville, 1852), p. 203.

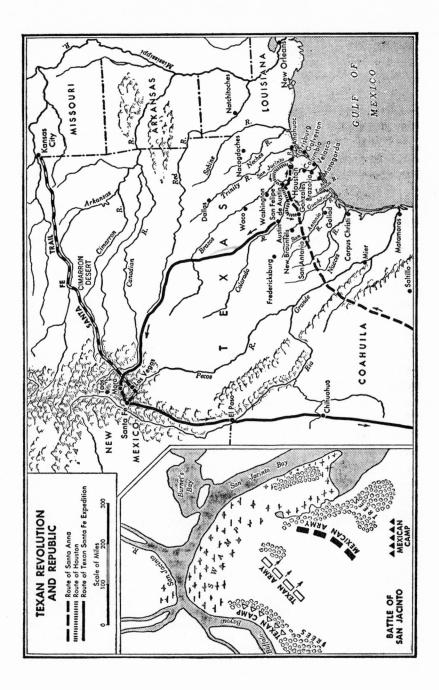

TEXAN REVOLUTION
AND REPUBLIC

- - - Route of Santa Anna
||||||| Route of Houston
━━━ Route of Texan Santa Fe Expedition

Scale of Miles
0   100   200   300

MISSOURI

ARKANSAS

LOUISIANA

Kansas City

Natchitoches

New Orleans

GULF OF MEXICO

SANTA FE TRAIL

CIMARRON DESERT

NEW MEXICO

Santa Fe

Las Vegas

San Miguel

El Paso

Chihuahua

Saltillo

COAHUILA

Matamoros

Mier

Corpus Christi

Goliad

Victoria

San Antonio

New Braunfels

Fredericksburg

Austin

Gonzales

San Felipe

Washington

Waco

Dallas

Nacogdoches

Houston

Anahuac

Harrisburg

Galveston

Columbia

Velasco

Matagorda

TEXAS

Red R.

Sabine R.

Neches R.

Trinity R.

Brazos R.

Colorado R.

San Antonio R.

Guadalupe R.

Nueces

Rio Grande

Pecos R.

Canadian R.

Cimarron R.

Arkansas R.

Mississippi R.

BATTLE OF
SAN JACINTO

Burnet's Bay

San Jacinto Bay

San Jacinto R.

Buffalo Bayou

TEXAN CAMP

TREES

TEXAN ARMY

SWAMP

MEXICAN ARMY

MEXICAN CAMP

and surged over the top of a slight hill two hundred yards from the enemy's defenses. Slowly they advanced, their Lone Star flag fluttering bravely, and an improvised band piping away merrily with the strains of a popular love song, "Will You Come to the Bower I Have Shaded For You." Before them rode Houston, warning "Hold your fire! God damn you, hold your fire!" When only sixty yards from Santa Anna's "Invincibles," the first Mexican volley sailed harmlessly over their heads. The shout of "Fire" ran along the line; when the smoke cleared there were gaps in the enemy forces. Then came the charge, as the Texans surged forward, yelling "Remember the Alamo." Within fifteen minutes all was over. The bodies of 630 Mexicans were strewn over the battlefield, while 730 more, including Santa Anna, were prisoners. The Texans lost only nine men killed and thirty-four wounded.[22]

The Battle of San Jacinto won Texas its independence. Some two thousand Mexican troops were still in the country, but they scurried for home as soon as the news reached them. Santa Anna was taken to Velasco, where the government was meeting, to sign two treaties, one declaring hostilities at an end, the other, a secret document, pledging his support for an independent Texas with the Rio Grande boundary. Time was soon to show that these treaties meant nothing, for they were repudiated by the Mexican Congress as soon as news of Santa Anna's capture reached Mexico City. With this repudiation came word that another Mexican army was approaching Goliad, bent on reconquest. The Texan force, now swelled to 2,500 men and led by Thomas J. Rusk (Houston was receiving treatment for a leg wound), marched away toward the border. When no enemy appeared, they settled down to plot revenge on their own government for refusing to hang Santa Anna. For a time Texas was threatened with the same type of military rule it had fought to avoid, but the crisis passed when an expedition against Matamoros was invented to occupy the men. While the soldiers planned the Matamoros jaunt that never took place, an election occurred that assured continued civil rule for Texas.[23]

[22] Houston's account of the battle is in Williams and Barker (eds.), *Writings of Sam Houston*, I, 416–420, and that of Santa Anna in Carlos E. Castañeda (ed.), *The Mexican Side of the Texan Revolution (1836) by the Chief Mexican Participants* (Dallas, 1928), pp. 23–33. A colorful contemporary description is in Chester Newell, *History of the Revolution in Texas* (New York, 1838), pp. 104–108, and the most complete modern history is Sam H. Dixon and Louis W. Kemp, *The Heroes of San Jacinto* (Houston, 1932), pp. 1–30.

[23] William C. Binkley, "The Activities of the Texan Revolutionary Army after San Jacinto," *Journal of Southern History*, VI (1940), 311–346.

This election was the first held under the newly ratified constitution. Stephen Austin and Sam Houston were the natural candidates; but the result was never in doubt, for Austin's popularity had declined sharply during the months of fighting. Houston was chosen President by an overwhelming majority, with Mirabeau B. Lamar his Vice-President. All but 61 of the 6,000 persons who cast ballots favored annexation to the United States as soon as opportunity offered. With his future policy established, Sam Houston was inaugurated at Columbia in October, 1836, firmly dedicated to the dual program of restoring sound civil government within Texas and winning eventual annexation.

The restoration of orderly government proved difficult, largely because the new Republic's finances were in a chaotic state. The war had cost heavily, while adequate sources of income were lacking even for normal expenditures. During Houston's three years in office poll taxes, direct property taxes, a tax on business, customs duties, and a tonnage duty were levied, but they returned only a small portion of the $2,000,000 needed; time and time again Houston had to pledge his personal credit to buy supplies for the army. Borrowing and the issue of paper money helped fill the gap, but the President was wise enough to see that strict economy was the only answer. His Indian policy was dedicated to keeping peace at all costs, while the army was reduced from 3,587 men to only 600. The administration was also responsible for laws creating twenty-three counties and establishing an efficient court system.

The second plank in Houston's platform—annexation by the United States—proved more difficult to achieve. William H. Wharton, the agent dispatched to Washington with instructions to "make every exertion to effect annexation with the least possible delay," found President Jackson cordial but uncooperative.[24] Annexation was impossible, Wharton was told, not only because this would almost certainly involve the United States in a war with Mexico, but because a sizable portion of the American public was opposed. Northern Whigs were already charging that the revolution had been engineered by Jackson and Houston to add another Democratic state to the Union; southern extremists were insisting that Texas was better off as an inde-

[24] George P. Garrison (ed.), "Diplomatic Correspondence of the Republic of Texas," American Historical Association, *Annual Reports for 1907 and 1908* (2 vols., Washington, 1908, 1911), I, 127–135.

pendent republic than under the domination of a slavery-hating, high-tariff, centralized government at Washington;[25] and abolitionists were noisily arguing that the Texan revolution was a "dark lanterned conspiracy of the slavocracy" to secure more slave territory. Jackson feared, and rightly, that annexation would stir up a hornets' nest of political conflict that might disrupt the Union.

Recognizing that the President would never budge from this position, Wharton directed his efforts toward securing official recognition by the United States. On this subject he found Jackson sympathetic, but still fearful of northern opinion. The wily agent suggested that Texas would soon expand its borders to the Pacific, adding the ports that were wanted by the shipping and whaling interests of the North. When this failed to convince the President, Wharton prodded Congress into action. A measure appropriating funds for a diplomatic representative to the Republic of Texas was finally adopted, and on March 2, 1837, Jackson officially extended recognition.[26]

With this step the Texans were assured freedom from Mexican reconquest and could settle to the happy task of developing their new Republic. Times were auspicious. In the United States the Panic of 1837 was displacing thousands who were anxious to escape their debts and begin life anew. To many of these, Texas offered a perfect haven, for the international boundary would protect them from their creditors, while land could be obtained almost for the asking. Under a law passed in December, 1836, the Texan Republic promised all newcomers who were heads of families 1,280 acres free of charge, and all single men 640 acres, as well as the right to pre-empt additional amounts at a price of fifty cents an acre. Here was inducement indeed. Why stay at home when life could start anew in a land where the air was "as elastic as a morning zephyr," the climate so healthy that men who wanted to die had to go elsewhere, the growing season so long that several crops could be harvested each year, and the soil blessed with such "exuberant fecundity" that bottom lands produced four thousand pounds of cotton or one hundred bushels of corn to the acre? Or so, at least, the immigrants were told by the Texas boosters of that day.

[25] Elizabeth H. West, "Southern Opposition to the Annexation of Texas," *Southwestern Historical Quarterly*, XVIII (1914), 74–82.
[26] Ethel Z. Rather, "Recognition of the Republic of Texas by the United States," *Quarterly of the Texas State Historical Association*, XIII (1910), 155–256.

And they came, some by steamboat from New Orleans, some on the little craft that plied the Red River, but most along the main road from Natchitoches in Louisiana to Nacogdoches. During the summer of 1837 six thousand persons crossed the Sabine at Gaines Ferry. "Loaded wagons," wrote one observer, "and travellers in carriages and on horseback, were all along the road, pressing on the far west." [27] Cities were crowded with jostling immigrants, standing in long lines before land offices to secure "certificates" that would entitle them to free land. At first migration was confined to individuals and families, but in 1841 the Texan Congress revived the *empresario* system, and group colonization became increasingly important. Of the colonies established, the Peters Colony near modern Dallas was most successful; there the Texas Emigration and Land Company planted some 2,205 families during the Republic era.[28] Others came from abroad, many from Germany, where the Society for the Protection of German Immigrants in Texas was formed in 1842. Although badly mismanaged and constantly plagued by debt, this company settled 5,247 Germans near the villages of New Braunfels and Fredericksburg by 1846. France also contributed its quota, lured by the wealthy Henri Castro, who dissipated a fortune but brought 2,134 persons to his Indian-infested *empresario* grant between the Nueces and the Rio Grande.

As they came, these homeseekers from the United States and Europe, they swelled the population of Texas from 30,000 in 1836 to 142,000 ten years later. Within that land, the newcomers blended to create a raw society typical of new frontiers. Farming was their principal occupation, with cotton the most important cash crop and corn the staff of life. Commercial activity was centered in a few villages: Galveston with four thousand inhabitants, San Antonio with less than one thousand, Houston with still a smaller number, and Austin, which became the capital in 1839, with hardly more. All were ramshackle collections of log structures, with here and there a spacious frame house attesting to the ambition of the more fortunate founders. But all were bustling with activity. Houston was typical. A traveler in 1838 found all "charming confusion" there with tree stumps blocking the streets and logs scattered everywhere as building went on. Only a year

[27] F. B. Page, *Prairiedom: Rambles and Scrambles in Texas* (New York, 1846), p. 65.

[28] Seymour V. Connor, "Kentucky Colonization in Texas; a History of the Peters Colony," *Register of the Kentucky Historical Society*, LI (1953), 5–33; LII (1954), 310–331.

later the village boasted a courthouse, a jail, two small theaters, a state house, twelve stores, and forty-seven saloons; after five more years it contained forty stores, three hotels, several newspapers, a large cotton press, an iron foundry, two packing houses, grist and saw mills, schools, and four churches attended by "an intelligent, industrious, and moral population" of some four thousand souls.[29]

Life in both village and farm was as rough and crude as it always was on such advanced frontiers, but elements of higher civilization were by no means lacking. Gambling and drinking were universal especially on the anniversary of the Battle of San Jacinto, while crime flourished despite the vigilance of hard-working peace officers. "Property," a traveler observed, "is more secure than life." [30] Yet the forces that were to lead to greater stability were already beginning to operate. Protestant clergymen began moving to Texas as soon as independence ended the predominance of Catholicism there; by 1840, Methodists were sufficiently numerous to organize a separate Texas Conference, while Baptists and Presbyterians were not far behind. With them came schoolmasters to found not only grade schools but such institutions of slightly higher learning as Rutersville College and McKenzie College. As the social order matured, newspapers blossomed until thirteen were published by 1840; in the villages literary societies, lyceums, choral groups, and "Thespian Corps" of amateur dramatists all waged a constant battle against the primitivism of frontier life. On few frontiers did society come of age so rapidly.[31]

Its lustiness was due partly to the unpleasant realization that Texas, unwanted by the United States, would have to carve out its own destiny as an independent nation. That this fate was fully realized was shown when the presidential election of 1838 rolled around. Sam Houston could not succeed himself, but had he been able to he would probably not have been re-elected. What was needed now, the people believed, was not economy and caution, but a bold policy that would elevate the Republic of Texas to a stable position among the nations

[29] Frédéric Leclerc, *Texas and Its Revolution* (Houston, 1950), p. 27; Edward Stiff, *The Texan Emigrant: being a Narration of the Adventures of the Author in Texas* (Cincinnati, 1840), pp. 79–81; Page, *Prairiedom,* pp. 85–86.

[30] Carl, Prince of Solms-Braunfels, *Texas, 1844–1845* (Houston, 1936), p. 57.

[31] The best description of Texan social life is William R. Hogan, *The Texas Republic. A Social and Economic History* (Norman, Okla., 1946), *passim.*

of the world. This could be achieved by stimulating commerce, driving back Indian tribes that blocked expansion, muscling into the international arena to win support from other powers, and especially by flinging back the borders of Texas until its area matched that of the great nations it was destined to rival. These were the results promised by one of the candidates in the election of 1838, Mirabeau B. Lamar, and those promises won him victory.

The contrast between the Houston and Lamar administrations was nowhere better illustrated than in their attitude toward the Indians. Houston had made every concession to keep the tribes at peace; Lamar believed they must be expelled to make room for more settlers even at the cost of war. Cherokee who lived in the northeastern corner of Texas felt the brunt of this change first, largely because their lands were in the course of the advancing frontier. During the summer of 1839 a force of militiamen and rangers marched into their country, defeated them in battle, and drove them over the border into Arkansas. On the western borderlands a vigorous campaign waged against the Comanche lasted until the autumn of 1840, when the red men finally sued for peace. Costly though these wars were, they opened rich lands to occupation and assured quiet on the frontiers for another generation.[32]

Lamar's foreign policy was equally forceful. His objectives were sensible: he would win recognition from the major European powers, then bludgeon Mexico into acknowledging Texan independence. The time seemed ripe for such a program, for periodic revolutions racked the northern Mexican provinces during those years, and the country's coast was under blockade during much of 1838 and 1839 by a French fleet sent to collect debts due that nation's citizens. These circumstances, combined with Lamar's outspoken insistence that Texas was destined to a long career as an independent nation, finally convinced France to extend official recognition in October, 1839. England followed in November, 1840, with the Netherlands and Belgium taking similar action a short time later. Despite this support from abroad, all efforts to force Mexico into acknowledging Texan independence proved futile. Three agents were sent to Mexico City, one after the other, between 1839 and 1841; but the first never got beyond Vera

[32] Anna Muckleroy, "The Indian Policy of the Republic of Texas," *Southwestern Historical Quarterly,* XXVI (1922), 128–148.

Cruz, and the others returned after waiting for months without even being allowed to present their cases.

These failures only accentuated Lamar's desire to expand the borders of Texas to the Pacific, thus creating a republic that could maintain itself among the world's powers. New Mexico, just to the west, was the first objective. There the people had shown their discontent with Mexican rule by staging a revolution which elevated Manuel Armíjo to the governorship; nine tenths of them, Lamar believed, were "anxious to come under the protection of that flag to which they really owed fealty." [33] He was wise enough to realize that attempted military conquest would unite the New Mexicans against a common enemy, but a caravan of trading goods sent to Santa Fe might work wonders. Once they learned they could enjoy such trade only by annexation, they would gladly cast their lot with Texas. If, on the other hand, they insisted on allegiance to Mexico, the trading caravan would do no harm and would bring in revenue needed by the Texans.

Thus decided, Lamar advertised for merchants who would risk the journey. None who joined had the slightest hint that the military conquest of New Mexico was planned; the subjugation of 150,000 New Mexicans by three hundred traders and adventurers was, as one of them put it, "a shade too Quixotical" to be considered.[34] The handful of soldiers who went along seemed needed to fight off Indians, while the three Texan commissioners who represented Lamar were surely necessary to care for the diplomacy of trade, not conquest. So there were no thoughts of anything but profits as the party of 303 men, with twenty-four ox-drawn wagons, pulled out of the little town of Austin on June 21, 1841, and started west along the Red River. By September 11 an advance party of one hundred men was at the village of Mora, one hundred miles from Santa Fe, while the bulk of the traders were some distance behind at the Palo Duro. All were exhausted by the 1,300-mile journey; for days they had been subsisting on the flesh of their horses and such snakes and horned toads as they could capture.

In this defenseless state they were surprised by an army that had been hurried eastward by Governor Armíjo as soon as he learned of the invasion. The Texans surrendered without firing a shot. All were bound with hair ropes and thongs of rawhide, while Armíjo hurried

[33] George W. Kendall, *Narrative of the Texan Santa Fé Expedition* (2 vols., New York, 1844), I, 14–15.
[34] *Ibid.*, I, 36.

1. STEPHEN F. AUSTIN

(The New York Public Library)

2. JAMES BRIDGER

(The New York Public Library)

3. NATHANIEL J. WYETH

From *A History of the Pacific Northwest*
by G. W. Fuller

4. SAM HOUSTON

(The New York Public Library)

5. Rancheros roping cattle during California's Pastoral Age, with the San José Mission in the background

From *California: A History of Upper and Lower California from Their Discovery to the Present Times* by Alexander Forbes

6. Arrival of the traders' caravan at Santa Fe

From *Commerce of the Prairies* by Josiah Gregg

7. The Hudson's Bay Company's Fort Vancouver

From *Sketches in North America and the Oregon Territory* by Henry J. Warre

8. The American Fur Company's Fort Union

From an engraving by Charles Bodmer, reproduced by permission of the Chicago Historical Society

9. A Methodist Mission in Oregon

From *A Report, in The Form of A Journal, To The Quarter-master General, of The March of The Regiment of Mounted Riflemen, to Oregon* by Osborne Cross

10. The Interior of Fort Laramie

A painting by Alfred Jacob Miller, from *The West of Alfred Jacob Miller* by Marvin C. Ross, copyright 1951 by the University of Oklahoma Press (Courtesy of the Walters Art Gallery, Baltimore, Maryland)

11. JOHN BIDWELL

(The New York Public Library)

12. THE REVEREND JASON LEE

(The New York Public Library)

13. JOHN A. SUTTER

From *Illustrated Historical Sketches
of California* by Dr. John F. Morse

14. The American village at the falls of the Willamette

From *Sketches in North America and the Oregon Territory* by Henry J. Warre

15. An emigrant caravan crossing the Rocky Mountains

From a print by Currier and Ives (Reproduced by permission of the Chicago Historical Society)

16. Hoisting a team over the Wasatch Mountains

From *California Gold Book* by William W. Allen and R. B. Avery

17. The storming of the Alamo

From *Pictorial History of Texas* by Homer S. Thrall

18. Texans drawing the black beans at Salado

From *Journal of The Texan Expedition Against Mier* by Thomas J. Green

19. JAMES P. BECKWOURTH

(Reproduced by permission of the State
Historical Society of Colorado)

20. STEPHEN KEARNY

(The New York Public Library)

21. KIT CARSON

(Reproduced by permission of the State
Historical Society of Colorado)

22. Mormon hand-cart emigrants in a snowstorm

From *The Rocky Mountain Saints* by T. B. H. Stenhouse

23. Salt Lake City in 1853

From *Route From Liverpool to Great Salt Lake Valley* by James Linforth

25. JOHN C. FRÉMONT

From *A History of the Pacific Northwest* by G. W. Fuller

24. BRIGHAM YOUNG
(Culver Service)

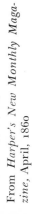

26. How the forty-niners mined the gold: panning, cradle rocking and washing with the long tom

From *Harper's New Monthly Magazine*, April, 1860

27. "A few days in the diggins."

From *Punch*, 1849

28. The winter of '49 in a mining camp

From *Mountains and Molehills* by Frank Marryat

29. Virginia City, Nevada

From *Harper's New Monthly Magazine,* January, 1861

30. Gold mining in Gregory Gulch, Colorado

From *Beyond the Mississippi* by Albert D. Richardson

31. Morning cattle yoking on an overland freight train

From *Frank Leslie's Illustrated Newspaper,* January 8, 1859

32. Changing the mails from stagecoach to celerity wagon

From *Frank Leslie's Illustrated Newspaper,* October 23, 1858

news of his "two great victories over the Texan invaders" to Mexico City and promised that the prisoners would soon follow. Thus began a "death march" of two thousand miles that would have tried the stamina of men more rugged than the Texans. Food was scarce, water lacking, the cold frequently intense. By the time they reached the Rio Grande their clothes had rotted away until most were nearly naked. Many were kept alive in the grim days ahead only by presents of food from Mexican women who "would follow us in large numbers for miles, weeping at the cruelties to which we were subjected." [35] Others dropped beside the road to die, or were shot when their weary feet lagged. Not until December, 1841, did the gaunt survivors reach Mexico City, where they were cast into dungeons or put to work on the streets under heavy guard.

The ill-fated Texan Santa Fe expedition sealed the doom of Lamar as President of the Texan Republic. His aggressive policies had won Texas recognition from abroad and peace from Indian attack at home, but they had cost the people dearly. Expenditures during his administration totaled nearly $5,000,000, while revenue from taxes and customs duties amounted to only a little over $1,000,000. The paper money issued to close this gap was already declining in value so rapidly that finances were in a chaotic state. Little wonder that dissatisfaction brewed, or that news of the Santa Fe expedition's fate brought opposition to a head. Congress voted to censure him publicly, and the election of 1841 placed Sam Houston in the Presidency by an overwhelming majority over Lamar's candidate, David G. Burnett.

The people had spoken for conservatism and economy, and Houston gave them both in the three years ahead. Offices were abolished, salaries reduced, the army disbanded save for a few companies of rangers, the navy sold, and treaties or councils with the border Indians substituted for conquest. Yet dedicated though he was to peace and parsimony, Houston soon found himself involved in a new war. Mexico, angered by the Santa Fe expedition, suddenly emerged from its lethargy with the announcement that the reconquest of Texas would begin at once and go on until the flag was planted on the banks of the Sabine. That this was no idle threat was shown in February, 1842,

[35] Franklin Combs, "Narrative of the Santa Fe Expedition in 1841," *New Mexico Historical Review*, V (1930), 310. The best modern account of the expedition is in William C. Binkley, *The Expansionist Movement in Texas, 1836–1850* (Berkeley, 1925), pp. 68–95.

when seven hundred troops crossed the border, captured San Antonio, and then retreated with all the plunder they could carry. In July Corpus Christi was attacked by another Mexican force, and in September San Antonio again fell before an army of 1,200 men under General Adrian Woll. As these raids went on panic swept through southern Texas; everywhere people abandoned their homes and fled eastward in a second "runaway scrape" which resembled that of the revolution.

This was too much, even for the economy-minded Sam Houston. Three retaliatory forces were hastily recruited. One under General Alexander Somervell started south in mid-November, but after scouting unsuccessfully along the Rio Grande for Mexicans until December, it was ordered back to San Antonio. The men refused to go; they were out to hunt Mexicans and hunt they would. Electing their own officers, they crossed the Rio Grande to occupy the Mexican town of Mier on Christmas Day, 1842. There they were surprised by an enemy force so large that resistance seemed suicidal. Surrendering peacefully, the 226 Texans were marched off toward Mexico City in chains. On the way they overcame their guards and started back, only to be recaptured almost at once. For this sin they were forced to draw beans from an earthen mug, with one in every ten drawing a black bean that meant death. After the condemned had been shot, the rest were taken to the village of Perote, where they were cast into dank dungeons with survivors of the Santa Fe expedition and some of the prisoners taken in General Woll's raid on San Antonio.[36]

The other two retaliatory forces fared almost as badly. One was formed in August, 1842, when the Texan government authorized Colonel Charles A. Warfield to recruit a small army for a march on Santa Fe. Visiting first the settlements in western Missouri and then the southern Rockies to enlist the help of Mountain Men, Warfield ordered his forces to rendezvous at Point of Rocks near New Mexico while he returned to Texas to raise his principal force. Unfortunately,

[36] Contemporary accounts by participants are in Thomas J. Green, *Journal of the Texan Expedition Against Mier* (New York, 1845), pp. 168–364; William P. Stapp, *The Prisoners of Perote, Containing a Journal Kept by the Author* (Philadelphia, 1845), pp. 2–162; Sterling B. Hendricks, "The Somervell Expedition to the Rio Grande, 1842," *Southwestern Historical Quarterly,* XXIII (1919), 112–140; and Frederick C. Chabot (ed.), *The Perote Prisoners. Being the Diary of James L. Trueheart* (San Antonio, 1934), pp. 91–302.

his followers were too ambitious for their own good. The twenty-four Mountain Men who volunteered could not resist attacking the New Mexican village of Mora as they moved toward the rendezvous, bringing a Mexican cavalry force into action that sent them scurrying to the protection of the mountains. The Missourians, in the meantime, had paused in their journey to Point of Rocks to murder a Mexican Santa Fe trader, an act of brutality that aroused bitter resentment in the United States. Fearful of the effect this hostility would have on annexation, President Houston reluctantly ordered Warfield to abandon his expedition.[37]

Nor did the last of the Texan forces to take up cudgels against Mexico in 1842 and 1843 fare better. Major Jacob Snively, its commander, was issued letters of "marque and reprisal" similar to those carried by privateers in time of war, and ordered north to raid Mexican caravans engaged in the Santa Fe trade. This was open robbery, and completely without justification, but most Texans applauded any attack on Mexico. With nearly 170 followers he marched northward to the trail at a point near the crossing of the Cimarron Desert. There, in June, 1843, the Texans defeated a small Mexican cavalry force, killing fifteen of the enemy and taking the rest prisoners, then settled down to await the arrival of the yearly caravan from Independence. To their horror this appeared under a strong Army escort; news of the Warfield raid had prompted the traders to request, and receive, the protection of a detachment of dragoons under Captain Philip St. George Cooke. Not daring to challenge such opposition, Snively's followers meekly surrendered, and by early July were straggling back toward Texas.[38] Thus did the Texans' plans for retaliation against Mexico end ingloriously.

There was no weeping at home, however, for by this time more dazzling prospects loomed on the Texan horizon. Bravely as they had planned their future as a republic, there was no question that the vast majority preferred a return to the United States of their birth. Annexation seemed the logical answer to their problems from the beginning; and as troubles beset them during their years of independence, this

[37] William C. Binkley, "The Last Stage of Texan Military Operations against Mexico, 1843," *Southwestern Historical Quarterly*, XXII (1919), 260–265.

[38] H. Bailey Carroll, "Stewart A. Miller and the Snively Expedition of 1843," *Southwestern Historical Quarterly*, LIV (1951), 261–286, is an excellent account of the expedition based on the unpublished diary of one of the party.

bulked as ever more desirable. Until 1844 the American government had viewed their ambitions with chilly indifference, but by the time Sam Houston's second administration drew to a close the situation there was changing. Hopefully the Texans renewed their pleas, and this time the United States, suddenly awakening to its "manifest destiny," was willing to listen.

CHAPTER 7

Manifest Destiny

EIGHTEEN FORTY-FOUR was America's year of decision. Overnight the American people awakened to their role in the Divine Plan: the "area of freedom" embraced within the boundaries of their nation must be flung westward to the Pacific! As this realization dawned the timidity that had held them back in the past was forgotten. Earlier Presidents had hesitated to annex Texas lest war with Mexico follow; now popular opinion not only demanded—and secured —that land but all of California as well. Former statesmen had avoided offending mighty England as the two nations contested ownership of the Oregon Country; by the end of 1844 politicians and the people alike clamored for "All of Oregon or None" and happily prepared for the war that seemed inevitable. An overwhelming shift in public opinion was taking place, with expansion to the Pacific its foreordained result.

This expressed itself first in the election of 1844. The Whigs' perennial candidate, Henry Clay, was on record as opposing the annexation of Texas; such a step, he had declared, would not only lead to war with Mexico but would be "dangerous to the integrity of the Union." [1] Although Clay hedged slightly before the election, the majority of the people viewed him as an opponent of expansion. The Democrats, on the other hand, met the issue squarely. Passing over the preconvention favorite, Martin Van Buren, because his antislavery principles led him to oppose annexing Texas, they chose a "dark horse," James K. Polk of Tennessee, as their standard bearer. Polk was an outspoken

[1] The "Raleigh letter," published in the *National Intelligencer*, April 27, 1844.

expansionist: "I have *no hesitation* in declaring," he wrote even before the convention, "that I am in favor of the Immediate Re-annexation of Texas." [2] To win northern votes, the Democrats coupled a demand for Oregon with that for Texas. Boldly the party platform declared "that the re-occupation of Oregon and the re-annexation of Texas at the earliest possible period are great American measures, which this convention recommends to the cordial support of the Democracy of the Union."

The election that followed was no clear mandate for expansion. Polk received a majority vote in fifteen of the twenty-six states, and an electoral vote of 170 to Henry Clay's 105. Yet seven of the fifteen Democratic states were in the North, where Texan annexation was unpopular, while Clay carried such strongly expansionist states as North Carolina, Kentucky, and Tennessee. As is so often the case, the truth was less important than the impression created by Polk's victory. Both he and the nation believed that the people had spoken for expansion, no matter what the cost. From the day of his inauguration the new President was determined to give them what they wanted.

Why this shift in the climate of opinion? Why were Americans ready to risk war with powers abroad and conflict over the slavery issue at home to secure more territories when millions of acres within the country were still unoccupied? The answer can be found in the persistence of the westward movement, the reawakening fear of other nations, and the emergence of a new spirit that came to be known as "manifest destiny."

Certainly the relentless advance of the pioneer made expansion inevitable. Wherever he went, whether to Texas or California or Oregon, the frontiersman demanded that his country's protective arm be extended over him. Loyalty to the land of his adoption was unthinkable; he was an American and an American he would remain. "They seem," wrote one who lived among the pioneers of California, "to look upon this beautiful land as their own Canaan, and the motley race around them as the Hittites, the Hivites, and the Jebusites, whom they are to drive out." [3] No extended reading of congressional debates is necessary to show that the statesmen of that day viewed expansion as inevitable, and believed that where the frontiersmen went the flag must follow. Possession, they felt, was nine points of the law. A New

[2] *Niles' Register*, LXVII (1844), 75.
[3] Walter Colton, *Three Years in California* (New York, 1850), p. 118.

York editor only reflected public opinion when he wrote: "There is in fact no such thing as title to the wild lands of the new world, except that which actual possession gives. They belong to whoever will redeem them from the Indian and the desert, and subjugate them to the use of man." [4] Here was justification enough for adding Texas and California and Oregon to the Union.

But more was forthcoming, for scarcely a loyal citizen but believed these lands would fall to some foreign power if the United States did not act at once. Of these potential rivals, the most dreaded was England. Hatred of Britain had persisted since the days of the Revolution and the War of 1812. In the 1840's this was heightened by British criticism of Americans as a "nation of swindlers" who had repudiated their just debts during the Panic of 1837, and by unfavorable reports of travelers who found little to their liking in the raw civilization of the United States. Charles Dickens, and others like him, hardly won favor when they painted the sturdy farmers of the Mississippi Valley as tobacco-spitting, eye-gouging, drunken, brawling, slave-beating semibarbarians. To make matters worse the two nations had been snarling at each other over American aid given insurgents in a rebellion that rocked Canada in 1837, and over a boundary dispute between Maine and New Brunswick.

With this background, rumors that England was working quietly to prevent the American annexation of Texas were enough to set indignation boiling. Nor were the rumors ill founded, for Britain was determined to keep the Texans independent by any means short of war. A strong Texas Republic would be an indispensable ally should the probable conflict with the United States develop, as well as a continuous brake on American expansion. Moreover both British capital and manufactured goods could find an outlet there; capitalists were wary of further investments within the United States since several states repudiated their debts following the Panic of 1837, while sellers were eager for a market in a tariff-free nation that could supply them with raw cotton for their textile mills. Humanitarians were also dedicated to preventing annexation. Fresh from their triumph in 1833, when all slaves in the British empire were freed, they were committed to a program of world-wide abolitionism. Texan union with the United States, they knew, would perpetuate slavery there, but an

[4] New York *Morning News,* November 15, 1845, quoted in Albert K. Weinberg, *Manifest Destiny* (Baltimore, 1935), pp. 140–141.

independent republic under British domination might be persuaded to adopt a program of gradual emancipation.[5] Strategic, economic, and humanitarian goals all dictated that Texas must remain free.

These British designs profoundly influenced American opinion, especially in the South. Not a Southerner but believed that slavery was essential to cotton production, and cotton production essential to England's economy. Having freed its own slaves throughout the empire, Parliament must force every other cotton-growing land into abolitionism, for only in this way could competition continue on even terms. So Southerners reasoned as they watched every British move for confirmation of their thesis. Nor were these lacking. When a world's antislavery convention, held in London in 1843, declared that a free Texas would be "a perpetual incitement to murder, insurrection and outrage by the slaves of the Southern states," and when a slave rebellion in Cuba that autumn immediately followed a visit by English agents, nothing more was needed to show that slaves were being goaded into revolt everywhere. The Mississippi legislature spoke for most of the South when it declared: "The annexation of Texas to this Republic is essential to the future safety and repose of the southern states." [6] Influential Whig planters who had hitherto opposed expansion leaped on the band wagon now, convinced that their way of life was at stake.

French designs on Texas aroused almost as much apprehension, and with some justification. Like England, France feared that annexation would deprive it of a profitable market for both manufactured goods and capital. Moreover war between the United States and Mexico would follow, with the inevitable Mexican defeat damaging the cause of Catholicism and the prestige of France's ally, Spain. These were the motives that led the government, in February, 1844, to instruct its minister in Washington to oppose annexation in every way. Even though he was cautioned to work behind the scenes, rumors of the French attitude were soon circulating, arousing Americans to new heights of indignation at this meddling in their affairs.[7]

[5] Ephraim D. Adams, *British Interests and Activities in Texas, 1838–1846* (Baltimore, 1910), pp. 227–228; Harriet Smither, "English Abolitionism and the Annexation of Texas," *Southwestern Historical Quarterly*, XXXII (1929), 193–205.

[6] *Niles' Register*, LII (1837), 258.

[7] R. A. McLemore, "The Influence of French Diplomatic Policy on the Annexation of Texas," *Southwestern Historical Quarterly*, XLIII (1940), 342–344.

Seeming designs of both France and England on California also fanned the flames of expansionism. Here the danger was more imagined than real, for neither had any serious intentions toward that distant land. Both, however, had allowed their nationals to loan money freely to the Mexican government, and, when repayments bogged down, both began thinking of compensation in the form of California land. As early as June, 1839, the Mexican Congress and British creditors agreed on a plan through which half the debt would be wiped out by grants of 125,000,000 acres there. In the end this speculation collapsed, but not before it had planted the seed of fear in the United States.

This was nurtured over the next years as the plan was revived over and over again. In 1839, Alexander Forbes, the British vice-consul at the Mexican port of Tepic, published his widely circulated *California: A History of Upper and Lower California,* which not only described the region in glowing terms but pleaded with his countrymen to take lands there in compensation for their debts. "I know of no place," he declared, ". . . better calculated for receiving and cherishing the superfluous population of Great Britain." [8] In 1841 the English minister in Mexico City, Sir Richard Pakenham, was infected by the California fever and began urging his home government to plant a colony there. Over the next years two private colonization schemes stirred American fears. One, engineered by Robert C. Wyllie, urged English bondholders to accept payment in California lands; the other, planned by a young Irish priest named Eugene McNamara, would have planted a colony of two thousand Irishmen in the lower San Joaquin Valley.[9]

News of each of these plans, sweeping the United States in distorted form, aroused a flurry of interest that soon swelled to immense proportions. Americans could not know that the British government steadfastly opposed expansion into California, partly because it feared war with the United States, partly because its "Little England" policy of that period discouraged further extension of the empire. Instead they quaked at each new rumor, and with each grew more insistent that

[8] Alexander Forbes, *California: A History of Upper and Lower California from Their First Discovery to the Present Times* (London, 1839), p. 321.

[9] Lester G. Engelson, "Proposals for the Colonization of California by England in Connection with the Mexican Debt to British Bondholders, 1837–1846," *California Historical Society Quarterly,* XVIII (1939), 136–148.

California be annexed at once. By the end of 1845 such a staid journal as the *American Whig Review* believed that Britain's designs must be frustrated by any means, while less restrained writers were asking: "Why not extend the 'area of freedom' by the annexation of California? Why not plant the banner of liberty there?" Even the American minister to Mexico believed that "it will be worth a war of twenty years" to prevent England from taking California.[10]

France also showed an alarming concern with that Mexican province. Its government, dreaming of reviving the empire lost in 1763, muscled into the scene in 1840 when a few French nationals were rumored killed during one of the periodic revolutions. From that time on a diplomatic agent, Duflot de Mofrás, was stationed there to keep his home government informed and to besiege it with demands to acquire "this magnificent heritage." This meddling bore fruit in 1844 when a French vessel, the *Angelina,* was attacked by insurgents during another revolution. For a time war threatened before ruffled feelings were calmed, but Americans never forgot that California was nearly lost to them forever. Why risk such a disaster when they could annex that golden land at once?

This blusteringly aggressive attitude was made possible by still another force that contributed to the expansion of the 1840's. During the early years of that decade the American people suddenly awakened to their God-given destiny in world affairs. Since the inception of the Republic they had known that their democratic institutions were too perfect to be confined within narrow boundaries, and that the "Americanization" of first North America and eventually all the world was inevitable. In this calm belief there was no hint of aggression; Thomas Jefferson summed up his countrymen's opinion when he spoke of the United States as a "standing monument and example" to freedom-loving people everywhere. "We can," the *North American Review* agreed, "wait the peaceful progress of our own principles." [11] By the beginning of the 1840's, however, this passive policy appeared insufficient. Not only were American institutions failing to alter Europe's monarchistic systems, but those backward nations were threatening to muddy the pure waters of democracy in America itself. Positive

[10] Alfred Robinson, *Life in California: During a Residence of Several Years in That Territory* (New York, 1846), p. 225; Waddy Thompson, *Recollections of Mexico* (New York, 1846), p. 235.

[11] *North American Review,* XXXIV (1832), 563.

steps were needed to extend the "area of freedom" (in Andrew Jackson's happy phrase), and prevent the spread of an "area of absolutism." As one congressman put it, the nation must repel "the contaminating proximity of monarchies upon the soil that we have consecrated to the rights of man." [12]

Once made, this decision was easy to rationalize. Expansion into contiguous lands would allow the United States to fulfill its role as the mother of liberty. It would elevate and enlighten the millions kept in chains by the archaic governments of Mexico or England, endowing them with a new spirit of enterprise. Wrote one enthusiast of the Mexican Californians: "They are only a grade above the aborigines, and like them will be compelled by the very nature of things, to yield to the swelling tide of Anglo-Saxon adventure." [13] Expansion would not only bring freedom to the downtrodden abroad, but would solidify the liberties of the American people by creating new states to challenge the centralized authority of the federal government and by luring men westward where the democratic forces of the frontier could radiate over all the land. Surely a benevolent Deity wanted nothing less than this for His chosen people.

One thing more was needed before this exuberant belief could be translated into action: a catchy phrase that would sum up the Americans' faith in themselves. This was provided by the editor of the New York *Morning News*, John L. O'Sullivan, who in December, 1845, wrote of "our manifest destiny to overspread and to possess the whole of the continent which Providence has given us for the development of the great experiment of liberty and federated self-government entrusted to us." [14] Manifest destiny! There was a pulse-tingling phrase indeed. Overnight the magic words swept the nation. Congressmen fastened upon them. "The right of our manifest destiny," declared one.

[12] Representative Lewis C. Levin of Pennsylvania in *Congressional Globe*, 29th Congress, 1st Session, Appendix, p. 95.

[13] Overton Johnson and W. H. Winter, *Route Across the Rocky Mountains, With a Description of Oregon and California* (Lafayette, Ind., 1846), pp. 88–89.

[14] New York *Morning News*, December 27, 1845. O'Sullivan had used the phrase "manifest destiny" in an unsigned article on "Annexation" in the *United States Magazine and Democratic Review*, XVII (July-August, 1845), 797–798, but the time was not then ripe for its general acceptance. The whole subject is thoroughly discussed in Julius W. Pratt, "The Origin of 'Manifest Destiny,'" *American Historical Review*, XXXI (1927), 795–798.

"There is a right for a new chapter in the law of nations." [15] Editors seized upon them as they urged on the nation its God-given duty to extend American blessings to the less fortunate. "Prophecy," one wrote, "looks forward to the time when the valley of the Mississippi shall overflow with a restless population, and Europe be subjected to a new migration." [16] This was America's destiny. This was the will of God. All who opposed expansion were traitors to their country and their Creator.

These, then, were the ingredients that shaped American opinion by the middle 1840's: the persistence of the frontier advance, fear of France and England, and a belief in manifest destiny. The transition that occurred as the people fell under their sway was admirably illustrated in the Texan problem. In the past John Quincy Adams, Andrew Jackson, and Martin Van Buren had flatfootedly rejected all overtures for annexation, fearful of war with Mexico and of political opposition from conservative southern Whigs and radical northern abolitionists. As late as the summer of 1842 Daniel Webster, President John Tyler's Secretary of State, refused a Texan proposal that the United States join with England and France in mediating its problems with Mexico, lest to do so court war. Clearly Americans had not yet realized their manifest destiny toward this little republic.

The shift in opinion began to appear in 1843, when the wily Sam Houston, then serving his second term as Texan President, devised a formula to interest the United States. Seizing on a Mexican proposal to grant Texas separate statehood if it would re-enter the Republic, Houston hinted that something along that line might be possible if Mexico would grant a temporary armistice. President Santa Anna rose to this bait at once, granting the armistice on June 15, 1843, and entering into negotiations with the Texan government. That these had no chance for success was clear, but Houston was playing a more complex game. The possibility that Texas might return to Mexican rule, he hoped, would arouse the United States from its lethargy. Nor was he disappointed. Alarmed by reports that the conferences were nearing success, and by rumors that Houston was falling under British influence, Abel P. Upshur, who had replaced Webster as Tyler's Secretary of State, on October 16, 1843, informed the Texan government that he was willing to negotiate a treaty of annexation.

[15] Robert C. Winthrop of Massachusetts in *Congressional Globe,* 29th Congress, 1st Session, Appendix, p. 99.
[16] *American Union* (Boston), October 13, 1849.

Upshur's untimely death, and the elevation of John C. Calhoun of South Carolina to his post, doomed the negotiations. Calhoun accepted the position only because southern friends convinced him that his influence was needed to secure Texas and thus save slavery from destruction; this was the spirit that motivated him as he drafted the treaty and laid it before the Senate on April 22, 1844. His argument for acceptance was enough to ensure a negative vote from every Northerner. Texas must be annexed, he insisted, to prevent it from falling into the hands of English abolitionists who would wipe out slavery there. Calhoun sincerely believed that the reasons he advanced would win the support of all who hated Britain; he failed to see that his defense of the slave system would touch off a chorus of vituperation through the entire North. This rose at once. Editorial writers sharpened their pencils; presses hummed as pamphlets were hurried into circulation. Everywhere north of the Mason-Dixon line the people demanded that their senators strike down the dragon of annexation with one blow.

This rising tide of opposition, combined with senators' fears that they might commit political suicide by voting for the treaty just before the election of 1844, ensured its defeat. When the vote was taken on June 8, 1844, only sixteen were in favor with thirty-five opposed. Seven Democrats, and all Whigs save one, cast their votes in opposition; only five southern states were recorded in support. Although the outcome was not unexpected in Texas, resentment there ran high. The negotiations had cost the Texans their temporary armistice with Mexico, which sent word at once that hostilities would be resumed. Bitter and disgruntled, they settled back to wait the next move in the diplomatic game.

This was not long in coming, for Calhoun's ill-fated treaty touched off two developments that led inevitably to annexation. One was Polk's victory in the autumn of 1844; his election on a program of expansion was viewed as a mandate for Texan annexation by both parties. "It is the will of both the people and the States," President Tyler told Congress in his annual message of December 3, 1844, "that Texas shall be annexed to the Union promptly and immediately." [17] The other was a scheme hatched by Lord Aberdeen, the British Foreign Secretary, as soon as he heard of Calhoun's treaty. Fearful lest this mean

[17] J. D. Richardson (ed.), *Compilation of the Messages and Papers of the Presidents, 1789–1897* (10 vols., Washington, 1897), IV, 344.

the end of the Texas Republic, he first sounded out the French government, then proposed that Great Britain, France, Mexico, and Texas join in a "diplomatic act" to guarantee the perpetual independence of Texas. Mexico would be compensated by assurance that its boundaries would be forever protected by the other contracting powers. If the United States persisted in seeking to acquire Texas, Aberdeen told the representatives of that Republic, England "would go to the last extremity . . . in support of her opposition to the annexation," providing that France was "perfectly agreed." [18]

This bold proposal, which in effect committed England and France to guarantee Texan independence even by war, was never adopted. Aberdeen's own enthusiasm began to wane when news of Polk's election awakened him to the extent of expansionist fervor within the United States, while France was sufficiently alarmed to inform Britain that Texan annexation hardly seemed "of sufficient importance to us to justify our having recourse to arms in order to prevent it." Hurriedly backing water, Lord Aberdeen contented himself with wringing from Mexico an official recognition of Texan independence, in the vain hope that this would still the demand for union with the United States.

The harm was done. News of the Anglo-French proposal spread over the United States like wildfire, and with it a rising tide of indignation. Here was proof that England was willing to go to war to keep the Americans from having Texas; let them have war then! "One or two doses of English *calomel* and French *quinine*," the Texan secretary of state remarked, had convinced the American people that annexation was necessary, slaves or no slaves.[19] President Tyler, sensing this shift in opinion and anxious to win the glory of adding the new state to the Union, promptly urged Congress to adopt a joint resolution of annexation, incorporating the terms of the Calhoun treaty which had already been agreed upon. This was hurriedly drafted, and on January 25, 1845, passed the House of Representatives by a vote of 120 to 98. The Senate followed, with twenty-seven votes

[18] Ashbel Smith to Anson Jones, June 24, 1844, in George P. Garrison (ed.), "Diplomatic Correspondence of the Republic of Texas," *American Historical Association, Annual Reports for 1907 and 1908* (3 vols., Washington, 1908, 1911), III, 1153–1154.

[19] Anson Jones, *Memoranda and Official Correspondence Relating to the Republic of Texas* (New York, 1859), pp. 335–336.

in favor and twenty-five opposed. In both houses the vote followed party rather than sectional lines, with all Democrats favoring the resolution and only two Whigs failing to vote in opposition. President Tyler signed the measure on March 1, 1845, three days before he retired from the Presidency; two days later his special agent, Andrew Donelson, departed for Texas to lay the official proposal for annexation before that government.

The decision was up to the Texans now. There the President, Anson Jones, who had assumed office in December, 1844, flirted for a time with British and French agents, who worked frantically to prevent annexation, but public opinion was too strong to be checked.[20] On June 16, 1845, the Congress of the Republic voted unanimously for re-entry into the United States rather than continued independence; three weeks later a popularly elected convention confirmed this decision by another unanimous vote and ratified a constitution for the new state of Texas. On December 29 President Polk signed the measure that admitted Texas to the Union. "This high evidence of the affection of her sons to the land of their birth and its institutions," wrote a Southerner, "gives assurance that she will shine as one of the brightest stars in our brilliant constellation." [21]

American support for annexation cannot be simply explained. To state that the South favored and the North opposed is to rely on a generality that does little justice to the complexity of human motivation. That a majority of Southerners wanted Texas is incontestably clear; that they wanted to increase the slave territory within the United States does not necessarily follow. Those who expressed themselves were more concerned with fear of England than with expansion of slavery, while a sizable segment opposed adding Texas to the Union. Some among these felt that Texans would enjoy a "brighter destiny" if they could remain free of meddling northern abolitionists and high-tariff advocates; others sought to avoid the sectional conflicts that loomed if more slave states were acquired, or disliked taking on new lands that would drain population westward. Similarly, a significant portion of Northerners violated the sectional pattern to favor annexation. These included speculators who had invested in Texan securi-

[20] Annie Middleton, "Donelson's Mission to Texas in Behalf of Annexation," *Southwestern Historical Quarterly*, XXIV (1921), 286.

[21] John C. Calhoun to Thomas J. Rusk, in Lois F. Blount, "A Brief Study of Thomas J. Rusk, Based on His Letters to His Brother, David, 1835–1856," *Southwestern Historical Quarterly*, XXXIV (1931), 199.

ties or lands and stood to gain fortunes when the United States assumed the obligations of the poorly managed Republic. Jay Cooke, a leading financier, believed that the "selfish exertion in their own interests" of this small but powerful group was responsible for the passage of the joint resolution.[22] Other Northerners welcomed Texas as a new area for commercial exploitation, or because the spirit of manifest destiny so dictated, or as a means of glorifying the national honor. Whatever the reasons, the American people had decided. The new spirit of expansionism had borne its first fruit.

Nor had they long to wait before another ripe plum fell their way. When the Democratic platform in 1844 spoke of the "re-occupation of Oregon" as well as the "re-annexation of Texas," it only recognized a situation that was crying for settlement. This distant land, which was claimed by both the United States and England, had been opened to settlement under the Treaty of Joint Occupation of 1827. So long as a few trappers roamed its forests this arrangement was satisfactory enough, but the migrations of the early 1840's were pouring thousands of American homeseekers into the Willamette Valley. As their numbers increased with each year, so did their demands that a stable government be provided for them. "Where the highest court of appeal is the rifle," they pointed out with masterly understatement, "safety in life and property cannot be depended on." [23] Clearly the answer was to divide the territory between its two claimants, thus allowing American jurisdiction to extend over the American settlers. But where should the dividing line be drawn?

The boundaries of the Oregon Country stretched from the forty-second parallel on the south to the line of 54° 40′ on the north, but the whole area was never in dispute. England was willing to settle at any time on a boundary that followed the Columbia River to the sea, thus assuring control of the area north of the river where the Hudson's Bay Company was dominant. The United States had, on four earlier occasions, offered to accept a line extending the forty-ninth-parallel boundary westward to the Pacific. Thus the region actually in dispute

---

[22] E. P. Oberholtzer, *Jay Cooke, Financier of the Civil War* (2 vols., Philadelphia, 1907), I, 73–74; Moses W. Ware, "Land Speculation and the Mexican War," *Historical Outlook,* XIX (1928), 217–223.

[23] "Petition of a Number of Citizens of the Territory of Oregon, Praying the Extension of the Jurisdiction of the United States over that Territory," 28th Congress, 1st Session, *Senate Document* No. 105, pp. 1–4.

lay between the Columbia and the forty-ninth parallel; this was the "core" of the Oregon controversy. In the 1844 election, however, the Democrats had shouted the campaign cry of "Fifty-four Forty or Fight" as they talked bravely of "All of Oregon or None." Hence Polk entered the Presidency with a dangerous commitment; he must wrest the whole land from England, even at the cost of war.

Nor did the temper of the people allow any delay. Since 1842 locaí "Oregon Conventions" had met regularly throughout the West to demand immediate occupation of the whole region; these were climaxed by a national convention held at Cincinnati in July, 1843, where speakers proclaimed that "the time has gone by when this nation shall agree to surrender a solitary just right to avoid war." Southerners were adding to the clamor, recognizing that their support for Oregon would win northern sentiment for the annexation of Texas. Congressmen, sensing the popular trend, debated a whole galaxy of measures during 1843 and 1844, all designed to force the President's hand. One would have fortified the Oregon Trail; another demanded the immediate abrogation of the treaty with England; still another insisted that a territorial government be set up at once. None of these warlike acts marshaled enough votes to pass both houses of Congress, but a less acute observer than President Polk would have recognized that an Oregon Bill of some sort would soon be adopted. A settlement with England was necessary before such a crisis arose.

Polk's answer was to deliver a belligerent warning to England in his inaugural address of March 4, 1845. "Our title to the country of the Oregon is 'clear and unquestionable,'" he declared, "and already are our people preparing to perfect that title by occupying it with their wives and children." [24] Then, as war headlines flamed on both sides of the Atlantic, he opened the door to compromise. The United States, he informed the British minister in Washington, Richard Pakenham, was entitled to all of Oregon; but because his predecessors had repeatedly offered to settle at the forty-ninth parallel, he was willing to make the same concession. This offer was flatly rejected by Pakenham, who did not even bother to refer it to his government. From that time on Polk was determined on the forty-ninth-parallel boundary, even at the risk of war. "I considered a bold & firm course on our part the pacific one," he wrote in his diary; ". . . if Congress faultered [sic] or

[24] Richardson (ed.), *Messages and Papers of the Presidents,* IV, 381.

hesitated in their course, John Bull would immediately become arrogant and more grasping in his demands." [25]

This bold policy was inaugurated in his annual message to Congress in December, 1845, when he asked for power to abrogate the treaty of joint occupation and extend the protection of American laws over settlers in the Oregon country. Three weeks later he coldly rejected a proposal from Pakenham that the matter be negotiated. Congress steadfastly supported him in these warlike steps, for debate over his measures showed all the nation save the Southeast solidly behind him. Even those opposed favored a policy of "wise and masterly inactivity" which would allow Oregon to be won by the continued flow of settlers there, "quietly, peacefully, and effectively." The people wanted the Oregon Country; there was no question of that. And Polk would have it, even if a fight was necessary.

In most such conflicts in history, the occupants of a disputed region have been only pawns in the hands of contending powers, but in the Oregon controversy they played a decisive role. When Polk uttered his warlike demands, at the end of 1845, about five thousand Americans and 750 British subjects occupied the region. The Americans, however, all lived in the Willamette Valley, in a region not in dispute, while the "core" area north of the Columbia was firmly held by the Hudson's Bay Company under its able local factor, Dr. John McLoughlin. Nor was this a tenuous hold by a few fly-by-night traders. Dr. McLoughlin had fostered farming from the beginning as a step toward self-sufficiency; by 1840 this had evolved into a major occupation, so important that the Puget's Sound Agricultural Company was chartered to raise food and market farm surpluses along the coast. Two giant farms were laid out between the Cowlitz River and Puget Sound; workers were brought in from England; cattle were imported from California. Within a year the company was supplying local needs and exporting thousands of bushels of wheat as well as quantities of cheese, butter, and salt meat.[26] Such a secure enterprise as this, backed by the wealth of the Hudson's Bay Company, could never be dislodged. Only if the company voluntarily decided to abandon the "core" region north of the Columbia was there any hope of a peaceful settlement.

[25] Milo M. Quaife (ed.), *The Diary of James K. Polk during His Presidency, 1845–1849* (4 vols., Chicago, 1910), I, 155.

[26] John S. Galbraith, "The Early History of the Puget's Sound Agricultural Company, 1838–1843," *Oregon Historical Quarterly,* LV (1954), 234–259.

That the company did take this step, and thus open the door to an American diplomatic victory, was due primarily to the influx of American settlers. True, they were not in the disputed area; Dr. McLoughlin had seen to that when he encouraged them to build their homes south of the Columbia. But their mere presence in the Willamette Valley doomed the Hudson's Bay Company's operations in the Puget Sound country. Their coming meant the dispersion of fur-bearing animals; since 1840 trading operations had been shifted gradually northward. More important, the presence of five thousand "desperate characters," who considered "the Bowie knife, Revolving Pistol and Rifle" the only sources of law, and who to a man hated the company for standing between them and the protection of the American government, constituted a threat to Fort Vancouver that no one could ignore. The fort was built of well-dried logs that would burn like tinder; within it in 1845 were goods worth £100,000. What if the rambunctious Americans should storm across the Columbia with guns and torches as they frequently threatened? Company officials spent sleepless nights worrying over such an attack, and finally decided that Fort Vancouver must be abandoned. On January 1, 1845, orders arrived from London to shift supplies and operations to Fort Victoria, a post built on Vancouver Island in 1843 in anticipation of this need.[27]

By this move the company was, in effect, abandoning the disputed "core" area and informing the British government that it would not object to the forty-ninth-parallel boundary. News of these developments reached Sir Robert Peel, the Prime Minister, on March 29, 1845. He was sufficiently interested to authorize two investigations, one by the Royal Engineers and the other by the Navy. Both reports, submitted on October 6, 1845, and February 10, 1846, agreed that the region could never be defended against American attack and that its eventual overrunning by frontiersmen from the United States was inevitable.

This was welcome news to Lord Aberdeen, the Tory Foreign Secretary, who must manage all negotiations. Having a low opinion of the Oregon Country—a "pine swamp," he called it—and recognizing the validity of the American claim to a good harbor on the Pacific coast, he had reconciled himself to a settlement at the forty-ninth parallel as early as March, 1844. To Aberdeen a war over this barren wilderness

[27] Frederick Merk, "The Oregon Pioneers and the Boundary," *American Historical Review,* XXIX (1924), 690–693.

seemed absurd when so many problems of world magnitude were pressing for solution: wars in China and Afghanistan, the reorganization of Canada, the settlement of long-standing difficulties with France. Yet to give the Americans what they wanted—the forty-ninth-parallel boundary—meant surrender; five times in the past the United States had offered to settle on this line, and five times England had refused. Sir Robert Peel, his Prime Minister, agreed with Aberdeen, and the whole Tory cabinet was ready to go along after the abandonment of Fort Vancouver. But what would the Whig opposition say? And how could public opinion be convinced that such a sellout did not taint Britain's honor?

Winning over the opposition came first. Lord John Russell, the Whig leader, was easy to persuade, for he was dedicated to aiding the Tories in repealing the corn laws, and disliked the thought of a war that would interfere with this reform. Far more dangerous was Lord Palmerston, the Whig expert on foreign affairs. A stormy, independent nationalist, Palmerston had carried on a constant attack on the "cowardice" and "truckling" of Aberdeen's policies; he had denounced the Webster-Ashburton Treaty of 1842—which settled a boundary dispute in northern Maine by giving Britain 893 square miles more than an impartial tribunal had earlier recommended—as "capitulation" and "one of the worst and most disgraceful treaties that England ever concluded." Tories naturally shuddered over what he might say at Oregon's surrender. Yet the spirit of the times played into their hands. Peace was in the air, and Palmerston's warlike bellowings were singularly unpopular. This the Whigs learned, to their sorrow, when the Tory government fell from power in December, 1845, and they were asked to form a ministry. News that Palmerston would be Foreign Secretary sent the price of securities tumbling as a war scare flamed; when other leading Whigs refused to serve in the cabinet with him, the Queen was forced to call upon the Tories once more. This was enough. Palmerston, convinced at last, took himself off to France, while on January 12, 1846, Lord John Russell responded to a banquet toast, "Peace with all nations," by speaking boldly in favor of compromise on the Oregon dispute. A few weeks later he secretly assured Aberdeen that his party would accept any treaty drafted by the Tories.[28]

[28] Frederick Merk, "British Party Politics and the Oregon Treaty," *American Historical Review*, XXXVII (1932), 653–675.

While Aberdeen and Peel labored to still the opposition, they also used their power over the press to convert public opinion to their stand. Here too they were favored by the spirit of the day; the "Little England" concept was so popular that all colonies were deemed burdens rather than assets, and the campaign for free trade that was to reach its climax a year later with the repeal of the corn laws bred a spirit of international good feelings. Amidst this atmosphere Aberdeen had little difficulty persuading his own Tory press to advocate an Oregon compromise, or in finding Whig journalists willing to fall into line. The London *Examiner,* a leading Whig paper, broke the ice on April 26, 1845, when it published an article which painted the Columbia River valley as a valueless waste and urged settlement at the forty-ninth parallel; the *Edinburgh Review* followed in July, 1845, and the independent London *Times* on January 3, 1846. With the capitulation of *The Times* the goal was won, for most of the press followed its lead. By the spring of 1846 a reader of England's newspapers would gain the impression that the whole land was clamoring for the forty-ninth-parallel boundary as a gesture of peace and good will.[29]

The rest was but a matter for negotiation. On June 6, 1846, the formal British offer to settle on the forty-ninth parallel reached Washington. Polk, mindful of his campaign promises to secure the line of 54° 40', was inclined to object at first, but his cabinet persuaded him to submit the treaty to the Senate. There a few jingoistic Westerners howled their anger at this "surrender," but theirs were voices crying in a wilderness of indifference. On June 10, 1846, the Senate by a vote of 38 to 12 authorized the President to accept the English offer; on June 15 the treaty was formally ratified with 41 in favor and 14 diehard expansionists opposed. Hardy pioneers who had trekked westward along the Oregon Trail to plant their homes in the Willamette Valley had won for their homeland a new empire.

Nor was the end of expansion in sight. The formula that had added Texas and Oregon to the Union was even then beginning to operate in California. There, as in Texas, a rich domain was but feebly held by a weak neighbor. In each case, too, the United States openly coveted the region and made futile efforts to buy from Mexico. In both a peaceful penetration of American settlers was followed by a revolu-

[29] Frederick Merk, "British Government Propaganda and the Oregon Treaty," *American Historical Review,* XL (1934), 38–62.

tion designed to win first independence, and then annexation. It is not surprising that the Mexican government, viewing these parallels, became convinced that its northern provinces were being deliberately dismembered, or that it felt a war justified to check this process.

American efforts to acquire California began during Jackson's administration when expansionists realized that Northerners would be more willing to accept Texas if they could be offered good Pacific harbors at the same time. Anthony Butler, Jackson's unscrupulous representative in Mexico, informed the President that $500,000, "judiciously applied," would secure not only Texas but upper and lower California as well, "an empire in itself, a paradise in climate." Interest did not die with Butler's recall; Tyler's agent, Waddy Thompson, kept the pot boiling with his glowing reports, and Tyler's secretary of state, Daniel Webster, made two attempts to secure the harbor at San Francisco for his commercial-minded constituents of New England. These negotiations came to an end when Commodore Thomas Ap Catesby Jones of the American Pacific Fleet committed an understandable error. Hearing that war had broken out between his country and Mexico, and fearful that a British fleet would capture the region unless he acted, he sailed into Monterey Harbor on October 19, 1842, with guns leveled. He found no British there and the garrison working peacefully in the fields, but troops were hurried ashore and the American flag raised. Only then did he discover that he had captured the port of a friendly power. Making the best of a bad situation, he returned Monterey to its rulers in an elaborate ceremony, staged a ball for the governor, and sent his ship's band ashore to entertain the people. Yet the harm was done. Even though the United States apologized and recalled Commodore Jones from his command, further peaceful negotiations were impossible.

If the United States was to secure California now, it must use more devious devices. Here the situation played into American hands. After the last of the numerous revolutions that racked the province, the Micheltorena Revolt of 1845, political anarchy descended on California. Pío Pico, who had been chosen governor, established his capital at Los Angeles, leaving the former capital at Monterey under the military commander, José Castro, a man "utterly deficient in strength and steadiness of purpose." This accentuated the normal jealousy between northern and southern California, nor was the situation eased when the two governors fell to squabbling between themselves. As they quarreled government ceased to function, the machinery of justice collapsed, finances disintegrated, and the tiny army degenerated into an uncontrolled rabble "with as little discipline, sobriety, and order, as would characterize a bear hunt." [30] Amidst this chaos respectable native Californians, most of whom were men of some property, reluctantly decided that the time had come to sever their ties with the home government. Some believed that an independent California under the protection of England or France was the answer; a larger faction led by the wealthy Sonoma ranchero, Mariano G. Vallejo, felt that law and order would best be restored by seeking annexation by the United States.

California was ripe for the plucking when Polk became President, yet careful manipulation was necessary to avoid war with Mexico or alienating the pro-American faction among native Californians. This he realized, but he was still determined to have the land at all cost, lawfully if possible, by intrigue if not. His first efforts were directed toward lawful purchase. Word from a confidential agent in Mexico City, William S. Parrott, indicated that this might be possible; the existing government under General Herrera was doomed to fall and might be persuaded to risk popular wrath by selling. As soon as this information arrived, on September 16, 1845, Polk called his cabinet together to reveal his plans. The cabinet agreed unanimously that John Slidell of New Orleans should be sent to Mexico; his instructions warned him not to arouse antagonisms but to help "restore those ancient relations of peace and good will which formerly existed between the governments and the citizens of the sister republics" by offering up to $40,000,000 for all of upper California and as much of the Southwest as could be secured. Slidell's only hope was to complete the sale and pay off President Herrera before his mission became known, but even before he reached Mexico City the news was out. Herrera, who could receive the American and precipitate a revolution or refuse to see him and risk war with the United States, decided on the latter course. Slidell was not received; with his failure ended the last hope of securing California peacefully.

President Polk, not at all disheartened, turned at once to intrigue. On October 17, 1845, an important letter was dispatched to Thomas O. Larkin, wealthy businessman and American consul at Monterey.

[30] Colton, *Three Years in California*, p. 14.

"Whilst the President will make no effort and use no influence to induce California to become one of the free and independent States of this Union," it read, "yet if the people should desire to unite their destiny with ours, they would be received as brethren, whenever this can be done, without affording Mexico just cause of complaint." [31] Larkin, correctly interpreting this to mean that he was not to foment a revolution but to further designs of Californians to separate from Mexico, set about his task with his usual skill. Prominent Americans, such as Abel Stearns of Los Angeles, John J. Warner of San Diego, and Jacob Leese of Sonoma, were enlisted in the cause, as well as influential native Californians who preferred American rule to the chaos that existed. Each dispatch Larkin sent to Washington showed that, if left to himself, he would eventually win California for the United States.

Such a peaceful solution, however, reckoned without Polk's impatience or the aggressiveness of American frontiersmen who were pouring westward over the California Trail. The President, increasingly alarmed by rumors that the British vice-consul at San Francisco was winning over Governor Pío Pico to favor English protection rather than American annexation, apparently succumbed to the war of nerves first; this is indicated by his connections with the "man of mystery," John Charles Frémont. Frémont, a former Army captain and son-in-law of Senator Thomas Hart Benton, had already gained fame as an explorer before he started from St. Louis in April, 1845, with a party of sixty men, bound for California and Oregon. By December 9 he was camped near Sutter's Fort, ready to launch that strange drama which was to undo all Larkin's plans and add California to the Union by force rather than intrigue.

The presence of these sixty buckskin-clad frontiersmen, all armed and bearded to the point of ferociousness, naturally caused concern among the Californians. "Frémont's conduct," wrote John A. Sutter, "was extremely mysterious. Flitting about the country with an armed body of men, he was regarded with suspicion by everybody." [32] Certainly the governor of northern California, José Castro, felt this way; for in March, 1846, he ordered the Americans to leave at once—a step he had every right to take, as they had not bothered to secure passports. Instead of complying, Frémont flew into a rage, moved his men

[31] George P. Hammond (ed.), *The Larkin Papers* (Berkeley, 1951–), IV, 44–46.
[32] Erwin G. Gudde, *Sutter's Own Story* (New York, 1936), p. 161.

to a steep hill named Hawk's Peak, raised the American flag, and defied the Mexicans to oust him. Fortunately Larkin and other peacemakers changed his mind before Governor Castro could marshal his forces; on March 9, 1846, he slipped away and started northward, leaving behind him a legacy of hatred and suspicion that undid much of the good accomplished by Larkin's campaign.[33]

For a time Frémont's party tarried in the lower Sacramento Valley, but by May 6, 1846, they were at Klamath Lake on their road to Oregon. Two days later, while still camped there, they were overtaken by news that a messenger from Washington was on their trail. Frémont, with ten men, started back south, and after an all-night ride met the dispatch bearer, Lieutenant Archibald H. Gillespie, at dawn on May 9. Just what passed between these two shadowy figures will never be known. Gillespie had been sent west by President Polk in late October, 1845, bearing secret instructions for Thomas O. Larkin and carrying a packet of family letters from Senator Thomas Hart Benton to Frémont, his son-in-law.[34] In the best cloak-and-dagger tradition he memorized and destroyed his dispatches to Larkin, then crossed Mexico disguised as a merchant, and reached Monterey on April 17, 1846. There he delivered his messages to Larkin before spending a short time in San Francisco and starting northward on Frémont's trail. Whatever Gillespie told Frémont, the latter gathered his forces and started at once for the lower Sacramento Valley. Wrote one of his men: "What we were to return to Cal. for no one knows (but to return was sure of creating a row with the yellow bellies)."[35]

Did Frémont return because Gillespie brought secret orders from President Polk to stir up a revolution? Or did he simply decide to become the Sam Houston of California? Evidence to support both of these views is surprisingly plentiful, and completely inconclusive. Frémont steadfastly maintained that he acted under secret orders which

[33] Allan Nevins, *Frémont: Pathmarker of the West* (New York, 1939), pp. 206–216.

[34] The best account of the early stages of the Gillespie mission is in John A. Hussey, "The Origin of the Gillespie Mission," *California Historical Society Quarterly*, XIX (1940), 46–58. Hussey shows that most of the Benton letters carried by Gillespie had originally been designated for the reguar mails across Mexico, and concludes that they could have contained no secret instructions for Frémont.

[35] E. M. Kern, a member of the party, in a letter of July 27, 1846, printed in Oscar Lewis (ed.), *California in 1846, Described in Letters from Thomas O. Larkin, "The Farthest West," E. M. Kern, and "Justice"* (San Francisco, 1934), p. 45.

"absolved me of my duty as an explorer," and "made known to me now on the authority of the Secretary of the Navy that to obtain possession of California was the chief object of the President." [36] On a later occasion he testified that one of the letters from Senator Benton, "while apparently of mere friendship and family details, contained passages enigmatical and obscure, but which I studied out, and made the meaning to be that I was required by the government to find out any foreign schemes in relation to the Californias, and to counteract them." [37] But were these explanations only rationalizations to justify his too-hasty action in the eyes of his countrymen? If they were, why did Gillespie travel in such secrecy and go six hundred miles out of his way to deliver a packet of family letters? If they were not, how can today's historian explain why Benton, an outspoken opponent of expansion, suddenly ordered his son-in-law to stir up a war in California, or the fact that in all the known correspondence between the two there is no evidence of a secret code? How can this theory be reconciled with the one surviving letter that Gillespie delivered—an innocent epistle from Mrs. Frémont hoping that her husband would be home soon? [38] Apparently Gillespie carried no secret instructions; Frémont's decision to return to California was his own.

That decision is easy to understand, however, in light of the information that Gillespie brought—not from Washington but from San Francisco. During his short stay in that village, the United States warship *Portsmouth* had arrived. Its commander, Captain John B. Montgomery, brought disturbing news: American and Mexican troops faced each other along the southern border of Texas; the Pacific fleet was anchored off Mazatlán preparing to attack; the next mail was expected to bring word of a declaration of war. Here were stirring events indeed; that the adventurous Captain Frémont could hide himself in the Oregon wilderness while they were transpiring was unthink-

[36] John C. Frémont, *Memoirs of My Life* (2 vols., New York, 1887), I, 488–489.

[37] John C. Frémont, *Defence of Lieut. J. C. Frémont before the Military Court Martial, Washington, January, 1848* (Washington, 1848), p. 6.

[38] In Catherine C. Phillips, *Jessie Benton Frémont, A Woman Who Made History* (San Francisco, 1935), pp. 104–107. The argument that Gillespie carried secret instructions is best presented in Ernest A. Wiltsee, *The Truth About Frémont: An Inquiry* (San Francisco, 1936), pp. 20–32, and Richard R. Stenberg, "Polk and Frémont, 1845–1846," *Pacific Historical Review*, VII (1938), 211–227. The opposite position is ably held in George Tays, "Frémont Had No Secret Instructions," *Pacific Historical Review*, IX (1940), 151–171, and Hussey, "Origin of the Gillespie Mission," pp. 43–58.

able. By May 30 he was camped at Marysville Buttes some sixty miles north of Sutter's Fort, ready to "take advantage of any contingency which I could turn in favor of the United States." [39]

This was not long in coming. The several hundred emigrants who had arrived during the past few years stirred up the hornet's nest. Clustered in their own settlements near Sutter's Fort, where their sense of racial solidarity was accentuated, they both despised and distrusted all Mexicans, whether pro-American or not. As tensions increased during those days of uncertainty, rumors flew among them: Indians were massing for an attack; Governor Castro had gathered six hundred cutthroats who were "foaming out vengeance" against all foreigners; all Americans who had been in the province less than a year were to be expelled! Understandably, many began drifting to Frémont's camp at Marysville Buttes, where his sixty stout followers offered some protection. There they waited, as tension mounted. Only a false move on either side was needed to start a shooting war.

Actually, an unhappy accident touched off fighting. Early in June Governor Castro secured nearly two hundred horses at Sonoma and sent two army officers to drive them to Monterey. The rumor spread that these were to be used by an army being formed to attack Frémont's camp. Hurriedly consulting, the Americans decided to nip this plan in the bud by stealing the horses—an occupation not unknown to many of them. A dozen recruits volunteered and set off under the command of Ezekiel Merritt, a tall, rawboned, tobacco-chewing illiterate. After an all-night ride they overtook the herd some fifteen miles from Sutter's Fort on the morning of June 10, just as the Mexicans were preparing breakfast. Profanely claiming the horses, they galloped back to their headquarters, which were now moved near Sutter's Fort.

Knowing that Mexican reprisals were certain, and overconfident as a result of their easy victory, Ezekiel Merritt and his followers decided that safety lay in continuing the attack. Why not fall on Sonoma, the leading settlement nearby and the home of the wealthy Mariano G. Vallejo? To think was to act with such characters; after only a short rest thirty-three of them were off again on another all-night ride. They found Sonoma sleeping quietly in the dim light of early morning as they rode across the plaza to hammer on Vallejo's door. With true Spanish courtesy, they were invited to send three of their members in to negotiate, while a bullock was killed to provide breakfast for the rest.

[39] Frémont, *Memoirs of My Life,* I, 508.

When the negotiators failed to emerge after some time, another was sent to make inquiries; he also vanished into the spacious Vallejo home. Once more the men met to elect a new delegate. This time their choice was the sober and scholarly William B. Ide. A strange sight met his eyes when he entered the conference room. At one side of the table sat Vallejo and two members of his family; across from them two Americans slept soundly with heads in arms, another lay sprawled in the corner, and a fourth was laboring with drunken concentration on articles of capitulation. Vallejo's hospitality had proved too much for the negotiators; "the bottles," Ide wrote, "had well nigh vanquished the captors." [40]

Ide restored order at once. An idealist who viewed this moment as the dawn of the California Republic, he drew up articles of surrender that Vallejo signed, then sent his prisoner off to Sutter's Fort while he and twenty-five of his followers stayed on to garrison Sonoma. Having gone this far, there was no turning back. Ide supervised his followers as they met to name him president of the new-born California republic and fashion a flag bearing the image of a grizzly bear. When this was raised over the Sonoma plaza on June 15, 1846, Ide read a proclamation inviting all "peaceable & good citizens of California" to assist in establishing "a Republican government which shall secure to us Civil & religious liberty, which shall encourage virtue and literature, which shall leave unshackled by fetters Agriculture, Commerce & Mechanism." [41] The Bear Flaggers had raised the standard of revolt; the war for Californian independence was begun.

All of this excitement was more than Frémont could resist. He had tainted his cloak of neutrality when he received Vallejo as a prisoner; now he threw it off entirely, marched his force on Sonoma, and on June 25 rudely shouldered William Ide from his post as leader. By this time the two Mexican governors, Pío Pico and José Castro, had forgotten their differences and were breathing fiery threats to "fall on and kill all the Bears of Sonoma." Pío Pico was still far to the south, advancing slowly northward with an army of one hundred men, but Castro was near at hand with 160 ill-equipped soldiers. Learning that this force had killed two American youths, Frémont set out on their

[40] Simeon Ide, *A Biographical Sketch of the Life of William B. Ide* (n.p., 1880), pp. 111–205, is a detailed description of the capture of Sonoma by a participant.

[41] The proclamation is in *ibid.*, pp. 138–140.

trail with 134 men, pausing only to kill three Mexicans to revenge the loss of the two Americans. These were the only casualties of the Bear Flag Revolt. By July 19, 1846, he was at Monterey, while Castro's army was fleeing toward southern California.

There Frémont learned that the minor uprising he had helped provoke had merged into a larger war. In the harbor lay the seven ships of the American Pacific Fleet; over the plaza floated the Stars and Stripes. In the streets all talk was of the war between Mexico and the United States that had begun three months before. Some of his men "made long faces, as they thought if the Bear flag would remain there would be a better chance to rob and plunder," [42] but most heard the news with rejoicing. Gladly they shifted the burden of conquest from their own shoulders to those of the American people, who were destined to win not only California but all the Southwest in the war that lay ahead.

[42] John A. Sutter, *The Diary of Johann Augustus Sutter* (San Francisco, 1932), p. 37.

CHAPTER 8

The West in the Mexican War

WAR with Mexico followed America's expansionist spree as inevitably as night follows day. The annexation of Texas and President Polk's blatant demands for California left a legacy of hatred that the best will in the world could not have resolved—and that will was lacking. To the Mexicans the United States was a ruthless colossus bent on dismembering its southern neighbor step by step. To the Americans Mexico was an irresponsible troublemaker, indifferent to its obligations and hopelessly sunk in anarchy. Against this backdrop of mutual suspicion, war could have been avoided only by ceaseless negotiation. Yet this was impossible after March, 1845, when the Mexican government broke off diplomatic relations with the United States. From that moment on, hope of orderly settlement was gone; mounting tensions were certain to bring on conflict.

America's grievances against Mexico had accumulated since that nation won its independence from Spain. Painfully adjusting from the absolutism of Spanish rule to the republicanism they had proclaimed their ideal, the Mexican people were by both training and inclination incapable of maintaining the orderly government that would allow them to live as good neighbors in the world community. Their periodic revolutions inevitably involved the lives and property of citizens of other powers, and of the United States especially; in one uprising alone twenty-two Americans were executed without trial. Since the days of Andrew Jackson constant efforts to collect for these losses had been frustrated by the indifference of Mexican governments or by their inability to pay. A claims commission established in 1839 finally set the sum due each creditor, but only three payments were made before defaulting began again. The United States seemed justified in concluding that Mexico was a dangerous menace in the family of nations, fully deserving punishment. That this view had some basis was shown when France and England adopted an even more belligerent tone in attempting to collect their own debts, even fighting the so-called "Pastry War" against Mexico in 1838.[1]

The "claims" question might, as Andrew Jackson believed, "justify in the eyes of all nations immediate war," but this was not the only grievance against Mexico. The massacre of Texans at the Alamo and Goliad convinced many that Mexicans were ruthless barbarians, too sunk in savagery to be trusted. Their refusal to sign an armistice with Texas only confirmed this belief; nothing less than more bloodshed would satisfy them. Their attempts to sell California to England or France showed their cold-blooded indifference to the wishes of the United States; so did their talk of establishing a Mexican monarchy under French protection, a step much discussed in the European press during the winter of 1845–46. Worst of all was their slight to the national honor when they refused to receive the Slidell mission. "Be assured," wrote John Slidell as he reported his failure, "that nothing is to be done with these people, until they have been chastised." Such insults might have been taken from equals, but the spirit of manifest destiny was breeding a sense of Anglo-Saxon superiority that transformed Mexicans into "ignorant Indians, debased by three centuries of worse than colonial vassalage"—"a semi-barbarous people." [2] Why accept insults from such lowly beings?

Especially when they could be punished with ease. Every traveler reported that Mexico boasted a mere caricature of an army, one so ill manned and ill equipped that its defeat would be "an adventure full of fun and frolic." Waddy Thompson, returning after his years as minister in Mexico City, revealed that the armed force contained less than half of the forty thousand troops claimed, and that these were mostly Indians dragged from the mountains to serve their time—"mere apologies for soldiers, or even men." [3] All were poorly equipped with dis-

[1] The classical argument that "claims" justified the United States in going to war is in Justin H. Smith, *The War with Mexico* (2 vols., New York, 1919), I, 58–101.

[2] 29th Congress, 1st Session, *House Report* No. 752, pp. 42–43.

[3] Waddy Thompson, *Recollections of Mexico* (New York, 1846), pp. 168–169; Philip St. George Cooke, *Scenes and Adventures in the Army* (New York, 1857), p. 86.

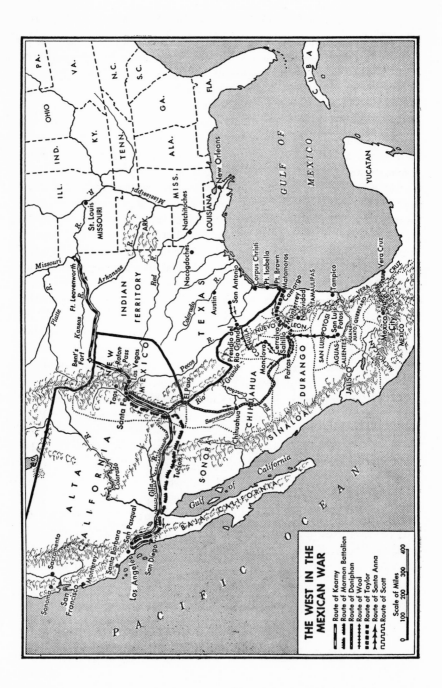

THE WEST IN THE
MEXICAN WAR

Route of Kearny
Route of Mormon Battalion
Route of Doniphan
Route of Wool
Route of Taylor
Route of Santa Anna
Route of Scott

Scale of Miles
0 100 200 300 400

carded English muskets of such amazing inefficiency that less than one ball in one thousand reached its target. Their uniforms were in tatters or nonexistent; Archibald Gillespie while crossing Mexico found one garrison where the men had not left the fort for months because they had no clothes to hide their nakedness. The conquest of such a Falstaffian enemy would be absurdly easy; one returning traveler estimated that "two hundred Tennessee riflemen could take the country," and another was sure that "in any conflict with our own own or European troops, it would not be a battle but a massacre." [4]

Did these jingoistic sentiments mean that the mighty United States simply launched an aggressive war to strip a weaker neighbor of wanted lands? Such a simple explanation ignores both the character of President Polk and the desires of the Mexican people. By nature Polk was no aggressive dictator. A lean, angular man with long grizzled hair, cold gray eyes, and somber face, he hardly fitted the role of international plotter assigned him by his political enemies. Cold rather than passionate, sly rather than bold, methodical rather than dashing, Polk, as one of his contemporaries put it, "never dreamed of any other war than a war upon the Whigs." Yet he was a stubborn man, and he was unmovable in his determination to secure California for the United States. If legal steps could succeed, he vastly preferred them, but if Mexico refused to negotiate, he was willing to resort to war. He reached this conclusion only after every effort to purchase California had failed, after commercial and diplomatic intercourse between the two nations had been broken off at Mexico's insistence, after foreign intervention seemed imminent, and after his own diplomats had assured him that a peaceful settlement was impossible.[5]

Nor does the picture of the United States as a land-grabbing colossus take into account the desire of the Mexican people for war. There was not a red-blooded man among them but felt the national honor could be redeemed and the nation saved from future aggression only

[4] Jefferson T. Farnham, *Travels in California, and Scenes in the Pacific Ocean* (New York, 1844), p. 115; Thompson, *Recollections of Mexico*, pp. 170–171.

[5] Both contemporaries and historians have differed sharply on Polk's motivation. His stanchest defender among the latter is Smith, *War with Mexico*, I, 127–137; while Richard R. Stenberg devotes two articles to arguing that the President maneuvered Mexico into war as a means of acquiring California and New Mexico: "The Failure of Polk's Mexican War Intrigue of 1845," *Pacific Historical Review*, IV (1935), 39–68, and "Intrigue for Annexation," *Southwest Review*, XXV (1939), 58–69.

by challenging America at once. "The real and effective cause of this war," one wrote shortly after it began, ". . . was the spirit of aggrandizement of the United States of the North, availing itself of its power to conquer us." [6] Why suffer such humiliations when the United States could easily be defeated? There was no question of victory in their minds. Was not the Mexican army five times as large as that of its enemy? Were not Mexican soldiers man for man more than a match for the lily-livered *Americanos* who had shown their impotence by failing to capture helpless Canada in the War of 1812? Would not the deserts of northern Mexico and that "terrible and faithful ally," yellow fever, stop any invasion of their homeland, while their own armies moved northward unchecked, growing constantly in size and power as freed slaves flocked to join their ranks? Was not the United States so torn by sectional differences that the northern states would withdraw from the struggle? Would not England and France join Mexico in this crusade to prevent Texas from falling into the hands of the slavocracy? Scarcely a Mexican but applauded when a leading newspaper proclaimed: "We have more than enough strength to make war. Let us make it, then, and victory will perch upon our banners." [7]

In such an inflammatory atmosphere only a spark was needed to ignite the flames of conflict. This was provided by the dispute over Texas' southern boundary. As part of the state of Coahuila-Texas, this had followed the Nueces River; yet when Texas declared its independence it laid claim to a boundary at the Rio Grande, partly as a device to be used in subsequent negotiations with Mexico. President Polk, however, took this claim seriously when Texas entered the Union. In the hope that a show of force would win the disputed territory and discourage Mexico from starting a war, he immediately ordered 1,500 troops under General Zachary Taylor to occupy the region south of the Nueces. By July 25, 1845, Taylor's force was camped near the hamlet of Corpus Christi. There they waited through the steaming summer as Taylor refused to march nearer the Rio Grande, fearful that such a move would launch a war.

Polk, in the more comfortable atmosphere of Washington, was also doing his best to keep peace through negotiation, but on January 12, 1846, he received word that Mexico had refused to receive John Sli-

[6] Ramón Alcáraz, *The Other Side: or Notes for the History of the War between Mexico and the United States* (New York, 1850), p. 32.
[7] *La Voz del Pueblo*, quoted in Smith, *War with Mexico*, I, 107.

dell and would afford any American agent similar treatment. On that same day he ordered General Taylor to march to the north bank of the Rio Grande. "It is not designed in our present relations with Mexico," read Taylor's instructions, "that you should treat her as an enemy; but, should she assume that character by a declaration of war, or any open act of hostility towards us, you will not act merely on the defensive, if your relative means enable you to do otherwise." [8] By March 28, 1846, the American force of four thousand men stood on the banks of the Rio Grande, gazing across its muddy waters to the adobe-hut town of Matamoros, where Mexicans climbed to the roof-tops to wave their greetings. There they began constructing a fortification that they called Fort Brown.

For a time all was peaceful as the soldiers went about their tasks by day and spent their evenings playing band concerts for the applauding Mexicans across the river or lining the banks to blow kisses at shapely *señoritas* who unabashedly followed their custom of bathing in the nude. On April 11, 1846, the first detachment of Mexican troops arrived at Matamoros, and as more followed, until 5,700 were quartered there, tension displaced gaiety as the prevailing mood. The first test came on April 24, 1846, when General Mariano Arista sent his cavalry thirty miles up the river with orders to cross to the north bank. Hearing of this, General Taylor ordered sixty-three dragoons to ride out and investigate. When this small force met the enemy party on the morning of April 25, 1846, it was ordered to surrender; instead firing broke out in which sixteen of the dragoons were killed or wounded before the survivors broke away to gallop back to Taylor's camp. Taylor interpreted this attack as Arista had intended: as an act of war. "All idea of their being *no fight* has ceased," wrote one of his excited soldiers that night. *"War has commenced,* and we look for a conflict within a few days." [9]

News of this skirmish reached Washington on the night of May 9, 1846, just after President Polk had adjourned a momentous cabinet meeting. War, he told his advisers, was inevitable; should the United States make the first move? Polk thought a declaration should be prepared at once, based on Mexico's refusal to pay its claims or deal with

[8] W. L. Marcy, Secretary of War, to Taylor, January 13, 1846, in 29th Congress, 1st Session, *House Executive Document* No. 196, pp. 77–78.

[9] W. S. Henry, *Campaign Sketches of the War with Mexico* (New York, 1847), p. 83.

the United States in a manner fitting a civilized nation. "I told them," he confided in his diary, "that I thought I ought to make such a message by tuesday next, that the country was excited and impatient on the subject, and if I failed to do so I would not be doing my duty." [10] Only George Bancroft, the Secretary of the Navy, disagreed; he counseled waiting until some warlike step by Mexico provided a better excuse. Scarcely had the meeting broken up when news of Taylor's engagements reached the President. The war message that he hurriedly prepared recited grievances that had accumulated over the past twenty years, but gave principal weight to this skirmish. "After repeated menaces," he wrote, "Mexico has passed the boundary of the United States, has invaded our territory and shed American blood upon the American soil. . . . As war exists, and, notwithstanding all our efforts to avoid it, exists by act of Mexico itself, we are called upon by every consideration of duty and patriotism to vindicate with decision the honor, the rights, and the interests of our country." [11]

Congress and the nation responded in the only possible way. Polk's message was read on May 10; two days later a resolution authorizing him to declare war against Mexico passed the House by a vote of 174 to 14 and the Senate by 40 to 2. All Democrats voted for war; 47 Whigs in the House and 16 in the Senate deserted their party to side with the majority. The same thumping majorities were mustered for measures that authorized fifty thousand volunteers and appropriated $10,000,000 for the initial effort. On May 15, 1846, the Secretary of War issued a call for enlistees, assigning a quota to each state and community. Overnight "Mexico Or Death" placards blossomed everywhere, while companies filled up so fast that "it soon became difficult even to *purchase* a place in the ranks." [12] In Illinois fourteen regiments volunteered where four had been called for; in Kentucky recruits were so numerous that enlistments had to be stopped after ten days; in Tennessee thirty thousand drew lots for the three thousand places available. Throughout the land the same scene was acted in town after town; as recruits gathered to march away, the populace turned out to

[10] Milo M. Quaife (ed.), *The Diary of James K. Polk During His Presidency, 1845 to 1849* (4 vols., Chicago, 1910), I, 384.

[11] J. D. Richardson (ed.), *Compilation of the Messages and Papers of the Presidents, 1789–1897* (10 vols., Washington, 1897), IV, 442.

[12] John B. Robinson, *Reminiscences of a Campaign in Mexico; by a Member of the "Bloody-First"* (Nashville, 1849), pp. 59-60.

cheer while the ladies with "a few beautiful and appropriate sentiments" presented them with a flag to carry, and the elected officers
replied "in behalf of the regiment, in a brief and characteristic
speech." [13]

These scenes concealed the fact that "Mr. Polk's War" was by no
means universally popular. In general, support declined proportionately with the distance from the center of conflict; in the Southwest
one in every thirty-three persons and in the Northwest one in every 110
enlisted; in the mid-Atlantic states the numbers fell off to one in every
1,000 persons, and in New England to one in every 2,500. To abolitionists and antislavery Whigs this was a war engineered by "Land-
Jobbers and Slave-Jobbers," and should be opposed by every civilized
humanitarian. One northern Congressman told his colleagues that if
he were a Mexican he would ask: "Have you not room in your own
country to bury your dead men? If they come into mine, we will greet
you, with bloody hands, and welcome you to hospitable graves"; [14]
another, a young unknown from Illinois named Abraham Lincoln,
gained momentary fame by introducing his "spot resolutions" defying
Polk to name the "spot" where American blood had been spilled on
American soil. These divisions meant that the Northeast, the nation's
wealthiest section, would refuse to give financial support needed for
the prosecution of the conflict.

The divided nation that faced Mexico was further weakened by the
inefficiency of its military establishment. The regular Army contained
only 7,200 men, all of them accustomed to garrison duty rather than
fighting. Militia companies formed by volunteers were relied on prin-
cipally, and few soldiers in history seemed as unlikely to win victory.
Equipment, uniforms, and discipline were alike unknown to them; one
observer watched a band of volunteers with "torn and dirty shirts—
uncombed heads—unwashed faces" as they tried to drill, "all hallow-
ing, cursing, yelling like so many incarnate fiends." "Holloa there,"
shouted their officer as one of the men wandered off by himself, "you
man there, you don't know how to file." "The he__l I don't," the
soldier yelled. "Da__n you, I've been marching all day, and I guess

[13] *Ibid.*, pp. 64–65.
[14] *Congressional Globe*, 29th Congress, 2nd Session, Appendix, p. 217. An
excellent study of sectional sentiment, both secular and religious, is Clayton S.
Ellsworth, "The American Churches and the Mexican War," *American Historical Review*, XLV (1940), 302–317.

I'm tired." [15] Nor was this unusual, for in every company the men elected their own officers, and were always ready to depose one captain and choose a new one if his conduct offended them. To make matters worse, many of the troops enlisted only to secure cash bounties and showed no loyalty; the rate of desertion was alarmingly high.[16]

These were the untrained, unreliable, and unpredictable troops that Polk must use to win his war, and to win it as rapidly as possible. Speed was essential, partly to secure California and the Southwest before the people tired of the conflict, partly to prevent the two generals, who were Whigs, from gaining such popularity that one of them could win the election of 1848. The administration, wrote Thomas Hart Benton, "wanted a small war, just large enough to require a treaty of peace, and not large enough to make military reputations, dangerous for the presidency." [17] With this in view, Polk planned a triple thrust against the enemy: an "Army of the West" large enough to conquer but small enough not to terrify the conquered would subdue New Mexico and California, an "Army of the Center" would hold Chihuahua and northern Mexico under control, and an "Army of Occupation" would thrust southward to Mexico City to dictate the terms of the peace.

Before this over-all plan could be put into operation, General Zachary Taylor had to dispose of General Arista's "invaders." On May 1 the Mexican army began crossing the Rio Grande some eight miles below Matamoros, thus threatening the American supply line between Fort Brown and the ocean base at Point Isabella. Hurriedly retreating to the sea, Taylor prepared his men and then on the afternoon of May 7 set out to face the enemy with 2,300 troops. The two forces sighted each other at noon the next day as they drew together on an open plain near the Palo Alto water hole. Forming lines, they first engaged in an artillery duel; the steady American fire opened wide gaps in the Mexican ranks, but the enemy's powder was so faulty that Taylor's troops could dodge the slow-moving cannon balls as they came skipping across the ground. Knowing that his men would soon wilt under this punishment, General Arista ordered a charge, only to have his

---

[15] George B. McClellan, *The Mexican War Diary of George B. McClellan* (Princeton, 1917), pp. 29, 38–39.

[16] Edward W. Wallace, "Deserters in the Mexican War," *Hispanic American Historical Review*, XV (1935), 374–383.

[17] Thomas Hart Benton, *Thirty Years' View* (2 vols., New York, 1854), II, 680.

troops flounder in a morass and hurriedly retreat. Once more cannonading was resumed, and once more whole platoons were mowed down. A charge by the Americans would have brought complete victory; instead Taylor kept up the bombardment until nightfall, then let his men sleep. Daybreak on the morning of May 9 revealed that the Mexicans had vanished. The United States had won the Battle of Palo Alto, but had failed to destroy the enemy.

Taylor soon had another chance, for General Arista elected to make a second stand in the dry bed of a river where four-foot banks protected his men and a rank growth of cactus and twisted bushes formed a belt through which attackers must charge. Snaking through this undergrowth in Indian fashion, the Americans burst upon the Mexicans late in the afternoon of May 9, charging so furiously that the two armies locked in hand-to-hand combat. For a time Arista's soldiers "fought like devils," as an admiring American wrote; but when their left flank was turned, resistance suddenly dissolved and they rushed pellmell toward the Rio Grande, leaving 547 men dead or wounded on the battlefield. American losses at this Battle of Resaca de la Palma were only 122. Instead of pursuing, the cautious Taylor camped on the spot, allowing the enemy to cross the Rio Grande. No plans had been made for boats; while men were hurried away to Point Isabella for lumber, Arista had time to lead his demoralized army out of Matamoros and vanish into the deserts beyond. When Taylor's men finally crossed the river on May 18 they found no soldiers, "nothing but old hags, worse looking than Indians," as one of the men wrote ruefully.[18]

The American general's overcautious leadership failed to impress either his followers or his Washington contemporaries, but his victories at Palo Alto and Resaca de la Palma caught the popular imagination. Overnight "Zach" Taylor was the national hero; newspapers screamed his praises; orators compared him to Caesar and Napoleon; and tailors wrung their hands in horror as orders poured in for duplicates of his unkempt pantaloons, tattered brown coat, and white linen roundabout. Everywhere the demand rose that he be made supreme commander for the conquest of Mexico. President Polk was not displeased. Taylor was hardly cut to the pattern of heroes; he was a thickset, corpulent man of sixty-one years, with a short body, stubby

[18] Smith, *War with Mexico*, I, 170–180, is particularly critical of Taylor's strategy at this point. The quotation is from George Meade, *The Life and Letters of George Gordon Meade* (2 vols., New York, 1913), I, 86.

legs, and a habit of contracting his heavy brows to appear constantly severe. Surely such an ungainly individual would be a less dangerous political rival than the one other general in the regular Army, Winfield Scott. Scott, a year younger than Taylor, was of proper social background and magnificent presence; moreover he was known to be politically ambitious. Polk felt that he was aiding the Democratic party as well as choosing the right leader when he elevated Taylor to the rank of major general and named him commander of the American forces, while relegating Scott to training enlistees at Washington.

With this done, the time had come to launch the President's overall campaign. The first task—the conquest of the northern Mexican provinces—was entrusted to the Army of the West. When fifty-two-year-old Brigadier General Stephen Watts Kearny was named commander of this force, the problem of recruits was automatically solved, for his long career in the West had made him a hero among the frontiersmen, and they flocked to his standard. Throughout Missouri men fought for places in the ten regiments authorized, organized their companies, and marched off to Fort Leavenworth. There they received a little training, but most were so skilled in horsemanship and the hunt that regular Army officers could teach them nothing. By June 26, 1846, the first detachments went swinging out of the fort on their way west, accompanied by miles of supply trains. "As far as the vision could penetrate," wrote one of the troops, "the long files of cavalry, the gay fluttering of banners, and the canvass-covered wagons of the merchant train glistening like banks of snow in the distance, might be seen winding their tortuous way over the undulating surface of the prairies." [19]

General Kearny had set Bent's Fort, 565 miles from Fort Leavenworth, as the rendezvous point; the first units came streaming in on July 22 after twenty-four days on the trail—twenty-four days of rain and mosquitoes and short rations during which the two companies of foot soldiers outdistanced the cavalry on more than one occasion. There they found the Santa Fe caravan of that year waiting to be escorted into New Mexico. For a few days the men were allowed to rest, while General Kearny made the preparations that allowed him to win Santa Fe without a shot.

Within that Mexican city news of the army's approach had caused

[19] John T. Hughes, *Doniphan's Expedition; Containing an Account of the Conquest of New Mexico* (Cincinnati, 1847), pp. 14–15.

less terror than confusion. The people had little reason to be loyal to their homeland; for years their economic ties had been with the United States, while Mexico provided them only corrupt governors and oppressive taxes. Yet they were Mexicans, and in time of crisis latent patriotic sentiments began to stir. These were encouraged by the governor, Manuel Armíjo, a mountainous man whose blue frock coat and flaming red sash compensated for a total lack of either principles or courage. Armíjo had seized the opportunity to bombard his subjects with proclamations urging resistance, but within his own heart he was terrified at the prospect of either fighting the Americans or facing punishment if he did not. Torn by these doubts, he was willing to swing to the side that offered him most, just as the people were so divided in their loyalties that they might turn either way.

General Kearny realized this situation, and acted accordingly. From Bent's Fort he sent three captured spies into Santa Fe with word that those who did not resist would be protected; then on July 31 he issued a proclamation promising civil and religious freedom for all who laid down their arms. This, with a letter to Governor Armíjo asking that New Mexico be yielded, was carried to Santa Fe by Captain Philip St. George Cooke and James W. Magoffin, a trader who bore secret instructions from Polk himself to talk Armíjo into surrender.[20] With a small escort of troops under a flag of truce, the emissaries reached the New Mexican capital on the night of August 12, 1846, and immediately went into conference with the governor. Just what passed between these three men will never be known, although Magoffin apparently did his best to persuade Armíjo to surrender the province. They parted in high spirits, met again for chocolate the next morning, and finally separated as Cooke rode back to join his commander.

Whether the ill-played drama that followed had been engineered by Magoffin or was inspired by Governor Armíjo's own cowardice will always remain a mystery. The governor led his poorly equipped army of three thousand men out of Santa Fe on August 16, taking up his position at Apache Canyon, an easily defended defile through which the invaders must pass. There they waited as General Kearny's army, with the "long-legged infantry" in the lead, struggled upward toward Raton Pass, pulling their wagons with ropes. As they neared Apache

[20] Documents dealing with Magoffin's appointment are in Stella M. Drumm (ed.), *Down the Santa Fé Trail and into Mexico; the Diary of Susan Shelby Magoffin, 1846–1847* (New Haven, 1926), pp. 263–265.

Pass, panic swept over the Mexican defenders. Governor Armíjo, who would have had little stomach for fighting even if Magoffin had not convinced him that resistance was futile, showed his taut nerves when he began quarreling with his officers; after a few hours of this he suddenly shouted orders for the whole force to disperse. By August 17, when Kearny's army arrived, Apache Canyon was deserted. The Americans marched through, marveling that it should have been abandoned without a fight; "had Armíjo's heart been as stout as the walls of rock which nature gave him to aid in defense of his country," one wrote, "we might have sought in vain to force this passage." [21] A day later they were in Santa Fe, complaining of the mud houses and the "contemptible set of swarthy thieves and liars" that formed its population, while Armíjo and his followers fled southward toward Chihuahua.

The formal surrender of New Mexico took place in the Santa Fe plaza on August 19. There Kearny spoke to the people, promising them protection for their lives, property, and religion. Amidst shouts of *"Viva el General"* leading citizens crowded forward to take the oath of allegiance. Three days later he issued a proclamation assuring the New Mexicans that the United States intended to provide them with a free popular government without delay; on September 22, 1846, Charles Bent was named civilian governor and an "organic law" established, with provisions for a popularly elected legislature. Kearny's skill had won—and apparently secured—the first of Polk's objectives without a shot being fired.

His work, however, was still far from done, for his orders required him to continue his march across the continent and aid in the conquest of California. Hence Kearny divided his command, swelled now by new troops from the East, into three units. He planned to lead one of these westward himself. Another under General Alexander W. Doniphan was ordered to subdue nearby Indians before starting southward to conquer the province of Chihuahua. The third, with Colonel Sterling Price in command, was told to continue the occupation of Santa Fe. The troops assigned to that prosaic task grumblingly settled down to wait the war out, complaining that the others were having all the fun. Yet the occupation had scarcely begun before they saw all the fighting they wanted.

[21] Frank S. Edwards, *A Campaign in New Mexico with Colonel Doniphan* (Philadelphia, 1847), pp. 44–45.

Conditions within Santa Fe that autumn and winter of 1846–47 were bound to breed trouble. Crowded into the town were hundreds of disgruntled troops who had little to do but curse their fate or seek forgetfulness in grogshops. Each night "crowds of drunken volunteers filled the streets, brawling and boasting," while sober citizens trembled behind their doors.[22] Racial tensions, inevitable when the lordly Americans were thrown in intimate contact with a people they considered inferior, contributed to the discontent of the Mexicans. "The Americans say they have come for our good," they said, and added, "yes, for all our goods." By December 1, irate citizens were beginning to plot a revolt against their conquerors; as the days passed this emerged as a full-scale rebellion. The blow fell on the night of January 19, 1847, at Taos, where Governor Bent and his staff were visiting. Moving silently across the snow-covered plaza, the rebels first killed the sheriff and one of his helpers, then swarmed into the house where the governor was staying. As his mangled body was paraded through the streets, mobs fell on all Americans they could find, killing ruthlessly. By the time the slaughter was over, fifteen were dead and the few survivors were fleeing toward Santa Fe to spread the alarm.[23]

Colonel Price rallied to the attack as soon as news of the "Taos Rebellion" reached him on January 20, 1847. With five companies of troops he started for Taos at once. Near the town of La Cañada they stopped to disperse 1,500 rebels; a little farther on another band of six or seven hundred Mexicans and Indians was dislodged from its mountain stronghold and sent flying. When Price entered Taos on February 3 he learned that seven hundred of the enemy were waiting behind the adobe walls of the Taos Pueblo, which towered seven stories tall. After cannonading failed to breach the stout defenses, he ordered his men to charge. Dashing forward to reach the protection of the pueblo, they battered a hole through the walls with axes and went storming in. By nightfall on February 4, 150 of the enemy lay dead, and the rebellion was over. From that day on New Mexico enjoyed a troubled peace as the conquest of its mother country went ruthlessly on.

General Kearny led one of the forces that helped achieve the inevi-

[22] George F. Ruxton, *Adventures in Mexico and the Rocky Mountains* (London, 1847), pp. 196–197.

[23] Documents concerning the rebellion are in 56th Congress, 1st Session, *Senate Document* No. 442, pp. 1–48, while a modern history of the affair is E. Bennett Burton, "The Taos Rebellion," *Old Santa Fe*, I (1913), 176–195.

table victory. With three hundred "wilderness-worn dragoons, in shabby and patched clothing," he had started westward on September 25, 1846. Scarcely had he taken the trail when he learned that the "Mormon Battalion" had arrived in Santa Fe; five hundred youths and men from that persecuted sect had enlisted in Iowa to secure their bonus money and salaries for their fellow Saints. Captain Philip St. George Cooke was hurried back to lead them them on to California, while Kearny pressed on more rapidly, mindful of his role as liberator of that province. On October 6, 1846, his force was stopped by a band of yelling frontiersmen under Kit Carson who had ridden hell-for-leather to tell them that California was already won by the Bear Flaggers and a naval force. Kearny sent most of his dragoons back to Santa Fe; with the remainder and with the reluctant Kit Carson pressed into service as guide, he pushed on westward, reaching his destination without difficulty if not without hardship.

The story of the Mormon Battalion under Captain Cooke was terrifyingly different. Aware that settlers would soon be crowding westward, Kearny had ordered Cooke to blaze a wagon trail to California. Cooke, knowing something of the difficulties this meant, reduced his force to 397 men by eliminating the old and infirm, then on October 19, 1846, led these out of Santa Fe on one of the most grueling marches in history. As they left the Rio Grande valley they found it necessary for some of the men to walk in double file before the wagons, beating down a track, while the rest pulled and tugged at the wheels. So they inched along, across New Mexico, over the rugged Sacramento Mountains, where double teaming was required; over the deserts of southern Arizona, where men and animals fought to drink muddy water in occasional pools; over the sun-blistered reaches of southern California, where for three days and two nights they had no water at all. They were on pitifully short rations by this time, with their clothing so worn that the men used all they had to wrap their feet against the burning sands in the daytime and at night walked barefoot that their bodies could be protected from the biting cold. Then came the climb over the mountains, and the sickening discovery that the narrow defile at the top was too narrow to let wagons through. For a time they tried to hack a wider opening with axes, then dismantled the wagons, carried them through, reassembled them, and in triumph made their way into San Diego on January 29, 1847. Captain Cooke scarcely exaggerated when he told his weary followers: "History may be searched in vain for an equal march of infantry." [24]

Neither Cooke's heroic followers nor the dragoons under Kearny who had preceded them into California played a vital role in the conquest of that province. Instead California was won with surprisingly little effort by naval forces under Commodore John D. Sloat and his successors, ably assisted by Captain John C. Frémont and his Bear Flaggers. Sloat, who commanded the Pacific Squadron of the Navy, had been anchored off the Mexican coast on June 7, 1846, when word reached him of the engagements along the Rio Grande. Sailing northward at once, he reached Monterey on July 2, and after a period of soul-searching (for no word of an official declaration of war had arrived) took possession of the town on July 7, 1846. Sloat was hailed as a liberator by most Californians, for even those who disliked the prospect of American rule preferred his orderly command to the uncertainties of life under the Bear Flaggers. The Mexican rulers, Governors Castro and Pío Pico, failed to appreciate these sentiments; with some eight hundred followers they fled southward, muttering threats of reconquest.

The glory of final victory was denied Commodore Sloat, for he was due to retire from the Navy, and on July 23 his replacement arrived in the person of Commodore Robert F. Stockton. More aggressive than Sloat, Stockton immediately enlisted Frémont and his 160 Bear Flaggers as the "California Battalion," and hurried them off to San Diego by sea to halt the Mexican forces fleeing toward the border. Stockton followed more slowly, stopping to take possession of Santa Barbara and Los Angeles. With his arrival in southern California, Castro and Pío Pico vanished into Mexico in a cloud of oratorical eloquence. By August 17, 1846, when word of the declaration of war finally reached California, the province was safely in American hands. The region was divided into northern and southern districts, with Frémont in charge of the former and Lieutenant Archibald Gillespie of the latter; by September orderly government had made such advances that local elections were held. This was the type of reform that the wealthier Californians wanted; Stockton and his officers were so popular that

[24] Henry W. Bigler, "Extracts from the Journal of Henry W. Bigler," *Utah Historical Quarterly*, V (1932), 57–58, prints Cooke's address. Cooke's journal of this expedition is printed in Ralph P. Bieber (ed.), *Exploring Southwestern Trails, 1846–1854* (Glendale, Calif., 1938).

their health was threatened by the round of *fiestas* given in their honor.

California, however, proved easier to have than to hold. Among poorer Californians and Mexicanized Indians the spirit of rebellion still flamed, especially in the south, where Gillespie had only fifty troops to give him aid. The rebels struck on the night of September 22, 1846, so suddenly that Gillespie had no choice but to accept the honorable terms of surrender they offered; four days later he and his men were sailing for Monterey as the rebellion spread behind them. By the end of October an estimated 1,200 insurgents roamed the land, all of them well mounted, at least, for they had stolen virtually every horse in the province. Yet the cause was by no means lost, for most were penniless drifters so untroubled by basic loyalties that they would desert to the winning side in a moment. Commodore Stockton had only to prove that his was the winning side.

Word of the insurrection reached him at San Francisco on October 1, carried by a messenger who had ridden 460 miles in fifty-two hours with the news hidden in a cigar. Sailing at once, Stockton reached San Diego early in November. In the meantime Frémont was moving southward by land, leading 428 formidable fighters who made up in valor what they lacked in style; "a single bugle (and a sorry one it is)" composed their band.[25] As he marched, affairs in southern California reached the boiling point with the arrival of General Kearny and his one hundred dragoons from Santa Fe. Kearny paused at Warner's ranch, near San Diego, until he was reinforced with thirty-eight men under Archibald Gillespie; then on December 6 advanced to the town of San Pasqual, where eighty well-mounted insurgents awaited him. Their attack on the weary Americans was devastating; after the first charge eighteen lay on the battlefield and fifteen others, including Kearny and Gillespie, were wounded. The survivors straggled into San Diego a day later, fully impressed with the might of the enemy.

Kearny's inglorious arrival convinced Commodore Stockton to attack at once, without waiting for Frémont's help. Four hundred sailors were brought ashore, armed, and started toward the rebel position on the San Gabriel River, twelve miles from Los Angeles. On January 8, 1847, they stormed across that stream; in a few moments all was over,

---

[25] Edwin Bryant, *What I Saw in California* (New York, 1848), pp. 365–394, describes the march as seen by one of Frémont's men.

with the insurgents fleeing toward Mexico and the road to Los Angeles open. Stockton entered the city on January 10, just after Frémont arrived from the north. The Treaty of Cahuenga offered such honorable terms of capitulation to the vanquished that the fears of those still in arms were quieted; overnight resistance vanished and California settled into its accustomed idyllic calm. For a time the transition to civil rule was delayed as Frémont and Kearny squabbled over the right to govern, but orders from Washington settled the dispute in Kearny's favor in February, 1847.[26] His able administration, and that of Colonel R. B. Mason, who succeeded him in May, 1847, soon convinced Californians that the change of masters had benefited them immeasurably.

With the Mexican War less than a year old the northern Mexican provinces were safely in American hands. There remained the task of convincing the government that these conquests should be permanent. This could be done only by carrying the war deep into Mexico, a task entrusted to General Zachary Taylor with orders to open the road to Mexico City by subduing Monterrey and Buena Vista. In this maneuver Taylor's right flank was guarded by two small armies that moved into Mexico from San Antonio and Santa Fe. One of these, led by Brigadier General J. E. Wool, occupied the important city of Monclova on October 29, 1846, without firing a shot, then continued south to rejoin Taylor at Saltillo. The other accomplished more, for its members were the self-styled "ring-tailed roarers" that Colonel A. W. Doniphan had scraped together from the frontier settlements and welded into one of the most effective fighting machines of the war.

There was little in either Doniphan or his half-wild followers to command the respect of West Pointers of that day. Doniphan himself was a giant of a man, standing six feet two inches tall, with carroty red hair, prominent chin, and dazzling hazel eyes. Scorning both formality and discipline, he dressed in slouchy, ragged clothes, pitched his own tent and cooked his own meals, consulted as freely with the humblest private as with his own staff, and spiced his speech "with strong expressions which many eastern men would call something like swearing." [27] His followers were of the same stamp. Enlisted from the

[26] Thomas Kearny, "The Mexican War and the Conquest of California. Stockton or Kearny Conqueror and First Governor?" *California Historical Society Quarterly*, VIII (1929), 251–261.

[27] Edwards, *Campaign in New Mexico*, p. 76.

backwoods as the First Missouri Regiment, they were "unwashed and unshaven, were ragged and dirty, without uniforms, and dressed as, and how, they pleased." Their camps were the despair of Regular Army officers, strewn with rubbish and the bones and offal of the animals they ate, and filled with unkempt semibarbarians who loafed about, "listless and sickly-looking, or were sitting in groups playing at cards, and swearing and cursing, even at the officers." [28] But these men could ride like Comanche and shoot like Mountain Men, and were as chock full of fight as gamecocks. Their exploits in the Mexican War form one of the sagas of the Far West.

Starting from Santa Fe in November, 1846, 856 strong and followed by a train of 315 wagons driven by Santa Fe traders willing to risk the hazards of war to peddle their goods, Doniphan's wild crew swung southward along the Rio Grande; crossed the dread Jornado del Muerto, where for three days they marched over a gravelly desert without water or rest; and at Brazito, near El Paso, fought their first engagement. Twelve hundred of the enemy, resplendent in bright scarlet coats, white belts, and brass helmets with waving plumes, barred their path; after waving away a Mexican demand for surrender with a "charge and be damned," Doniphan calmly strode among his men while they alternately fired and knelt, fired and knelt, until one hundred of the enemy lay dead and the rest were fleeing in panic.

At El Paso, Doniphan learned that the Taos Rebellion had cut his source of supplies, but there was no thought of turning back. They would live off the country as they marched; a habit already forming in El Paso to the disgust of the inhabitants, who soon changed their salutation of "omegas" (as one of the men heard it) to more explosive phrases. No tears were shed when the Americans took the trail again on February 11, 1847, moving southward into an unknown land of deserts and mountains. For day after day they forged ahead, across deserts where scorching days alternated with freezing nights. Storms blew away their tents, and grass fires endangered their lives; food was scarce and their clothing so worn that "shoes were a luxury, and hats a very doubtful article." [29] Yet not a word of complaint was heard and not a mention of turning back.

On February 27, 1847, as they neared the city of Chihuahua, dis-

---

[28] Ruxton, *Adventures in Mexico and the Rocky Mountains*, p. 178.
[29] Edwards, *Campaign in New Mexico*, p. 99.

quieting news greeted them. Twenty-seven hundred well-armed soldiers and one thousand rancheros equipped with machetes waited
them on an elevated tongue of land where the Sacramento River
joined a dry canyon known as the Arroyo Seco. So confident were the
Mexicans, Doniphan heard, that they were planning the division of
goods brought by the Santa Fe traders, and were fashioning short
lengths of rope to tie their prisoners. That night the invaders sharpened their sabers and loaded their rifles; the next morning they swung
down the four-mile-wide valley with their band piping "Yankee
Doodle" until the enemy's shining lances were sighted just at noon.
Knowing that a frontal attack would be suicidal, Doniphan ordered
his men across the dry Arroyo Seco and up the steep bank beyond;
after a flurry of dirt, sweat, and profanity his whole force faced the
Mexicans on a wide, open plain. The usual artillery duel began at
three o'clock, and as usual, too, inferior Mexican powder allowed the
Americans to dodge every ball while their own chain shot ripped great
holes in the opposing lines. Through it all Doniphan sat calmly on his
horse, whittling gravely, and remarking now and then: "Well, they're
giving us hell now, boys." At last the defenders broke for the earth-
works they had prepared; Doniphan ordered a charge at this moment.
By five o'clock the Battle of Sacramento was over. Eight hundred
frontiersmen had routed four thousand Mexican troops, killing three
hundred of them and wounding as many more, with a loss of only one
man killed and five wounded.[30]

For a time the Missourians rested in the city of Chihuahua, where
the fifteen thousand inhabitants greeted them with shouts of *"amigo"*
and welcomed the Santa Fe traders with open pocketbooks. Doniphan
was sorely perplexed as to the future; he was deep in enemy country,
a thousand miles from his nearest countryman, and unable to move
until the traders sold their goods. The answer was provided by General
Zachary Taylor when he was located by messengers who rode thirty
days across one thousand miles of unknown country "with no other
passports than their rifles." [31] The force was to join Taylor's army at
Saltillo. In late April they pulled out of Chihuahua as the happy cit-

[30] Doniphan's report on the battle is in James M. Cutts, *The Conquest of
California and New Mexico by the Forces of the United States in the Years
1846 & 1847* (Philadelphia, 1847), pp. 81–86.
[31] Adolphus Wislizenus, *Memoir of a Tour to Northern Mexico, Connected
with Col. Doniphan's Expedition, in 1846 and 1847* (Washington, 1848),
p. 62.

izens shouted, "The gringos are gone, hurrah." Again a grueling march followed, across deserts where scorpions and lizards scurried from their path and the sharp thorns of prickly-pear cactus raked their bodies, but on May 21, 1847, they reached Saltillo, only to find that Taylor had moved on. Doggedly they followed, to catch him at last at Monterrey. In one year Doniphan's men had traveled six thousand miles and defeated two armies, yet in all this time had served without supplies, instructions, or pay. Here was an exploit unique in the annals of war.

Colorful as the deeds of Doniphan's regiment were, they played little part in bringing Mexico to her knees. This task fell first on General Taylor, who had begun his invasion in August, 1846, with an army of six thousand men. Moving out of the border town of Matamoros, where his first victories had been won, he pushed southward along the San Juan valley through Mier and Cerralvo until September 19, when he camped with the stone buildings of Monterrey in view. Seven thousand enemy troops awaited him there, commanded by General Pedro de Amudia, a mean little man noted for his polished mustaches rather than his military valor. The Americans attacked in the gloom of misty morning on September 20. All that day they battered at the defenses in vain, but on the next the western approaches gave way and the Mexicans retreated to the heart of the city. Hopelessly surrounded, and fearful that each American shell would set off his powder magazines, General Amudia offered to surrender on the morning of September 24. The terms granted him could hardly have been more generous; the Mexican force was allowed to withdraw with its arms, while the Americans pledged not to advance deeper into Mexico for at least eight weeks.

As Taylor settled down to wait out this ill-advised armistice, conditions within Mexico changed rapidly. The early disasters of the war had brought the existing government under President Mariana Paredes y Arrillaga into such disrepute that even the often-discredited Antonio López de Santa Anna seemed acceptable by comparison. He returned from his exile in Cuba in mid-August, 1846, breathing fire and brimstone as he boasted of leading an army of 25,000 men northward to drive Taylor from the land. Such grandiose projects were beyond the means of poverty-stricken Mexico, but by the end of January, 1847, Santa Anna did have eighteen thousand so-called troops at the rallying point, San Luis Potosí, and with them started toward Buena Vista where Taylor awaited him. Worn by the march, hampered by lack of equipment or leadership, and panicky lest they follow the pattern of defeat established by earlier Mexican armies, they were no match for the well-trained Americans. After vainly battering Taylor's defenses for two days, Santa Anna's forces fell back. The Battle of Buena Vista opened the road to Mexico City and brought victory within sight.

The glory of winning the war was not to be General Taylor's. For some time differences between him and President Polk had been multiplying. Polk was scornful of the general's military ability after his failure to capitalize on his victories at Palo Alto and Resaca de la Palma, and resentful of the eight weeks' truce after the Battle of Monterrey. He was also jealous of the fame of "Old Rough and Ready," who seemed headed straight for the White House—on a Whig ticket —in 1848. When Taylor was so imprudent as to publish a letter in January, 1847, insisting that the war could be won without further bloodshed by holding the line he had established, Polk made up his mind. Taylor was publicly rebuked, and General Winfield Scott named supreme commander. Scott's instructions called for a giant force to invade Vera Cruz from the sea, then march inland to the Mexican capital.

These plans were carried through without a hitch. On March 9, 1847, the American army of invasion landed just south of the strong fortress at Vera Cruz, which capitulated after an eighteen-day siege. The road to Mexico City that was now opened was not an easy one to follow, for it twisted upward into the mountains through narrow canyons. General Santa Anna chose the steepest of these, the Cerro Gordo, to defend; there he stationed eight thousand of his best troops while Mexicans from miles around gathered to cheer the victory that seemed certain. The fireworks they carried to celebrate Santa Anna's triumph were never used. Scott realized that a frontal attack would be suicidal; instead he sent troops experienced in New England's mountains to cut paths up the steep slopes on either side. By the morning of April 18, 1847, the Mexican force was retreating in panic, with Santa Anna leading the way. At their heels came the Americans, fighting constant small engagements as they moved upward over the rim of mountains that surrounded the high interior plateau. Beating down opposition in battle after battle, they stood before the gates of Mexico City by the end of August, 1847. Two weeks later the heavily fortified Chapultepec hill which guarded the main causeway to the lake-enclosed city was won; out over the causeway the attackers moved, leaping from pillar to pillar like so many Indians, until they knocked on the stone walls that surrounded the capital. On the evening of September 13 they entered the narrow streets, where fierce hand-to-hand fighting continued until Santa Anna finally ran up the white flag on September 17, 1847. The war was over.

Polk had anticipated this victory from the beginning. As early as April 10, 1847, when news arrived of Scott's capture of Vera Cruz, he had decided to send a commissioner with the invading army, "ready to take advantage of circumstances, as they might arise to negotiate a peace." Nicholas P. Trist, a pompous man with modest abilities and an overbearing conceit, was plucked from his post as chief clerk of the State Department and started southward, bearing instructions to secure California, New Mexico, and the Rio Grande border for a payment of no more than $15,000,000.[32] For a time Trist and General Scott quarreled so bitterly that they reached the "not speaking" point, for Scott resented both Trist's pomposity and the action of the President in naming this "clerk" to a position that seemingly challenged his own authority. For days on end they bombarded each other and Washington with angry letters (Trist was never happier than when filling thirty or more pages with solidified Victorian oratory), but before Mexico City was won they had composed their differences and were bosom friends.

This was the situation when dispatches from Polk reached them on November 16, 1847, ordering Trist back to Washington at once. Trist was willing to obey, but Scott insisted that he draft a treaty before the tottering Mexican government degenerated into complete anarchy. These arguments carried the day, even though Trist knew that he was committing political suicide. After justifying his conduct in an extraordinary sixty-five-page letter to Polk, he settled down with the Mexican commissioners in the little town of Guadalupe Hidalgo near the capital. Haggling went on for some time before the last differences were settled, but by February 2 Mexico had agreed to accept payment

---

[32] Trist's instructions are in 30th Congress, 1st Session, *Senate Executive Document* No. 52, pp. 81–84. Accounts of his mission are in Louis M. Sears, "Nicholas P. Trist, a Diplomat with Ideals," *Mississippi Valley Historical Review*, XI (1924), 85–98, and Robert A. Brent, "Nicholas P. Trist and the Treaty of Guadalupe Hidalgo," *Southwestern Historical Quarterly*, LVII (1954), 454–474. A challenging interpretation of Trist's diplomacy is in Norman A. Graebner, *Empire on the Pacific* (New York, 1955), pp. 191–216.

of $15,000,000 in return for a boundary that followed the Rio Grande and Gila rivers, and for the cession of both California and New Mexico. President Polk, still bristling at "the exceptional conduct of Mr. Trist," hesitated to accept the Treaty of Guadalupe Hidalgo at first, but he could hardly repudiate his own agent for following his own instructions. On March 10, 1848, it was ratified by the Senate with 38 votes in favor and 14 opposed. Wrote a disgruntled Whig: "The treaty negotiated by an unauthorized agent, with an unacknowledged government, submitted by an accidental President to a dissatisfied Senate, has . . . been confirmed." [33]

Polk's hesitancy in accepting the Treaty of Guadalupe Hidalgo was due less to his annoyance with Trist than to a new spirit of expansionism that flamed during the summer and autumn of 1847. The ease of the American conquest seemed to confirm all the arguments of those who had preached America's manifest destiny. Surely a benevolent Deity intended that such a backward and powerless people as the Mexicans should be absorbed and regenerated! Why take only the northern provinces when God had shown them that all Mexico could be theirs? This would not only fulfill America's destiny, but provide compensation for a war that had proved more costly than anyone had imagined. By the autumn of 1847 the "All Mexico" campaign was in full cry, with scarcely a newspaper in the land demanding anything less than the absorption of every inch of the conquered nation. Even violent racists who had railed against contaminating Anglo-Saxon blood with the "inferior" fluid of Mexican peons found that the government, not the people, was responsible for that unhappy land's plight; even abolitionists who had rallied to prevent the annexation of more "slave pens" discovered that Mexico's arid lands were so unsuited to slave labor that their addition would deal slavery a fatal blow.[34]

This tide of opinion had its effect on the politics of the peace. The Democrats, having lost the congressional elections of 1846, were quick to seize upon the issue as a means of recapturing their popularity. By midwinter of 1847–48 virtually every Democrat in Congress was baying at the All Mexico moon, while party conventions vied in adopting

[33] Bayard Tuckerman (ed.), *The Diary of Philip Hone, 1828–1851* (2 vols., New York, 1910), II, 347.

[34] The "All Mexico" campaign is described in Albert K. Weinberg, *Manifest Destiny* (Baltimore, 1935), pp. 160–180, and more fully in John D. P. Fuller, *The Movement for the Acquisition of All Mexico, 1846–1848* (Baltimore, 1936), *passim.*

resolutions asking the government to be content with nothing less. Among Polk's closest advisers, many were clambering aboard the bandwagon; Robert J. Walker, his Secretary of the Treasury, believed that the Mexican people should be "benevolently assimilated," as did James Buchanan, the Secretary of State, and Vice-President George M. Dallas. In such an atmosphere the President was not long in realizing that his initial war demands, as embodied in the instructions to Nicholas Trist, were altogether too modest. As early as September, 1847, he told his cabinet that Mexico's refusal to consider peace offers inclined him to favor taking "more territory than the provinces named," while an early draft of his December, 1847, message to Congress declared that if the Mexicans would not end the war at once "additional territory must be required as further indemnity." [35]

In the light of this rolling tide of expansionist opinion, there is little doubt that Trist saved Mexico from further dismemberment when he drafted a peace treaty based on instructions that were months old. That the United States would have taken "All Mexico" is extremely unlikely, despite pressure from jingoists. That it would have been content with only California and New Mexico is equally improbable. Such were the fruits of that mounting wave of emotionalism that had, by adding Texas and all the Southwest to the United States, opened a new stage for the further development of the Far West.

[35] Quaife (ed.), *Polk Diary,* III, 161, 217.

CHAPTER 9

Mormons Move Westward

VICTORY in the Mexican War opened millions of acres of fertile pasturage and farmlands to the pioneers. Yet the first newcomers, paradoxically enough, were not frontiersmen in search of verdant fields, but Easterners who sought a region so inhospitable and so isolated that it would be wanted by no one else. For these intruders on Mexico's former domain were members of the Church of Jesus Christ of Latter-day Saints, or Mormons as they were popularly called, and their goal was the founding of a desert Zion so separated from the haunts of men that they could live their lives and worship their God as they pleased.

Persecution drove them westward. Joseph Smith, their prophet, had aroused popular ire when, as a youth in upper New York State, he told neighbors of visits from God and the Saviour and of Their divine message that he had been selected to reveal the one true religion to man. Hostility had increased when he published the Book of Mormon, and in 1830 organized his church with its first six members; so intense was feeling against him that he had led his few converts to the little hamlet of Kirtland in northern Ohio. For a time the Mormons prospered there, but with hard times following the Panic of 1837 attacks began again. Once more Smith guided the faithful westward, this time to a Zion in northwestern Missouri, where they built their homes about the towns of Far West and DeWitt. And once more mobs soon were at their heels as the governor branded them "public enemies" who must be "exterminated or driven from the State, if necessary, for the public good." [1] This time Smith guided his followers east-

[1] Herman C. Smith, "Mormon Troubles in Missouri," *Missouri Historical*

ward into Illinois. "Shrewd and vindictive" as a result of his Missouri experiences, he took advantage of an even split between Whigs and Democrats to wring concessions from both parties; by the time bargaining was over, he had secured a charter for a new Mormon city of Nauvoo that made him virtually sovereign.

Once more the Saints knew peace as they built their city on a tongue of land projecting into the Mississippi. So industriously did they labor that soon two thousand neat homes pushed back the forest, "almost all of them brick, built in the New England style, neat as well as substantial, surrounded by garden plats . . . and without any of that unfinished temporary *makeshift* appearance that characterises the new settlements of the West." [2] Dominating all was the temple, a giant structure of stone and gilt. Here gathered the faithful from all the East and from England as missionaries won converts and dispatched them to the wilderness Zion. Most came from settled agricultural areas or from England's industrial slums; Mormonism's appeal was to the submerged classes, who were promised not only salvation but the chance to begin life anew amidst the plentiful opportunities provided by a virgin land. "In this place," wrote an English convert who had settled in a Mormon community, "there is a prospect of receiving every good thing both of this world and that which is to come." [3] This emphasis on a gospel of practical living helps explain the loyalty of the people to their leaders, and the remarkable unity with which they faced renewed persecutions.

These began in 1844, when Nauvoo was Illinois' largest and most prosperous city, with 15,000 contented Saints within its gates. Neighbors resented this prosperity, just as they did the Mormons' dismissal of all other sects as creations of the Devil, but nothing could be done so long as they held their ranks closed against the outside world. But when Joseph Smith received his last revelation, which allowed certain Mormons to practice polygamy, some Saints branded him a fallen prophet and denounced him to the world. Smith retaliated by sending the Nauvoo marshal to destroy the presses of a newspaper established

Review, IV (1910), 238–251; Rollin J. Britton, "Early Days on Grand River and the Mormon War," *Missouri Historical Review*, XIII (1919), 112–134; XIV (1920), 459–473.

[2] Oscar O. Winther (ed.), *The Private Papers and Diary of Thomas Leiper Kane, a Friend of the Mormons* (San Francisco, 1937), pp. 6–7.

[3] Quoted in M. Hamlin Cannon, "Migration of English Mormons to America," *American Historical Review*, LII (1947), 440.

by his enemies, the *Nauvoo Expositor;* they, in turn, signed warrants asking for the Prophet's arrest. Joseph Smith surrendered to the civil authorities meekly enough and was taken to a jail in nearby Carthage. There, on June 27, 1844, he and his brother were killed by a mob of two hundred anti-Mormons. This touched off a mass outbreak. In all that part of Illinois mobs roamed the countryside, crying for the blood of the Saints and threatening to launch a mass attack on their city. Once more the decision must be made: should they defy their tormentors, or flee to still a newer land?

Fortunately this decision rested on an individual remarkably well equipped to provide the correct answer. With Joseph Smith's martyrdom, his mantle of leadership fell to the president of the Council of Twelve Apostles of the Church, Brigham Young. An early convert to Mormonism, Young was forty-three years of age, with a stocky body tending to corpulence, fleshy features, sharply pointed nose, and thin, close lips. His long, sandy hair, slightly stooped walk, and somber clothes, "neat and plain as a Quaker's," created the impression of an honest farmer rather than a religious leader. This ordinary exterior hid a mind that was sharp and incisive, a memory that was remarkable, a will that was indomitable, and powers of leadership that rivaled those of history's heroes. Brigham Young had been favored with little formal education, but he spoke readily if ungrammatically, and when aroused could lash out at opponents in a manner no one ever forgot.[4] Few men were as well equipped to lead the Mormons to a new land.

For to Young there was only one answer to the problem facing his people. They had suffered persecution in both the settled East and the Mississippi Valley frontier. Hence they could find repose only by fleeing to an isolated and unwanted spot far beyond the settlements. Nor did Brigham Young take long to decide where that spot must be. He was familiar with the journal kept by John C. Frémont on his 1842 exploring expedition, and with the famous guidebook of Lansford W. Hastings, *The Emigrants' Guide to Oregon and California.* Both told him that the most isolated area in all the West lay beside the Great Salt Lake, where towering mountains blocked access from the east and arid deserts from the west and south. Water for farming must be available there, Young knew; Frémont's account spoke of streams fed by

---

[4] Richard F. Burton, *The City of the Saints* (London, 1861), pp. 291–293; Horace Greeley, *An Overland Journey, from New York to San Francisco, in the Summer of 1859* (New York, 1860), p. 216; Jules Remy and Julius Brenchley, *A Journey to Great Salt Lake City* (2 vols., London, 1861), I, 201.

perpetual mountain snow, and of "good soil and good grass, adapted to civilized settlements." [5] There the Saints would find their haven. So Brigham Young decided, and the Council of the Twelve Apostles agreed, when, in mid-September, 1845, they promised the Illinois authorities to vacate Nauvoo the following spring in return for immunity from persecution until then.

All that winter preparations for the migration went on. Some labored to complete the temple at Nauvoo as a last gesture of defiance toward their persecutors, but more wandered the countryside trading their valuables for oxen, or prepared wagons and food for the journey. In early February a pioneer band crossed the frozen Mississippi to Iowa, there to build Camp of Israel as the first of a string of way stations across that territory. All that spring others followed, amidst snow and sleet and chilling rain, cheerfully abandoning their worldly goods as they turned their faces toward an unknown future, childishly confident that God and Brigham would look after them. By June, Nauvoo was a deserted city, its orderly gardens rank with weeds, its neat streets silent as the grave.

As Saints poured into Camp of Israel through that spring of 1846, another stream moved out of the camp to begin the march westward. In this journey across Iowa, Brigham Young first displayed the organizing genius that endowed the Mormon migrations with an order and comfort unrivaled in the history of overland trails. He explained his system on February 17, 1846, when he called his followers together and, mounted on a wagon, spoke to them of the course they would follow. They would move, he told them, not as a group but in a series of small parties. He would start westward with the first band at once, with others following at regular intervals. All must keep strict order and live in peace with the people they met; young men must seek work along the way to buy food and equipment. "If you do these things," Young promised them, "faith will abide in your hearts; and the angels of God will go with you, even as they went with the children of Israel when Moses led them from the land of Egypt." [6] Then,

[5] John C. Frémont, *Report of the Exploring Expedition to the Rocky Mountains in the Year 1842, and to Oregon and California in the Years 1843–44* (Washington, 1845), pp. 275–276. In 1877 Young told an interviewer that he had led the Mormons to the Great Salt Lake because of Frémont's account of the region. John C. Frémont, *Memoirs of My Life* (2 vols., New York, 1887), I, 415–416.

[6] John R. Young, *Memoirs of John R. Young, Utah Pioneer of 1847* (Salt Lake City, 1920), p. 16.

with two hundred wagons, he started westward toward the Missouri.

As this pioneer group moved across Iowa, Brigham Young ordered halts at set intervals to build rest camps for those who would follow. At Garden Grove, 155 miles from Camp of Israel, a major way station was constructed; when the party moved on, some were left to plant crops so that later migrants would have food. Again, in the valley of the Lewis River, where sweet William and blue indigo flowers waved in the spring breeze, they stopped to build Mount Pisgah, with building, planted fields, a gristmill, and shops where carpenters, blacksmiths, and wagon makers remained to provide for the major migration. By June 14, 1846, Young and his pioneers were at the Missouri, where they laid out a third principal encampment. This was christened Winter Quarters, because here the Mormons would spend the winter before moving on to the Far West. On a high plateau overlooking Council Bluffs they built a meetinghouse, workshops, a gristmill, and, over the course of the summer, almost one thousand cabins.

So well had Brigham Young and his pioneers labored that the caravans which followed their trail experienced few difficulties. The first left Camp of Israel on March 1, 1846, "without confusion, without hurrying or even discord"; others followed at regular intervals until they formed a giant procession three hundred miles long. Each wagon train, following Young's instructions, was divided into "hundreds" or "fifties" under a captain; these in turn were subdivided into "tens" controlled by a lieutenant who kept order, settled disputes, and supervised the day's march and nightly encampment. Rarely in history had a mass migration been accomplished with so little difficulty. Of hardship, of course, there was plenty; not even Young's genius could control the weather or ease the pangs of hunger among those too poor to buy food. Those who started first floundered through drifts of snow by day and at night spread their blankets on the frozen ground. Those who came later plodded through sleet and pelting rain which slowed progress to a half mile a day. But scarce a word of complaint was heard. "We were happy and contented," one wrote, "and the songs of Zion resounded from wagon to wagon, reverberating through the woods while the echo returned from the distant hill." [7] By autumn all 15,000 were safe in Winter Quarters, or in one of the way stations of Iowa.

[7] Thomas L. Kane, *The Mormons. A Discourse Delivered before the Historical Society of Pennsylvania, March 26, 1850* (Philadelphia, 1850), p. 34.

The winter tried their patience even more. Huddled in drafty cabins or tents, they seldom had enough fuel or food, while a plague that spread among them carried off no less than six hundred before spring. Yet little heed was paid these discomforts, for all were too busy planning the migration that would begin in April. Brigham Young and his fellow leaders spent their time questioning travelers who had visited the West or poring over the few guidebooks available; the rest of the Saints listened to regular lectures on methods of plains travel or perfected the organization that they would use on the trail.[8] That Brigham Young had already decided to plant his desert Zion on the shores of the Great Salt Lake was indicated when one of the lecturers, a Mormon trained in science, spoke to his fellows on devices to use in irrigating arid soil. Few immigrants began their journey westward as well versed in the arts of travel as did the Saints.

The first group started west on April 9, 1847—a "Pioneer Band" of 143 men, three women, and two children, with Brigham Young as their leader and with their belongings stored in seventy-three wagons. All had been carefully selected for endurance and skills; most were between thirty and fifty years of age, while a proper proportion of farmers, artisans, and craftsmen assured efficiency in founding their settlement. As they moved out of Winter Quarters they blazed a path along the north bank of the Platte, largely to avoid conflicts with Missourians who were streaming westward along the usual overland trail. Over this they traveled day after day, following a rigid schedule that Young revealed to them after a week on the road. Each morning a bugle sounded at five o'clock, to be followed by prayers and breakfast while draft animals grazed. Another bugle blast signaled the start of the day's march. The caravan moved forward in single file except in dangerous Indian country, when a double column was used; each group of ten wagons had its lieutenant who kept the ranks closed and watched over his men as they plodded along. At 8:30 each evening the train halted after wheeling the wagons into a circle; supper and prayers took such a short time that by nine the whole camp was asleep.[9]

With such an efficient organization, the Pioneer Band moved rapidly. At the crossing of the North Platte they fashioned a boat which

[8] Charles Kelly (ed.), *Journals of John D. Lee, 1846–47 and 1859* (Salt Lake City, 1938), pp. 17–146.

[9] The best contemporary account of the migration is in William Clayton, *William Clayton's Journal* (Salt Lake City, 1921), pp. 81–315.

they not only used to cross the river themselves, but to ferry across another party bound for Oregon, in return for food and supplies, then left some of their number to operate a service for later comers. As they passed through South Pass they heard disquieting news; first an old trapper and then the Mountain Man, Jim Bridger, warned them that the valley of the Great Salt Lake was an arid desert that would support nothing but cactus and sagebrush. Bridger even offered Brigham Young a thousand dollars for the first bushel of corn grown there. A few miles beyond, temptation beckoned again. Near the Green River they met Elder Samuel Brannan, a Mormon leader who had taken 238 Saints to California by sea the year before, and who had come eastward now to urge them to follow him into the San Joaquin Valley. Once more Brigham Young refused to be deterred. "God has made the choice—not Brigham Young," he patiently explained.[10] Nor did a single Saint raise his voice in protest.

So they pressed on, past Fort Bridger, along the faint trace of the Hastings Cutoff, over the Bear River, as they neared the looming Wasatch Mountains. There, on July 12, Brigham Young took to his bed with "mountain fever," but he ordered Orson Pratt to take twenty-three wagons and push on. By July 14 this advance party was wending its way between the red-walled cliffs of Echo Canyon as it skirted the mountains, while canyon after canyon was explored for a passage through the barrier. Finally settling on the route the Donner party had followed, they labored with picks and spades to clear a way for their wagons as they climbed steadily upward, then crossed the summit to plunge into the narrow defile of Emigration Canyon. As this broadened near its western outlet, the Saints had their first glimpse of their future home. There was little in the sight to gladden their hearts. They saw only "a broad and barren plain hemmed in by mountains, blistering in the burning rays of the midsummer sun. No waving fields, no swaying forests, no verdant meadows . . . but on all sides a seemingly interminable waste of sagebrush . . . the paradise of the lizard, the cricket and the rattlesnake."[11]

[10] Paul D. Bailey, *Sam Brannan and the California Mormons* (Los Angeles, 1943), pp. 63–66.

[11] Orson F. Whitney, *History of Utah* (4 vols., Salt Lake City, 1892–1904), I, 325. According to Mormon legend, Young rose from his pallet on first sighting the valley and said: "This is the place." There is no contemporary evidence that he made such a remark, which was first attributed to him by Wilford Woodruff in 1880.

There was no hint of despair in such comments, for all had supreme faith that God would send rain if they remained faithful to His word. So Orson Pratt and eight others entered the valley on the morning of July 22, 1847, with joy in their hearts. Turning northward, as Young had instructed them, they camped on the banks of a clear stream which they called City Creek. The sun-baked earth shattered their plows at first, but when they flooded the ground they could plant with ease. By the time Brigham Young and the rest of the Pioneer Band arrived on July 24, all were busily planting potatoes, or building a dam across the creek to turn more water onto the land. That night a heavy rain fell, convincing the Saints of God's watchfulness. By the time the second caravan reached the valley on July 29, green fields welcomed them. A month later the third arrived, with 566 wagons and 1,500 men, women, and children. When migration ended that fall some 1,800 Saints lived on the shores of the Great Salt Lake, while 108 of the men had returned to Winter Quarters with Brigham Young to arrange the next year's migration.

That first year would have tried the souls of a less devout people. Only twenty-nine cabins had been built before winter struck; the rest of the Mormons lived in tents or dugouts or canvas-covered wagons which proved woefully inadequate against the cruel winds of that high country. Food was so scarce that the daily family ration of a handful of grain was supplemented with wild mustard, roots of the sego lily, thistles, and soup made from old oxhides. "I used to eat thistle stalks," one reminisced later, "until my stomach would be as full as a cow's." [12] With the spring of 1848 their spirits revived as all turned to planting the five-thousand-acre "Big Field" laid out the year before. But again fate was unkind. Late frosts killed part of their crop; in June swarms of black crickets descended in such multitudes that all seemed lost. In this darkest moment the Saints' prayers were answered when clouds of seagulls appeared to gorge on the insects, but half of all that had been planted was already destroyed. Even the crops that survived withered and died amidst the searing drought of July and August, for the Saints trusted to God to water their fields that year and paid little attention to irrigation. By autumn, as the prospect of another winter without decent food or shelter faced both older settlers and the 1,891 new-comers who reached the valley that year, some were beginning to

[12] Young, *Memoirs of John R. Young*, p. 64.

grumble that their leaders should forsake this "dry, worthless locality" for the greener lands of California or Oregon.[13] This was the situation that faced Brigham Young when he returned from the East on September 20, 1848. To one of his abilities, both the problem and its solution were clear. The Saints, he realized, had relied too much on God and too little on themselves. They could prosper in that inhospitable environment only by constant effort; this, moreover, must be a joint effort, for the forces of nature were too powerful to be combated by individuals. To secure this, leadership must be provided by the church, for such was the devotion of the Mormons that they would obey its dictates unquestioningly. Thus guided, they could be welded into an effective group in which the ambitions of each person were directed toward aiding society rather than himself. Only in this way could they make the desert bloom. This realization on the part of Brigham Young launched one of the most successful cooperative experiments in all history.

During that autumn, Young revealed his program to his followers. No longer, he told them, could each person live where he chose or farm as he wished. Instead they would dwell together and work together under the leadership of their church. Their homes would be in a great city that would follow a plan he and the Twelve Apostles had devised. This was of magnificent proportions; in the center was a Temple Square of ten acres; about this wide streets marked off blocks of the same size, each divided into eight lots for houses and gardens. These were surveyed by a committee under Brigham Young that fall, and each family assigned a plot. Work began at once on both homes and a giant temple which would, the Saints believed, "surpass in grandeur of design and gorgeousness of decoration all edifices the world has yet seen." [14] So rapidly did building go on that most families were living in snug adobe houses by the time winter struck, while fences had been built by cooperative effort, irrigation ditches dug beside each street, and trees planted everywhere.

Brigham Young also laid down principles that would govern farming in a message delivered on September 30, 1848. There would be no sale of land, he told them, and no private ownership of streams or

[13] James S. Brown, *Life of a Pioneer. Being the Autobiography of James S. Brown* (Salt Lake City, 1900), p. 120; John Brown, *Autobiography of Pioneer John Brown, 1820–1896* (Salt Lake City, 1941), p. 102.

[14] Howard R. Egan, *Pioneering the West, 1846 to 1878; Major Howard Egan's Diary* (Richmond, Utah, 1917), p. 125.

timber or anything else essential to the social welfare. "These," he said, "belong to the people: all the people." Instead each person would be given just the amount of land that he could till most effectively. A vigorous young man with a large family might be assigned forty or eighty acres, while an older farmer whose children had left home would be allotted only ten acres. "Do not be anxious to have large farms," Young told his people, ". . . but divide your lands with your brethren and make yourselves humble and happy." [15] All farming would be done in tiers of fields laid out around Salt Lake City. Nearby would be a band of five-acre plots for young artisans and mechanics who had little time to cultivate the soil; beyond would be ten-acre lots for those with larger families, and beyond these farms of from twenty to eighty acres. These plots were assigned by lot during October, 1848, and the work of fencing started.

Water was as essential as land in that arid country, as the Mormons had discovered during 1848. That Brigham Young could devise a workable irrigation system was truly remarkable, for the practice was completely foreign to the Anglo-American tradition, yet that put into operation during the autumn of 1848 was so efficient it might have been planned by a modern engineer. A main irrigation ditch was built by cooperative effort, leading from the mouth of Big Cottonwood Canyon through the farming lands. Side ditches were then dug, with bishops assigning each farmer an amount of work proportionate to the water he would use. When they were completed, water was allotted each user in rotation, with first the bishops and later elected "water masters" designating the exact time it could be drawn from the main ditch. In the use of water, as in the use of land, exacting supervision by the church assured society protection from greedy individuals.

This closely knit economic structure could operate successfully only if the governmental system provided absolute controls. The "Theo-Democracy" that Brigham Young proclaimed in 1848 was more a theocracy than a democracy, for it simply extended the rule of the church hierarchy over civil affairs. At its pinnacle was Young himself, in the office of the presidency, with supreme authority on all legislative and judicial as well as executive matters, as befitted one who alone understood the Divine will. Directly responsible to the president was the Quorum of Twelve Apostles, which supervised spiritual affairs,

[15] Quoted in Milton R. Hunter, *Brigham Young the Colonizer* (Salt Lake City, 1940), p. 140.

and the Presiding Bishopric, which ruled the temporal world of the Mormon community. These governed the large geographic units, the "Stakes," and the smaller "Wards" into which each "Stake" was divided. The bishop in each ward was the spiritual and temporal guide on all matters; he helped his people establish their homes, advised them on plowing or rearing their families, settled disputes among them, and gave them both material help and heavenly comfort when either was needed.

There was little room for popular rule in this system. True, all officers of the church were elected after being nominated by higher officials, but no Saint would think of voting against a candidate selected by God through Brigham Young. This gave the president absolute control over every subordinate down to the lowest ward bishop; the Mormon system was not a democracy but an oligarchy, "working under and deadening the forms of democracy," as one traveler put it.[16] This, to the Saints, was the ideal government. By delegating to Young complete control over their affairs, spiritual and temporal alike, they assured themselves the guidance of Divine will which he alone understood. Upon him they lavished the love of a child for its father, of a zealot for his God. No problem could be solved, no decision made, without "asking counsel" of this infinitely wise man. "An old woman," wrote an amused traveler, "will go to the president to know whether she had better change her old cloak for a tippet, or the new calf for a pig." [17] Nor was his judgment ever questioned, whether he was ordering one of his followers into a distant mission field or proclaiming a new religious doctrine. More remarkable was the fact that passing Gentiles found the Mormon governmental system so just they frequently submitted their own disputes to its courts for settlement, always with satisfaction.[18]

This theocratic state was first tested when the 1849 gold rush to California sent a stream of immigrants pouring through Salt Lake City. Brigham Young had little trouble stopping his people from joining the rush, partly because he explained that this was the Lord's will, partly because they found that greater profits could be made at home.

[16] William Chandless, *A Visit to Salt Lake* (London, 1857), p. 178.
[17] *Ibid.*, pp. 188–189.
[18] John W. Gunnison, *The Mormons, or, Latter-Day Saints, in the Valley of the Great Salt Lake* (Philadelphia, 1852), p. 65; J. Howard Stansbury, "Report to the Government on the Survey of the Great Salt Lake," 32nd Congress, Special Session, *Executive Document* No. 3, pp. 134–135.

Most of the forty-niners reached the Mormon settlements with over-loaded wagons and worn-out teams; they were willing to sell their surplus clothes, tools, and furniture at a fraction of cost, and to buy flour at one dollar a pound or pay $200 for a horse or mule that normally sold for $25. For a time the Saints enjoyed unexpected prosperity, but at the price of the isolation they had sought, for a number of newcomers settled among them. As Gentile population increased, Brigham Young realized that his simple church government must be displaced by one more suited to the needs of Saints and non-Saints alike, and at the same time acceptable to the United States. In forming these plans, Young had no thought of an independent republic, as his enemies charged; he was simply responding to the situation that had forced frontiersmen to form their own states from the days of the Mayflower Compact and Watauga Association down.

This became clear when a convention to deal with the problem met in March, 1849. Because Congress had failed to provide them with a civil government, they decided, they must form their own state. Deseret, they called it, from a term meaning "honeybee" in the Book of Mormon; its constitution was patterned after those of eastern states, with four-year terms for governor and members of the two-house legislature, manhood suffrage, religious toleration, and no mention of slavery.[19] Its boundaries were generous, extending from the Rockies to the Sierras and on to the Pacific in southern California. When the constitution was ratified on March 12, 1849, an election named Brigham Young governor and placed other church officials in all offices. "This intimate connection of church and state," wrote a non-Mormon, "seems to pervade every thing that is done. The supreme power in both being lodged in the hands of the same individuals, it is difficult to separate their two official characters and to determine whether in any one instance they act as spiritual or merely temporal officers." [20] When the legislature met on July 2, it devoted its nine-day session to a petition begging Congress to accept Deseret as a state.

This reached Washington when Congress was so busy debating the extension of slavery into lands acquired from Mexico that the troublesome Mormon religious issue was temporarily overlooked. Had congressmen been reminded of the Saints' polygamous doctrines, their

[19] The constitution is in Dale L. Morgan, "The State of Deseret," *Utah Historical Quarterly,* VIII (1940), 156–163.

[20] J. Howard Stansbury, *An Expedition to the Valley of the Great Salt Lake of Utah* (Philadelphia, 1852), pp. 131–133.

request would probably have been shelved indefinitely; instead their petition was transformed into one of the elements from which Henry Clay and Stephen A. Douglas fashioned the Compromise of 1850. Under this the Territory of Utah was created, with boundaries roughly those of Utah and Nevada today. The change in government was not extensive. Brigham Young was named territorial governor, with four of the officials under him Mormons and four Gentiles. Time soon showed that these four outsiders were powerless to meddle with Young's benevolent rule. As in the past, his word was law and his church supreme in both religious and secular matters. "Nominally," one Gentile wrote, "the civil authority is Utah: *de facto,* it is Deseret." [21]

To the Saints this was of vital importance, for they were now free to build their desert Zion under the official sanction of the United States. The first need was manpower, and to supply this converts must be lured to Utah. Wholesale missionary activities were launched in the autumn of 1849; within a few months hundreds of zealous Mormons were laboring in England, France, Italy, Denmark, Sweden, and the Society Islands; over the next years the program was extended to the rest of Europe, the Far East, and Latin America. Wherever they went their special appeal was to the poor and the dispossessed; to them was offered not only salvation but Heaven on earth in the valley of the Great Salt Lake. "Come . . . to the place of gathering," Brigham Young urged, "even in flocks, as doves fly to their windows before a storm." [22] The response was astounding. In England alone 32,894 converts were ready to depart by the end of 1851, while in the Scandinavian countries the appeal was almost as successful.

To aid these flocks in reaching the place of gathering, the Mormons devised a system of wondrous efficiency. A Perpetual Emigrating Fund, established in 1849, provided loans to all the needy, with the understanding that the money be returned after they reached Utah. Central embarkation points were designated in each country, where converts were allotted space on chartered ships or portions of vessels where they were apart from other passengers. Each group was assigned a leader who cared for every detail of their lives, from the assignment of sleeping space to the preparation of meals, as well as directing social activ-

[21] Thomas B. H. Stenhouse, *The Rocky Mountain Saints* (New York, 1873), p. 275.

[22] Quoted in Hunter, *Brigham Young,* p. 98.

ities, arranging dances or concerts, and conducting religious services. When the immigrants reached America, they were welcomed by agents who arranged passage to St. Louis; there other agents sent them on to Kanesville or Kansas City, where they were provided with teams and wagons and given instruction in plains travel.[23] Even on the trail they were not forgotten, for the Mormons maintained ferries across streams and outfitting posts at regular intervals. When they finally arrived in Utah work was provided until they were trained in desert life and ready to fit into society. Protected and encouraged at every step of their journey, the immigrants were transplanted from one social group to another half a world away with a minimum of hardship.

As the tide rolled toward Utah, reaching 4,225 persons in 1855, the financial burdens on the Mormons became so excessive that Brigham Young decided to experiment with a cheaper method of plains travel. Why not, he reasoned, substitute handcarts for expensive covered wagons? Pushing these, immigrants could average fifteen miles daily, crossing the plains in seventy days. That autumn Mormon carpenters in Iowa began building carts, which were waiting by the hundreds when new arrivals began flocking in during the spring of 1856. On June 9 and June 11 the first two companies of 497 persons, with one hundred handcarts, went rolling out of Iowa City, singing as they trudged along:

> Who cares to go with the wagons?
> Not we who are free and strong;
> Our faith and arms, with right good will,
> Shall pull our carts along.[24]

By September 26, 1856, they were in Salt Lake City, "somewhat fatigued," but still buoyant and cheerful, having outdistanced every wagon train on the trail. A third party arrived safely on October 2.[25]

Their happy fate was not shared by the other two "Handcart Brigades" that started west that summer. Delayed until carts could be completed for them, they did not leave until late in August. Breakdowns were frequent at first, as carpenters had used green lumber that

---

[23] The most complete description of these techniques is in James Linforth, *Route from Liverpool to Great Salt Lake Valley* (Liverpool, 1855), pp. 17–22.

[24] Stenhouse, *Rocky Mountain Saints*, p. 333.

[25] LeRoy R. Hafen, "Hand Cart Migration Across the Plains," in James F. Willard and Colin B. Goodykoontz (eds.), *The Trans-Mississippi West* (Boulder, Col., 1930), pp. 103–121; Jay Monaghan, "Handcarts on the Overland Trail," *Nebraska History*, XXX (1949), 3–18.

shrank in the arid plains air. Too, the carts were overloaded, for not enough wagons were available to carry heavier foodstuffs. They intended to replenish their stocks at Fort Laramie, only to find supplies exhausted there. So they pushed into South Pass on such short rations that children and older persons gave out under the strain, further slowing progress. In this weakened state, the brigades were caught by early winter snows. Deaths were frequent as they inched through the drifts; "we soon thought it unusual," one immigrant wrote, "to leave a campground without burying one or more persons." [26] Finally the towering drifts stopped them entirely and they settled down to wait, confident that Brigham Young would care for them. There they were found by a relief train sent out from Salt Lake City. Of the thousand Saints in the two parties, 225 perished in one of the major disasters of overland travel.

Such sacrifices were not in vain, for the eight thousand converts who reached Utah during the decade allowed Brigham Young to rear a commonwealth that assured the Mormons security for all time to come. His plan was boldly ambitious: he would occupy every site that could be irrigated, every spot where mineral or forest wealth was available, every strategic approach, in all the Great Basin. With that giant empire in the hands of the Saints, they would be free to live their own lives without fear of further persecution. "If the people of the United States will let us alone for ten years," he is reputed to have said, "we'll ask no odds of them." From the time the Pioneer Band reached the Great Salt Lake, Young had planned his colonization program, sending parties to explore the Bear River Valley, the beautiful shores of Lake Utah, and the regions southward to the tropical Virgin River country. From their reports Young compiled information on every spot where water made farming possible, or where mineral or forest wealth seemed promising.

Armed with this knowledge, he was ready to launch a program of expansion as soon as immigration provided man power. His colonization process was the most efficient in the history of the frontier. When a new outpost was to be planted, a party was sent out to survey town lots, locate irrigation ditches, and mark out farms. Then settlers were carefully selected, with a bishop at their head, and with a proper proportion of farmers, artisans, shopkeepers, millers, blacksmiths, and professional men. Care was taken, too, to include experienced colonizers

[26] Hafen, "Hand Cart Migration," p. 114.

as well as newcomers to Utah, who could profit by their example. All chosen cheerfully sold their homes and bade their friends farewell, for colonization was the expansion of God's kingdom and to share in such a divine task was compensation enough.[27]

Certainly expansion proceeded with an efficiency that suggested heavenly help. The process began in the winter of 1847–48, when a band of Saints was sent northward to buy lands in the Weber River valley from an old Mountain Man, Miles Goodyear; there the town of Ogden took shape. In 1849 the valley of Lake Utah was occupied with the founding of Provo and Fort Utah; before the year was out five other valleys were being peopled and twenty-six towns had been laid out. During 1851 another thrust southward led to the planting of Parowan in the Little Salt Lake Valley, and of Nephi and Fillmore in the San Juan and Pauvan valleys. To guard the fringes of this empire a band of pioneers was sent 550 miles westward along the route to San Francisco to establish Carson City under the shadow of the Sierra Nevada Mountains; another moved eastward to build Fort Supply on the road to South Pass and later to purchase Fort Bridger nearby. More ambitious was extension into the Southwest, for Young dreamed of a "Mormon corridor" through California to the Pacific. In 1851 the principal settlement along this route was established at San Bernardino in the fertile valley of southern California. By 1855 twenty additional towns had been founded along the "Corridor," including one at Las Vegas.[28] Slowly but surely the Saints were carving out their empire and guarding its approaches.

Within this domain they labored mightily to achieve economic independence from the hostile Gentile world. In each community farming was the principal occupation. At times—as during 1855—farmers suffered when black crickets descended in such clouds that the beat of their wings "resembled the passage of a train of cars on a railroad"; at others bitter winter winds carried off cattle or ruined crops. But these near-disasters were forgotten as orchards bloomed, cattle multiplied, and wheat production skyrocketed from 107,702 bushels in 1850 to 384,892 bushels a decade later.

Industry was as important to the Mormons as agriculture if they

[27] The process of colony planting is described by an observer in Stansbury, *Expedition to the Valley of the Great Salt Lake*, pp. 142–143, and by a modern scholar in Hunter, *Brigham Young*, pp. 55–60.

[28] Hunter, *Brigham Young*, pp. 361–366, lists and locates 358 towns founded by the Mormons between 1847 and 1877.

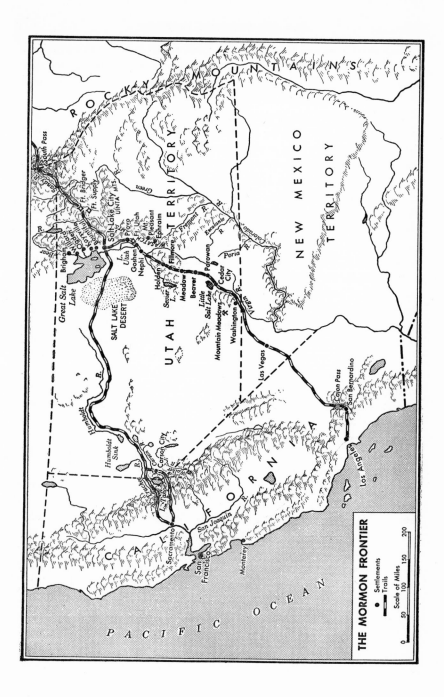

THE MORMON FRONTIER

● Settlements
— Trails

Scale of Miles
0   50   100   150   200

were to win economic independence, but here they were less successful. Certainly the will was there. In 1852 the territorial legislature offered $1,000 to the person who would "produce the greatest quantity of manufactured goods of good quality," while four years later the Deseret Agricultural and Manufacturing Society was organized to "encourage the production of articles from the native elements of this Territory." [29] Thus inspired, Mormons built saw- and gristmills, opened a pottery works, and began textile production. Others erected a small blast furnace near Parowan, where iron ore was discovered, but not even the dedicated devotion of the Saints could overcome the handicaps that faced them, and by 1856 mining was at a standstill. The industrial development of Utah was forced to wait until capital and manpower were available in larger quantities.[30]

Although the Mormon Church failed to effect economic miracles, it did create a social and intellectual atmosphere in Utah Territory markedly different from that of any other frontier. This, to Brigham Young, was as important as physical prosperity. Properly directed social activities would solidify the group consciousness of the people, keep them happy and contented, quicken their religious interests, and provide relief from the drabness of life in a new community. These were proper objectives for a church dedicated to the improvement of man's lot in this world as well as the next. So bishops in each community arranged evening lectures on everything from stock raising to literature; organized a Deseret Literary and Musical Association, a Polysophical Society, and a Horticultural Society; and played a prominent role in founding the Deseret Theological Institute in 1855, with branches in every community where men and women could gather for social intercourse. In lighter vein they planned dances, from elaborate balls in Salt Lake City to Friday-night gatherings in the smallest hamlets, for the Mormons had none of the prejudices against such pleasures exhibited by their Protestant brethren of that day.

Intellectual life was as rigidly prescribed and as enthusiastically stimulated as social activity, for Mormons believed that God had gone through a period of corporal existence before becoming the Supreme

[29] Delila G. Hughes, *The Life of Archibald Gardner, Pioneer of 1847* (West Jordan, Utah, 1939), p. 42.

[30] The economy is described in Andrew L. Neff, *History of Utah, 1847–1869* (Salt Lake City, 1940), p. 238, and Leland H. Creer, *The Founding of an Empire: The Exploration and Colonization of Utah, 1776–1856* (Salt Lake City, 1947), pp. 338–341.

Intelligence, and that man could enjoy a similar evolution by improving his own mind. "It is impossible," stated the basic creed, "for a man to be saved in ignorance." [31] Yet strive as they did, the Saints were unable to surmount the obstacles of poverty and materialism that slowed cultural growth on every frontier. The gulf between theory and practice was especially clear in their school system. Schools were opened in every new community, and were attended by the old as well as the young, but most were poorly manned and worse equipped, while efforts at improvement were steadfastly resisted. Thus when an attempt was made to extend the school year beyond three months, parents insisted that their children were needed in farm and shop. Nor did higher education fare better, for a University of Deseret that opened in a private home in February, 1850, expired a year later with no mourners to follow it to the grave. Only a more mature social order could support such institutions.

Efforts to stimulate reading among Mormons also succumbed to the inhospitable frontier atmosphere. A newspaper, the *Deseret News,* began publication in June, 1850, but paper was so scarce that it remained a tiny, uninfluential sheet until after the Civil War. Books were also rarely found in Mormon homes, although Brigham Young urged immigrants to bring any volumes they owned, and many responded by tucking "an old text book among the blankets." Yet not a bookstore existed in Utah in 1855, and libraries and reading rooms were conspicuous by their absence. Only in the realms of music and the theater did the Saints show any cultural interest. In every community choirs were formed, while some boasted bands as well. Salt Lake City had an amateur theatrical company as early as 1850, and five years later opened its first theater for performances that ranged from the plays of Shakespeare to such ear-offending offerings as *Luke the Laborer.* In Provo, Parowan, and other towns dramatic performances were given by local companies before the close of the decade.[32]

The social and intellectual progress of the Mormons demonstrated, as effectively as did their economic development, the ability of a strongly centralized social group to vary, but not upset, the normal

[31] *The Doctrine and Covenants of the Church of Jesus Christ of Latter-Day Saints, containing the Revelations given to Joseph Smith, the Prophet* (Salt Lake City, 1923), Sec. 131:6.

[32] William J. McNiff, *Heaven on Earth: A Planned Mormon Society* (Oxford, Ohio, 1940), *passim,* is the best description of Mormon social and intellectual life.

frontier pattern. Dominated by an all-powerful church, the Saints were directed into social activities and cultural pursuits that their leaders felt would be beneficial, just as they were regimented to found towns or industries essential to the community. Yet no amount of prodding could overcome the cultural apathy normal among people who lacked both leisure and an educational heritage, any more than such pressure could establish an iron-manufacturing plant when skilled workers and adequate capital were lacking. The Mormon community was hurried along the path to civilization by Brigham Young and his cohorts, but not even they could deny a frontier environment its corrosive effects.

To make matters worse for those planning a desert renaissance, the Saints were not destined to enjoy their new-won isolation long. As the United States began exploiting its newly acquired territories in the Southwest, first friction and then interference from the East were inevitable. Such conflicts between frontier communities and older societies were normal, but in Utah they were unusually intense. To Americans, the Saints were immoral eccentrics bent on establishing their own commonwealth; to Mormons, their fellow countrymen were persecuting bigots plotting the complete destruction of Mormonism. In this atmosphere of mutual suspicion, the first contacts were certain to blossom into a conflict of unbelievable intensity.

Hard feelings began to develop when overland emigrants spread tales of the merciless prices charged by the Mormons, little knowing that these were normal "mountain prices." Distrust mounted when official United States surveyors, seeking a route for a transcontinental railroad, entered Utah Territory. Rumors that their purpose was the destruction of all land titles hardly assured them a cordial reception, yet trouble might have been avoided had not a party under Captain John W. Gunnison been attacked by Indians in 1853, with a loss of eight men. The Mormons had no part in this massacre, but this the people of the United States refused to believe. These incidents prepared the way for a major conflict over control of Utah. Brigham Young, with the support of a vast majority of the settlers, dominated the executive and legislative branches of the territorial government from his post as governor. In 1852 he extended church rule over the judicial branch as well as by prodding the legislature into creating local courts with original jurisdiction over both civil and criminal cases, thus depriving federal courts of all business. From this time on he was completely supreme.

This tight little monopoly was challenged in 1855 when three federal judges were appointed for the Utah Territory. Few worse jurists could have been found; two were apostate Mormons who hated their former brethren, and the third, W. W. Drummond, was a political appointee who made no secret of his low opinion of the Saints. Hence, when they reached the territory Mormons continued to take their cases to the county courts while the federal judges presided over empty rooms. For a time they endured these insults, then in the spring of 1857 hurried back to Washington breathing fire at every step. Brigham Young, Judge Drummond charged, was a ruthless dictator who employed a band of "destroying angels" to stamp out all who disobeyed him. Federal officials were "constantly insulted, harrassed and annoyed"; some had been killed and countless government records destroyed.[33] The absurdity of these charges was obvious to any rational being, but prejudice too often ruled over reason where the Saints were concerned. Too, Judge Drummond's widely heralded statement coincided with others: a stagecoach operator who had lost his mail contract to a more efficient Mormon contractor charged they were plotting to kill all Gentiles; an Indian agent on the Upper Platte hinted that the red men were being armed to aid in the massacre. In the wake of these warnings, public opinion flamed against the Saints. The time had come, everyone agreed, to let them know they were not as powerful as the American government.

Even now the imagined differences might have been resolved but for a changing atmosphere among the Mormons. During the winter of 1856–57 a fiery religious revival—"The Reformation," they called it—swept their ranks. This began in the little town of Kaysville, twenty-five miles from Salt Lake City, when the congregation gathered on September 13, 1856, to hear a sermon by Jedediah M. Grant, second counselor to Brigham Young. Annoyed because some mules he had loaned to neighbors had been abused, Grant lashed out at the Saints for their hypocrisy and carelessness, calling on them to repent and "do their first works over again." His words struck a responsive chord, for crops had been poor and uncertainty was in the air. So the flame

[33] 35th Congress, 1st Session, *House Executive Document* No. 71, pp. 212–214. These events are described in Leland H. Creer, *Utah and the Nation* (Seattle, 1929), pp. 115–127.

spread, gaining in fanaticism as it moved from village to village. Grant added to the fire a short time later when he urged his overwrought listeners to "have your blood shed to atone for your sins." Overnight this doctrine of "blood atonement" raged across Utah, as elders roamed the land urging all to seek forgiveness, even by shedding their own blood.[34] A people thus plunged into fanaticism was hardly equipped to use diplomacy in settling conflicts with Gentiles, nor did exaggerated tales of bloodspilling which reached the East lessen the hostility universal there.

Amidst this inflammatory atmosphere, President Buchanan decided the time had come to assert federal authority over the Saints. On May 26, 1857, he ordered a force of 2,500 men under Colonel Albert Sidney Johnston to march against Utah; three weeks later the force started westward. News of its coming sent the Mormons into a flurry of fear and preparation. They believed that the soldiers were coming to kill them, destroy their property, and ravage their wives; "Beauty and Booty," it was whispered, was the slogan of the troops. Better to die than accept such a fate. So they talked among themselves as they rallied to Brigham Young's call. Some were hurried east or west to urge Saints everywhere to rally for the defense of their Zion; at San Bernardino, at Carson City, and elsewhere, towns were abandoned as their inhabitants flooded into Salt Lake City. Others were sent eastward to delay the approaching army by raiding its supply trains, driving off its stock, and burning the grass before it. Still more were ordered to defend the passes through the Wasatch Mountains, while those left at home packed their houses with dried straw that could be ignited when the army entered the valley. "There shall not be," Brigham Young declared, "one building, nor one foot of lumber, nor a stick, nor a tree, nor a particle of grass and hay that will burn, left in reach of our enemies." [35]

Guerrilla attacks on Johnston's approaching forces began in late September, 1857, when the troops were twenty miles east of Fort Bridger. Every stray animal was driven off by Mormon bands, trains of wagons loaded with food were put to the torch, and the grass

[34] Stenhouse, *Rocky Mountain Saints*, pp. 392–394.

[35] Matthias Cowley, *Wilford Woodruff, Fourth President of the Church of Jesus Christ of Latter-Day Saints, History of His Life and Letters as Recorded in His Daily Journals* (Salt Lake City, 1909), pp. 383–410; Creer, *Utah and the Nation*, p. 135.

burned for miles around until no fodder was left for horses or oxen.[36]
Not until November 17, 1857, did the army struggle into Fort Bridger
amidst a blinding snowstorm, having taken two weeks to cover the last
thirty-four miles. All hope of pushing on to Utah was gone now;
instead, Johnston ordered his men into winter camp.

The harm was done, however, for the army's approach had raised
tensions among the Mormons so high that panic rather than reason
governed their reactions. The result was the Mountain Meadows Massacre. This occurred in the southern part of the territory, where the
reformation spirit raged uncontrolled. In this mood the Saints were
visited by a band of 140 emigrants bound for California. Most were
respectable farmers from Arkansas, but traveling with the party was a
group of "Missouri Wild Cats" who abused Indian converts, turned
their cattle into Mormon fields, killed chickens with their bull whips,
and shouted profane insults at Mormon women in which the word
"whore" was frequently used. Near Cedar City their inexcusable conduct aroused the Indians to the point of attack. This came on September 7, 1857, when the emigrants were camped in an open valley
named Mountain Meadows. Seven were killed before the red men
were beaten back and a barricade of wagons formed. Then the two
forces settled down for what promised to be a long siege.[37]

While this went on, both sides sought aid. Three emigrants tried to
slip through the lines, but two were cut down by the Indians and the
third, William Aiden, was killed by a fanatical Mormon. The Indians
were more successful. A delegation hurried to the home of John D.
Lee, a farmer who had worked among them as a missionary. Lee, instead of trying to restrain the red men, sent a message to Cedar City
asking for reinforcements. Fifty men responded. On September 10
these Saints gathered to decide their course: should they help the
emigrants, or should they aid the Indians in their bloody work? The
memory of insults shouted by the Missouri Wild Cats, the tensions of
the hour, and the fear that they would be blamed for the murder of
William Aiden carried the day. Every emigrant must be killed, they
decided, to prevent news of that murder from reaching California.

---

[36] Journals kept by Mormon raiders are in John Crook, "John Crook's Jour-
nal," *Utah Historical Quarterly,* VI (1933), 58–60, and Jesse W. Crosby,
"History and Journal of the Life and Travels of Jesse W. Crosby," *Annals of
Wyoming,* XI (1939), 211–214.

[37] The standard account of the massacre is Juanita Brooks, *The Mountain
Meadows Massacre* (Stanford, 1950), *passim.*

The next day their grim plan was put into effect. John Lee entered
the camp with word that a safe passage had been arranged through
the Indian lines. As the emigrants marched out the Mormons began
firing, killing the men while the Indians were given a free hand with
the women and children. Within a few minutes 120 persons lay dead,
while seventeen children had been saved. Before scattering, the Saints
bound themselves to spread the tale that the whites had been mas-
sacred by red men.[38]

The American people, however, laid the Mountain Meadows Massacre at the door of the Mormon church. Throughout the United
States editorial writers screamed their indignation and demanded that
the "beastly heresy" of Mormonism be crushed forever. President
Buchanan reflected the hysteria when he asked for four additional
regiments to be sent to Utah. "This," he declared, "is the first rebellion
which has existed in our territories, and humanity itself requires that
we should put it down in such a manner that it shall be the last." [39]
These warlike gestures only drove the Mormons to more fanatical
resistance. All that winter they drilled, or manufactured gunpowder, or
prepared to burn their homes as they retreated, even to Mexico, to
escape their oppressors. Both sides in this useless conflict knew that
spring would bring victory or death.

That further bloodshed was avoided was due to the intervention of
a self-appointed peacemaker. Thomas L. Kane, a Philadelphia lawyer,
had been a stanch friend of the Mormons since the Nauvoo persecutions interested him in their plight. During the winter of 1857–58 he
offered himself as mediator to President Buchanan, and was allowed
to conduct negotiations on his own authority. He reached the Saints'
capital on February 25, 1858, and there had little difficulty persuading
Brigham Young to receive the newly appointed territorial governor,
Alfred Cumming, providing the army did not enter the valley.[40] Thus
armed, Kane hurried to Colonel Johnston's headquarters at Fort
Bridger, where he convinced Governor Cumming to return with him.
The two men, accompanied only by two servants, arrived at Salt Lake

[38] The events are described by a participant in John D. Lee, *Mormonism
Unveiled; or the Life and Confessions of the Late Mormon Bishop, John D.
Lee* (St. Louis, 1877), pp. 213–293, which reproduces his confession.

[39] J. D. Richardson (ed.), *Compilation of the Messages and Papers of the
Presidents, 1798–1897* (10 vols., Washington, 1897), V, 456.

[40] Winther (ed.), *Private Papers and Diary of Kane*, pp. 65–77; Oscar O.
Winther, "Thomas L. Kane, Unofficial Emissary to the Mormons," *Indiana Historical Bulletin,* XV (1938), 83–90.

City on April 12, 1858. Brigham Young received them warmly; the new governor was told that his authority would be respected and every aid tendered him in his duties. But when Cumming told four thousand Mormons assembled in the Tabernacle that Colonel Johnston's army must be allowed to occupy their land, the harm was done.

Suddenly, almost unaccountably, panic swept northern Utah. Throughout the land families packed their belongings, loaded their wagons, and started south toward safety. In all some thirty thousand persons joined this mad rush; within two months northern Utah was deserted save for bands of men left behind to fire buildings and crops when the enemy appeared.[41] As news of this "Grand Move" filtered east, a rapid reversal of sentiment occurred there. Overnight the Saints became martyrs, ready to sacrifice all they possessed to worship God in their own way. This shift in opinion, combined with Governor Cumming's friendly reception by Brigham Young, convinced President Buchanan that peaceful gestures should be made. On April 6, 1858, he offered full pardon to all Mormons who would submit to the authority of the United States, and at the same time hurried two peace commissioners westward. After two days of negotiations, it was agreed that the army should enter Utah but camp at least forty miles from Salt Lake City, and that the territory should accept civilian officials.[42]

Thus did the tragic and useless "Mormon War" come to an end. On June 26, 1858, Johnston's troops marched through the deserted city on their way to Camp Floyd, where they remained until called east by the outbreak of the Civil War. The Mormons, by unwavering devotion to their God and unswerving allegiance to their leaders, had won the respect, if not the affection, of their rulers in Washington. From that day on they were allowed to develop their desert Zion in peace; for while Gentile governors might sit over them, their true leader was Brigham Young. His genius had transformed Utah Territory from a barren desert to a thriving frontier community; his leadership in the future would help mold the higher civilization that was Utah's destiny.

[41] Cumming's report describing these events is in 35th Congress, 2nd Session, *Senate Executive Document* No. 1, Pt. II, pp. 91–97.

[42] The commissioners' report is in *ibid.*, pp. 167–168.

CHAPTER 10

The California Gold Rush

THE trickle of population flowing westward over the trails to Oregon, California, and the Great Salt Lake country was swelled to a flood by an accidental event—the discovery of flakes of yellow metal in one of the rivers that cascaded westward from the Sierras. Gold had been rumored to exist, and had been found, in a dozen spots, without arousing more than a ripple of interest. But suddenly, unaccountably, the whole nation caught fire now. Overnight the wildest mining rush in history was under way, and before it subsided one hundred thousand men had been swept westward, to transform California from a half-tamed wilderness to a settled commonwealth. The rush of the forty-niners was primarily responsible for the conquest of America's most westerly frontier.

For the discovery, John A. Sutter was indirectly responsible. As pioneers clustered about his famous fort in the lower Sacramento Valley, his economic activities multiplied and with them his greed for more profits. Mindful of the demand for lumber created by the influx, he determined to build a sawmill in the Sierra foothills where timber and water power were advantageously combined. James W. Marshall, a moody eccentric whose strange ways had earned him the title of "queer old codger" despite his thirty-five years, was sent eastward to supervise construction in the Coloma Valley of the American River, some forty miles from Sutter's Fort. In January, 1848, tests showed that the millrace must be deepened before water pressure would turn the twelve-foot wheel. While Marshall was inspecting progress on this excavation on the morning of January 24, his sharp eyes detected the glint of yellow metal at the bottom of the stream. Curious, he collected several samples, which responded to every test for gold that he knew.[1]

Sutter, when informed of the find, was concerned only that the news be kept secret until his mill was completed, but that proved impossible. Still there was no excitement for another month. The workers finished the mill faithfully, although they did use their spare time to scrape up gold with their knives. Some were members of the disbanded Mormon Battalion. Their letters to friends attracted a few curiosity seekers, who began prospecting nearby, then wandered on to a spot along the American River twenty-five miles away where more gold was found. On March 7 the first of Marshall's men deserted to start mining at these Mormon Diggings, as they came to be known. Clearly all would soon be infected with the fever. So Sutter reasoned as he quietly began leasing sites along streams from the Indians and preparing to start mining himself.

He acted none too soon. Early in May the miners at Mormon Diggings were visited by Sam Brannan, a prominent Mormon who owned various San Francisco properties as well as a store near Sutter's Fort. Perhaps because he hoped to create business for his store, perhaps because he had succumbed to the fever, Brannan returned to San Francisco in mid-May, wildly excited. Rushing through the plaza with a bottle of dust in his hand, he shouted to all who would listen: "Gold! Gold! GOLD from the American River." [2] Sophisticated San Franciscans, who for two months had read accounts of the discoveries at Coloma and Mormon Diggings in their newspapers without showing any interest, suddenly were swept by the gold fever. "Never, I think," wrote a resident, "has there been such excitement in any country of the world." [3] Overnight carpenters dropped their hammers, masons

[1] Marshall's own account of the discovery, "The Discovery of Gold in California," *Hutchings' Illustrated California Magazine*, II (1857–58), 194–195, is less authentic than that of one of his companions, James S. Brown, *California Gold: An Authentic History of the First Find* (Oakland, Calif., 1894), pp. 8–18. The most complete modern history of the event is Aubrey Neasham, "Sutter's Sawmill," in *California Gold Discovery: Centennial Papers of the Time, the Site and Artifacts* (San Francisco, 1947), pp. 3–27.

[2] This scene, which is described in Hubert H. Bancroft, *History of California* (7 vols., San Francisco, 1884–90), VI, 56, rests only on tradition, although the reminiscences of three witnesses record that Brannan did display a bottle of dust and swing his hat while "shouting aloud in the streets." James A. B. Scherer, *The First Forty-Niner and the Story of the Gold Tea-Caddy* (New York, 1925), pp. 51–52.

[3] Walter Colton, *Three Years in California* (New York, 1850), pp. 247–248.

their trowels, bakers their loaves, clerks their pens, to rush to the American River. Schools were closed as both teachers and pupils deserted; shopkeepers hung signs on their doors—"Gone to the Diggings," "Off to the Mines"—and disappeared. By June 15 San Francisco was a ghost town, with houses and shops empty, and all who could walk, ride, run, or crawl rushing toward the Sierras.

From there the contagion spread over northern California, and beyond. During June, Sonoma, San José, Monterey, and Santa Cruz succumbed; at Monterey so many deserting sailors and soldiers joined the rush that not a utensil capable of holding sand and water could be had at any price. Santa Barbara and Los Angeles began stirring with excitement in July, as did the Hawaiian Islands. Within a few weeks natives from southern California and Kanakas from the Islands were pouring into the mines, to be joined soon by Mexicans from Sonora Province as word spread there in August. About the same time the influx from Oregon began, to continue until two thirds of the territory's able-bodied males were in the mines. "The whole country," lamented a San Francisco editor as he announced the suspension of his paper because of lack of readers, "from San Francisco to Los Angeles, and from the sea shore to the base of the Sierra Nevadas, resounds with the sordid cry of '*gold!* GOLD! GOLD!' while the field is left half planted, the house half built, and everything neglected but the manufacture of shovels and pickaxes." [4]

As the gold-seekers swept over the Sierra foothills, excitement was constantly rekindled by new discoveries. Lumbermen cutting timber ten miles north of Coloma observed that the country resembled that where gold was found, began digging, and opened mines on a spot dubbed Weberville. A farmer on the Feather River noted a similar parallel, and found rich deposits on that stream. A rancher found pockets of metal on Clear Creek; others successfully prospected the Stanislaus and Mokelumne rivers of the lower San Joaquin Valley and the valley of the Shasta far to the north. As word of each "strike" spread, a rush to that spot occurred, until nearly ten thousand miners were busily grubbing away in a belt of hilly land that extended 150 miles from the Feather River on the north to the Tuolumne River on the south. Nearly all were Californians or from Oregon, with a sprin-

[4] *The Californian,* May 29, 1848, quoted in Rodman W. Paul, *California Gold: The Beginning of Mining in the Far West* (Cambridge, Mass., 1947), p. 19.

kling of Mexicans and Hawaiian natives. The first phase of the rush was a local affair.

Few had any knowledge of mining, but none was needed as the surface wealth was skimmed away. "Crevice mining" was universally used at first; working with knives and spoons in dry gulches or ravines, the men scraped away surface dirt, then spooned out dust or dug out nuggets of the prized metal. The more ambitious shoveled gravel from former river beds until they reached bed rock, where they frequently found "pockets" of gold that could be lifted out by the handful. This was then "winnowed" by tossing in a blanket while the wind blew away the dirt, leaving the heavy gold dust behind. "Dry washing" was extremely wasteful, but why bother about losses when more gold could be had for the taking?

By the closing months of the 1848 season some miners were shifting from "dry diggings" to "wet diggings" and more efficient practices. Gold, they soon found, was plentiful not only in dry beds of former streams, but in rivers and creeks as well. It could be separated from gravel and sand by using a "washing pan," a shallow metal vessel introduced into California during the summer by Isaac Humphrey, an experienced miner from Georgia. Filled with "pay dirt," this was submerged in a stream and gently rotated while water carried away the light gravels, leaving the gold behind. The work was cruelly difficult, for each pan had to be held under numbingly cold water for ten or twelve minutes, but this mattered little when half a cup of gold was the reward. Isaac Humphrey also built the first "cradle" in California that summer. This simple device consisted of an oblong box mounted on rockers; dirt was shoveled into a hopper at one end, water was poured in, and the cradle rocked violently until the sand was washed away and the heavier gold captured by cleats along the bottom. Three or four men with a cradle could wash out as much dirt as a dozen with washing pans.

This was important in the lush early days of the California mines, for some finds were unbelievably rich. Two men took $17,000 in dust and nuggets from one canyon; in eight days five men at Mormon Diggings made a profit of $1,800; a lone prospector on the Yuba River panned out $5,356 in sixty-four days; an editor touring the mines averaged $100 daily by pausing now and then to use his washing pan. Such fortunes fell to few men, although profits of from $300 to $500 a day for short periods were not uncommon. On the whole, miners in

1848 averaged about one ounce of dust daily, worth about $20, but this was a handsome wage when laborers in the East were paid only one dollar a day. Even the exorbitant prices charged for the necessities of life—flour at $400 a barrel, sugar at $4 a pound, whisky at $20 a quart, picks and shovels at $10 each—could be cheerfully endured when such earnings were certain and a fortune-making strike always possible.[5]

Best of all, operations in 1848 had barely touched a vast mining country that still waited exploitation. This extended in a wide belt from LaPorte on the north to Mariposa on the south, and was called the Mother Lode. Here in past ages the earth's convulsions had shattered the surface crust, allowing masses of molten magma from the interior to pour upward. This had hardened into rocks that formed the core of the Sierra range, but separating the rocks were veins of copper, tungsten, and gold. Over the course of centuries erosion had carried these metals into streams where they were ground into small pieces and deposited, the heavier chunks high in the river bed, the lighter farther down. The miners understood little geology, but they did reason that more and more "placer gold," as they called the dust and nuggets, would be found as they followed rivers toward their sources. The prospect of such finds filled their dreams during the winter months.

These golden visions were never realized, for the spring of 1849 brought such a rush of miners to California that not even the riches of the Mother Lode could provide for them all. The East first heard of Marshall's discovery on August 19, 1848, when the New York *Herald* printed a letter describing the event and reporting that prospectors were making thirty dollars daily, but neither this nor later dribbles of information created even a flurry of interest. Both editors and their readers were skeptical; speculators had invented so many similar stories to lure the gullible westward in the past that they refused to be fooled.[6] But when President James K. Polk devoted a paragraph in his December 5, 1848, message to Congress to an enthu-

---

[5] A long letter on the subject of prices is in Walker D. Wyman (ed.), *California Emigrant Letters* (New York, 1952), pp. 23–26.

[6] Newspaper extracts reflecting this point of view are collected in Ralph P. Bieber (ed.), *Southern Trails to California in 1849* (Glendale, Calif., 1937), pp. 51–56, 67–100, 116–125. The best discussion of the subject is Ralph P. Bieber, "California Gold Mania," *Mississippi Valley Historical Review*, XXXV (1948), 16–22.

siastic account of California mining, the whole nation was filled with excitement. "The accounts of the abundance of gold in that territory," the President reported, "are of such an extraordinary character as would scarcely command belief were they not corroborated by the authentic reports of officers in the public service." [7] As if to lend weight to these words, an agent sent east by Governor Richard B. Mason of California reached Washington just two days later, carrying a tea caddy crammed with 230 ounces of pure gold. When this was placed on display in the War Office, the last skepticism vanished.

Not even the most rational man could keep his sanity now. Editors, as though to compensate for their earlier doubts, filled their columns with caution-shattering phrases: "the Eldorado of the old Spaniards is discovered at last"; "we are on the brink of the Age of Gold"; "now have the dreams of Cortez and Pizarro become realized." [8] Lecturers told eager audiences of miners who averaged $1,000 daily or of soil so rich that every handful contained half an ounce of pure gold. Guidebooks appeared as if by magic; during the winter of 1848–49 some thirty were published, most of them by hack writers who employed imagination rather than knowledge to inflame their readers. A typical volume described an Indian who had found a lump of gold as large as his fist which he gladly traded for a red sash, of a mine that paid $20,000 in six days, of a stream bed solid with metal that could be flaked away with a pickax.[9] So extravagant were these claims that when a humorist told of a miner who had been sitting on an 839-pound nugget for sixty-seven days to keep it from being stolen, and was at last reports offering $27,000 for a plate of pork and beans, some were inclined to take him seriously.[10]

Amidst the feverish atmosphere created by this barrage, California's mines became the topic of the day. Merchants did a land-office business in rough clothes, broad felt hats, bowie knives, shovels, and a fantastic array of mining machinery ranging from patented cradles to "goldometers" guaranteed to reveal hidden wealth. Pawnbrokers were

[7] Polk's message is in 30th Congress, 2nd Session, *House Executive Document* No. 1, pp. 10–15.

[8] Bieber, "California Gold Mania," p. 21.

[9] Henry I. Simpson, *The Emigrant's Guide to the Gold Mines* (New York, 1848), pp. 7, 14, 16–17; David T. Arnsted, *The Gold-Seeker's Manual* (London, 1849), p. 102.

[10] Fred W. Lorch, "Iowa and the California Gold Rush of 1849," *Iowa Journal of History,* XXX (1932), 321–333, reprints this and similar stories from Iowa newspapers.

inundated with watches, rings, and every possible item that could be hocked as men raised money to pay their passage west. Ministers devoted sermons to the evils of Sunday travel or pleaded with soon-to-be-departed parishioners not to leave their morals at the Missouri. Daguerreotype operators reaped small fortunes from those wanting to leave a handsome likeness with loved ones. Even musicians leaped upon the band wagon with such numbers as "The Gold Digger's Waltz" and "The Sacramento Gallop." All America was deliciously, deliriously, delightfully mad as it sang

> Oh Susannah, don't you cry for me,
> I'm gone to California with my wash-bowl on my knee

and made the last hurried preparations to depart for the gold fields.

First to leave were those who could afford passage on one of the leaky vessels rescued from well-earned retirement to collect the exorbitant sums that gold-seekers would gladly pay. By mid-December, 1848, the docks at New York and Philadelphia and Boston were jammed with starry-eyed men and teary-eyed women as ship after ship sailed away. "I say, Bill," shouted a friend to a would-be miner, "if you send me a barrel of Gold Dust don't forget to pay the freight on it." Another, as the vessel left the dock, tossed his last five-dollar gold piece overboard with, "I'm going where there is plenty more!" [11] The rush had begun.

Those who went by sea had their choice of the "Panama Route" or the "Cape Route." The first was favored by those who could pay $380, largely because they would reach the gold fields in weeks rather than months—or so they were told. The journey from New York to Chagres in Panama was novel enough to be exciting; travelers could wear their new flannel shirts and heavy boots, and pepper passing dolphins with their shiny new revolvers. But at Chagres, a steaming cluster of mud huts holding back the jungle, hardships began. First they haggled with natives for canoe transportation up the Chagres River. Then for two days they made their way inland amidst constant rainfall and oppressive heat, marched another two days through a snake-ridden jungle, and at last reached the ancient city of Panama on the shores of the Pacific, where they settled down amidst heat, moisture, and filth to wait a ship to San Francisco.

[11] Katherine A. White (ed.), *A Yankee Trader in the Gold Rush; the Letters of Franklin A. Buck* (New York, 1930), p. 31.

The wait was always long. On January 17, 1849, the first vessel of the Pacific Mail Line reached Panama, to find seven hundred gold-seekers clamoring for the 250 places available. By trickery, bribery, mayhem, and overpayment—one paid $1,000 for steerage passage—365 passengers managed to cram aboard, reaching San Francisco a month later. This scene was repeated over and over again in the year ahead, with the backlog at Panama City numbering hundreds and graves in the American cemetery multiplying daily. Yet the Panama Route continued to be popular, as miners were assured they could reach California in from six to eight weeks.

For those who preferred comfort to speed, the Cape Horn Route was favored. Some paid passage on freight vessels bound for the coast, but more would-be miners formed companies, sold stock to raise money, and chartered either an entire vessel or space aboard a larger ship.[12] The days that followed combined dreary monotony with unbelievable discomfort. For weeks they sailed southward, then spent as many as two or three months beating their way around the Horn amidst tempestuous waves, then faced another eon of boredom as the ship plowed northward toward the Golden Gate. By the time they arrived the companies formed in the East had succumbed to conflicts inevitable on such a voyage, and the men piled ashore to face that strange new world alone. Some had money enough to pay the outrageous fares demanded for steamship passage to Sacramento or Stockton, the western gateways to the Mother Lode country, but more had to hunt jobs or auction off the last of their meager belongings to raise the sums necessary. "A graduate of Yale," wrote an observer, "considers it no disgrace to sell peanuts on the *Plaza,* a disciple of Coke and Blackstone to drive a mule-team, nor a New York poet to sell the *New York Tribune* at 50 cents a copy." [13]

Perhaps 25,000 miners reached California in 1849 over the Cape Horn or Panama routes, but they were a mere handful compared with the thousands who preferred the overland trails. The principal attraction of land travel was financial; young men from the Mississippi Valley could borrow the family wagon and oxen, lay in a few dollars'

[12] The 124 companies that left Massachusetts are described in Octavius T. Howe, *Argonauts of '49. History and Adventure of the Emigrant Companies from Massachusetts, 1848–1850* (Cambridge, Mass., 1923), pp. 46–135.

[13] Samuel C. Upham, *Notes of a Voyage to California via Cape Horn, together with Scenes in El Dorado, in the Years 1849–'50* (Philadelphia, 1878), p. 226.

worth of food, and start west with no other investment save their own brawn and bravery. No one knows exactly how many did so, but the best estimates indicate that more than 80,000 persons reached California during 1849. Of these probably 55,000 went overland, 45,000 along the central trail through South Pass, and the remainder over either the Santa Fe route, the Southern Route via El Paso, or one of several trails that crossed northern Mexico.[14]

Whatever the route, all who traveled overland spent the winter of 1848–49 in breathless excitement. Some sought odd jobs to raise money necessary for supplies; others fitted the hickory bows and white canvas that would convert the farm wagon into a "prairie schooner," or spent happy hours wrapping bacon and sugar and flour in waterproof packages. All used every leisure moment poring over guidebooks and planning their routes on the information—or misinformation—that they gleaned. Few of these guides were reliable. Some older works, reprinted in fabulous quantities now, had long since been discredited by emigrants; Lansford Hastings' *Emigrants' Guide* and John C. Frémont's *Report of the Exploring Expedition to the Rocky Mountains in 1842* were two of the most popular, yet Hastings' advice had led the Donner party into disaster, and Frémont had crossed the Rockies over virtually unscalable mountains and followed desert trails across Utah rather than the easier Humboldt River route. Nor were books specially written to meet the demand any better. Most described the terrifying trail along the Gila as a verdant path that offered no obstacles to a man on horseback, or recommended routes across the Sierras that would have tried the skill of a mountain goat.

No less fascinating than reading guidebooks was the task of organizing mining companies. There was scarcely a newspaper in the Mississippi Valley during the winter of 1848–49 that was not filled with advertisements asking "all who are interested in the California expedition" to meet "at candlelight in the court house." At these gatherings committees were appointed to draw up rules and regulations and to recommend the equipment to be taken. The committees on rules occasionally devised absurdly complex systems—one company was burdened with a "president and vice-president, a legislature, three judges, and court of appeals, nine sergeants, as well as other officers" [15]

---

[14] 31st Congress, 1st Session, *Executive Document* No. 5, Pt. 1, p. 225.

[15] Alonzo Delano, *Life on the Plains and Among the Diggings* (New York, 1853), p. 85.

—but most suggested simple organizations with few officers and easily followed regulations. Similarly, the members in charge of equipment succumbed to the charm of the flamboyant now and then, suggesting gaudy uniforms and an array of guns and knives that converted members into walking arsenals. Yet the companies provided companionship and protection along the trail, even though quarrels disrupted nearly all of them before they reached the gold fields.

They began flocking into the embarkation towns—Independence, St. Joseph, Westport, Kanesville—while winter snows covered the ground, for every would-be miner was obsessed with the fear that all the gold fields would be appropriated before he reached California. As they came, by the tens of thousands, every hotel room was jammed, every boardinghouse crowded to the doors, every field covered with tents and wagons. Storekeepers jacked up prices mercilessly as miners made last-minute purchases; gambling halls and saloons blossomed like magic to lighten their pocketbooks before they started. "Their is," wrote a forty-niner as he left Kanesville, "some of the greatest scoundrels I ever saw here." [16] Even when the time for departure finally arrived the "skinning" did not stop, for all had to cross the Missouri River and ferry operators did a huge business at fantastic prices. In the first rush men were killed fighting for places on the few boats, but order was gradually restored and lines formed stretching back for miles. Although ferries operated twenty-four hours a day, a two weeks' wait was not unusual.

With this obstacle surmounted, the wagon trains rolled out upon the prairies. They moved in a procession of caravans, so close together that the lead wagon of one train was often only a few hundred yards behind the last wagon of the train ahead. Rain fell almost constantly that spring, from mid-May until well into the summer. "The very clouds seemed to sweep the earth," wrote a forty-niner, while another, with equal feeling if less elegant grammar, added: "it blew, rained, thundered & lightened tremendous heavy." [17] Day after day the men slogged through ankle-deep mud in soaking clothes, then ate supper

[16] Thomas Turnbull, "T. Turnbull's Travels from the United States across the Plains to California," State Historical Society of Wisconsin, *Proceedings for 1913* (Madison, 1914), p. 161. A modern account is in Walker D. Wyman, "The Outfitting Posts," *Pacific Historical Review*, XVIII (1949), 14–23.

[17] Ralph P. Bieber (ed.), "Diary of a Journey from Missouri to California in 1849," *Missouri Historical Review*, XXIII (1928), 18; David DeWolf, "Diary of the Overland Trail, 1849," *Transactions of the Illinois State Historical Society*, XXXIII (1925), 190.

of wet hardtack and raw bacon before lying down to sleep in water-soaked blankets. With the rains came disease. Colds, malaria, and diarrhea took a frightful toll, but these were as nothing compared to the dread killer of 1849: Asiatic cholera. This followed the miners westward, sweeping through wagon train after wagon train. When it struck, panic struck with it. Those not afflicted whipped up their teams to escape, but as well flee the wind. The graves of five thousand forty-niners marked the trail before the trains entered the high plains country and left the disease behind.

When diarists of well-equipped parties suffered hardships such as these, what can be said of those who started westward with no other protection than their own audacity? Now and then the journals made passing mention of such persons: three men and a boy plodding along with all their possessions on their backs, a lone traveler pulling a cart containing his worldly goods, two men leading a scrawny white cow with their supplies in a pack on her back. How those foolhardy souls must have suffered. Occasionally a diarist recorded the results of their reckless optimism: a lone traveler who had cut his throat and lay beside the road, another driven insane, another begging food along the way. California's gold was a heartless taskmaster.

So they marched westward, these pilgrims of the Golden Grail: out along the Platte, past Fort Laramie, and ever onward toward the dim mountains on the western horizon. As the road grew steeper they lightened their wagons by discarding useless items until the trail was littered with "goldometers, gold washers, pins and needles, brooms and brushes, ox shoes and horse shoes, lasts and leather, glass beads and hawksbells, jumping jacks and jewsharps, rings and bracelets, pocket mirrors and pocket-books, calico vests and *boiled shirts*." [18] The country aroused their scorn, with its sun-dried hills and interminable distances. "I can't see," one wrote, "what God Almighty made so much land for!" [19] And still they climbed, until their caravans wound through South Pass and they could marvel at the sight of westward-flowing waters from Pacific Spring.

At the Big Sandy River the more cautious turned south to Fort Bridger, but most followed the shorter Sublette's Cutoff across the

[18] Ansel J. McCall, *The Great California Trail in 1849. Wayside Notes of an Argonaut* (Bath, N.Y., 1882), p. 5.

[19] Anna P. Hannum (ed.), *A Quaker Forty-Niner; the Adventures of Charles Edward Pancoast on the American Frontier* (Philadelphia, 1930), p. 231.

fifty-two-mile-wide desert that separated them from the Green River. This was a grim crossing, usually made in a night and day of steady plodding through choking dust. At the Green they found a Mormon ferry that charged up to eight dollars for a single wagon, but once across they could rest for a day or two while fiddles sang and the rough-clad forty-niners staged dances, even without the blessings of the gentler sex. Then they pushed on, fearful that all the gold would be mined before they reached California. Through the grass-carpeted Bear Valley they went, over the Wasatch Mountains, and into Salt Lake City to be hospitably received by the Mormons.

Ahead lay an arid land where the firstcomers had almost exhausted the scant supply of grass and water. As they marched the dust rose in such blinding clouds that men coughed constantly, mules blundered into clumps of sagebrush, and meals tasted of sand rather than bacon and beans. Men and animals alike began to drop along the trail, until bodies lined the path for miles on end. Others, their supplies exhausted, wandered from wagon train to wagon train, begging for food. Wrote one traveler: "It is hard to turn away a starving man 1500 miles one way, and 300 the other, from any source of supply, but we are obliged to do it." [20] The grassy marshes about Humboldt Sink gave them momentary relief, but beyond lay the Humboldt Desert. Along a trail marked by the bones of animals and men they struggled for thirty or forty hours before sighting the waters of the Carson or Truckee rivers.

The forty-niners who believed nothing could be so bad as the desert were to be sadly disillusioned as they climbed into the Sierras, following the Carson if their objective was the San Joaquin Valley, the Truckee if bound for the Sacramento gold fields. As the trail wound back and forth across the racing streams, men stood for hours waist deep in icy water to aid worn-out teams, or watched wagons jolt over giant boulders until they fell apart. "One time cracking she goes," wrote one with more realism than rhetoric; "another time grind & another time hop & another time bounce she goes it is awful to see it." [21] To add to their miseries, an early snow clogged the road for latecomers. Nor was the worst over when the summit was reached, for the descent was so steep that wagons had to be lowered on ropes

[20] Lorenzo Sawyer, *Way Sketches Containing Incidents of Travel across the Plains from St. Joseph to California in 1850* (New York, 1926), pp. 85–86.
[21] Turnbull, "Travels," p. 215.

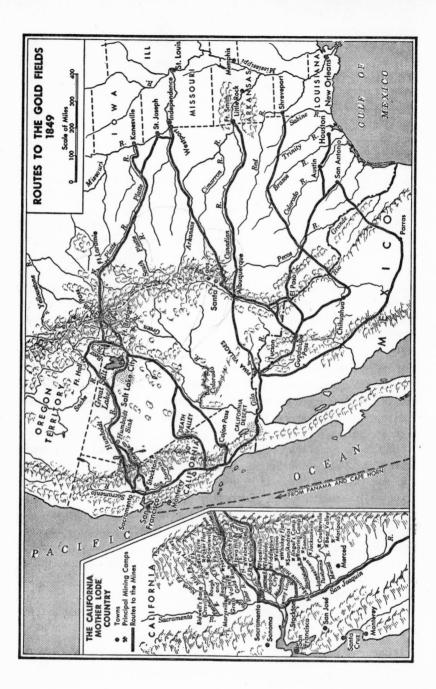

snubbed around rocks and stumps. Those who reached the diggings over the central route had indeed been tried and not found wanting.

Yet their trail was a paradise when compared with that followed by forty-niners who started so late in the year that they dared not risk the assault on the Sierras. Congregating in Salt Lake City in September and early October, five hundred of these unfortunates finally started for southern California over the desert route that Jedediah Strong Smith had blazed. Those who followed the Mormon hired to serve as guide reached their destination safely, but part of the Sand Walking Company broke away in southern Utah after a trader promised to lead them to the mines by a shorter path. When this scoundrel abandoned them in the middle of a desert the miners split into several bands. One managed to catch up with the main party; another was never heard from again, although some of its members apparently reached Cajon Pass; and still another, known as the "Jayhawkers," stumbled through Death Valley before a few survivors made their way to safety.[22]

Those who followed the southern trails west—through Santa Fe or El Paso or northern Mexico—fared somewhat better, although their journey was hardly idyllic. Some reached Santa Fe over the old traders' path, while more moved directly west from Fort Smith, Arkansas, under the watchful eye of a detachment of federal troops; still others journeyed to El Paso along two new "roads" that had been opened across Texas, battling cholera and thirst the entire distance. From Santa Fe or El Paso the forty-niners moved together along the Gila River, where barren hills alternated with scorching deserts until one cried out in despair: "what this God-forsaken country was made for, I am at loss to discover." [23] They ended their journey crossing the ninety-mile-wide desert of southern California; here the road was lined with skeletons of men and animals, and scarcely a party passed without adding to these grim markers. The lot of those crossing northern Mexico was somewhat less trying, although their journals recorded days of thirst and searing heat: "how little," wrote one, "do people in

[22] Diaries of these parties are collected in LeRoy R. Hafen and Ann W. Hafen (eds.), *Journals of Forty-Niners, Salt Lake to Los Angeles* (Glendale, Calif., 1954). A vivid description by a survivor is William L. Manly, *Death Valley in '49* (San José, Calif., 1894).

[23] H. M. T. Powell, *The Santa Fé Trail to California, 1849–1852* (San Francisco, 1931), p. 159.

the States know how to appreciate their cold and sweet-tasting water."[24] Most who followed this route reached the gold fields before those using trails in the United States.

However they came, the miseries of overland travel were forgotten as soon as they reached the mining country. "It seemed," one recorded in that ecstatic moment of arrival, "that every rock had a yellow tinge, and even our camp kettle, that I had thought in the morning the most filthy one I had ever seen, now appeared to be gilded—and I thought with more than one coat. During the night, yellow was the prevailing color in my dreams." [25] Tired as they were, none thought of resting. Instead they scattered through the mines, some north to the newer fields along the Klamath and Scott rivers, some south to the Mariposa district, but most to the central mining area east of Sacramento. With washing pan in hand, and with feverish gleams in their eyes, they set out to reap the fortunes that the guidebooks told them were there.

How tragic was their disillusionment. All good mining sites were already appropriated, leaving only abandoned mines or marginal regions for the newcomers. In these they spent hours of backbreaking toil, with pitifully small returns. One typical party of five young men, bursting with optimism, started working an abandoned mine near Hangtown. Their first shovelful disclosed a nugget worth thirty cents, and excitement flamed. But ten more hours of hard labor yielded dust worth only three dollars. Day after day they worked for these meager profits, until in disgust they turned to farming. Nor was theirs a unique experience. Diary after diary, letter home after letter home, told the same story: wild hope, hard work, gradual disillusionment, and the final realization that they had been "humbugged." One, after three months of toil, found he had cleared only one penny a day; another averaged three dollars daily after work that would have killed a horse. Little wonder they reworded the gay "Oh Susannah" that had been sung so lustily on the outward trail:

> But I'm bound off, I've got my load, my shovel I've laid down,
> My pick and crow and pan and spoon, I've left upon the ground.
> My cradle I can rock at home, if ever there I get,
> And there I'm bound with empty purse and pockets all to let.

[24] George W. B. Evans, *Mexican Gold Trail: The Journal of a Forty-Niner* (San Marino, Calif., 1945), p. 61.
[25] John M. Letts, *California Illustrated* (New York, 1852), p. 72.

To make matters worse, most forty-niners had been in California only a month when October rains ended the mining season, leaving them to cope with astronomically high prices without dust or nuggets.

The picture reflected in these diaries was hardly accurate, for the mines did yield about $10,000,000 during 1849, on the average paying each miner daily an ounce of gold worth sixteen dollars. That most of these returns went to a few fortunates who happened on rich sites made no difference to most of the forty-niners. Disillusioned as they were, wild horses would have been unable to drag them from California. Once they were infected with the gold fever, mining became more of a disease than a profession. Why admit defeat when the next shovelful of dirt might gleam with nuggets? Throughout the mines tales were told of men who had "struck it rich": of a miner near Stockton who had uncovered a pocket hiding $400 in gold, of another in the San Joaquin district who found five pounds of precious metal with the turn of his spade, of a gulch in the Mokelumne diggings that yielded fourteen pounds of dust daily? Scarcely a person but believed Dame Fortune would cast such wealth in his path. So the forty-niners stayed, to labor endlessly, and usually in vain.

Their influx, however, forced a revolution in mining methods. In 1848 and early 1849 unprospected streams were so numerous and yields so high that miners could afford to employ the individualistic techniques usual in frontier communities. Working alone with their washing pans, or in groups of three or four with cradles, they could support themselves adequately while waiting to "strike it rich." With the flood of newcomers these methods no longer sufficed. Cooperative effort was needed if men were to live. Hence, with the usual adaptability of frontiersmen, they began experimenting with group methods of mining that would allow untapped ores to be exploited, and with group techniques that would produce greater yields from known mines. In late 1849, as a result, they turned more and more to "river mining" and "coyoting," and they perfected the sluice box as a means of extracting more gold from pay dirt.

River mining was based on the sensible belief that gold had been trapped in beds of existing rivers, just as it had in ravines and dry gulches where streams formerly flowed. It could be obtained only by diverting the river with a dam, a task that required the cooperative effort of many men. "River companies" sprang up like magic, with members agreeing to contribute their labor for a share of the profits.

In some cases they exposed gold-bearing sands by digging a diversion channel or a wooden aqueduct; more often a "wing dam" was built by extending a barrier halfway across the stream, then blocking the water from the river bed behind the dam. Days of toil were needed for either device, with miners standing waist deep in icy water, and the constant danger that a sudden freshet would carry away their dams and themselves as well. But at last, if they were lucky, the happy day would come when they could rush out over the exposed river bed with their washing pans. When one found an unusual "show" of "color" he would sing out: "Well, boys! I say, just look a here." All would come running, and if the "show" was exceptional, use the term miners employed only in highest praise: "Well! that's real lousy! that is!" [26] As often as not, however, the weeks of labor were wasted when no gold was found, or the yield was hardly enough to pay a living wage for the time consumed.

"Coyoting" was no less arduous, but somewhat more rewarding. Experience taught that pockets of dust frequently had collected in bedrock below the floors of ravines; logically, similar pockets might be expected everywhere in the Mother Lode country where streams flowed. To find them, crews of miners sank shafts or dug tunnels to bedrock, which usually lay from twenty-five to forty feet below the surface along the edges of rivers. Once the rock was reached, side tunnels were extended in all directions, until the whole region was honeycombed. Not only was this cruelly hard work, but cave-ins were frequent, water seeped in, and the air at the bottom of shafts was so foul that miners lapsed into unconsciousness as they dug. Such grueling labor, one wrote, "was really unworthy of a rational being." [27] Yet returns were usually sure, if not spectacular, and "coyoting" was widely employed for several years.

Finding gold-bearing ore was only half the battle, for something more efficient than the cradle was needed to separate the precious metal from gravel before California could sustain its swelling population. The "long tom" was the answer. This was made by fashioning two coffinlike boxes, each twelve feet or more long, and placing one on top of the other. Pay dirt was shoveled into the top box and water run through, carrying away light stones and gravel while the heavier

[26] George Payson, *Golden Dreams and Leaden Realities* (New York, 1853), pp. 265–266.
[27] *Ibid.*, p. 145.

gold and sand descended to the bottom "riffle box" through holes in a
perforated iron floor. There more water carried away the sand, while
the dust was lodged against cleats. The long tom required a crew of
men, some to shovel in the dirt, others to stir the contents, and still
others to scrape away the gold; but far less dust was lost than with a
cradle and greater quantities of pay dirt could be washed. When introduced in the autumn of 1849 they were not only generally adopted,
but gradually lengthened to one hundred feet or more, with longer
riffle boxes to capture more gold. These sluice boxes, as they were
called, required even larger crews of miners, not only to operate, but
to bring in water. Frequently viaducts miles long were built across the
mountains, sometimes by "water companies" which sold the fluid to
miners. The cooperative labor employed in these enterprises during
1850 showed how completely the forty-niners had shifted from complete reliance on individual effort.

These developments brought sufficient promise of permanence to
the mines that a relatively stable social organization could begin to
take shape. And what a unique society that was! Formed from the
flotsam and jetsam of half the world, and shaped in an environment
where luck rather than thrift brought men fortunes, it caricatured
rather than typified the social organisms usual on the American frontier. Yet in this mere fact the miners provide a case study of real significance. In their society could be found an extreme example of the
transition that occurred when men left their homes to grapple with
the strange new world that lay beyond the borders of civilization. The
changes wrought in their characteristics and institutions showed, even
if in exaggerated form, the impact of the frontier on all who came
under its influence.

The units in their social order were the "mining camps." These
sprang up wherever a prospector made a strike; as news of his good
fortune spread, a "rush" occurred until several hundred men had
staked their claims and settled down to dig gold. There was little to
distinguish one mining camp from another save their colorful names:
Whisky Bar, Humbug Creek, Jesus Maria, Devil's Retreat, Jackass
Gulch, Hell's Half Acre, Flapjack Canyon, Murderer's Bar, Shirt Tail
Canyon, Red Dog, You Bet, Gouge Eye, Lousy Level, Gomorrah,
Rough and Ready. In all, the meandering single street was ankle deep
in dust during the dry season and knee deep in mud when rains fell,
and always littered with old boots, empty sardine boxes, discarded

bottles, gnawed hambones, broken shovels, and everything else that could be thrown away. Each boasted crazily built eyesores that housed the saloons and gambling halls where social life centered; each was lined with "brush shanties" or "cabins" of the miners—the latter usually made by tacking old blankets or shirts over a wooden frame to save the high prices asked for lumber. There was little in a typical California mining camp to please the eye or any other of the senses.

In them lived the most remarkable conglomeration of individuals that accident had ever cast together. Americans were in the majority, representing 68 per cent of the population in 1850; most of these came from the Mississippi Valley and were known as "Pikes" because of the predominance among them of round-shouldered, sallow-faced, greasy-clothed farmers from Pike County, Missouri. Mingling with the "Pikes" were "Yankees" from the East Coast, "Sonorans" from Mexico, "Sydney Ducks" from Australia, "Kanakas" from the Hawaiian Islands, "Limies" from London, "Paddies" from Ireland's old sod, "Coolies" from China, and "Keskydees" from Paris—for this was the name assigned all Frenchmen from their habit of asking: *"Qu'est-ce qu'il dit?"* [28] They came, as one wrote, "from every hole and corner in the world," to blend into a social organism as unique as it was colorful.

Dedicated to the pursuit of wealth through backbreaking toil, their lives were dully monotonous. Laboring the day long with feet immersed in icy water and bodies baked by the hot California sun, they returned to their cheerless shacks at night to cook their own dismal meals and gulp down the same uninspired dishes. Bread, leavened with saleratus and baked on a hot stone or fried in a skillet, was eaten three times a day, usually with beans or greasy pork, and always with coffee "strong enough to float a millstone." There was no time to prepare better dishes when gold could be dug, nor could miners vary their diet when potatoes sold for one dollar a pound, eggs for fifty cents each, cheese for a dollar fifty, chickens for four dollars, and apples at two for seventy-five cents, as was the case in the winter of 1849–50. Even cleanliness lost its godliness when laundresses charged eight dollars to wash a dozen shirts; miners sometimes found it cheaper to send their dirty clothes to China to be laundered.

Subsisting on this stomach-abusing diet, sleeping in drafty cabins, wearing sweat-dampened clothes, and laboring long hours in cold

[28] J. D. Borthwick, *Three Years in California* (Edinburgh, 1857), p. 252.

streams beneath a scorching sun, the forty-niners were constantly racked by disease. Diarrhea, dysentery, and scurvy were regular visitors at the mining camps; "chills and fever," or malaria, also took a frightening toll; and contagious diseases swept through their ranks like wildfire. Those struck down had to cure themselves, for the few physicians in the mines were too busy digging gold to care for the sick. Most dosed themselves so liberally with calomel, quinine, and laudanum that the cure sometimes proved more fatal than the disease.[29] They dreamed of the comforts of home and the fostering care of mothers when illness laid them low. "Am poisoned again," one wrote, "down sick, no medicine, no bed but the ground. I wish I could have some chicken broth, or some such thing that I could get at home." [30]

Men who lived such lives could be pardoned for taking their pleasures in boisterous form. In the mining camps, normal social restraints were completely lacking; no one had a reputation to maintain while respectable representatives of the gentler sex were so conspicuous by their absence that in one camp a lady's bonnet and boots were exhibited for one dollar a look. Thus uninhibited, the forty-niners delivered themselves with abandon into the hands of saloonkeepers and gamblers. Drinking was universal except during working hours; "liquoring" usually began early Sunday morning with a few "flashes of lightning," and continued all day. Gambling was so common in every camp that monte tables sometimes were set up in the streets. Losses were taken philosophically, for there was always more gold in the earth. On more than one occasion a miner who had made his "pile" and started home stopped off for one last bet, saying, "Now for it! Home or the diggings." Usually he turned away with "The diggings, by Heaven!" [31] Yet not a word of complaint was uttered, not even when professional gamblers were rumored banking $17,000 monthly.

This lack of restraint meant that both bad and good features of civilization would be sloughed away. The miners were thoroughly democratic within their own limits. "All distinctions indicative of means have vanished," one observer wrote; "the only capital required is

[29] John E. Baur, "The Health Factor in the Gold Rush Era," *Pacific Historical Review,* XVIII (1949), 97–108.

[30] Florence E. Muzzy (ed.), "The Log of a Forty-Niner," *Harper's Magazine,* CXIII (1906), 922.

[31] William Kelly, *A Stroll through the Diggings of California* (London, 1852), p. 48.

muscle and an honest purpose." [32] No one expressed surprise when
saints and sinners labored side by side over a sluice box, or when a
former Yale professor drove a mule team, "mixing in his vocabulary
Gee Haw Buck with his *veni vidi vici.*" [33] Yet absence of social pressures also inspired a completely undemocratic nativism. Mexicans,
Chinese, and Indians were shamefully abused by the "Yankee" majority, under the theory that "coloured men were not privileged to
work in a country intended only for American citizens." [34] In nearly
all camps Mexicans were driven from their claims by mobs, Chinese
were heavily taxed or forced to work mines abandoned by others, and
Indians mercilessly slaughtered. That Americans could be converted
into such heartless nativists was indicative of the corrosive effect of the
environment.

If the characters of men were altered by the strange world of the
mining camp, so were their institutions. Machinery for law enforcement was required from the autumn of 1849 on, for by that time
miners were crowding into the country in such numbers that not all
could find claims. In this situation the temptation to drive an established forty-niner from his mine was sometimes too strong to resist, and
"claim jumping" began. The flow of gold also attracted the dregs of
world society to California, with saloonkeepers, gamblers, dance-hall
girls, harlots, and desperadoes flocking from everywhere. The law-
abiding elements clearly must unite for their own protection until the
federal government's arm could be extended over California.

Faced with this need, they fell back upon the precedents of frontier
self-government that had been accumulating since the Mayflower
Compact. At each camp a mass meeting assembled on the main street,
chose a temporary chairman, and organized a "mining district," which
included the area adjacent to the town. Officers were elected, and a
committee named to draw up a "mining code" which was adopted at
a second meeting. The five hundred codes drafted in California varied
little, for miners drifted about so constantly that the good features of
one were soon made known. All defined the size of the claim that each
man could appropriate, and provided that the process of "locating"
this claim gave him the right to work it. All established methods of

[32] Colton, *Three Years in California,* p. 255.
[33] Linville J. Hall, *Around the Horn in '49. Journal of the Hartford Union
Mining and Trading Company* (Wethersfield, Conn., 1898), p. 176.
[34] William Shaw, *Golden Dreams and Waking Realities; being the Adventures of a Gold-Seeker* (London, 1851), pp. 86–87.

marking claims, varying from merely leaving a pick and shovel on the ground to elaborate rules for surveying boundaries, and all established a system of recording claims with an elected "district recorder." Once a claim had been recorded, the whole force of the camp was directed against a "jumper" who tried to wrest it from its owner. All codes set up machinery for settling disputes over claims, sometimes by the mass meeting as a whole, sometimes by a committee of miners. All discriminated against absentee owners by ruling that mines must be worked regularly or forfeited. Most, in addition, contained restrictive covenants barring Asiatics, Mexicans, or other foreigners from mining in the district.[35]

Protection of mining claims was one function of the districts; safeguarding life and property was another. Most codes provided for an alcalde or sheriff to arrest lawbreakers, and a court of all the miners to mete out punishment. In such trials justice was administered with more haste than discretion, although legal forms were carefully followed. With one of the miners elected judge, two others named to represent the prosecution and defense, and either the whole camp or an elected jury of twelve sitting in judgment, criminals were sentenced to banishment, a flogging, or hanging with a minimum of nonsense. Wrote one European observer after such a trial: "I never saw a court of justice with so little humbug about it." [36] In the end these peoples' courts accomplished their purpose by ridding the camp of disturbing elements, but they were conducted in such an atmosphere of drunkenness and sadistic hate that miscarriages of justice were common.

The legal institutions perfected in the mining camps showed the miners' ability to adapt practices known in the East to the unique environment of the gold fields; the cultural institutions demonstrated their unwillingness to sever the ties that bound them to civilization's heritage. Established societies, the miners knew, boasted schools, theaters, literary societies, and newspapers; hence California must have these hallmarks of culture even though it had no real need for them. And have them it did, for money was plentiful and money talked even among the most aesthetic.

Schools were founded in the most primitive mining camps, where

[35] Typical articles of association are in Daniel B. Woods, *Sixteen Months at the Gold Diggings* (New York, 1851), pp. 126–130, and Borthwick, *Three Years in California*, pp. 153–156.

[36] Borthwick, *Three Years in California*, p. 155.

pupils and teachers alike were nonexistent; literary societies were established by profane illiterates who were as unfamiliar with books as with morality. The cultural significance of these efforts may be doubted, although California's educational system was based on the miners' schools and one "literary" society, at least, provided entertainment for members who spent evenings spinning a hat to see who would pay for drinks.[37] Newspapers flourished more readily; the San Francisco *Alta Californian* published its first issue on January 4, 1849, and inspired so many imitators that California soon boasted more newspapers per capita than any other part of the United States. Theaters also blossomed. A visitor to the remote mines along the Yuba River was astounded to find a Shakespearean company performing in a comfortable theater, while in a concert hall nearby the "American Glee-Singers" were attracting large audiences. Another realized why even the best actors were not ashamed to squander their talents on the Californians when he saw a bearded miner rise after one performance, cough bashfully, and express the hope that the ladies of the company would honor him by accepting a bag filled with $500 worth of gold dust as a tribute to their excellence.[38]

This striving after culture reflected a growing social stability in California as surely as did the drafting of mining codes and the establishment of legal systems. This trend was even more noticeable in subsequent years as new settlers continued to pour in. By the end of 1850, estimates placed the number of miners at fifty thousand, and two years later one hundred thousand were busily grubbing out gold. This expansion was made possible by the opening of new mining regions as improved techniques allowed hitherto untapped resources to be exploited. One such discovery was made late in 1850, when miners found that several large gravel hills near Nevada City were rich in dust and nuggets. They had unwittingly stumbled upon deposits formed along banks of gold-bearing streams in the Tertiary era. Further exploration revealed a number of similar hills just below the mining camp of Placer, and others high in the Sierras, where such camps as Dutch Flat, Gold Run, and Iowa Hill blossomed overnight. Similar expan-

[37] Frank Marryat, *Mountains and Molehills or Recollections of a Burnt Journal* (London, 1855), p. 224.

[38] Upham, *Notes of a Voyage to California*, pp. 271–272; Bayard Taylor, *Eldorado, or, Adventures in the Path of Empire* (2 vols., London, 1850), II, 30–31; Borthwick, *Three Years in California*, pp. 217–218.

sion took place in the Klamath River mines in 1850 and 1851, for their isolation seemed less of an obstacle as older fields showed signs of exhaustion.

Important as these discoveries were, profits were yearly distributed among more and more miners. Production mounted from 10,151,360 ounces of gold in 1849 to 81,294,700 ounces in 1852, the peak year; but miners' daily wages fell from twenty dollars in 1848 to sixteen in 1849, ten in 1850, less than eight in 1851, and six in 1852.[39] As competition increased, miners who had in 1849 abandoned claims when the yield fell below an ounce or two a day were glad to find a quarter ounce of dust in their sluice box at the end of ten hours of work. Most kept on digging, living on the hope that sustained all prospectors, but the day when California's treasures could lure increasing hordes to the West was drawing to a close.

Nor was the time far distant when even this mineral empire would be wrested from its first exploiters by a new breed of men. "The Miners," wrote the editor of the *Alta Californian* late in 1851, "are beginning to discover that they are engaged in a science and a profession, and not in a mere adventure." [40] Only a few could make this transition. With the help of eastern capital, these sunk shafts to tap gold deposits far beneath the ground, using scientific timbering instead of older "coyoting" techniques. Others developed sluicing to wash out low-grade surface ores that could not profitably be worked by hand; water was used to flush gravel into giant sluice boxes that could trap the small quantities of dust it contained. Still more began experimenting with "quartz mining." In this process tunnels were driven down to gold-bearing veins of quartz rock, which was then blasted out, brought to the surface, and crushed in large "stamp mills" until the gold could be extracted. Quartz mining became the rage in the fall of 1851, with crushing mills sprouting like mushrooms throughout the Mother Lode country. By the end of 1852 at least 108 were operating, although sluicing and Tertiary gravels continued to supply the bulk of California's gold through the 1850's.

With these changes, mining passed from the hands of the forty-niners into those of capitalists whose plush offices were in far away San Francisco or New York. Gone was the day when the lone prospector could make his strike in a forest-shaded stream, or a crew of

[39] Paul, *California Gold,* pp. 120–123, 345.
[40] Quoted *ibid.,* p. 66.

flannel-shirted "Pikes" scoop a panful of dust from the bottom of their cradle. Mining had become a big business in which the individual miner had no place. As he drifted away, washing pan in hand, to continue his search for illusive fortune elsewhere, his place was taken by farmers and ranchers, carpenters and bookkeepers, merchants and businessmen, all dedicated to the task of rearing an enduring civilization on the foundations laid by California's gold.

CHAPTER 11

The Miners' Frontier Moves Eastward

THOSE who dug California's gold not only built a permanent empire beyond the Sierras but set in motion a chain of events that led to the peopling of much of the Far West. Their eternal restlessness was responsible. Hopelessly infected with gold fever, placer miners could no more settle down as workers in quartz mines than they could resist a faro game. "What a clover-field is to a steer," wrote one who knew them well, "the sky to the lark—a mudhole to a hog, such are new diggings to a miner." [1] So it was that when the Mother Lode country underwent the transition from placer to quartz mining in the mid-1850's, thousands of nomads shouldered their picks, hung their washing pans on a mule, and set out to prospect the mountains and deserts of all the West for gold. Most found scarcely enough dust to replenish their "grub stakes," but the few who "struck it rich" touched off rushes rivaling that of the forty-niners. These, in turn, were responsible for the permanent occupation of the Inland Empire of the Northwest, the Fraser River country of British Columbia, the desert lands of Arizona, the western fringes of the Great Basin, and the Pike's Peak region of the Rocky Mountains.

The first exodus was toward the plateau that nestled between the northern Rockies and the Cascade Mountains. There the swift-flowing Columbia and Fraser rivers cut their way to the sea through canyons where gold-bearing gravels awaited discovery; there outcroppings of mineral-bearing quartz could be found in the Bitter Root, Cariboo, Boise, and Salmon River ranges. Gold was discovered in the Columbia

[1] *The Oregonian*, July 12, 1862, quoted in William J. Trimble, *The Mining Advance into the Inland Empire* (Madison, Wis., 1914), p. 158.

River in the fall of 1854 by a servant at Fort Colvile, a Hudson's Bay Company post, but the rush that started in the spring of 1855 was soon halted by an uprising of Yakima Indians. For the next three years fighting continued intermittently; not until the summer of 1858 did troops from newly established Fort Walla Walla administer such a crushing defeat that the red men sued for peace. An Army order of October 31, 1858, opening the region to settlement, was followed the next spring by a rush of two thousand prospectors to the Fort Colvile mines. Most were doomed to disappointment, for gold deposits were soon exhausted. Their mining camps—Calfax, Pataha, and Fort Colvile—were destined to find glory only as supply bases for a much richer mining country farther to the north.

This lay in the valley of the Fraser River, a turbulent stream that coursed through British Columbia's forested mountains with few of civilization's scars to mar its natural beauty. Blocked by snags and sandbars, and closed to navigation by high water much of the year, the Fraser had attracted no settlers save Hudson's Bay Company trappers, who lived at three posts along its banks: Fort Langley on the lower river, Fort Hope sixty miles beyond, and Fort Yale fifteen miles farther inland. The wilderness calm of their existence was broken in the fall of 1857, when prospectors from the Fort Colvile country made the first strikes on sandbars north of Fort Langley. News filtered out to costal towns, growing with each retelling, until Victoria in British Columbia and Whatcom and Bellingham in Washington Territory heard tales of riches dwarfing those of the Mother Lode country. The season was too advanced for a rush that autumn, but in each of these hamlets the winter was spent in dreams and preparations; before spring was more than a week or two old the coal mines at Bellingham had shut down for lack of laborers, ships in the harbors were deserted by their crews, and the entire floating population had vanished into the interior.[2]

The trickle of migration swelled to a flood when word of the Fraser River strikes reached California. The news, as usual, lost nothing in the telling; Californians heard of one man who had taken out $600 worth of nuggets in sixteen days, of another who could count on six ounces of dust daily, of two men who took $250 in gold from their

[2] Kinahan Cornwallis, *The New Eldorado; or, British Columbia* (London, 1858), p. 255; R. C. Mayne, *Four Years in British Columbia and Vancouver Island* (London, 1862), p. 93; William C. Hazlitt, *British Columbia and Vancouver Island* (London, 1858), pp. 134–140.

rocker in a day and a half. They were too familiar with miners' tall tales to believe entirely, but who could be sure when the Mother Lode country had produced finds that were just as improbable? Too, even seasoned prospectors pricked up their ears when they learned that the Fraser dust was very fine, indicating that coarser dust and nuggets

THE FRASER RIVER GOLD RUSH

would be found higher up the river. Why stay in crowded California when such opportunities beckoned? "Where else in the world," asked one who caught the fever, "could the river-beds, creeks and cañons be lined with gold? Where else could the honest miner 'pan out' $100 per day every day in the year?" [3]

And so the rush was on. All over California in the spring of 1858 men abandoned their mines or quit their jobs to join; some sections

[3] J. Ross Browne, "A Peep at Washoe," *Harper's Magazine*, XXII (1860), 3.

lost one third of their population overnight. In San Francisco wharves were jammed with men fighting to pay the sixty-dollar fare demanded of "nobs" or the thirty dollars asked of "toughs" for deck passage on the leaky wrecks that were pressed into service; streets leading to the docks were so densely packed that it was impossible to walk along them. Five hundred miners sailed in April, double that number in May, more than seven thousand in June, and almost as many again in July, while eight thousand more who could not afford even deck passage made their way overland. In all some thirty thousand Californians started for the Fraser River mines that spring and summer.[4]

Those who expected to step ashore on river banks yellow with gold were destined to a whole series of disappointments. Some landed at the towns in Washington Territory nearest the mouth of the Fraser, Bellingham and Whatcom, only to find that flood waters on the river blocked all transportation. A few of the more daring paid outlandish prices for canoes that could be worked slowly up the stream, but most stayed on until high prices or gamblers exhausted their resources and turned them back to California. More of the miners were deposited at Victoria, a peaceful Canadian village of eight hundred inhabitants that was transformed within two months into a roaring metropolis of twenty thousand "gamblers, pickpockets, swindlers, thieves, drunkards and jail birds." [5] There they waited for some means of crossing the 160-mile-wide strait that separated them from the Fraser River, complaining constantly of "English fogyism" and the lack of "American enterprise." Some hired Indians to take them across in canoes; others built their own boats; more fought for passage on the two small steamships operated by the Hudson's Bay Company or the five additional vessels imported from Sacramento to serve as ferries. By early June they were pouring ashore at Fort Langley, ready to begin their conquest of the newest Eldorado.

Those who expected to fill their pockets with nuggets were to have still another disappointment, for in mid-June the Fraser rose again with the runoff from mountain snows, stopping all mining until late July. A few managed to eke out an existence by digging gold from dry ravines or the upper edges of sandbars, but more departed for home, loudly denouncing the whole rush as a "humbug." As the

[4] E. W. Wright (ed.), *Lewis and Dryden's Marine History of the Pacific North-West* (Portland, Ore., 1895), p. 69.

[5] Alfred Waddington, *The Fraser River Mines Vindicated* (Victoria, B.C., 1858), pp. 9–10.

waters fell, those who had stayed on staked their claims and began mining. The gold, they found, lay from three to eighteen inches below the surface of the sandbars that dotted the river. In all some thirty bars between Fort Hope and Fort Yale were prospected successfully, and fifty more bars on the "upper river" beyond Fort Yale.[6] Few yielded much gold, however, and prices were exorbitantly high, especially above Fort Yale, where navigation ended and goods had to be packed in on men's backs. Rare indeed was the mine that paid a profit when its operators were charged seventy-five cents for a pound of flour, two dollars a pound for meat of any kind, and one dollar a pound for beans. One disgusted miner found that for a fifty-mile stretch along the river not a single person was "making his grub." [7]

That such a potentially rich country should prove so disappointing was due, the miners agreed, to the dictatorial rule of the Hudson's Bay Company's chief factor, James Douglas. A giant of a man physically, with a masterful self-assurance, Douglas was determined that the turbulent disorder of the California mining camps should not be duplicated in his domain. In January, 1858, he ruled that every miner was to pay a monthly tax of twenty-one shillings—about five dollars—and that all who refused or whose conduct was reproachable should not be allowed to mine. Every effort was made to enforce this licensing law: a ship at the mouth of the Fraser River turned back all who had not complied, and revenue agents regularly visited each camp. When, on August 2, 1858, Parliament created the colony of British Columbia with Douglas as its first governor, he acted at once to tighten his authority. An elaborate legal code, based on that of Australia, was proclaimed, calling for a "gold commissioner" in each camp who not only would enforce the twenty-one-shilling tax law but had absolute power over the administration of justice. From that date a miner judged guilty of any offense by the commissioner could have his license revoked; when this was done anyone could jump his claim without punishment.[8]

[6] A contemporary letter describing these developments is in Hazlitt, *British Columbia and Vancouver Island*, pp. 131–132. See also Donald Sage, "Gold Rush Days on the Fraser River," *Pacific Northwest Quarterly*, XLIV (1953), 161–165.

[7] Charles C. Gardiner, "To the Fraser River Mines in 1858," *British Columbia Historical Quarterly*, I (1937), 253.

[8] *Papers Relative to the Discovery of Gold on the Fraser River* (London, 1858), pp. 7–10; *Papers Relative to the Affairs of British Columbia* (2 vols., London, 1859–1860), I, 13–15.

That these measures ended disorder in the Fraser River camps there can be no question. Yet they also doomed the Fraser mines. Historians who have praised Douglas' orderly regime have ignored the fact that civilization must evolve at its own pace on any frontier, and that the process cannot be markedly accelerated.[9] The miners, whether British or American, agreed to a man that the license fees, trade regulations, and moral codes stifled progress; without them, they insisted, more men would flock in to share the work, prices would fall as competition increased, and carriers would vie for profits until transportation costs were lowered. One miner felt this so strongly that he established a Victoria newspaper, the *British Colonist,* to berate Douglas, while those less articulate showed their hostility first by refusing to pay the license fees, and then by leaving the Fraser River country as rapidly as possible. By the spring of 1859, when the mining season was at its height, a mass exodus was under way; by autumn once-booming Victoria resembled a ghost town, with street after street of boarded-up shops as reminders of its day of prosperity.[10]

Most of the disappointed miners made their way back to California, but some stayed on to prospect in the remote wilds of British Columbia where Douglas had not yet extended his authority. They struck it rich first in the Cariboo country, a land of forest-clad mountains lying beyond the farthest northward bend of the Fraser River. There, in the summer of 1860, prospectors discovered pockets of gold, some producing nuggets of seventeen ounces. During the next three years the diggings were extended as canyon after canyon yielded up precious metals; at the height of the rush in 1863 four thousand miners were braving the bitter winter cold, the incessant spring rains, and the exorbitant prices charged by traders. As the Cariboo mines lost their lure, prospectors in 1863 found new deposits on the Kootenai River, fifty miles north of the border. The rush that followed reached a climax two years later, although mining continued in the Kootenai country for some years.[11]

[9] Competent historians who have praised Douglas' efforts include Trimble, *Mining Advance into the Inland Empire,* pp. 187–210; Frederic W. Howay, Walter N. Sage, and Harry F. Angus, *British Columbia and the United States: the North Pacific Slope from Fur Trade to Aviation* (Toronto, 1942), p. 176; and Rodman W. Paul, "Old Californians at British Gold Fields," *Huntington Library Quarterly,* XVII (1954), 161–172.

[10] The exodus is described in Raymond E. Lindgren, "John Damon and the Fraser River Rush," *Pacific Historical Review,* XIV (1945), 184–195.

[11] Matthew Macfie, *Vancouver Island and British Columbia* (London, 1865),

"Yonder siders" from California also opened a new page of history when they began prospecting the Inland Empire of the Pacific Northwest on their return from the Fraser River rush. Gold was discovered on Oro Fino Creek in the Nez Percé country during the summer of 1860, attracting miners who fanned out over all of southern Idaho, making strike after strike as they moved. From Idaho the miners' frontier swept eastward into Montana, where rich finds in Grasshopper Creek during the spring of 1863 touched off a major rush. Nor did these mines prove as ephemeral as those of British Columbia. Instead tunneling and quartz crushing began, farmers flocked in to feed the miners, and a permanent civilization gradually evolved. Idaho achieved territorial status in 1863, and Montana in 1864.

While some disappointed forty-niners roamed the mountains of British Columbia and the northern Rockies in their quest for gold, others sought the will-o'-the-wisp of fortune among the barren hills of the Southwest. Rumors of fabulous "lost mines" in the Arizona country, which had persisted since the days of Spanish occupation, could not be tested so long as the fierce Apache Indians guarded that land. In 1850, however, Fort Yuma was built at the junction of the Colorado and Gila rivers. Prospecting along both streams followed as a matter of course, with the first strike in 1853, when Jacob Snively of Texas, with a few followers, began washing out gold about twenty miles up the Gila. The 1,200 miners who rushed to that isolated spot founded a mining camp, Gila City, which rapidly established itself as the West's most wide-open town. "It opened up," as a visitor put it, "with a saloon to supply the necessities of life and later added a grocery store and a Chinese restaurant for the luxuries," and soon boasted all the elements of a civilization "except a church and a jail." Gila City's Gomorrah-like existence was short-lived; by 1864 its mines were exhausted, but not until they yielded some $2,000,000 in gold.[12]

More enduring were the gold and silver fields of the Tucson area of southern Arizona, which was added to the United States in 1853 with the Gadsden Purchase. The occupation of the region began three years later when federal troops built Fort Buchanan, twenty miles east of the border village of Tubac, as a screen against Apache attacks. Lured by

pp. 245–252; Alexander Rattray, *Vancouver Island and British Columbia* (London, 1862), pp. 93–94.

[12] Rufus K. Wyllys, *Arizona* (Phoenix, 1950), p. 120; Sylvester Mowry, *Arizona and Sonora: the Geography, History and Resources of the Silver Region of North America* (3rd ed., New York, 1864), pp. 37–39.

the hope of finding "lost mines," prospectors flocked in at once, led by a group of San Franciscans organized as the Arizona Mining and Trading Company. While some stopped to appropriate the long-abandoned Ajo Copper Mine, ninety miles southeast of Fort Yuma, the rest pushed on to search the Gadsden country for the fabled Planchas de la Plata Mine, where, rumor had it, Spaniards had found one silver lump weighing 2,700 pounds. The Californians found the mine, but Mexican troops soon found them and convinced them they were in Mexican territory. Shipments of copper ore from the Ajo Mine did reach San Francisco in 1856, carried westward in sacks by pack mules.

These pioneering efforts were dwarfed by those of Charles D. Poston and Hermann Ehrenberg, a Kentuckian and a German who joined forces in San Francisco to become the first important exploiters of Arizona's mineral wealth. Reaching the Gadsden country in 1854, they made their headquarters at Tubac while searching nearby mountains for gold and silver. Encouraging finds soon attracted enough eastern capital to allow their Sonora Exploring and Mining Company to transform Tubac into a thriving community of three hundred Mexican laborers and to bring into production eight mines in the nearby Santa Rita and Cerro Colorado mountains. Although the yield was high, the cost of exporting ore on muleback across desert trails prevented the expansion that might have been expected.[13] With the withdrawal of troops during the Civil War, Apache attacks stopped mining completely. This was also the fate of mines in the Santa Cruz Mountains opened in 1860 by Sylvester Mowry, a West Point graduate.

The Arizona mines made up in color for what they lacked in permanence. Their center was the miserable little town of Tucson, situated halfway between the Poston and Mowry mines in a sun-dried desert where only distant hills and the fantastically shaped saguaro cactus broke the monotony of the landscape. Here lived five hundred Mexicans, Indians, and Americans scraped from the bottom of society's barrel. "If the world were searched over," one traveler observed, "I suppose there could not be found so degraded a set of villains." [14]

[13] Poston's description of his experiences is in J. Ross Browne, *Adventures in the Apache Country; a Tour Through Arizona and Sonora* (New York, 1869), pp. 236–254.

[14] *Ibid.*, pp. 131–132. The best account of social conditions is in Clement Eaton, "Frontier Life in Southern Arizona," *Southwestern Historical Quarterly*, XXXVI (1933), 180–188.

Recruited from the dregs of two civilizations, and with neither trade nor agriculture to occupy their time, they gave themselves over to indolence or crime. All went about heavily armed, as they had to in a land where law was carried in holsters rather than books; shootings were so common that in 1860 the Tucson cemetery contained the graves of only two men who had died of natural causes. Yet this first "Wild West" town was not rugged enough to withstand the Apache attacks that began in 1861, and was virtually deserted by the end of the Civil War. Tucson's golden day, and that of Arizona as well, was yet to come.

Such was not the fate of another mining district that was just entering its heyday as the Apache were reasserting their control in the remote Southwest. This was in the Nevada country, where the Washoe Mountains, a range of sagebrush-covered hills, jutted eastward into the Great Basin from the Sierras. Some two thousand feet below the summit of the most easterly of these, Mount Davidson, a vein of decomposed quartz resembling a giant curbstone was sunk into the southeastern side of the mountain, extending nearly five miles from north to south. Although as much as half a mile wide far beneath the earth, the vein's surface outcroppings were few, and were hidden beneath rocky debris. At only two points were they partially exposed: at Gold Canyon, a shallow ravine cut by centuries of erosion down the southeastern side of Mount Davidson, and a mile away at Six Mile Canyon, which ran down the northeastern side. This was the stage setting for the most dramatic mining discovery in America's history, for the vein was the fabulous Comstock Lode, which was destined to yield $300,000,000 in gold and silver during the next twenty years.

As in most rich districts, miners were first attracted to the Washoe country not by the fortune hidden in the lode, but by gold washed from smaller veins and trapped in the two canyons. Probably members of the disbanded Mormon Battalion bound for Utah panned the first dust there in the summer of 1848,[15] but not until a year later did other Mormons spread news of the discovery. A band bound for the San Joaquin gold fields whiled away three weeks washing dust from the sands of Gold Creek, but found so little they gladly moved on as soon as the Sierra snows melted. News of their discovery spread, and within a few months the first miners began trickling in from Calif-

[15] This is the conclusion reached after extensive research by Effie M. Mack, *Nevada. A History of the State* (Glendale, Calif., 1936), pp. 194–197.

ornia, hoping that the meager returns reported by the Mormons would increase as they worked their way up the canyons. The opposite proved to be the case. Over the course of the next years deposits grew steadily scanter, until the average take of five dollars a day fell off to four dollars in 1855 and two dollars in 1857. By this time most miners had drifted away, leaving behind only a few ne'er-do-wells who hated to leave a country where they could work only three months of the year. Their shacks were clustered in a ramshackle camp called John-town that had grown up around "Dutch Nick's" saloon in Gold Canyon.

Among those who remained, however, were two men of a different stamp. Ethan A. Grosh and Hosea B. Grosh were young brothers from Pennsylvania who reached the Washoe mines in 1851 and stayed on because they believed their superior education would allow them to discover the source of the placer gold. With a Mexican partner named "Old Frank" who was experienced in silver mining, they spent their days mapping the quartz veins that honeycombed the mountain. Each letter to their clergyman father told of exciting new discoveries: "we found two veins of silver at the forks of Gold Canyon," they wrote in November, 1856. ". . . One of these is a perfect monster." [16] A year later they were ready to seek capital to develop their claims, but in September Hosea Grosh died from a mining wound, and before Ethan could pay off debts contracted during his brother's illness, snows blocked the Sierra passes. With a lone companion, his maps, and bags of ore samples he tried to reach California, only to be so severely frost-bitten that he died on December 19, 1857. Had Ethan Grosh lived he would probably have altered the history of Washoe mining but little, for the best evidence indicates that he and his brother had discovered not the Comstock Lode, but subsidiary veins which later proved to be unprofitable.[17]

The lode itself was found not once, but twice, and each time by accident. The first discoverer was James Finny—"Old Virginny," he was universally called—a simple, generous man whose well-earned reputation as a bibulous reprobate has obscured the fact that he was

[16] The letters are quoted in Eliot Lord, *Comstock Mining and Miners* (Washington, 1883), p. 27, and Myron Angel, *History of Nevada* (Oakland, Calif., 1881), pp. 52–53.

[17] This is the conclusion of two careful students: Grant H. Smith, *The History of the Comstock Lode, 1850–1920* (Reno, 1943), p. 4, and Thomas A. Rickard, *A History of American Mining* (New York, 1932), p. 87.

the best judge of placer ground in all the Washoe country. Always alert for pay dirt, he had noted promising gravel on the side of a flat-topped hill in upper Gold Canyon, but Old Virginny was on a hunting trip then, and too busy to investigate. In January, 1859, with placer mining halted by cold, he returned with three friends, cleared away the snow, and began digging. The results were far from startling, but the traces of dust in their washing pans seemed justification enough for naming the spot Gold Hill and locating fifty-foot claims. When the whole population of Johntown came trooping up to look over the situation, most were so unimpressed that only four bothered to stake out claims. Old Virginny and his partners, however, spent the spring digging further into the hill, and were delighted to find the dirt growing steadily richer. In early April, when they were ten feet down, they unearthed a vein of reddish, decomposed quartz that was rich in gold. Unwittingly they had stumbled on Old Red Ledge, a vein of the Comstock Lode itself. Yet their find aroused no excitement; a few nearby miners and ranchers took out claims on Gold Hill, but not a word of the discovery reached the outside world.[18]

Not until the lode was rediscovered did Washoe catch the imagination of the West. The heroes in this drama were two prospectors, Peter O'Riley and Patrick McLaughlin, who decided to try their luck high in Six Mile Canyon in the hope of accumulating the $100 grub stake needed to move on to a more promising gold country. Selecting a spot near a spring known as "Old Man Caldwell's," they set up their cradle and started washing dust early in 1859. The labor was backbreaking and the yield only four dollars a day, but instead of giving up they agreed to dig a reservoir to catch the spring waters in hope of lessening their work. As they dug, on the morning of June 10, 1859, they came upon a heavy, dark soil similar to that of Gold Hill. Acting on an impulse, the partners carried a pan to the spring. To their delighted amazement, when they finished washing away the dirt they found a thick layer of flakes and dust. They had uncovered the fabulous Ophir vein of the Comstock Lode. O'Riley and Mc-Laughlin posted notices claiming forty feet each, then set to work digging and washing furiously.[19]

[18] An account of these events, written by one of the discoverers, is in Dan De Quille, *The Big Bonanza: An Authentic Account of the Discovery, History, and Working of the World-Renowned Comstock Lode of Nevada* (Hartford, 1877), pp. 42–43.
[19] A similar account of this discovery, written by Emanuel Penrod, is in *ibid.*, pp. 47–54.

While they were thus engaged, Henry T. P. Comstock appeared, riding a mule so small that his long legs dangled in the sagebrush. A shiftless man, Comstock had drifted into Johntown in 1856 and had fast earned the undisputed title of laziest man at the diggings; his friends called him "Old Pancake" because he was too lazy to bake bread. But Comstock could exercise his tongue if not his back, and when he had run his fingers through the $300 worth of dust and scales that O'Riley and McLaughlin had to show for their day's work, he announced that he deserved his share. The spring, he said, belonged to him; he and Old Virginny and "Manny" Penrod had bought it from Old Man Caldwell the winter before. The partners were not impressed with his bluster, but claims in the Washoe mines usually played out so quickly they were not worth arguing over. Hence they added Comstock and Penrod to their partnership, while Old Pancake agreed to buy out Old Virginny's share—a task accomplished a few days later at the price of a blind horse and a bottle of whisky. A fifth partner was soon added in the person of Joseph D. Winters.

With the problem of ownership settled, four of the partners settled down to digging while the fifth, Henry Comstock, either superintended or held forth at length to anyone who would listen on "my mine" and "my gold" until all were referring to "Comstock's Lode." Within a few days the mine was yielding $300 in dust and scales for every cradle of dirt washed, and the best was yet to come. On June 11 the vein of decomposed black rock gave way to one of heavy bluish quartz that clogged their cradles. Manny Penrod insisted that it might be valuable, and on his suggestion each of the partners located a quartz claim of six hundred feet in addition to the placer claims they already had. It was well that they did, for when samples were sent across the Sierras to Nevada City, California, for assay on June 27, the report was unbelievable. The troublesome "blue stuff" was three fourths pure silver and one fourth gold, and was worth $3,876 a ton! The Ophir Mine, as the partners called it, was the richest in mining history.

The wild rush to the Washoe country that inevitably followed enriched few and impoverished many. Those who gained were a few experienced men with enough capital to buy proven property and enough common sense to hold it. In the vanguard were Judge James Walsh, a millowner of Nevada City, who started east on June 28 before the express that carried news of the assay to the Ophir owners; George Hearst, another Californian, whose acumen was to lay the basis for one of America's greatest fortunes; and a few others of the same type. To later generations the sums they paid in buying out the Ophir partners seemed pitifully small: McLaughlin received $3,500, Comstock $10,000, and O'Riley, who held out longest, $40,000. Yet the sellers were convinced they had driven a hard bargain and they were right, for the chance the veins would "run out" was high. Certainly the partners enjoyed their new wealth briefly before squandering it on liquor, women, and worthless mining stocks; all died in poverty.

While canny investors were buying the only proven mines in the Washoe country, a major rush was taking shape. Judge Walsh set the tide rolling when he returned to Nevada City on July 9, 1859. The Washoe mines, he reported, were so rich that men were making from $100 to $400 daily with old-fashioned rockers, while gold found in a single washing pan ran as high as $107. Little matter that the judge went on to warn that lack of water and wood made mining virtually impossible, and that extensive capital investment would be necessary before the lode could be developed.[20] These words of caution were forgotten as tales of the Comstock's wealth spread like wildfire. Overnight all California seemed bent on reaching Washoe; within a few weeks Nevada County lost one third of its population, and elsewhere the story was the same. The village of Placerville, which straddled the best road across the Sierras, was jam-packed with struggling humanity, all pleading with livery-stable owners for a horse or fighting for a seat on stagecoaches. There stores were jammed with goods for Washoe, the express office bulged with packages for Washoe, streets were piled with boxes for Washoe, and newspapers contained news of nothing but Washoe. "There was nothing but Washoe to be seen, heard, or thought of," wrote an observer.[21]

On the trail across the mountains all was similar confusion. The road itself was a primitive affair, wide enough at best for two wagons to meet, and at places only a single track with a cliff falling away a thousand feet on one side. From the day the rush began this was crowded with men on foot, men pushing wheelbarrows, men riding horseback, men in wagons, men in buggies, each trying to outdistance the other lest the $400-a-day placers be all taken. Through them

[20] Judge Walsh's account, as first published in the *Nevada Journal*, is reprinted in Mack, *Nevada*, p. 209, and similar extracts from other California newspapers are in Angel, *History of Nevada*, pp. 59–60.

[21] Browne, "A Peep at Washoe," p. 7.

careened overloaded stagecoaches, their drivers yelling constantly to clear the road. Accidents were common, until the trail was littered with broken wagons, discarded dry goods, and empty whisky barrels. The one inn along the way was so crowded that guests ate in six shifts and slept eight to the bed; on one occasion the landlord reprimanded a boarder who objected to a ninth being added, saying he liked to see a man "accommodating." [22] The snows of late autumn ended the rush, but only briefly, for the winter of 1859–60 was mild, and by February miners were braving the Sierras again, beating down ten-foot drifts as they marched. All through that spring the tide of humanity flowed unchecked, until July, 1860, when Californians were at last convinced that Washoe held no fortunes for the individual, capital-less miner.

Never in history had a rush created such problems. In the past newcomers in any district could be kept busy grubbing for gold, even if yields were small, but in the Comstock country the only possible mines were already appropriated and even these could not be worked until more capital flowed in. How could the influx be housed and occupied on barren Mount Davidson? Fortunately common sense helped solve the problem, for most of those who arrived in the 1859 rush took one look and turned tail for California. But the three hundred miners who shivered through the near-zero temperatures of that winter, and four thousand of the ten thousand new arrivals in the spring of 1860 who did not return at once, were something else again.

The matter of housing was solved when the miners laid out a new town, just below the Comstock Lode. There in the autumn of 1859 they threw up a remarkable collection of shanties fashioned from brush, blankets, potato sacks, and old shirts, which they dignified with the name of Virginia City.[23] Improvements were not long in coming: the first saloon was opened in a canvas tent with a sluice box as bar, a pitcher and a few tin cups as equipment, and two barrels of flavored

<hr>

[22] *Ibid.*, p. 17; Adolph Sutro, *A Trip to Washoe* (n.p., 1942), pp. 1–2; Susan M. Hall, "Diary of a Trip from Ione to Nevada in 1859," *California Historical Society Quarterly*, XVII (1938), 75–80.

[23] According to a story written by "Old Virginny" for the New York *Herald*, December 30, 1878, this bibulous character, stumbling home in a drunken state, fell and broke a bottle of whisky he was carrying. Staggering to his feet, he sprinkled the few remaining drops on the ground, and said: "I baptize this ground Virginia town." Unfortunately there is no other evidence to substantiate this colorful episode; the town's name was actually chosen at a mass meeting of the inhabitants in September, 1859.

alcohol optimistically labeled "brandy" as supplies; a second soon followed when "Dutch Nick" moved his establishment from Johntown and began ladling out his famous "tarantula juice" whisky, so called because "when the boys were well charged . . . it made the snakes and tarantulas that bit them very sick." [24] At first accommodations were so scarce that two hundred men paid one dollar a night each to sleep on the floor of a room twenty feet square, wrapped in blankets rented from a shrewd trader at an additional dollar a night. But during the spring of 1860 new streets were laid out, lots peddled for $1,000 each, a road to the mountains cut to allow lumber to be brought in, and Virginia City gradually assumed a permanent appearance. By the close of that year it boasted a theater, thirty-eight stores, eight hotels, nine restaurants, and twenty-five saloons, all charging such outlandish prices that old timers were reduced to a diet of pork, beans, and the region's alkaline water, which could, the miners maintained, be made palatable only by mixing a teaspoon of water with half a tumbler of whisky.[25]

This remarkable prosperity rested on shaky foundations. Just before snow fell in 1859 the first shipment of ore from the Ophir Mine reached San Francisco, where its sale at $3,000 a ton created a sensation. Overnight every Californian with money in his pocket experienced an overwhelming desire to buy "feet" in a Washoe mine. This urge kept Virginia City alive in its early days. Miners might not be able to produce wealth, but they could produce "feet" in any quantity. So they swarmed over Mount Davidson and all the surrounding countryside, staking claims to every quartz vein they could find, and peddling shares to gullible Californians, who never seemed to wonder whether a lode contained gold or not. What a happy dream world they lived in, those Washoe miners, as they traded "feet" in their own worthless properties for others equally worthless or tried to persuade the grocer to accept a foot or two of their latest find for a pound of bacon and a quart of beans. Not a person in Virginia City but owned "feet" in a dozen "mines" that had never been worked save by a Mexican hired to grub out a few choice ore samples; not one but carried a pocket full of "croppings" from the Flowery Diggings, or Wake-up-Jake, or Let-Her-Rip, or Root-Hog-or-Die, or some other equally fab-

[24] De Quille, *The Big Bonanza,* pp. 40, 63–64.
[25] Browne, "A Peep at Washoe," p. 159; Chester W. Cheel, *The Truth About Virginia City* (n.p., n.d.), p. 23.

ulous property. No two men could meet without pulling samples of ore from their pockets, spitting on them, peering at them through magnifying glasses, and like as not walking away with a few shares that were certain to make their fortunes. Amidst this speculative craze everyone in Washoe was a potential millionaire, but hardly a man among them had enough cash to pay his grocery bill.[26]

For of real wealth in Virginia City there was very little. Mining was confined to a few properties on the Comstock Lode: the Ophir, the Mexican, the Central, the Gould & Curry, and a few others. Even in these progress was alarmingly slow. All work was done by hand, with miners driving drills into the rock with sledges, blasting out the quartz, and carting it off to one of the stamp mills built in 1859 and 1860. To make matters worse, open shafts were used instead of tunnels, necessitating windlasses to haul ore to the surface, and exposing every mine to work-slowing floods with every rain or snowfall. In the spring of 1860 a new obstacle was encountered when the vein of blue-black sulphides that contained gold and silver widened from three or four feet to nearly two hundred. The miners had struck a real "bonanza" at last, but their find threatened to end mining as cave-ins crushed workers in caverns opened by removal of the ore. Not until a German expert devised a new "square set" method of timbering could operations be resumed.[27]

Even now progress remained slow. Less than four hundred newcomers reached Washoe in 1861, partly because new mines discovered that year at nearby Esmeralda and Humboldt drained off drifters for a time before the veins "ran out." Yet signs of future prosperity were beginning to appear: the Ophir and Gould & Curry mines reported the lode still widening at three hundred feet; mills were multiplying so rapidly that there was not enough ore to keep half busy; Congress created the Territory of Nevada in March, 1861, with James B. Nye as governor and Orin Clemens as secretary, thus assuring the region immortality in the classic *Roughing It* of Orin's brother, Samuel L. Clemens. A year later these promises were realized when the steadily deepening shafts revealed undreamed-of riches; stock in the Ophir leaped from $1,225 a foot in April to $3,800 in October, and of the Gould & Curry from $500 to $2,500. A new rush of settlers skyrocketed

[26] De Quille, *The Big Bonanza*, pp. 111–112; Browne, "A Peep at Washoe," pp. 155–157.

[27] Max Crowell, *A Technical Review of Early Comstock Mining Methods* (Reno, 1941), pp. 4–10.

Virginia City's population from four thousand in early 1862 to fifteen thousand in 1863, while faith in the future was revealed with the opening of an opera house, three theaters, and restaurants that rivaled those of San Francisco. Washoe's palmiest days were still ahead, but when Nevada became a state in 1864 it was already passing beyond the frontier stage.

While the Comstock Lode was enriching a few fortunates, another mining district farther eastward was capturing the nation's imagination. Rumors of gold in the country about Pike's Peak had bandied about the Mississippi Valley for years: of Arapaho Indians who fired golden bullets, of the old Mountain Man who stumbled on a fabulous mine and was unable to locate it again, of the trapper who appeared in Missouri with his "possibles sack" stuffed with nuggets. No metal was found, however, until the spring of 1850, when a party of miners bound for California stopped to pan the waters of Ralston's Creek on the South Fork of the Platte River.[28] They found gold, but not enough to detain them when California beckoned, and moved on.

One of the group, a Cherokee from the Indian Territory named John Beck, was to remember the incident eight years later with important results. In June, 1858, he and a friend from Georgia, William Green Russell, reached the Cherry Creek country with a party of seventy Indians and Georgians. They panned their way down that stream toward the South Platte without finding color, then pushed on to Ralston's Creek, where they were joined by a few Missourians. By July 4 most had lost heart and drifted homeward, leaving only Russell and twelve followers. They made their strike two days later, on the South Platte some eight miles above the mouth of Cherry Creek; and although the yield was far from spectacular, they built cradles and settled down to washing out gravel.[29] By mid-August the diggings had "played out" and they were on their way again, exploring the eastern edge of the Rockies as far north as present-day Wyoming before turning back to Cherry Creek in early September. There the Russell party stumbled on a second large group that had invaded the Rockies that

[28] An earlier party that made the same trip in 1849 is often credited with the discovery. That the 1850 party was responsible is demonstrated in LeRoy R. Hafen, "Cherokee Goldseekers in Colorado, 1849–1850," *Colorado Magazine,* XV (1938), 101–109.

[29] An account of the adventures of this party, written by a member, Luke Tierney, is in LeRoy R. Hafen (ed.), *Pike's Peak Gold Rush Guidebooks of 1859* (Glendale, Calif., 1941), pp. 95–105.

summer to search for gold. Led by J. H. Tierney, and enlisted from the adventuresome of the town of Lawrence, Kansas, they had prospected unsuccessfully in the southern mountains since early July before drifting northward to the South Platte country.[30]

The two parties joined forces at once, not to hunt gold, but to engage in another activity as dear to the hearts of frontiersmen: laying out a town. "They desired," wrote a cynical traveler, "not to pitch into, but on to the ground. They cared less for good placers than promising places." [31] Scarcely had they formed the St. Charles Town Association and laid out a town just east of the junction of Cherry Creek and the South Platte than new arrivals began to flock in from Missouri and eastern Kansas. In all nearly one thousand persons arrived that fall, even though mining had ended for the season. Needing homes, and unwilling to pay the high prices asked by the St. Charles Town Association, they organized the Auraria Town Company and laid out their settlement on the South Platte just west of Cherry Creek. Nor did the process stop there. On November 16 a party under William Larimer arrived from Leavenworth, Kansas, with town planting in mind. Realizing that the two earlier companies had claimed the best sites, Larimer decided to appropriate the lands of the St. Charles Town Association, since most of its members had departed for the East. This was accomplished by dosing its few remaining agents with whisky and promising them shares in a new company, the Denver City Company. Before snow fell streets were laid out and work begun on the first cabins.[32] All this in expectation of a rush, even though prospectors had found no more than a few ounces of gold in all the Pike's Peak country!

The speculators actually had sized up the psychology of their countrymen well, for in the Mississippi Valley preparations were under way for a mass exodus rivaling that of the forty-niners. The Panic of 1857 was primarily responsible. Unemployed laborers or evicted farmers were willing to grasp at any straw; when they heard tales of Pike's

[30] An extended account of this 'Lawrence party's" journey, written by a member, is in *ibid.*, pp. 322–335. The only known diary kept by a member is in LeRoy R. Hafen (ed.), "The Voorhees Diary of the Lawrence Party's Trip to Pike's Peak, 1858," *Colorado Magazine*, XII (1935), 41–54.

[31] Henry Villard, *The Past and Present of the Pike's Peak Gold Regions* (St. Louis, 1860), pp. 11–12.

[32] William Larimer and William H. H. Larimer, *Reminiscences of General William Larimer and His Son William H. H. Larimer, two of the Founders of Denvey City* (Lancaster, Pa., 1918), pp. 117–127.

Peak gold from agents hired to stimulate business by spreading false rumors, or read glowing accounts of imaginary strikes from the pens of editors seeking to revitalize trade, they forgot their usual caution in their eagerness to believe. Rumors began to fly in August, 1858, when a trader who had visited the Russell party on the South Platte arrived at Kansas City with a sackful of dust, which was washed out in the streets, yielding twenty-five cents to the pan. That day the Kansas City *Journal* carried screaming headlines:

THE NEW ELDORADO!!! GOLD IN KANSAS TERRITORY!! THE PIKE MINES! FIRST ARRIVAL OF GOLD DUST IN KANSAS CITY!!!

From then on editors vied in inventing fantastic tales of Pike's Peak wealth: one reported the arrival of a miner with $6,000 worth of nuggets; another proclaimed the diggings richer than those of California; another described a small boy who had dug $1,000 worth of dust "and the little fellow says he can get all he wants." The motive behind these ingenious fabrications was revealed by parallel advertisements proclaiming that Kansas City, or Independence, or Leavenworth was the ideal place to outfit for the mines.[33]

Under this barrage of propaganda the Mississippi Valley caught fire with excitement. In every town, "what's the news from the diggings?" was the usual method of salutation; in every store, hats and shirts and boots and shovels "designed especially for the use of emigrants and miners" filled the racks. Knots of starry-eyed men gathered at every corner to read guidebooks, and to believe unquestioningly that nuggets were "scattered around miscellaneously and loosely," and that "gold is to be found everywhere you stick your shovel." Amidst this feverish atmosphere the youth seen collecting empty meal sacks at Council Bluffs could be pardoned when he told a questioner that he was going to stuff them all with gold dust at Pike's Peak, and that he would do so if he had to stay until fall.[34]

Disappointment and tragedy were to follow. Those succumbing to the propaganda were not experienced plainsmen but hopeful youths, needy farmers, out-of-work shopkeepers. They started west in early

[33] LeRoy R. Hafen (ed.), *Colorado Gold Rush; Contemporary Letters and Reports, 1858–1859* (Glendale, Calif., 1941), pp. 30–31; James F. Willard, "Spreading the News of the Early Discovery of Gold in Colorado," *Colorado Magazine,* VI (1929), 98–104.

[34] Jerome C. Smiley, *History of Denver* (Denver, 1901), p. 236. Most of the guidebooks are reproduced or summarized in *Pike's Peak Gold Rush Guidebooks,* pp. 93–145, 153–295.

March, long before there was grass for their animals, for they discounted all words of caution as attempts to keep them home until the best mines were taken. Some traveled in wagons or buggies, others with handcarts and wheelbarrows, a few in dogcarts or "wind-wagons" that were supposed to fly before the prairie winds, and more on foot with packs on their backs—"each a domestic Atlas, with his little world upon his shoulders." [35] One party of eleven young men was sighted pulling a buggy westward under the direction of a gay dandy in fine cloth coat, stovepipe hat, and patent-leather shoes; others were reported with picks on their shoulders and all their possessions in a carpetbag. When asked how they would live on the long journey, they blithely answered that they would kill game and sleep in barns! Most of these "greenhorns" narrowly missed death by starvation and some were reduced to cannibalism; the three Blue brothers gained questionable fame when one reached the mines only after subsisting on the bodies of the two who had succumbed.[36]

The degree of hardship was governed both by the inexperience of the fifty-niners and the trail they selected. Of the three that were most popular, the "Platte Route" along the Platte and South Platte rivers, and the "Santa Fe Route" along the Arkansas River and Fountain Creek, were relatively safe and served as highways for most of the miners. The third, the "Smoky Hill Route," led across arid plains between the Smoky Hill River and Cherry Creek; in all this dreary distance there was not a landmark, not a spring, not a bite of food—only a sandy plain where travelers wandered until they died, or turned back in panicky search of water and civilization. Yet merchants at Leavenworth lured thousands into making the attempt by advertising it as hundreds of miles shorter than other trails.

Even those who reached the Pike's Peak country without suffering such agonies were doomed to heart-sickening disappointment. The first arrivals straggled into Denver in April, to find all mining sites along the ice-choked South Platte appropriated, and the passes into the mountains clogged with snow that would not melt for weeks. Most of them, after one look at the stratospheric prices asked for bacon, beans, and gritty Mexican bread, started home at once, loudly denouncing Pike's Peak as the greatest humbug of the century. As these

---

[35] Albert D. Richardson, *Beyond the Mississippi* (Hartford, 1867), p. 157.
[36] James F. Willard, "Sidelights on the Pike's Peak Gold Rush, 1858–59," *Colorado Magazine*, XII (1935), 8–10.

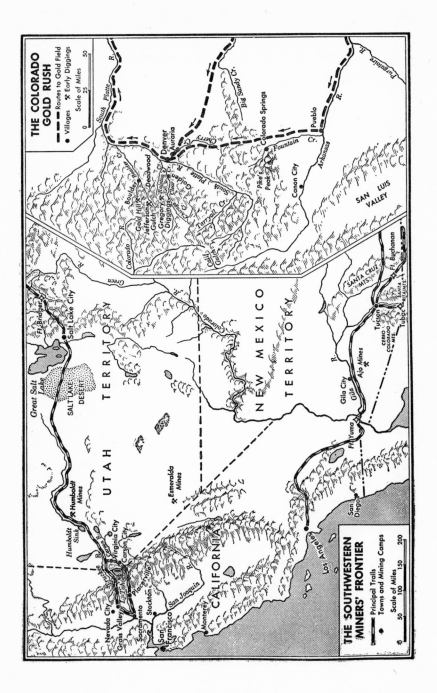

THE COLORADO
GOLD RUSH

Routes to Gold Field
● Villages ✕ Early Diggings

Scale of Miles
0   25   50

South Platte R.
Big Sandy Cr.
Denver
Auraria
Colorado Springs
Fountain Cr.
Pueblo
Arkansas R.
Purgatoire R.
Pike's Peak
Canon City
SAN LUIS VALLEY
Boulder
Deadwood
Gold Hill ✕
Jefferson ✕
Gulch
Gregory ✕
Diggings
Russian Gulch
Golden
Clear Cr.
Tarryall Cr.
Cache
Gulch
Colorado R.
Green R.
South Platte R.
Cherry Cr.

Ft. Bridger
Salt Lake City
Great Salt Lake
SALT LAKE DESERT

UTAH TERRITORY

NEW MEXICO TERRITORY

Colorado R.
Gila City
Gila R.
Ajo Mines ✕
Ft. Yuma
SANTA CRUZ MTS.
Tucson
CERRO COLORADO MTS.
Tubac
Ft. Buchanan
SANTA RITA MTS.

Humboldt R.
✕ Humboldt Mines
Humboldt Sink
Nevada City
Grass Valley
Virginia City
Carson City
Placerville
Stockton
Sacramento
San Francisco
Monterey
San Joaquin R.
Sacramento R.

✕ Esmeralda Mines

CALIFORNIA

San Diego
Los Angeles R.

THE SOUTHWESTERN
MINERS' FRONTIER

━ Principal Trails
● Towns and Mining Camps

Scale of Miles
0   50   100   150   200

"Pilgrims" moved back along the trail, cursing guidebook writers, Denver land speculators, and their own gullibility, panic spread among the throngs on their way west. One by one they turned tail and fled eastward; about half of the hundred thousand who started west never saw the mountains. By late spring the rush of the "stampeders" eastward surpassed that of the fifty-niners westward, most of them with the jaunty "Pike's Peak or Bust" scratched from their wagons and "Busted, by Thunder" written in instead.[37] The "rush of the fifty-niners" was over, leaving thousands sadder and poorer, if not wiser.

The "stampeders" left too soon, for even as they fled homeward discoveries were made that launched the Pike's Peak country on the road to prosperity. George A. Jackson, a Missourian with experience in the Mother Lode country, found pay dirt on Chicago Creek during January, 1859, but kept his find a secret until late April, when he returned with a few companions to set up a cradle.[38] The news sent hope throbbing through Denver, for if one gold deposit existed, others would almost certainly be found. The optimists were right. Within days prospectors found color at Gold Hill in Boulder Canyon. Neither Jackson's Diggings nor Gold Hill proved very rich, but no one was pessimistic. Surely the time for the big strike was near.

The hero was John H. Gregory, a full-whiskered Georgian, whose uncombed red hair and ragged clothes concealed his talents as a prospector. With one companion, Gregory set out in the spring of 1859 for a canyon on the North Branch of Clear Creek where he remembered seeing promising-looking dirt. Scraping away snow-covered pine needles and aspen leaves, he dug until May 6, when he came upon a quartz vein. Quickly crumbling the rock, he scrambled down to the stream, washed out a panful, and gazed happily at four dollars' worth of dust and nuggets. Here was a rich strike indeed! Gregory tossed with excitement all that night; a wanderer who visited him a few days later found him haggard from lack of sleep, but with nine hundred dollars worth of gold hidden in a frying pan.[39]

[37] These scenes are described in Richardson, *Beyond the Mississippi*, p. 166; E. Dunsha Steele, "In the Pike's Peak Gold Rush of 1859," *Colorado Magazine*, XXIX (1952), 300–301, 308; and LeRoy R. Hafen (ed.), *Overland Routes to the Gold Fields, 1859, from Contemporary Diaries* (Glendale, Calif., 1942), pp. 36, 99, 127, 143.

[38] LeRoy R. Hafen (ed.), "George A. Jackson's Diary, 1858–1859," *Colorado Magazine*, XII (1935), 201–214.

[39] The visitor was W. N. Byers, who described the incident in *Encyclopedia of Biography of Colorado* (2 vols., Chicago, 1901), I, 36. For the best account

The news of Gregory's find electrified Denver. The first gold to arrive was passed from hand to hand and from cabin to cabin as men laughed with joy or shouted at each other: "We are all right now," "the stuff is here after all," "the country is safe." A rush to Gregory Gulch began at once as storekeepers locked their doors, carpenters abandoned their half-completed houses, and laborers jostled with lawyers on the trail into the mountains. As the news spread east many of the "go-backs" turned about and joined the mad pack bound for the new Eldorado. For the next month as many as five hundred persons a day poured into Gregory Gulch, to stake their claims along Clear Creek or the small tributary stream where Gregory had made his strike. In all directions the hillsides were dotted with miners, all digging pay dirt from quartz veins, sliding it down to the streams in leather bags, and washing out the gold in sluice boxes and cradles. Gregory moved among them in a daze of happiness, having sold out his claim for $21,000 to accept a fee of $100 a day to prospect for others.[40]

Gregory Diggings enjoyed a short life; many of the veins ran out or "drifted" so deeply into hillsides they could not be followed. Yet no one was discouraged, for gold was there and only tunneling and quartz-crushing machinery were needed to bring it out. More important, news of John Gregory's find had brought such a rush of prospectors to the Rockies that even richer discoveries were certain. Horace Greeley, the famed editor of the New York *Tribune*, was responsible. Visiting the Gregory Gulch mines during their June heyday, he had joined with two other journalists—A. D. Richardson and Henry Villard—in a widely published statement that told of the fabulous fortunes being unearthed, as well as venturing the prophecy that the Pike's Peak country would produce similar wealth for years to come.[41] Such assuring words from a man as reliable as Horace Greeley set all doubts at rest. Once more an influx into the region began, but this time with experienced miners or sober farmers predominating. As

of Gregory, see Caroline Bancroft, "The Illusive Figure of John H. Gregory, Discoverer of the First Gold Lode in Colorado," *Colorado Magazine*, XX (1943), 121–135.

[40] Villard, *Pike's Peak Gold Regions*, pp. 38–39; Richardson, *Beyond the Mississippi*, pp. 180–184; and Horace Greeley, *An Overland Journey, from New York to San Francisco, in the Summer of 1859* (New York, 1860), pp. 124–125, all describe these events after visits to Gregory Gulch.

[41] The statement is reproduced in Hafen (ed.), *Colorado Gold Rush; Contemporary Letters and Reports*, pp. 376–382.

they fanned out over the mountains in quest of another Gregory Gulch, they made strike after strike until Greeley's words were justified.

During the rest of 1859 and throughout 1860 most of the central Rockies were prospected. Gold was discovered at Russell Gulch and Spanish Diggings along the South Fork of Clear Creek, near Idaho Springs, at Jefferson Diggings and Twelve Mile Gulch of the Boulder River, and in the waters of Tarryall Creek and Fairplay Creek of the South Park region, each resulting in a wild rush. A few miners crossed the continental divide to strike pay dirt on Blue Creek, a tributary of the Colorado River. During 1860 the influx from the East added as many as five thousand miners a week to these mines. Some of these struck it rich in California Gulch of the upper Arkansas River near Leadville, or in the San Juan Mountains. In each of these diggings rock-crushing mills were erected, tunneling was started, and the task of digging out deposits of gold-bearing quartz hidden below the surface was begun.

Denver reflected this new atmosphere as its population doubled during 1860; so did other towns that sprang up to supply the mining camps: Boulder at the mouth of Boulder Creek, Golden on Clear Creek, Canon City and Colorado Springs athwart roads to the South Park country, and Pueblo at the gateway to the Arkansas River gold fields. In all of these the transition from camp to city was amazingly rapid. By the autumn of 1860 Denver boasted an Irish schoolmaster, a barber who urged customers to "get your beards mowed," a theater, two newspapers, a circulating library, and the Rocky Mountain Debating Club. Even the most skeptical "old-timers" were forced to agree that civilization had triumphed when the bartender in the leading saloon announced that the community sport of taking "pot shots" at him was "about played out," and that he would shoot the next man who fired. Denver's wild and woolly days were nearly over.

⤷ The social transition occurring in the remote mining camps was even more marked. There the institutions that evolved showed the dependence of one frontier area on another, for the Pike's Peak mines borrowed directly from those of California. This was not surprising; Horace Greeley estimated that three of every ten miners had spent some time in the California mines, and few among these hesitated to give advice.[42] Moreover, the problems were the same; in both the

---

[42] Greeley, *Overland Journey,* pp. 157–158; Francis S. Williams, "The In-

Mother Lode and Pike's Peak countries the law-abiding majority was compelled to find means of protecting claims, keeping order, and establishing a workable government. The methods used in the Rockies were identical with those originated beyond the Sierras, but the speed with which they were introduced, the improvements in techniques, and the extent of social control applied illustrated the tendency of frontier lawmakers to hurry the transition to civilization whenever possible.

The problems of claim protection and law enforcement were solved, as they had been in California, by forming "mining districts." The constitutions of those established in 1859 showed a greater maturity than similar documents drafted in the Sierra foothills a decade before, just as those adopted in 1860 were more complex than those written in 1859. In the Pike's Peak country the names given the camps were usually functional rather than ornamental—Mining District No. 1, Jackson District, Gregory District, and the like—boundaries were more exactly defined, governmental machinery more carefully organized, and the powers of officials more specifically stated. The constitutions sometimes contained additional provisions for settling disputes between districts, keeping minutes at miners' meetings, building roads by joint labor, taxation, and a variety of other subjects omitted from the more primitive documents usual in California. Punishments for criminals were also more exactly defined, usually by providing that murderers and horse thieves be hanged, and thieves given from ten to twenty-five lashes on the bare back before banishment. So successful were these codes that by the summer of 1860 claim jumping and crime were virtually nonexistent, while so many desperados fled from the mining camps to Denver that the citizens of that city set up their own "People's Government" that autumn.[43]

Like the Californians, the Pike's Peak miners looked upon these compacts as temporary expedients, to be abandoned as soon as a legally based government could be created. Steps in this direction were

---

fluence of California upon the Placer Mining Methods of Colorado," *Colorado Magazine,* XXVI (1949), 127–143.

[43] Records of the mining districts are in Thomas M. Marshall (ed.), *Early Records of Gilpin County, Colorado, 1859–1861* (Boulder, 1920), and the same author discusses these constitutions in "The Miners' Laws of Colorado," *American Historical Review,* XXV (1920), 426–439. A similar discussion is in Percy S. Fritz, "The Constitutions and Laws of Early Mining Districts—in Boulder County, Colorado," *Colorado University Studies,* XXI (Boulder, 1934), 127–148.

taken absurdly early. "Congregate a hundred Americans anywhere beyond the settlements," a traveler wrote, "and they immediately lay out a city, form a State constitution and apply for admission into the Union, while twenty-five of them become candidates for the United States Senate." [44] Scarcely more than one hundred lived in the Pike's Peak country in November, 1858, when thirty-five elected delegates assembled to draft a memorial to Congress asking the admission of the region as a territory. When this received scant attention they met again in the spring of 1859, this time to proclaim the State of Jefferson and to authorize a constitution for the new commonwealth. This met opposition when submitted to the voters that autumn, for opponents of statehood argued that the federal government would pay part of the bills if they sought only territorial status. When these arguments carried the day, a memorial was hurried to Washington asking that the Territory of Jefferson be created. Impatient as usual, the miners chose their governor, elected their legislature, and had their government functioning long before Congress began debate on the matter. Not until January, 1861, did a congressional measure create the Territory of Colorado.[45]

These governmental developments did not portend the end of the mining frontier; for the next two decades prospectors roamed the Far West, constantly revealing new gold fields in the Colorado country, as well as in the Northwest, the South Pass region, and the Black Hills. The role of these later-comers, however, was to consolidate advances made by miners of the pre-Civil War era, rather than to open new empires. By the beginning of that conflict America's far western domain had been defined. The forty-niners, the "yonder siders" who ravaged the streams of the Inland Empire, the desert rats who dug the silver of Arizona's mountains, the exploiters of the Comstock Lode, and the fifty-niners had scattered islands of settlement over all the trans-Mississippi country. There remained only the task of linking these far-flung frontiers with each other and with the East.

[44] Richardson, *Beyond the Mississippi*, p. 177.
[45] Milo Fellows, "The First Congressional Election in Colorado (1858)," *Colorado Magazine*, VI (1929), 46–47; Frederic L. Paxson, "The Territory of Colorado," *American Historical Review*, XII (1906), 55–60.

CHAPTER 12

The Reuniting of East and West

THE unique settlement pattern of the Far West, shaped as it was by accidental location of mineral wealth, brought the United States face to face with a troublesome problem. How could the far-flung miners be kept in touch with the East and with each other? Almost one thousand miles of prairies separated the nearest mining camps—those of the Pike's Peak country—from the frontier of farms and villages in the Mississippi Valley; beyond these lay nearly one quarter of the continent, broken only by islands of settlement in the Inland Empire, the Great Salt Lake country, Arizona, New Mexico, the Washoe region, California, and Oregon. That the pioneers in these distant outposts must be reunited with the land of their origin was unquestioned. They wanted, and demanded, letters from home, newspapers, and merchandise; moreover politicians feared that separatist tendencies manifest on former frontiers would exert themselves unless the new territories were bound more closely to the old. But how could this be accomplished?

As this question was pondered in the 1850's, certain things became clear. Private enterprise, all agreed, must build the transportation network; since the Panic of 1837 state-operated systems had been frowned upon. All agreed, too, that animal power rather than steam power must be utilized; for even if the newfangled railroads were sufficiently advanced technologically (which many doubted), the use of rails seemed foolish where nature had provided its own highway in the Great Plains. Stagecoaches for fast travel and wagon trains for freight were obvious. But how could they pay for themselves in a land of vast distances where way traffic was lacking? The answer was government subsidies, in two forms: mail contracts for stagecoach operators, and military contracts for freighters to supply western Army posts.

When the nation first grappled with the problem at the beginning of the 1850's, the communications network soon to be extended over the Far West was taking shape in the East and in California. In the East small, independent stagecoach lines had multiplied over the years, then gradually retreated westward before the advancing railroad system. By 1850, coaching was centered in the frontier regions, where the Western Stage Company had a virtual monopoly. There, too, the express business had mushroomed into a major enterprise, dominated by three individuals destined to make their mark in western annals: Alvin Adams, Henry Wells, and William G. Fargo.

These developments were paralleled by those in California, for there too a denser population and an abundance of wealth allowed transportation to flourish without government aid. Stagecoaching began in 1849, when a pioneer put a secondhand French omnibus pulled by half-broken mustangs in service between San Francisco and San José. Its center soon shifted to Sacramento and Stockton, the gateways to the Mother Lode country, where a dozen small lines were competing for business by 1853. The inevitable merger occurred in January, 1854, with the formation of the California Stage Company. Under its president, James Birch, the company soon controlled five sixths of the coaching business of northern California and most of that of southern California and the Oregon Country as well, operating 2,690 miles of stage routes in all. With the extension of mining to the Washoe country, another concern, the Pioneer Line, began running daily coaches to Virginia City over a hastily cut road across the Sierras.[1]

The express business inevitably followed staging into California, for no financial genius was needed to see that miners would pay exorbitant rates to have their gold transported to a place of safety or to secure letters from home. One Alexander H. Todd was the first to capitalize on their isolation; appearing at the mining camp of Jacksonville one day in 1849, he offered to deliver letters from San Francisco at an ounce of dust (about sixteen dollars) a letter! Such prices

---

[1] Oscar O. Winther, *Express and Stagecoach Days in California* (Stanford, 1936), pp. 76–96, 135–138, 150–158. The construction of the road is described in Chester L. White, "Surmounting the Sierras," *California Historical Society Quarterly*, VII (1928), 3–19, and a classic description of travel over the route is in J. Ross Browne, *Adventures in the Apache Country* (New York, 1869), pp. 312–313.

lured others into the business, until dozens of "one-man companies" were operating; these gradually merged and were in turn absorbed by a large eastern concern, Adams & Company.[2] By 1852 "Adams' Express" seemed destined to monopolize California expressing, and might have done so had not a rival from the East entered the lists. Wells, Fargo & Company, the western branch of the powerful American Express Company, showed its mettle from the first; ruthlessly cutting prices, it soon challenged Adams & Company for control of the field. So bitter was competition that the older firm was driven into bankruptcy in 1855; from that time on "Wells Fargo" dominated western expressing.[3] Hardly an ounce of gold left California except in a Wells Fargo treasure chest; hardly a package or letter was delivered to a mining camp except by a well-armed agent of the company.

These developments accentuated rather than solved the West's transportation problem. As each improvement stimulated business in the Mississippi Valley or California, the demand increased for a link between them, and with it pressure on the federal government to act. Under prodding from business-hungry merchants and news-hungry miners, Congress launched experiments with Army contracts for freighters and mail contracts for coachers that finally reunited East and West.

Subsidies for overland freighters came first. During the Mexican War the Army had tried to supply General Stephen W. Kearny's forces itself, and had failed dismally; hence when peace posed the task of supplying seven forts maintained in the West, it turned to private contractors with plains experience. Here was a golden opportunity for such men. Scattered along the frontier were communities where goods were in great demand—in New Mexico, in mines of the Southwest and California, in the Northwest. If freighters could secure government subsidies to cover their expenses, they could earn additional profits by supplying these outposts. So they thought, at least, as the scramble for contracts began.

James Brown of Independence, Missouri, received the first, and by doing so started the chain of events that brought the West's most

[2] Ernest A. Wiltsee, *The Pioneer Miner and the Pack Mule Express* (San Francisco, 1931), pp. 22–46, lists and describes all the one-man companies.

[3] Ruth Teiser and Catherine Harroun, "Origin of Wells, Fargo and Company, 1841–1852," *Bulletin of the Business Historical Society*, XXII (1948), 70–83; Anson S. Blake (ed.), "Working for Wells Fargo—1860–1863," *California Historical Society Quarterly*, XVI (1937), 30–42, 172–181.

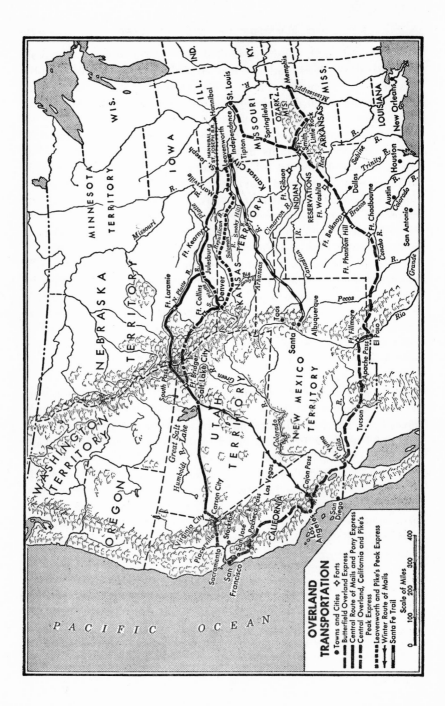

spectacular freighting firm into being. Brown's contract, granted in May, 1848, called for the delivery of 200,000 pounds of goods at Santa Fe for a fee of $11.75 for each one hundred pounds. When these arrived on schedule the War Department was so pleased that he was awarded new contracts in 1849 and 1850, this time in partnership with William H. Russell of Lexington, Missouri, whose name was soon to become symbolic of freighting to all the frontier.[4] Brown died in 1850 of typhus contracted on the trail, allowing Russell to align himself with a partner destined to share his fame, William B. Waddell. For the next three years the firm of Russell & Waddell prospered, until it was ready to take a final step needed to monopolize the overland carrying trade. On December 28, 1854, the two partners signed articles of agreement with Alexander Majors of Westport, Missouri, their principal rival. Thus was born the firm of Russell, Majors & Waddell, which dominated western freighting until the Civil War.

One could have searched the West in vain for three more unlikely partners, or three whose differing temperaments merged with such strength. Russell was a New Englander who affected carefully tailored clothes, enjoyed gracious living, and would have been thoroughly uncomfortable on the seat of a freight wagon or cooking beans over a buffalo-chip fire. Yet his conservative façade hid a gambler's temperament; nervous, volatile, and supremely confident of his own abilities, he was ready to plunge recklessly into new ventures or assume staggering debts in hope of turning a profit. Waddell, a Virginian, was a cautious, penny-pinching sort of man, who vastly preferred a sure 6 per cent to a possible 60 per cent; his contribution was to slow down the impetuous Russell and keep the firm on an even keel. The third partner, Alexander Majors, was the plainsman of the group; he was never happy save when on the trail, working with his men, spreading his blankets beneath their wagons, or sharing their greasy pork and beans over an open fire. His experience, and his ability to deal with wagoners on their own terms, gave the partnership an asset that neither the business acumen of Waddell nor the vision of Russell could supply.[5]

---

[4] The contracts are in 31st Congress, 1st Session, *Senate Executive Document,* No. 26, pp. 3–45, and freight shipments over the trail are listed in Walker D. Wyman, "Freighting: A Big Business on the Santa Fe Trail," *Kansas Historical Quarterly,* I (1931), 19–21.

[5] Raymond W. and Mary L. Settle, *Empire on Wheels* (Stanford, 1939), pp. 4–12.

The scale on which Russell, Majors & Waddell built their empire on wheels reflected the partners' determination to monopolize overland freighting. The hamlet of Leavenworth, Kansas, was selected as headquarters. There an army of workmen was assembled, to build wharves, offices, warehouses, wagon and blacksmith shops, packing plants, and a store; ten miles away on Shawnee Creek a sawmill was built to cut lumber for wagons. While Waddell supervised and Russell bought up nearby real estate for speculative purposes, Majors was busily hiring the 1,700 men needed as wagon masters, drivers, stock tenders, and messengers, or was sending out buyers to purchase 7,500 oxen and five hundred wagons. Intensely religious and prudishly moral, he demanded that each employee pledge himself "not to use profane language, nor to get drunk, nor to gamble, nor to treat animals cruelly, and not to do anything else that is incompatible with the conduct of a gentleman." [6] Majors selected his wagons as carefully as his men, buying only those built to his specifications: bodies of seasoned wood curved slightly to prevent the load from shifting, a shiplike prow, a square rear end to make loading easier, and a white canvas cover to protect the five-thousand-pound cargo.

As men and animals and wagons came pouring into Leavenworth that spring, Majors divided them into "outfits" of twenty-six wagons, each under a wagon master, or "bull boss," and an assistant wagon master. Each wagon was pulled by twelve oxen driven by a "bull-whacker" who was supplied with a rifle and Colt revolver. In addition every outfit included a "herder" who drove forty or fifty oxen for use as replacements and a "night herder" to watch the animals at night. All were carefully instructed. Bullwhackers were warned not to excite their beasts by "hallooing and cracking whips at them," to use a "long, deep-toned 'whoa,' " and to yoke "in a quiet gentle manner." They were told to stop ten minutes after leaving each camp to let the cattle "breathe and urinate, particularly if the weather is warm and cattle full," to rest for two or three hours after a "morning drive" of six or eight miles, and to end the "evening drive" in time to allow their animals to be bedded down after feeding. The men were to eat only two meals a day, Majors warned, as well as to "observe the Sabbath, and whenever an opportunity offers to hear preaching, embrace it." [7]

[6] Alexander Majors, *Seventy Years on the Frontier* (Chicago, 1893), p. 72.
[7] Majors' rules are in Settle and Settle, *Empire on Wheels*, pp. 29–31. That they were not generally followed is attested by nearly all travelers, who reported

That these exacting rules were always followed may be doubted; that they did have a sobering effect on the men there can be no question.

There was little sobriety in Leavenworth, however, as these preparations went on. All was hurrah and bustle: coughing steamboats nudging into the wharves, singing stevedores carrying bale after bale ashore, wagon masters supervising the loading of wagons, bullwhackers leading oxen about in pairs to accustom them to pull together, blacksmiths adding to the din by hammering the great iron tires into place. And everywhere mountain on mountain of merchandise waiting to be packed, or row on row of canvas-covered wagons ready for the trail, "Such acres of wagons!" wrote a traveler, "such pyramids of extra axletrees! such herds of oxen! such regiments of drivers and other employees!" [8] In early May, when the grass was turning green on the prairies, the first trains lumbered westward, some bound for Santa Fe, some for distant forts beyond the mountains, some for isolated mining camps. The firm of Russell, Majors & Waddell was in business, and in business with a vengeance.

Wherever they went, the routine of the company's outfits varied little. Each day began when the night herder drove the cattle into camp, singing to awaken the teamsters. As they rolled out of their blankets the cook in each "mess" of five bullwhackers began preparing the inevitable pork and coffee; the others rounded up their oxen and began "yoking," with the "wheelers" cared for first, then the "pointers," then the "swing teams," and finally the "leaders." So well were the men trained that the six teams could be harnessed in sixteen minutes. With breakfast over, the bull boss shouted his "lave, lave ho," and the caravan creaked into motion, each driver walking beside his team swishing his bull whip with its twenty-foot lash and its frayed "popper." If an animal lagged, the lash flashed out to "pop" against his rump like a small cannon; bullwhackers were so expert that every beast had a spot the size of a silver dollar worn on his flank where the whip descended. Hour after hour they plodded along, for Majors' outfits were all too well organized to be plagued by breakdowns. At

that swearing was universal among drivers and drinking common. One stated that he "scarcely ever saw a sober driver," and that their favorite drink was a potent brew called "tangle leg" made from alcohol, nitric acrid, pepper, and tobacco juice. A tenderfoot, it was said, began to stagger when he approached within four hundred yards of a demijohn of this fluid. Richard F. Burton, *The City of the Saints* (New York, 1862), pp. 5, 24–25.

[8] Horace Greeley, *An Overland Journey, from New York to San Francisco, in the Summer of 1859* (New York, 1860), pp. 47–48.

midday the caravan halted for two or three hours while the oxen grazed and the men dozed or played poker for plugs of chewing tobacco, then the march was resumed until the campsite selected by the wagon master was reached. There the wagons swung apart to form a circle as cooks lighted their fires and the night herder drove the stock out to pasture. By nightfall supper was over, and the men wrapped in blankets for the night's sleep.[9] Day after day this routine was repeated, with fifteen miles covered each day.

With such efficiency, there was little wonder that Russell, Majors & Waddell yearly tightened their grip on western freighting. Their contract in 1857 called for transporting nearly 5,000,000 pounds westward, a task requiring eight hundred wagons and so many men that the supply of bullwhackers was almost exhausted. Yet scarcely had the trains left Leavenworth when the outbreak of the "Mormon War" and the decision to send a force of 2,500 men to Utah created a new demand. The firm, the War Department insisted, must supply the Utah Expedition with an additional 3,000,000 pounds of supplies. As the partners hurriedly tried to buy oxen and recruit drivers, prices they had to pay mounted to 25 or 50 per cent above normal, yet by mid-July forty-one outfits were on the road to Utah. They were, it appeared, well on the road to a fortune.

Instead disaster struck. Three wagon trains were burned by Mormon guerrillas; others were lost when caught by winter snows as they moved toward Fort Bridger. Before the year was out the firm had lost nearly $500,000. This was bad enough, but to make matters worse the War Department informed the partners that it had exhausted its appropriation and could pay them nothing. Nor did a contract that kept nearly one hundred wagons on the road in 1858 allow them to recover their losses.[10] Plagued by debt, and discredited by their association with a "Mormon War" that had become extremely unpopular, Russell, Majors & Waddell were never able to recover their former pre-eminence. Yet all might not have been lost had the partners not been goaded by William Russell into entering a growing new business —stagecoaching.

[9] William F. Hooker, *The Prairie Schooner* (Chicago, 1918), pp. 30–31, 35–38; Burton, *City of the Saints*, pp. 24–25; Majors, *Seventy Years on the Frontier*, p. 105.
[10] Settle and Settle, *Empire on Wheels*, pp. 17–26; Charles R. Morehead, Jr., "Personal Recollections," in William E. Connelley, *Doniphan's Expedition and the Conquest of New Mexico and California* (Topeka, 1907), pp. 603–613.

That an attempt to bridge the miles between the Mississippi Valley and California with something speedier than lumbering freight wagons was inevitable; that stagecoaches should be employed was equally logical in view of their demonstrated success in both East and West. Yet how could coach service be maintained along a two-thousand mile trail where dangers were constant and way traffic nonexistent? The government found the answer in mail contracts.

Experiments began with the rush of the forty-niners; until that time letters for the West Coast were deposited at Independence or St. Joseph to be picked up by any traveler who cared to take them. In 1849, ocean mail service was begun, with letters carried from New York to the Isthmus of Panama by the government-subsidized United States Mail Steamship Company, and from Panama to San Francisco by the similarly supported Pacific Mail Steamship Company.[11] At the same time two contracts were let for the overland transportation of mail, one to Salt Lake City, and the other to Santa Fe. The former was undertaken by an optimist named Almond W. Babbitt who thought regular mail fees would provide adequate compensation; after one journey over the route in a light wagon he realized there were easier roads to bankruptcy and resigned. Nor was service to Santa Fe much better, for mails were carried irregularly on pack animals accompanying caravans of traders. These halfhearted trials only whetted the appetites of Westerners, who were clamoring by the end of the year for faster service.

Yet few improvements were made during the next half-dozen years. In 1850 a contractor agreed to maintain monthly service between Independence and Salt Lake City for a subsidy of $19,500 a year, and in 1851 another was found who would carry the mails on to California for $14,000 yearly. The experiences of these foolhardy hopefuls and their successors form one of the saddest sagas in frontier annals. Time after time carriers beat off Indian attacks and conquered nature's terrifying obstacles to complete their journeys. The trip between Salt Lake City and California was especially hazardous; on more than one occasion the mail wagon was preceded by crews of men with mauls to beat down snow in the Sierra passes, or was stopped entirely by high drifts for weeks at a time. After 1852, the southern route through

[11] John H. Kemble, "Pacific Mail Service between Panama and San Francisco, 1849–1851," *Pacific Historical Review*, II (1933), 405–417; John H. Kemble, "The Panama Route to the Pacific Coast, 1848–1869," *Pacific Historical Review*, VII (1938), 3–5.

Cajon Pass was usually followed during the winter, but this was so roundabout that the contractors regularly lost money.[12]

Nor did the service satisfy Westerners. Eastern letters and news-papers reached California fairly regularly over the ocean route via Panama, but thirty days were needed for the journey and prices charged were high. Overland service was hopelessly inadequate. Usually more than two months were consumed between Independence and San Francisco under the best of conditions; during the winter the route was sometimes blocked for months at a time. With typical frontier brashness, the Californians not only protested these conditions but suggested means of improvement. What was needed, they said, was a subsidy large enough to allow stagecoach service with way sta-tions where teams could be changed at regular intervals. This would allow coaches to run constantly, rather than stopping while men slept or animals grazed. Scarcely a newspaper that did not harp on this theme through the 1850's and scarcely a legislature that did not shower Congress with resolutions; in 1856 a petition signed by 75,000 Californians was sent east to add its weight to the cause.[13]

Congress was willing enough to respond, but as soon as debate began the sectional issue intervened. Should the government subsidize the "Central Route" through South Pass, or a "Southern Route" via El Paso and Fort Yuma? Given the tense state of nerves of the nation, there was no backing down on this matter for either Northerners or Southerners, especially as all believed that a railroad would eventually follow the mail coaches. As discussion raged, western congressmen realized that a formula to obscure sectional divisions must be found. The bill they devised authorized the Postmaster General to let con-tracts for semimonthly, weekly, or semiweekly service between the Missouri River and San Francisco over any route selected by the suc-cessful bidder. The trip was to be made in twenty-five days or less, in coaches or spring wagons that would carry passengers as well as the mails; the subsidy was to vary from $300,000 to $600,000 depending

[12] LeRoy R. Hafen, *The Overland Mail, 1849–1869* (Cleveland, 1926), pp. 56–73. Contemporary descriptions of travel over this route are in Burton, *City of the Saints,* p. 4, and Frank A. Root and William E. Connelley, *The Over-land Stage to California* (Topeka, 1901), pp. 1–2.

[13] The newspaper campaign is described in Virginia L. Rebbing, "Some Aspects of the Southern Overland Mail, 1857–1861," *Missouri Historical Re-view,* XL (1946), 482–485, and the sectional conflict in Curtis Nettels, "The Overland Mail Issue in the Fifties," *Missouri Historical Review,* XVIII (1924), 521–523.

on the frequency of the service. With neither a southern nor northern route specified, the sectional conflict was forgotten. In both the debate and vote on the measure, the division was along East-West rather than North-South lines, with an eastern "economy bloc" insisting that such an expenditure was unwarranted. In the end the bill passed Congress on March 3, 1857, by a substantial majority.[14]

The Postmaster General, Aaron V. Brown, was elevated to a position of unique importance by this measure, for his was the sole decision on the route to be followed. Actually, he found the choice easy when nine bids were submitted. That by a syndicate of prominent coachers headed by John Butterfield suited his purposes to a T; not only were wealth and experience represented among the incorporators, but the route proposed followed the thirty-fifth parallel through Albuquerque—and Postmaster Brown, a Tennessean, was determined to grant no contract that specified the South Pass road. The Butterfield syndicate, moreover, stated its willingness to accept any variation that Brown suggested. Fastening on this opportunity, he informed the Butterfield Overland Mail Company that it could have the contract if it would run coaches from St. Louis and Memphis to Fort Smith, Arkansas, then westward through El Paso and Fort Yuma to Los Angeles before swinging northward to San Francisco. This extensive alteration was accepted, and on September 16, 1857, the agreement was signed. The company guaranteed semiweekly service in twenty-five days or less for an annual subsidy of $600,000.[15]

The storm of northern protest rocked the nation for weeks to come. Why, the press asked, should the Postmaster burden the West with this "oxbow route" through impassable deserts when the Central Route was hundreds of miles shorter? "One of the greatest swindles ever perpetrated upon the country by the slave-holders," thundered the Chicago *Tribune,* and its charge was echoed everywhere. Through all the turmoil Brown stood his ground with one unanswerable argument. "There was," he stated, "no other all-the-year route between the Mississippi and the Pacific than the one chosen by the department." [16] Whether he was right or wrong had by this time become irrelevant;

14 *Congressional Globe,* 34th Congress, 3rd Session, Appendix, pp. 298–321; LeRoy R. Hafen, "Butterfield's Overland Mail," *California Historical Society Quarterly,* II (1923), 211–222.

15 The contract is in 35th Congress, 1st Session, *Senate Executive Document No.* 11, pp. 989–992.

16 "Report of the Postmaster General for 1857," *ibid.,* pp. 993–1005.

the decision was made and the nation committed to a grand experiment in overland transportation.

Certainly no one could have acted more vigorously to prove Postmaster Brown correct than John Butterfield. Fifty-six years old at the time, and an imposing figure of a man with his broad, square face and his massive frame impeccably clad in frock coat, pantaloons tucked into high boots, linen duster, and "wide-awake" hat, Butterfield had earned his spurs as a founder of the American Express Company and one of the East's leading stagecoachers. Drawing upon this experience, he set out to mold the Overland Mail Company into the West's most efficient line. Tipton, Missouri, the western terminus of the railroad from St. Louis, was selected as the starting point. The 2,812-mile-long route between that hamlet and San Francisco was divided at El Paso into an Eastern Division and a Western Division; these in turn were subdivided into nine "divisions" with a superintendent over each. The experienced plainsmen selected for these posts recruited gangs of men to bridge streams, cut down banks approaching fords, remove boulders, and fashion a makeshift road; others were set to work on the two hundred "stations" that were scattered along the route from twenty to eighty miles apart. Some were "home stations," designed to house a stationmaster, herders, harness makers, and blacksmiths; others were "swing stations," where two or three men would have the relays of horses ready for the flying coaches. All this was accomplished with remarkable speed as Butterfield drove his men relentlessly.[17]

He was equally busy buying equipment and hiring men. Eighteen hundred horses and mules were purchased and scattered along the route. Freight wagons and tankers to distribute hay and water were brought in lavish quantity, for many stations were located in country so barren that (as one stationmaster put it) "the grasshoppers have even perished from want of sustenance." [18] Even more care went into the selection of vehicles. The company planned to use "celerity wagons" in the unsettled country between Fort Smith and Los Angeles; these were light covered wagons carrying nine passengers and built so low to the ground that the danger of upsets was slight. More romantic were the 250 "Concord coaches" purchased to operate at either end of

[17] Roscoe P. Conkling and Margaret B. Conkling, *The Butterfield Overland Mail, 1857–1869* (3 vols., Glendale, Calif., 1947), I, 27–35, 128–129.

[18] Archer B. Hulbert (ed.), "Letters of an Overland Mail Agent in Utah," *American Antiquarian Society Proceedings*, n.s., XXXVIII, Pt. 2 (Worcester, 1929), p. 242.

the line. Built in Concord, New Hampshire, these were meticulously fashioned from seasoned hardwoods, and were the most elegant vehicles that ever the West had beheld. The oval-shaped body, painted red or dark green, was suspended on leather straps known as "thoroughbraces"; nine passengers could crowd themselves within and as many more find places on the roof, while mail was carried in a leather "boot" at the rear. Each cost $1,400; in all Butterfield spent about $1,000,000 before the first went into service.

Men were hired with equal care and extravagance. Some were "conductors" to accompany each coach, carefully selected for their sobriety and endurance, for each had to survive five hundred miles of jolting travel at a time. Others were stationmasters, herders, freighters, blacksmiths, and representatives of the multitudinous other occupations needed to keep such a line functioning smoothly. But those who captured the popular imagination were the drivers, or "whips," who handled the six half-tamed horses that pulled each coach. All were young, all were swaggering extroverts, all were sublimely profane, and nearly all "could get away with more double-rectified, copper-distilled, trigger-lightning, sod-corn juice" than a Mountain Man or an overland freighter. Yet most of them hid a solid sense of responsibility beneath their rough exteriors, for John Butterfield would hire no others. And not a man among them but could flick a fly off a lead horse's flank with a twelve-foot bull whip while at full gallop, or who would not lay down his life to live up to Butterfield's oft-stressed command: "Remember, boys, nothing on God's earth must stop the United States mail!" [19]

Extensive as these preparations were, they were completed at last, and all was in readiness for the first running of the Butterfield Overland Mail. On the sparkling clear morning of September 16, 1858, John Butterfield and Waterman L. Ormsby, a newspaper correspondent who was the lone passenger, loaded two bags of mail on the cars of the Pacific Railroad at St. Louis, swung aboard themselves, and were off. By 6:15 that night they were in Tipton, where only nine minutes were needed to shift mail and riders to the waiting coach, driven by John Butterfield, Jr. As this swept away toward the setting sun there was only a faint cheer from the few curious who had gathered. John drove well, despite frequent warnings from his father to

[19] Conkling and Conkling, *Butterfield Overland Mail*, I, 130; William Banning and G. H. Banning, *Six Horses* (New York, 1930), pp. 399–402.

"Be careful, John." At 2:05 on the morning of September 19 they galloped into Fort Smith, Arkansas, where the whole town was out to greet them. Butterfield stopped there, leaving the whole wagon to Ormsby for the rest of the journey.[20]

What a journey that was. Out across the Choctaw Indian reservation first, where stations were fairly frequent and fresh horses waiting in response to the terrifying yell of "Ah-wooh-wah" that the driver used to signal his coming. Delays increased after they crossed the Red River and began scattering mile after mile of Texas landscape behind them, for stations were farther apart now, or not yet built. In some, draft animals were unbroken and fought wildly against hitching; in others, no stock had arrived, forcing drivers to go on with tired beasts, sometimes for more than one hundred miles at a stretch. Beyond the Pecos the road was so strewn with boulders that the jolting "mud wagon" threatened to fall apart. These delays proved so costly that they rolled into El Paso nearly two days behind schedule. Some time was regained on the flat deserts of Arizona; more as they climbed the mountains that fringed the Los Angeles valley and flew across the fertile fields of southern California while inhabitants cheered or beat on anvils to show their enthusiasm. Up the San Joaquin Valley they swept on smooth roads, then over the rugged Pacheco Pass, where the driver used his whip rather than his brakes with the remark, "It's best to keep the wheels rolling, or they'll slide." [21] Just at sunrise on the morning of Sunday, October 10, the hills of San Francisco were sighted. Whipping up his horses, the driver went flying through the still-deserted streets to the company office on the plaza, after twenty-three days and twenty-three hours on the road.

San Francisco celebrated that night, with a great mass meeting, salutes, and speeches, including one from the badly worn Ormsby, who concluded feelingly: "Had I not just come over the route, I would be perfectly willing to go back by it." [22] Two thousand miles away in St. Louis a similar celebration was taking place, marking the arrival of the first eastbound stage. This had left San Francisco shortly after

[20] The description of the trip by the lone passenger, reprinted from the New York *Herald*, September 26—November 19, 1858, is in Waterman L. Ormsby, *The Butterfield Overland Mail* (San Marino, Calif., 1942), pp. 1–130. The route is traced and located in Conkling and Conkling, *Butterfield Overland Mail*, I, 153–412, II, 13–321.

[21] Ormsby, *Butterfield Overland Mail*, p. 124.

[22] Hybernia Grace, "The First Trip West on the Butterfield Stage," *West Texas Historical Association Year Book*, VIII (1932), 73.

midnight on September 15, 1858, with six passengers, and had reached
Fort Smith on October 7, to be greeted by a torchlight parade, a
barbecue supper, and the usual flood of oratory. At Tipton the mails
were shifted to railroad cars at 9:05 A.M. on October 9, reaching St.
Louis that night at 4:45, just twenty-four days and eighteen hours
after leaving San Francisco. Once more, cheering crowds led by the
St. Louis Silver Band escorted driver and passengers to the Planters
Hotel; once more, toasts were drunk to the success of John Butterfield
and his bridging of the continent. From Washington the President of
the United States wired: "I cordially congratulate you upon the result.
It is a glorious triumph for civilization and the Union." [23]

When the fanfare and the shouting had died, the Butterfield Overland Mail settled to the prosaic—but by no means easy—task of providing regular service over nearly three thousand miles of the unsettled
West. Each Monday and Thursday its coaches left Tipton and San
Francisco. The volume of mail increased steadily until by 1860 the
company was carrying more than went by sea; receipts from this
source mounted during the period from $27,229.94 to $119,766.76.
Passengers also accounted for a sizable revenue, for places on the
Butterfield coaches were in such demand that a ten-day wait was
necessary to secure a seat. The number of through passengers who
could afford the $200 fee was not large, but enough Westerners were
willing to pay the ten cents a mile charged for transportation between
points to bring in about $200,000 a year.[24]

These numbers attested to the stamina of that generation, for travel
on a Butterfield coach would have tested the strength of a Hercules or
the patience of a Job. Each journey began with the mail stowed in the
"boot" or, in case of overflow, on the floor of the coach. Passengers
then packed themselves in, for the Overland Mail, as an English traveler remarked, operated on the principle that a vehicle is never full.
When all were jammed in place or hanging precariously to the roof,
the swaggering driver mounted to his box, gathered up his "ribbons,"
and shouted "Turn 'em loose." Away scampered the horses as the
coach rocked wildly on its thoroughbraces, throwing the passengers
against each other as the iron-tired wheels clattered over the rocky

[23] Accompanying the first eastbound coach was G. Bailey, an agent of the Post
Office Department, whose report is in 35th Congress, 2nd Session, *Senate
Executive Document* No. 1, Pt. 4, pp. 739–744.

[24] Rupert N. Richardson, "Some Details of the Southern Overland Mail,"
Southwestern Historical Quarterly, XXIX (1925), 6–8, 15.

road amidst a cloud of choking dust. "Three in a row," wrote one traveler, ". . . we would solemnly rise from our seats, bump our heads against the low roof, and, returning, vigorously ram the again-rising seat we had incontinently left." [25] For the first few hours novelty sustained the riders, but as night fell the hardships of coach travel were brought home to all. Some managed to doze fitfully, but never for long, amidst the rumble of the coach, the shouts of the driver, or the din at a station while horses were changed. Sheer exhaustion allowed some to sleep after one or two nights on the road, but others were driven insane by the ordeal.

The only alternative to deadening fatigue was a stop at one of the stations. This appealed to few. One who did was marooned for a month until he could find a seat on another coach, while more were appalled by the dirt and squalor that greeted them. Built of adobe mud, with floors "much like the ground outside, only not nearly so clean," [26] and interiors black with flies, there was little in the usual Butterfield station to attract the discriminating traveler. Furnishings were less than primitive: a rickety table surrounded by boxes in lieu of chairs, a grease-encrusted stove, a few "bunks" littered with old rags and jumbled buffalo robes, a dingy tin bowl and a bit of gritty soap for the fastidious. Meals were even worse: every station served tough beef or pork fried in a grime-blackened skillet, coarse bread, mesquite beans, a mysterious concoction known as "slumgullion," lethally black coffee, and "a nasty compound of dried apples" that paraded under the name of apple pie. Day after day this deadening diet was inflicted on the passengers. Famous along the route was the tale of the stationmaster who placed a plate of fat pork before a traveler. "Thank you," said he, "but I never eat it." "Very well," that worthy replied, "just help yourself to the mustard." [27]

Monotonous food, monotonous countryside, monotonous companions—these were the lot of the overland traveler, except when even less-welcome danger threatened. Coaches sometimes stuck fast in snowdrifts at Apache Pass or other high spots, or overturned as they careened down a mountainside at breakneck rate. Occasionally an axle or thoroughbrace would snap, scattering riders and mail over the high-

[25] Joseph C. Tucker, *To the Golden Goal and Other Sketches* (San Francisco, 1895), p. 194.

[26] William Tallack, *The California Overland Express, the Longest Stage-Ride in the World* (Los Angeles, 1935), p. 61.

[27] Root and Connelley, *Overland Stage*, p. 97.

way. In western Texas or Arizona, Indians might sweep down upon the coach while the driver whipped up his horses and passengers cowered on the floor. Ten Butterfield drivers were killed by Apache and Comanche, especially during 1859, when attacks were alarmingly frequent. Mark Twain met one later who complained that he "came as near as anything to starving to death in the midst of abundance, because they kept him so leaky with bullet holes that he 'couldn't hold his vittels.' " [28] Coach travel under these conditions was no picnic, but the hardy souls of that generation enjoyed few comforts anywhere. And not a traveler but admired the enterprise of the Butterfield Overland Mail as its coaches swirled back and forth across the continent, never deviating more than a few hours from their scheduled time.

If few criticized service on the Overland, the same could not be said for the "oxbow route" followed by the coaches. Northerners and Westerners never forgave Postmaster General Brown for rejecting the shorter route through South Pass, which would, they insisted, allow mails to reach California in far less time. These grumblings did not become serious until the death of Brown in 1859 elevated Judge Joseph Holt of Kentucky to the office. Brown, despite his southern bias, had been a friend to the West, but Holt aligned himself with the eastern "economy bloc" as soon as he familiarized himself with his new domain. In all, he found, six routes were used for western mails: by sea via Panama, across Mexico to Tehuantepec, San Antonio to San Diego, the Butterfield route, Kansas City to Stockton, and St. Joseph to Placerville. On most lines weekly service was maintained with small subsidies, but the few items carried failed to justify even this support; thus the contractor delivering mails from Kansas City to Stockton had handled only two letters and twenty-six newspapers in nine months. Appalled by these figures, Judge Holt canceled contracts for the Stockton and Tehuantepec routes, reduced service between San Antonio and San Diego and between St. Joseph and Placerville to every other week, and decreased the subsidy granted carriers on the Panama route.

This was the blow that brought a competitor into the field to pioneer fast service over the Central Route. William H. Russell, the uncontrollable plunger of Russell, Majors & Waddell, was the West's champion. His motives, as always, were financial rather than patriotic. During the autumn of 1858 Russell heard much of the coming gold rush to the Pike's Peak country, and convinced himself that any com-

[28] Samuel L. Clemens (Mark Twain), *Roughing It* (Hartford, 1872), p. 76.

pany providing stagecoach service between Denver and the Mississippi Valley would profit enormously. His partners, William B. Waddell and Alexander Majors, were more cautious; they pointed out that no decent government subsidy could be secured and that without this no coach line could operate. Undeterred, the irrepressible Russell decided to go ahead on his own. With another western freighter, John S. Jones, he formed the Leavenworth and Pike's Peak Express Company, borrowed capital, and during the winter of 1858–59 hurried forward preparations needed to have coaches running when the promised rush began in the spring.

The route selected followed the Kansas and Solomon rivers before swinging on a straight line to Big Sandy Creek and Denver; along this an army of workers built stations, leveled down river banks, and fashioned what was called a road through country so barren that it would, as a later traveler reported, "hardly suffice when dry to nourish a prairie-fire." [29] Russell, in the meantime, was buying fifty Concord coaches, one thousand mules, and the mountains of equipment needed for such an ambitious enterprise. By April 18, 1859, all was ready for the first trip, although most stations were still only tents or dugouts. That morning two spanking-new coaches swept out of Leavenworth as the citizens cheered them on their way. Traveling day and night as their ten passengers dozed and jolted, they rolled into Denver on May 7 after nineteen days of wearisome travel. When the first returning coach reached Leavenworth on May 20—after ten days on the road— there was "naught but marching and feasting and enthusiastic acclaims" for twelve hours as the citizenry hailed William Russell as the savior of the West. [30]

Something more than huzzahs was needed to keep the Leavenworth and Pike's Peak Express Company alive, for expenses amounted to almost $1,000 a day while revenue dwindled alarmingly with the collapse of the 1859 rush. Too late Russell realized that no service could make money without a government subsidy. His answer was to buy out the John M. Hockaday Stage Line, a concern carrying semi-

[29] Greeley, *Overland Journey*, p. 99. The route is described in George A. Root and R. K. Hickman, "Pike's Peak Express Companies: Solomon and Republican Route," *Kansas Historical Quarterly*, XIII (1944), 173–180, 221–242, and Margaret Long, "The Route of the Leavenworth and Pike's Peak Express," *Colorado Magazine*, XII (1935), 186–194.

[30] A letter from a passenger describing the first trip is in LeRoy R. Hafen (ed.), *Overland Routes to the Gold Fields, 1859, from Contemporary Diaries* (Glendale, Calif., 1942), pp. 238–239.

monthly mails between Independence and Salt Lake City under a contract that granted it $130,000 yearly. This proved costly; John Hockaday drove such a hard bargain that Russell had to part with $144,000 to secure the franchise and a few mules and wagons. Moreover the mail contract called for use of the Platte River route, forcing him to build a completely new set of stations. On July 2, 1859, service began, with a seven-day schedule to Denver twice weekly and less frequent coaches to Salt Lake City. Travelers never tired of praising the smooth road, the swift stagecoaches, the clean stations, and even the meals, which would, as one put it, "throw many an eastern brag house in the shade." [31]

Popular good will, however, would not pay bills, and these mounted so steadily that by the fall of 1859 the Leavenworth and Pike's Peak Express Company tottered on the brink of bankruptcy. Russell's two original partners, William Waddell and Alexander Majors, watched these developments with foreboding, knowing that Russell's collapse would mean the end of their own freighting firm. To save themselves, they agreed to take over the stagecoaching company, and to nurture it with profits from freighting until it could secure a sufficiently lucrative mail contract. The concern was reorganized as the Central Overland, California & Pike's Peak Express, a contract secured to carry mails between Salt Lake City and Placerville, and triweekly service begun. Waddell and Majors' decision was a calculated risk. If they could prove the superiority of the Central Route over that followed by the Butterfield Overland Mail, they would win a large enough mail subsidy to make a profit; if they did not, they would end in bankruptcy. To win this gamble they must focus the attention of all the nation on their flying coaches.

Their attempt to do so provided the West with one of its most romantic interludes. Even before helping launch the Central Overland, William Russell had toyed with the idea of a "Pony Express" between the Missouri River and California; relays of horsemen, riding constantly at full speed and changing mounts frequently, would, he believed, be able to deliver light mails over the route in less than ten days. With the need of publicizing the Central Overland the plan took on new importance, for no more dramatic means of advertising the South Pass route could be found. When Russell, on a visit to Wash-

[31] George A. Root and R. K. Hickman, "Pike's Peak Express Companies: the Platte Route," *Kansas Historical Quarterly*, XIII (1945), 506–509.

ington, found Senator W. M. Gwin of California equally enthusiastic —and willing to work for a government subsidy—he hesitated no longer. On January 27, 1860, he announced his plan in a telegram to his son: [32]

> HAVE DETERMINED TO ESTABLISH A PONY EXPRESS TO SACRAMENTO, CALIFORNIA, COMMENCING THE 3RD OF APRIL. TIME TEN DAYS.

Only then did he seek out his partners to explain the scheme to which he had committed them. They agreed reluctantly, partly because Russell had gone too far to back down, partly because he convinced them that a Pony Express would win their stagecoach line the needed government contract.

Once the die was cast, preparations were pushed so feverishly that service could begin in two months. "Home stations" were constructed along the route at intervals of thirty miles, with "swing stations" every ten miles; riders, it was planned, would cover the distance between home stations, changing horses at each swing station. Five hundred horses were selected for their speed and stamina, all such untamable "outlaws" that they could be shod only with all four feet roped to the floor. Their specially designed saddles were light in weight with a short horn and the skirt reduced to a minimum. Over these a square of soft leather, called a *mochila,* was fitted; when a driver changed horses this was thrown in a twinkling from one saddle to another, for the mail was carried in four pockets in its corners. The total equipment weighed only thirteen pounds, and extra speed was assured by hiring riders who were tough and wiry, but weighed in at less than 135 pounds. Each was allowed to carry a knife and a repeating revolver but nothing else, for every gram was at a premium when the company charged five dollars for each one-half-ounce letter and $3.50 for every ten-word telegram.

With all in readiness, the first mail—forty-nine letters and a few special newspaper editions—reached St. Joseph late in the afternoon of April 3, 1860. For a time the first rider, "Billy" Richardson,[33] waited impatiently in his red shirt, blue pants, and high-topped boots

[32] Quoted in Olaf T. Hagen, "The Pony Express Starts from St. Joseph," *Missouri Historical Review,* XLIII (1948), 2.

[33] A dispute still rages over the question of whether the first rider was Johnson William Richardson or John Frye. The best case for Frye is in Howard R. Biggs, *The Pony Express Goes Through* (New York, 1935), pp. 38–40; more convincing is the argument for Richardson in Louise P. Hauck, "The Pony Express Celebration," *Missouri Historical Review,* XVII (1923), 435–439.

while a band played and the inevitable speechmaking dragged on, but at last he swung into the saddle and was away as the citizenry of St. Joseph shouted themselves hoarse. On the ferry across the Missouri the silver-embossed saddle and Richardson's fancy clothes were discarded; as soon as the boat touched shore he galloped through another cheering crowd to vanish into the night. The telegraph reported the Pony Express at Marysville, Kansas, 140 miles away, the next morning, then the world heard no more until Californians cheered their welcome. All the population of Placerville lined the streets when the rider flashed through on April 13; Sacramento gave him a similar welcome late that afternoon as he boarded a steamboat for San Francisco. When he arrived there at one the next morning, the lateness of the hour was forgotten as cannon boomed, bonfires flamed, bands ground out their discords, and a galaxy of speechmakers "uncorked the bottles of their eloquence." Well might Californians cheer, for Russell had made good his promise by delivering the mails in one hour less than ten days.

As the huzzahs died away, the partners settled to the task of maintaining their grueling schedule. Eighty riders were constantly in the saddle during the sixteen months the Pony Express operated, forty flying east and forty west. At first each rider rode from thirty to fifty miles, using three horses; but runs were later extended to seventy-five or one hundred miles, with the horses constantly at full gallop and changed every ten miles. Each change of mount was made in the twinkling of an eye; as the rider came crashing into the swing station his fresh beast stood saddled and waiting, ready for him to swing the *mochila* into place, throw himself upon it, and dash away. For the riders there was no rest until they reached their home stations after hours in the saddle, and even there word might wait them that a relief rider was sick and that they would have to ride on. One rode 280 miles in twenty-two hours without a rest when this happened; another, the famous "Buffalo Bill" Cody, was once in the saddle for almost as long as he rode 320 miles to get the mails through. All had a fanatical devotion to duty. The annals of the Pony Express abound with instances of riders who swam icy floods with the precious mails, or tramped through breast-high drifts and below-zero blizzards to lead their half-frozen horses into stations, or flew through bands of Indians gathered along the trail to waylay them.[34] And all for the salary of $50 to $150 a month that the Pony Express paid them.

[34] William L. Visscher, *A Thrilling and Truthful History of the Pony Express*

Such devotion meant that the mails would go through (in sixteen months riders traveled 650,000 miles with the loss of only one mail), but did not spell financial success for Russell, Majors & Waddell. The number of letters carried increased steadily, but rates were lowered from five dollars to two dollars for each half ounce under pressure from the public, and expenses mounted until the partners estimated that it cost thirty-eight dollars to deliver each letter.[35] Some loss was justified to advertise the Central Route, but not such a staggering one as this. To make matters worse, the Pony Express had scarcely begun operating when a competitor entered the field. The electric telegraph was less than a generation old in 1860, when Hiram Sibley, the dynamic president of the Western Union Telegraph Company, brought together two groups of promoters as the Pacific Telegraph Company and the Overland Telegraph Company, with authority from Congress —and a generous financial grant—to bridge the continent by wire. The first pole was set on July 4, 1861; from that date crews moved east from California and west from Nebraska until their wires were linked on October 24, 1861.[36] For a time the Pony Express operated in the ever-narrowing gap; but when the telegraph reduced the time from the Missouri to the Pacific from ten days to a fraction of a second, its doom was sealed. America's most romantic experiment in transportation had met its master.

Its collapse helped seal the doom of Russell, Majors & Waddell's other enterprises, for the partners poured almost $500,000 into the Pony Express. Business for their Central Overland, California and Pike's Peak Express did improve with their advertising of the South Pass route, but the needed mail contract failed to materialize. For a time in the summer of 1860 their hopes soared as Congress debated an Overland Mail Bill to consolidate all services in a single line with a million-dollar subsidy, but once more Southerners rallied to the defense of the Butterfield Overland Mail and defeated the measure. Still a worse blow fell that autumn when a rival company, the Western Stage Company, was awarded a contract to carry weekly mails to

(Chicago, 1908), pp. 39–48; W. R. Honnell, "The Pony Express," *Kansas Historical Quarterly*, V. (1936), 69–71; William F. Cody, *An Autobiography of Buffalo Bill* (New York, 1920), p. 47.

[35] Arthur J. Denney, "The Pony Express Trail: Its Dramatic Story," *Nebraska History*, XXI (1940), 16. Figures on the amount of mail carried are in Hafen, *Overland Mail*, pp. 180–181.

[36] Robert L. Thompson, *Wiring a Continent. The History of the Telegraph Industry in the United States, 1832–1866* (Princeton, 1947), pp. 345–371.

Denver, depriving the Central Overland of this lucrative business. By the time the first snows fell that winter, Russell, Majors & Waddell were so near bankruptcy that only a miracle could save them.

The exuberant William Russell tried to provide that miracle, and as usual failed. Visiting Washington that fall, he chanced to meet a young man named Goddard Bailey, who was reputedly a dealer in state bonds. Into his sympathetic ears Russell poured the whole sad story of his company's plight, ending by asking the loan of $150,000 in state securities. With these, Bailey was told, the company could borrow enough money to meet its obligations. Only when the bonds were delivered and Bailey approached for a second loan did Russell learn the truth: he was not a dealer but a clerk in the Department of the Interior who had goodheartedly embezzled the securities from the Indian Trust Fund. Instead of exposing this fraud, Russell persuaded him to take more and more, until $870,000 worth were turned over in all. Even this was not enough to save the firm. When Bailey realized this he sent a brokenhearted confession to President James Buchanan on December 22, 1860. A day later he and Russell were lodged in jail as a congressional investigation got under way.[37]

Had this unsavory affair not blackened the firm's name, it might possibly have survived in the unreal world created by the outbreak of the Civil War. The federal government, clearly, could no longer subsidize the southern Butterfield route and must supply the Pacific coast with mails through South Pass. This became clear as Congress began debating the Annual Post Route Bill in February, 1861, but as the debate progressed it became equally clear that the contract would never be awarded to a company associated in the popular mind with embezzlement and bankruptcy. The bill that finally passed on March 2, 1861, provided for a subsidy of $1,000,000 yearly to support daily stagecoach service over the Central Route, and stated explicitly that this should be awarded to the Butterfield Overland Mail. The contract was signed on March 12; a few days later the Overland began moving its equipment northward. William Russell had no choice but to swallow his pride and enter into an agreement that allowed the Central Overland a share of the subsidy in return for operating coaches and the Pony Express east of Salt Lake City.

[37] The report of the congressional committee is in 36th Congress, 2nd Session, *House Report* No. 78, pp. 1–365. See also Settle and Settle, *Empire on Wheels*, pp. 98–120.

Neither company enjoyed the fruits of this contest for long. The Butterfield line began operating over its new route on July 1, 1861, but John Butterfield had retired and the lesser men in control had little stomach for their task. Hence when the opportunity rose they sold out lock, stock, and barrel to the California express firm of Wells, Fargo & Company. For the next years Wells Fargo operated stage-coaches between Salt Lake City and Placerville, with branch lines running northward to the gold fields. The eastern end of the line changed hands a few months later. To secure money for improvements, Russell, Majors & Waddell in July, 1861, mortgaged their Central Overland to Ben Holladay, a rising figure in western freighting and commerce. These loans kept the company afloat for a time, but on March 21, 1862, the Central Overland went on the auction block, to be purchased by Holladay for a total price of about $500,000.[38] Holladay operated the line so efficiently that its profits allowed him to spread a stagecoach empire over most of the West before he in turn sold out to Wells, Fargo & Company in 1866. By this time the steel rails that would spell the doom of the frontier's romantic experiments in transportation were already stretching across the continent.

The death of overland coaching signaled the end of one phase of American frontier history. The pioneers who had aided in the conquest of the Far West—the Santa Fe traders, the Mountain Men, the farmers who followed the Oregon and California trails westward, the Mormons in their desert Zion, the forty-niners, the prospectors who dug their gold in remote mining camps—had founded not one but a galaxy of empires, scattered widely over a vast and distant land. These the freighters and stagecoachers had welded together, and these they had brought once more into contact with the East. In the future new and equally bold frontiersmen were to follow the trails they had blazed, but they were to be borne westward on rattling railroad cars, and they were to carry with them the artifacts of a machine civilization: mining machinery, steel plows, harvesters, windmills, and all the rest. Man had begun his battle against nature with only his hands and his brawn to aid him; man was to continue that battle with such efficient tools that only thirty years later the continent had been conquered and all the Far West subjected to the elevating forces of civilization.

[38] J. V. Frederick, *Ben Holladay: The Stagecoach King* (Glendale, Calif., 1940), pp. 21–25, 63–66.

Bibliography

The Mexican Borderlands

The literature on California's pastoral period is extensive. Two of the older histories, Hubert H. Bancroft, *History of California* (7 vols., San Francisco, 1884–1890), and Theodore H. Hittell, *History of California* (4 vols., San Francisco, 1885–1897), contain details not found in such modern studies as Robert G. Cleland, *From Wilderness to Empire* (New York, 1944), and John W. Caughey, *California* (New York, 1940). Social life is delightfully described in Nellie V. Sánchez, *Spanish Arcadia* (Los Angeles, 1929). The biographies of three pioneers also shed light on social conditions: Susanna B. Dakin, *A Scotch Paisano: The Life of Hugo Reid in California, 1832–1852* (Berkeley, 1929); Rockwell Hunt, *John Bidwell, a Prince of California Pioneers* (Caldwell, Ida., 1942); and James P. Zollinger, *Sutter: The Man and His Empire* (New York, 1939).

The diaries and reminiscences of early settlers also are invaluable in reconstructing the California scene. Of these the most useful are Edwin Bryant, *What I Saw in California* (New York, 1846; repr., Santa Ana, Calif., 1927); Walter Colton, *Three Years in California* (New York, 1850; repr., Stanford, 1949); William H. Davis, *Seventy-Five Years in California* (San Francisco, 1929); and Alfred Robinson, *Life in California: During a Residence of Several Years in That Territory* (New York,, 1846; repr., San Francisco, 1925). Among the descriptive accounts left by travelers, the fullest are Charles F. Carter (ed.), "Duhaut-Cilly's Account of California in the Years 1827–28," *California Historical Society Quarterly,* VIII (1929), 131–166, 214–250, 306–336; Eugene Duflot de Mofrás, *Travels on the Pacific Coast* (2 vols., Santa Ana, Calif., 1937); and "Edward Vischer's First Visit to California," *California Historical Society Quarterly,* XIX (1940), 193–216.

Brief but reliable accounts of the late Mexican period in Arizona and New Mexico are in Rufus K. Wyllys, *Arizona* (Phoenix, 1950); Cleve Hallenbeck, *Land of the Conquistadores* (Caldwell, Ida., 1950); and Erna Fergusson, *New Mexico: A Pageant of Three Peoples* (New York, 1951). Social life in New Mexico is described in Lynn I. Perrigo, "New Mexico in the Mexican Period, as Revealed in the Torres Documents," *New Mexico Historical*

Review, XXIX (1954), 28–40, and the best of the contemporary accounts is W. W. H. Davis, *El Gringo; or, New Mexico and Her People* (New York, 1857).

The Mexican period in Texan history is briefly surveyed in Rupert N. Richardson, *Texas, the Lone Star State* (New York, 1943), and more fully in Mattie A. Hatcher, *The Opening of Texas to Foreign Settlement, 1801–1821* (Austin, 1927). The best description of the governmental system is in Eugene C. Barker, *Mexico and Texas, 1821–1835* (Dallas, 1928). The same author's *The Life of Stephen F. Austin, Founder of Texas, 1793–1836* (Nashville, 1925) is a near-classic biography which tells the story of American colonization; he has also edited "The Austin Papers," American Historical Association, *Annual Reports for 1919 and 1922* (3 vols., Washington, 1924, 1928; Austin, 1926). The colonization process may also be studied in the histories of *empresario* grants, of which the most usable are Mary V. Henderson, "Minor Empresario Contracts for the Colonization of Texas," *Southwestern Historical Quarterly,* XXXI (1928), 295–324; XXXII (1928), 1–28; Lois Garver, "Benjamin Rush Milam," *Southwestern Historical Quarterly,* XXXVIII (1934–35), 79–121, 177–202; and E. Z. Rather, *DeWitt's Colony* (Austin, 1905).

The Road to Santa Fe

Of the older general histories the most useful is Henry Inman, *The Old Santa Fé Trail: The Story of a Great Highway* (New York, 1898); the best modern account is R. L. Duffus, *The Santa Fe Trail* (New York, 1930), which is popularly written but reasonably accurate. The origins of the trade can be reviewed in journals kept by members of the first three parties to reach Santa Fe: William Becknell, "Journal of Two Expeditions from Boon's Lick to Santa Fe," *Missouri Historical Society Collections,* II (1906), 55–67; Elliott Coues (ed.), *The Journal of Jacob Fowler* (New York, 1898); and Thomas James, *Three Years Among the Indians and Mexicans* (Waterloo, Ill., 1846; repr., St. Louis, 1916).

Journals and reminiscences of traders or travelers provide the most colorful sources on the Santa Fe trade. Of these the outstanding is Josiah Gregg, *Commerce of the Prairies* (2 vols., New York, 1844, and many later editions, including Max L. Moorhead [ed.], Norman, Okla., 1954). A day-by-day diary kept by Gregg on one of his return trips is in Maurice G. Fulton (ed.), *Diary and Letters of Josiah Gregg* (Norman, Okla., 1941), and Gregg's career is explored in R. E. Twitchell, *Dr. Josiah Gregg, Historian of the Old Santa Fé Trail* (Albuquerque, 1923). Journals of several other traders have been collected in Archer B. Hulbert (ed.), *Southwest on the Turquoise Trail; the First Diaries on the Road to Santa Fe* (Overland to the Pacific Series, II, Denver, 1933). Other useful diaries or reminiscences include F. F. Stephens (ed.), "Major Alphonse Wetmore's Diary of a Journey to Santa

Fe, 1828," *Missouri Historical Review,* VIII (1914), 177–197; F. A. Sampson (ed.), "Santa Fe Diary: M. M. Marmaduke Journal," *Missouri Historical Review,* VI (1911), 1–10; Benjamin F. Taylor, *Short Ravelings from a Long Yarn, or Camp March Sketches of the Santa Fe Trail* (Chicago, 1847); James J. Webb, *Adventures in the Santa Fé Trade, 1844–1847* (Southwest Historical Series, Glendale, Calif., 1931), and Jacob S. Robinson, "Sketches of the Great West. A Journal of the Santa Fé Expedition, 1846," *Magazine of American History,* Extra Numbers, XXXII (1927), 213–268.

A number of special studies deal with the government's efforts to protect the traders. The survey of the route in 1825–26 is described in Kate L. Gregg (ed.), *The Road to Santa Fe* (Albuquerque, 1952), which also reproduces many documents, and efforts to extend the surveys into Mexico are discussed in William R. Manning, "Diplomacy Concerning the Santa Fe Road," *Mississippi Valley Historical Review,* I (1915), 516–531. The military escorts of 1829, 1834, and 1843 are briefly treated in Fred S. Perrine, "Military Escorts on the Santa Fe Trail," *New Mexico Historical Review,* II (1927), 175–193, 269–304; and two of the expeditions receive more extended treatment in Otis E. Young, *The First Military Escort on the Santa Fe Trail, 1829; from the Journal and Reports of Major Bennet Riley and Lieutenant Philip St. George Cooke* (Glendale, Calif., 1952), and Henry P. Beers, "Military Protection of the Santa Fe Trail to 1843," *New Mexico Historical Review,* XII (1937), 113–133. Contemporary accounts written by participants are James Hildreth, *Dragoon Campaigns to the Rocky Mountains; being a History of the Enlistment, Organization, and First Campaigns of the Regiment of United States Dragoons* (New York, 1836), and Philip St. George Cooke, *Scenes and Adventures in the Army* (New York, 1857). The latter is especially valuable, as Cooke accompanied the 1829 expedition and commanded that of 1843.

Business aspects of the trade are discussed in F. F. Stephens, "Missouri and the Santa Fe Trade," *Missouri Historical Review,* X (1916), 223–262; XI (1917), 289–312; and in Lewis E. Atherton, "Business Techniques in the Santa Fe Trade," *Missouri Historical Review,* XXXIV (1940), 335–341. Letters of two leading merchants are in Ralph P. Bieber (ed.), "Letters of James and Robert Aull," *Missouri Historical Society Collections,* V (1927–28), 267–310.

The Era of the Mountain Men

The only general work on the Far Western fur trade is Hiram M. Chittenden, *The American Fur Trade of the Far West* (3 vols., New York, 1902; rev., New York, 1935). Chittenden's neglect of the southwestern trade is corrected in Robert G. Cleland, *This Reckless Breed of Men: The Trappers and Fur Traders of the Southwest* (New York, 1950), a sound and entertaining book. To recapture the excitement of the trade, this should be supplemented by narratives of two trappers: Charles L. Camp (ed.), "The Chronicles of George C. Yount," *California Historical Society Quarterly*, II (1923), 3–66, and James Ohio Pattie, *The Personal Narrative of James O. Pattie of Kentucky* (Cincinnati, 1831, and many later eds.). The most comprehensive study of the trade between Santa Fe and Los Angeles is LeRoy R. Hafen and Ann W. Hafen (eds.), *Old Spanish Trail: Santa Fé to Los Angeles* (Glendale, Calif., 1954).

The extension of British trading operations from the Northwest are surveyed in the histories of the Hudson's Bay Company and biographies of Dr. John McLoughlin, of which the best are Douglas MacKay, *The Honourable Company* (Indianapolis, 1936), and Frederick V. Hollman, *Dr. John McLoughlin, The Father of Oregon* (Cleveland, 1907), but more fully in the scholarly introduction in Frederick Merk (ed.), *Fur Trade and Empire, George Simpson's Journal* (Cambridge, Mass., 1931). The records of the principal brigades that invaded the Great Basin and Rocky Mountain country are in E. E. Rich (ed.), *Peter Skene Ogden's Snake Country Journals, 1824–25 and 1825–26* (London, 1950), and T. C. Elliott (ed.), "The Peter Skene Ogden Journals," *Oregon Historical Quarterly*, X (1909), 331–365; XI (1910), 201–222, 355–396.

The definitive history of early American trade west from St. Louis is Dale L. Morgan, *Jedediah Smith and the Opening of the West* (Indianapolis, 1953). Documents dealing with the activities of Smith, William Ashley, and other early traders are in Harrison C. Dale (ed.), *The Ashley-Smith Explorations and the Discovery of a Central Route to the Pacific, 1822–1829* (Cleveland, 1918, rev., Glendale, Calif., 1941); Maurice S. Sullivan (ed.), *The Travels of Jedediah Smith* (Santa Ana, Calif., 1934); and Donald M. Frost, "Notes on General Ashley, the Overland Trail, and South Pass," *American Antiquarian Society Proceedings*, CIV (1944), 161–312.

Two brief but significant studies that serve as an introduction to any understanding of the Mountain Men are Frederick E. Voelker, "The Mountain Men and Their Part in the Opening of the West," *Missouri Historical Society Bulletin*, III (1947), 151–162, and Carl P. Russell, "Wilderness Rendezvous Period of the American Fur Trade," *Oregon Historical Quarterly*, XLII (March, 1941), 1–47. More essential are the diaries of the Mountain Men themselves. Among these the most accurate is Osburne Russell, *Journal of a Trapper, or Nine Years in the Rocky Mountains, 1834–1844* (Boise, Ida., 1921), which is apparently an actual journal. Only slightly less reliable are Warren A. Ferris, *Life in the Rocky Mountains, 1830–1835* (Salt Lake City, 1940); Zenas Leonard, *Narrative of the Adventures of Zenas Leonard, Written by Himself* (Clearwater, Pa., 1839, repr., Cleveland, 1904); Rufus B. Sage, *Scenes in the Rocky Mountains and in Oregon, California, New Mexico, Texas and the Grand Prairie* (Philadelphia, 1846); Elliott Coues (ed.), *Forty Years a Fur Trader on the Upper Missouri: the Personal Narrative of Charles Larpenteur, 1833–1872* (2 vols., New York, 1898); and Lewis H. Garrard, *Wah-to-Yah, and the Taos Trail* (Cincinnati, 1850, repr., Glendale, Calif., 1938). All are based on notes or journals kept by traders.

Among reminiscences written or dictated by Mountain Men, the best are Charles L. Camp (ed.), *James Clyman, American Frontiersman, 1792–1881* (San Francisco, 1928); James P. Beckwourth, *The Life and Adventures of James P. Beckworth* (New York, 1856; repr., New York, 1931); and Frances F. Victor, *The River of the West* (Hartford, 1870). The latter was dictated to Mrs. Victor by Joseph L. Meek. In the same category are James B. Marsh, *Four Years in the Rockies; or, the Adventures of Isaac P. Rose* (New Castle, Pa., 1884); William H. Ellison (ed.), *The Life and Adventures of George Nidever, 1802–1883* (Berkeley, 1937); David L. Brown, *Three Years in the Rockies* (n.p., 1950); and Howard L. Conrad, *"Uncle Dick" Wootton, the Pioneer Frontiersman of the Rocky Mountain Region* (Chicago, 1890).

Travelers also left valuable impressions of the fur trappers. The most readable accounts are from the pen of George F. Ruxton: *Adventures in Mexico and the Rocky Mountains* (New York, 1848), and an autobiographical novel, *Life in the Far West* (Norman, Okla., 1951). Albert Pike, *Prose Sketches and Poems* (Boston, 1834), contains an account of his experiences, and two works by Thomas J. Farnham, *Travels in the Great Western Prairies, the Anahuac and Rocky Mountains, and in the Oregon Country* (London, 1843; repr., Cleveland, 1906), and *Travels in California and Scenes in the Pacific Ocean* (New York, 1844), describe the author's experiences at a rendezvous.

The Mountain Men have also inspired numerous biographers. Among the most accurate accounts are Alpheus H. Favour, *Old Bill Williams, Mountain Man* (Chapel Hill, 1936); J. Cecil Alter, *James Bridger, Trapper, Frontiersman, Scout and Guide* (Salt Lake City, 1925); Edwin L. Sabin, *Kit Carson Days, 1809–1868* (2 vols., New York, 1914; rev., New York, 1935); LeRoy R. Hafen and W. J. Ghent, *Broken Hand, the Life Story of Thomas Fitzpatrick, Chief of the Mountain Men* (Denver, 1931); and Charles Kelly, *Old Greenwood. The Story of Caleb Greenwood* (Salt Lake City, 1936).

The expansion of American Fur Company activities is described in Kenneth W. Porter, *John Jacob Astor, Business Man* (2 vols., Cambridge, Mass., 1931), and the most useful works on the Nathaniel Wyeth expeditions are Frank G. Young (ed.), *The Correspondence and Journals of Captain Nathaniel J. Wyeth, 1831–1836* (Eugene, Ore., 1899), and John B. Wyeth, *Oregon; or A Short History of a Long Journey* (Cambridge, Mass., 1833, repr., Cleveland, 1905). Jennie B. Brown, *Fort Hall on the Oregon Trail: A Historical Study* (Caldwell, Ida., 1932), is also useful. Two standard works on other forts prominent in the later days of the trade are LeRoy R. Hafen and Francis M. Young, *Fort Laramie and the Pageant of the West, 1834–*

1890 (Glendale, Calif., 1938), and David Lavender, *Bent's Fort* (Garden City, N.Y., 1954).

The Coming of the Pioneers

Of the general histories of the Pacific Northwest, the most recent and readable is Oscar O. Winther, *The Great Northwest. A History* (New York, 1947). William H. Gray, *A History of Oregon, 1792–1849, Drawn from Personal Observation and Authentic Information* (Portland, Ore., 1870), was written by an old settler. One of the most thorough and reliable histories of the settlement process is Robert C. Clark, *History of the Willamette Valley, Oregon* (3 vols., Chicago, 1927). Valuable collections of documents are in the Overland to the Pacific Series edited by Archer B. Hulbert: *Where Rolls the Oregon: Prophet and Pessimist Look Northwest* (III, Denver, 1933), *The Call of the Columbia: Iron Men and Saints Take the Oregon Trail* (IV, Denver, 1934), *The Oregon Crusade. Across Land and Sea to Oregon* (V, Denver, 1935), and *Marcus Whitman, Crusader* (VI-VIII, Denver, 1936–41). Materials dealing with missionary activities not in these volumes are in LeRoy R. Hafen and Ann W. Hafen (eds.), *To the Rockies and Oregon, 1839–1842* (The Far West and the Rockies Historical Series, III, Glendale, Calif., 1955).

The best account of awakening Congressional interest in the Northwest is Charles H. Ambler, "The Oregon Country, 1810–1830: A Chapter in Territorial Expansion," *Mississippi Valley Historical Review*, XXX (1943), 3–24. Hall Jackson Kelley's career is described in Fred W. Powell, "Hall Jackson Kelley—Prophet of Oregon," *Oregon Historical Quarterly*, XVIII (1917), 1–53, 271–295, and the same author has edited most of Kelley's important works in *Hall J. Kelley on Oregon; a Collection of Five of His Published Works and a Number of Hitherto Unpublished Letters* (Princeton, 1932).

The literature on the missionary invasion of Oregon is extensive, as indicated by Clifford M. Drury, "Protestant Missionaries in Oregon: A Bibliographic Survey," *Oregon Historical Quarterly*, L (1949), 209–221. Cornelius J. Brosnan, *Jason Lee, Prophet of the New Oregon* (New York, 1932), is a satisfactory biography, and Lee's diary is in "Diary of Rev. Jason Lee," *Oregon Historical Quarterly*, XVII (1916), 116–146, 297–430. Two of his co-workers describe their activities in Daniel Lee and J. H. Frost, *Ten Years in Oregon* (New York, 1844), and Elijah White, *Ten Years in Oregon* (Ithaca, N.Y., 1848). An excellent study of Marcus Whitman is Clifford M. Drury, *Marcus Whitman, M.D., Pioneer and Martyr* (Caldwell, Ida., 1937), and the same author has admirably described the careers of two other Presbyterian missionaries in *Henry Harmon Spaulding: Pioneer of Old Oregon* (Caldwell, Ida., 1936), and *Elkanah and Mary Walker, Pioneers among the Spokanes* (Caldwell, Ida., 1940). The standard biography of the first

Catholic missionary is Letitia M. Lyons, *Francis Norbert Blanchet and the Founding of the Oregon Missions (1838–1848)* (Washington, 1940). No modern biography of the first Catholic missionary from the United States has been written, but documents illustrating his career are in Hiram M. Chittenden and A. T. Richardson (eds.), *Life, Letters and Travels of Father Pierre-Jean de Smet, S.J., 1801–1873* (4 vols., New York, 1905). Brief but of some value is William N. Bischoff, *The Jesuits in Old Oregon, 1840–1940* (Caldwell, Ida., 1945).

Early settlers who attracted immigrants to California can best be studied through their biographies or writings. Standard works are George D. Lyman, *John Marsh, Pioneer* (New York, 1930), and James P. Zollinger, *Sutter: The Man and His Empire* (New York, 1939). A fragmentary diary kept by Sutter is in Douglas S. Watson (ed.), *The Diary of Johann Augustus Sutter* (San Francisco, 1932), and Sutter's reminiscences, liberally expanded by the editor, have been printed in Erwin G. Gudde, *Sutter's Own Story* (New York, 1936).

The Overland Trails

Jay Monaghan, *The Overland Trail* (Indianapolis, 1937), contains readable chapters on the Oregon and California trails. Less useful is James C. Bell, *Opening a Highway to the Pacific 1838–1846* (New York, 1921), which stresses the forces leading to migration. Among general works on the Oregon Trail, W. J. Ghent, *The Road to Oregon* (New York, 1929), is both colorful and sound. Many of the best-known diaries have been reproduced in Maude A. Rucker (ed.), *The Oregon Trail and Some of Its Blazers* (New York, 1930). The best brief account of the compacts that provided government for the emigrants is Harrison C. Dale, "The Organization of the Oregon Emigrating Companies," *Oregon Historical Quarterly,* XVI (1915), 205–227, and Helen B. Kroll, "The Books That Enlightened the Emigrants," *Oregon Historical Quarterly,* XLV (1944), appraises the role of guidebooks in shaping the migration.

The most useful sources for the principal emigrant party of 1841 are from the pen of its leader, John Bidwell: *Journey to California* (Liberty, Mo., 1842; repr., San Francisco, 1937), and *Echoes of the Past* (Chico, Calif., n.d.; repr., Chicago, 1928). The former is a day-by-day journal; the latter contains two articles reprinted from *Century Magazine.* The standard biography of Bidwell is Rockwell D. Hunt, *John Bidwell, a Prince of California Pioneers* (Caldwell, Ida., 1942). Two other journals kept by members of the party are Joseph Williams, *Narrative of a Tour from the State of Indiana to the Oregon Territory in the Years 1841–2* (Cincinnati, 1843; repr., New York, 1921), and Nicholas Dawson, *Narrative of Nicholas "Cheyenne" Dawson (Overland to California in '41 and '49, and Texas in '51)* (San Francisco, 1933).

The "Great Migration" of 1843 inspired a number of diarists and contemporary historians. The classic account is Jesse Applegate, "A Day with the Cow Column," *Oregon Historical Quarterly,* I (1900), 371–383 (repr., Chicago, 1934). Jesse A. Applegate, *Recollections of My Boyhood* (Chicago, 1934), are the reminiscences of a nephew of Jesse Applegate, and Peter H. Burnett's reminiscences have been published as *Recollections and Opinions of an Old Pioneer* (New York, 1880). Another memoir, written many years later, is Edward H. Lenox, *Overland to Oregon in the Tracks of Lewis and Clarke* [*sic*]. *History of the First Emigration to Oregon in 1843* (Oakland, Calif., 1904). Brief diaries kept by members of the party include Overton Johnson and W. H. Winter, *Route Across the Rocky Mountains, with a Description of Oregon and California* (Lafayette, Ind., 1846; repr., Princeton, 1932); James W. Nesmith, "Diary of the Emigration of 1843," *Oregon Historical Quarterly,* VII (1906), 329–359; Harry N. M. Winton (ed.), "William T. Newby's Diary of the Emigration of 1843," *Oregon Historical Quarterly,* XL (1939), 319–324; and John Boardman, "The Journal of John Boardman. An Overland Journey from Kansas to Oregon in 1843," *Utah Historical Quarterly,* II (1929), 99–121.

George R. Stewart (ed.), *The Opening of the California Trail* (Berkeley, 1953), includes the only known reminiscences of the Stevens-Murphy party of 1844, and the classic journal of the 1845 migrations is Joel Palmer, *Journal of Travels over the Rocky Mountains to the Mouth of the Columbia River; Made During the Years 1845 and 1846* (Cincinnati, 1847, repr., Cleveland, 1906). John E. Howell, "Diary of an Emigrant of 1845," *Washington Historical Quarterly,* I (1907), 138–158, is brief and factual.

Each of the three parties reaching California in 1846 had its chroniclers. Edwin Bryant, *What I Saw in California* (New York, 1848; repr., Santa Ana, Calif., 1936), describes the Russell Party, and William W. Allen and R. B. Avery, *California Gold Book. First Nugget. Its Discovery and Discoverers* (San Francisco, 1893), contains a journal of the Harlan-Young party. Journals of these and other parties using the Hastings Cutoff that year are collected in J. Roderick Korns (ed.), *West from Fort Bridger; the Pioneering of the Emigrant Trails Across Utah, 1846–1850* (Salt Lake City, 1951). The third party, that led by the Donners, is described in Charles F. McGlashan, *History of the Donner Party; a Tragedy of the Sierra* (Truckee, Calif., 1879; 4th ed., 1881; repr., Stanford, 1947), and J. Quinn Thornton, *Oregon and California in 1848* (2 vols., New York, 1849). Both contain reminiscences of and interviews with survivors. Two briefer reminiscences are Eliza P. Donner Houghton, *The Expedition of the Donner Party and Its Tragic Fate* (Chicago, 1911; repr., Los Angeles, 1920), and Patrick Breen, "Diary of Patrick Breen. One of the Donner Party," *Academy of Pacific Coast History Publications,* I (1910), 271–284. An excellent modern study is

George R. Stewart, *Ordeal by Hunger. The Story of the Donner Party* (New York, 1936).

Texas: Revolution and Republic

An interpretative introduction to this period of Texas history is William C. Binkley, *The Texas Revolution* (Baton Rouge, 1952), although the earlier work by Eugene C. Barker, *Mexico and Texas, 1821–1835* (Dallas, 1928), is useful. Another essential study is Samuel H. Lowrie, *Culture Conflict in Texas, 1821–1835* (New York, 1932), a sociological interpretation, and Gerald Ashford, "Jacksonian Liberalism and Spanish Law in Early Texas," *Southwestern Historical Quarterly,* LVII (1953), 1–37, argues convincingly that the relative freedom enjoyed by the Texans inspired their revolution as soon as restrictions were imposed. Documents are in William C. Binkley (ed.), *Official Correspondence of the Texan Revolution, 1835–1836* (2 vols., New York, 1936).

The diplomacy of the prerevolutionary years is described in detail in William R. Manning, *Early Diplomatic Relations between the United States and Mexico* (Baltimore, 1916). Eugene C. Barker, "President Jackson and the Texas Revolution," *American Historical Review,* XII (1907), argues that President Jackson did not help foment the revolution; the opposite thesis is maintained, not quite convincingly, in three works by Richard R. Stenberg: "The Texas Schemes of Jackson and Houston, 1829–1836," *Southwestern Social Science Quarterly,* XV (1934), 229–250; "Jackson's Neches Claim, 1829–1836," *Southwestern Historical Quarterly,* XXXIX (1936), 255–274; and "President Jackson and Anthony Butler," *Southwest Review,* XXII (1937), 391–404.

Conflicts between Texans and Mexicans centered about colonization, land sales, and customs duties. The colonization issue is considered in Ohland Morton, *Terán and Texas: A Chapter in Texas-American Relations* (Austin, 1948). The conclusions of Eugene C. Barker, "Land Speculation as Cause of the Texas Revolution," *Quarterly of the Texas State Historical Association,* X (1906), 76–95, are more valid than those of Elgin Williams, *The Animated Pursuit of Speculation: Land Traffic in the Annexation of Texas* (New York, 1949).

No satisfactory biography of Sam Houston has been written for the war years. Marquis James, *The Raven. A Biography of Sam Houston* (Indianapolis, 1929), is popular, and Llerena Friend, *Sam Houston, the Great Designer* (Austin, 1954), emphasizes the post-1845 period of his life. His works have been collected in Amelia W. Williams and Eugene C. Barker (eds.), *The Writings of Sam Houston, 1813–1863* (8 vols., Austin, 1938–1943), and more briefly in Donald Day and Harry H. Ullon (eds.), *The Autobiography of Sam Houston* (Norman, Okla., 1954). The three principal military engagements are best described in Amelia W. Williams, "A Critical

Study of the Siege of the Alamo and the Personnel of Its Defenders," *Southwestern Historical Quarterly,* XXXVI (1933), 251–287; XXXVII (1934), 237–312; Harbert Davenport, "The Men of Goliad," *Southwestern Historical Quarterly,* XLIII (1939), 1–41; and Sam H. Dixon and Louis W. Kemp, *The Heroes of San Jacinto* (Houston, 1932).

The political history of the Texas Republic can be traced in the biographies and papers of its presidents. Those dealing with the Houston administration are listed above; the papers of the second president are in C. A. Gulick, *et al.* (eds.), *The Papers of Mirabeau Buonaparte Lamar* (6 vols., Austin, 1921–27), and Asa K. Christian, *Mirabeau Buonaparte Lamar* (Austin, 1922), is the most useful biography. Herbert P. Gambrell, *Anson Jones: The Last President of Texas* (New York, 1948), is a scholarly book. The best study of social developments is William R. Hogan, *The Texas Republic. A Social and Economic History* (Norman, Okla., 1946). Barnes F. Lathrop, *Migration into East Texas, 1835–1860* (Austin, 1949), brilliantly describes population growth, and Rudolph L. Biesele, *The History of the German Settlements in Texas, 1831–1861* (Austin, 1930), deals less thoroughly with the principal foreign settlement.

A thorough history of Texas efforts to expand is William C. Binkley, *The Expansionist Movement in Texas, 1836–1850* (Berkeley, 1925), although no modern history can duplicate the atmosphere of George W. Kendall, *Narrative of the Texan Santa Fé Expedition* (2 vols., New York, 1844), and Thomas Falconer, *Letters and Notes on the Santa Fe Expedition, 1841–1842* (New York, 1930), two contemporary accounts. Narratives of the ill-fated Mier expedition have been collected in Frederick C. Chabot, *Texas Expeditions of 1842* (San Antonio, 1942), and the same author has edited the diary of one of the survivors: *The Perote Prisoners. Being the Diary of James L. Trueheart* (San Antonio, 1934). Thomas J. Green, *Journal of the Texas Expedition against Mier* (New York, 1845), and William P. Stapp, *The Prisoners of Perote, Containing a Journal Kept by the Author* (Philadelphia, 1845; repr., Austin, 1935), are also valuable.

Manifest Destiny

The most detailed history of the diplomacy of manifest destiny is in Vols. IV and V of Hunter Miller (ed.), *Treaties and Other International Acts of the United States of America, 1776–1863* (8 vols., Washington, 1931–48); briefer accounts are in Samuel F. Bemis (ed.), *The American Secretaries of State and Their Diplomacy* (10 vols., New York, 1927–29). The standard biographies of the presidents are also useful: Oliver P. Chitwood, *John Tyler, Champion of the South* (New York, 1939), and Eugene I. McCormack, *James K. Polk; A Political Biography* (Berkeley, 1922). Essential for the era is Albert K. Weinberg, *Manifest Destiny* (Baltimore, 1935), which is a history of expansionism rather than of expansion.

A detailed history of the diplomacy of Texan annexation is Justin H. Smith, *The Annexation of Texas* (New York, 1911); more readable is Joseph W. Schmitz, *Texan Statecraft, 1836–1845* (San Antonio, 1945). Two articles by Richard R. Stenberg attempt to show, without success, that Polk tried to goad the Texans into an attack on Mexico in 1845: "President Polk and the Annexation of Texas," *Southwestern Social Science Quarterly*, XIV (1934), 333–356, and "The Failure of Polk's Mexican War Intrigue of 1845," *Pacific Historical Review*, IV (1935), 39–68. Ephraim D. Adams, *British Interests and Activities in Texas, 1838–1846* (Baltimore, 1910), should be supplemented with Harriet Smither, "English Abolitionism and the Annexation of Texas," *Southwestern Historical Quarterly*, XXXII (1929), 193–205. French relations with the Republic are described in R. A. McLemore, "The Influence of French Diplomatic Policy on the Annexation of Texas," *Southwestern Historical Quarterly*, XLIII (1940), 342–347. Essential documents are in George P. Garrison (ed.), "Diplomatic Correspondence of the Republic of Texas," American Historical Association, *Annual Reports for 1907 and 1908* (2 vols., Washington, 1908, 1911).

The diplomacy of the Oregon controversy is conveniently summarized in Melvin C. Jacobs, *Winning Oregon* (Caldwell, Ida., 1938), although this should be supplemented with the interpretative study by Richard W. Van Alstyne, "International Rivalries in Pacific Northwest," *Oregon Historical Quarterly*, XLVI (1945), 185–218. Norman A. Graebner, *Empire on the Pacific* (New York, 1955), argues convincingly that expansion into both Oregon and California was dictated at least partly by a desire for ports. The diplomacy of the 1846 treaty is most thoroughly explored in articles by Frederick Merk: "The Oregon Pioneers and the Boundary," *American Historical Review*, XXIX (1924), 681–699; "British Party Politics and the Oregon Treaty," *American Historical Review*, XXXVII (1932), 653–677; and "British Government Propaganda and the Oregon Treaty," *American Historical Review*, XL (1934), 38–62. In "The British Corn Crisis of 1845–46 and the Oregon Treaty," *Agricultural History*, VIII (1935), 95–123, Mr. Merk argues convincingly that economic factors did not greatly influence the settlement.

The growth of American interest in California is traced in Robert G. Cleland, "The Early Sentiment for the Annexation of California: An Account of the Growth of American Interest in California, 1835–1846," *Southwestern Historical Quarterly*, XVIII (1914–15), 1–40, 231–260; and in Norman A. Graebner, "American Interest in California, 1845," *Pacific Historical Review*, XXII (1953), 12–28. The fear of foreign designs on California that whetted this interest is appraised in Ephraim D. Adams, "English Interest in the Annexation of California," *American Historical Review*, XIV (1909), 744–763, and A. P. Nasatir, "French Activities in

California before Statehood," Pacific Coast Branch of the American Historical Association, *Proceedings,* III (1928), 76–88. An unsatisfactory biography of the principal American diplomatic agent in California, Thomas O. Larkin, is Reuben L. Underhill, *From Cowhides to Golden Fleece* (2nd ed., Stanford, 1946), and Larkin's letters are being reproduced in George P. Hammond (ed.), *The Larkin Papers* (10 vols., Berkeley, 1951–).

Literature on the Frémont expedition is voluminous. The best biography is Allan Nevins, *Frémont: Pathmarker of the West* (New York, 1939). Many of the documents concerning his adventures in California are in "The Frémont Episode," *California Historical Society Quarterly,* III (1924), 270–289, to IX (1930), 81–88. Whether or not Frémont precipitated the Bear Flag Revolt has long divided historians. Ernest A. Wiltsee, *The Truth About Frémont: An Inquiry* (San Francisco, 1936), holds that he acted on secret instructions from Polk, as does Richard R. Stenberg, "Polk and Frémont, 1845–1846," *Pacific Historical Review,* VII (1938), 211–227. More convincing is the opposite conclusion reached by George Tays, "Frémont Had No Secret Instructions," *Pacific Historical Review,* IX (1940), 151–171, and John A. Hussey, "The Origin of the Gillespie Mission," *California Historical Society Quarterly,* XIX (1940), 43–58.

A colorful contemporary account of the Bear Flag Revolt, written by a participant, is Simeon Ide, *A Biographical Sketch of the Life of William B. Ide* (n.p., 1880; repr., Oakland, Calif., 1944); the career of Ide's principal antagonist is described in Myrtle M. McKittrick, *Vallejo, Son of California* (Portland, Ore., 1944). Comments of observers have been collected in Oscar Lewis (ed.), *California in 1846, Described in Letters from Thomas O. Larkin, "The Farthest West," E. M. Kern, and "Justice"* (San Francisco, 1934).

The West in the Mexican War

The standard history of the Mexican War is Justin H. Smith, *The War with Mexico* (2 vols., New York, 1919); such later histories as Robert S. Henry, *The Story of the Mexican War* (New York, 1950), add little save readability. Eugene I. McCormac, *James K. Polk: A Political Biography* (Berkeley, 1922), is standard, as is the basic document for the period, Milo M. Quaife (ed.), *The Diary of James K. Polk During His Presidency, 1845 to 1849* (4 vols., New York, 1910). The best biographical studies of the leading military figures are Brainerd Dyer, *Zachary Taylor* (Baton Rouge, 1946); Charles W. Elliott, *Winfield Scott: The Soldier and the Man* (New York, 1937); and Wilfred H. Callcott, *Santa Anna. The Story of an Enigma Who Once Was Mexico* (Norman, Okla., 1936).

An invaluable history of Kearny's "Army of the West" is the introduction to Ralph P. Bieber (ed.), *Journal of a Soldier under Kearny and Doniphan, 1846–1847* (Southwest Historical Series, III, Glendale, Calif., 1935), containing the diary of George R. Gibson. Other diaries of the campaign are in Ralph P. Bieber (ed.), *Marching with the Army of the West, 1846–1848* (Southwest Historical series, IV, Glendale, Calif., 1936), and Ross Calvin (ed.), *Lieutenant Emory Reports* (Albuquerque, 1951). Three additional firsthand accounts are John S. Griffin, *A Doctor Comes to California. The Diary of John S. Griffin, Assistant Surgeon with Kearny's Dragoons, 1846–1847* (San Francisco, 1943); Philip St. George Cooke, *Conquest of New Mexico and California* (New York, 1878); and Jacob S. Robinson, *Sketches of the Great West. A Journal of the Santa-Fé Expedition* (Portsmouth, N.H., 1848; repr., Princeton, 1932). The Emory, Griffin, and Cooke accounts also describe the march from Santa Fe to California as do Ralph B. Bieber (ed.), *Exploring Southwestern Trails, 1846–1854* (Southwest Historical Series, VII, Glendale, Calif., 1938), and Frank A. Golden (ed.), *The March of the Mormon Battalion from Council Bluffs to California; taken from the Journal of Henry Standage* (New York, 1928). The most reliable history of the Mormon Battalion is Daniel Tyler, *A Concise History of the Mormon Battalion in the Mexican War* (Salt Lake City, 1881).

Among the fullest of the numerous journals kept by members of the Doniphan expedition is John T. Hughes, *Doniphan's Expedition; Containing an Account of the Conquest of New Mexico* (Cincinnati, 1847; repr., Washington, 1914). Others are William H. Richardson, *Journal of William H. Richardson, a Private Soldier in Col. Doniphan's Command* (Baltimore, 1847); Frank S. Edwards, *A Campaign in New Mexico with Colonel Doniphan* (Philadelphia, 1847); and Adolphus Wislizenus, *Memoir of a Tour to Northern Mexico, Connected with Col. Doniphan's Expedition, in 1846 and 1847* (Washington, 1848). William E. Connelley, *Doniphan's Expedition and the Conquest of New Mexico and California* (Topeka, 1907), reproduces many documents and also tells the story of the expedition.

The diplomacy of the war and peace is described in Hunter Miller (ed.), *Treaties and Other International Acts of the United States of America, 1776–1863* (8 vols., Washington, 1931–48), V, 207–428, although the older account, Jesse S. Reeves, *American Diplomacy under Tyler and Polk* (Baltimore, 1907), is still of use. Two scholarly studies of the Trist mission are Louis M. Sears, "Nicholas P. Trist, A Diplomat with Ideals," *Mississippi Valley Historical Review*, XI (1924), 85–98, and Robert A. Brent, "Nicholas P. Trist and the Treaty of Guadalupe Hidalgo," *Southwestern Historical Quarterly*, LVII (1945), 454–474. The "All Mexico movement" is described in John D. P. Fuller, *The Movement for the Acquisition of All Mexico, 1846–1848* (Baltimore, 1936).

Mormons Move Westward

The most satisfactory history of the founding of Mormon settlements in Utah is Nels Anderson, *Desert Saints: The Mormon Frontier in Utah*

(Chicago, 1942), although additional details may be gleaned from the voluminous work by Brigham H. Roberts, *A Comprehensive History of the Church of Jesus Christ of Latter-Day Saints* (6 vols., Salt Lake City, 1930). The outstanding biographies of the Mormon leaders are Fawn M. Brodie, *No Man Knows My History. The Life Story of Joseph Smith* (New York, 1945), and Preston Nibley, *Brigham Young, the Man and His Work* (Salt Lake City, 1936). The latter is strongly biased in favor of Young.

The persecutions in Missouri are best described in Rollin J. Britton, "Early Days on Grand River and the Mormon War," *Missouri Historical Review,* XIII (1919), 112–134; XIV (1920), 459–473; while Jacob Van der Zee, "The Mormon Trails in Iowa," *Iowa Journal of History and Politics,* XII (1914), 3–16, is still the most satisfactory account of the migration across Iowa. Life in Winter Quarters is the theme of E. Widstoe Shumway, "Winter Quarters, Nebraska, 1846–1848," *Nebraska History,* XXXV (1954), 115–125. Charles Kelly (ed.), *Journals of John D. Lee, 1846–47 and 1859* (Salt Lake City, 1938), is a contemporary account.

The most complete diary of the 1847 migration to Utah is William Clayton, *William Clayton's Journal* (Salt Lake City, 1921), although Appleton M. Harmon, *Appleton Milo Harmon Goes West* (Berkeley, 1946), is also thorough. Other valuable journals of this migration are Howard R. Egan, *Pioneering the West, 1846 to 1878; Major Howard Egan's Diary* (Richmond, Utah, 1917); Matthias F. Cowley (ed.), *Wilford Woodruff, Fourth President of the Church of Jesus Christ of Latter-Day Saints. History of His Life and Labors as Recorded in His Daily Journals* (Salt Lake City, 1909); and Orson F. Whitney (ed.), *Life of Heber C. Kimball, an Apostle* (Salt Lake City, 1888). Reminiscences that are especially valuable include Parley P. Pratt, *The Autobiography of Parley Parker Pratt* (New York, 1874); Delila G. Hughes, *The Life of Archibald Gardner, Pioneer of 1847* (West Jordan, Utah, 1939), which reprints Gardner's memoirs; and John R. Young, *Memoirs of John R. Young, Utah Pioneer of 1847* (Salt Lake City, 1920). Two useful biographies are John H. Evans, *Charles Coulson Rich, Pioneer Builder of the West* (New York, 1936), and Reva Stanley, *A Biography of Parley P. Pratt; the Archer of Paradise* (Caldwell, Ida., 1937).

The development of Mormon civilization in Utah is treated in the various histories of the state, of which the most complete is Andrew L. Neff, *History of Utah, 1847–1869* (Salt Lake City, 1940); useful also is the collection of documents in J. Cecil Alter, *Utah, the Storied Domain. A Documentary History of Utah's Eventful Career* (3 vols., Chicago, 1932). More specialized, and hence more valuable, is L. H. Creer, *The Founding of an Empire: The Exploration and Colonization of Utah, 1776–1856* (Salt Lake City, 1947). Milton R. Hunter, *Brigham Young the Colonizer* (Salt Lake City, 1940), is an excellent history of expansion within the Great Basin, and the social structure is surveyed in Ephraim E. Ericksen, *The Psychological and Ethical*

Aspects of Mormon Group Life (Chicago, 1922), and especially William J. McNiff, *Heaven on Earth: A Planned Mormon Society* (Oxford, Ohio, 1940). Economic beginnings are the theme of Levi E. Young, *The Founding of Utah* (New York, 1923). Travelers who left particularly full descriptions of Mormon life include Richard F. Burton, *The City of the Saints* (London, 1861); William Chandless, *A Visit to Salt Lake* (London, 1857); Horace Greeley, *An Overland Journey, from New York to San Francisco, in the Summer of 1859* (New York, 1860); John W. Gunnison, *The Mormons, or Latter-Day Saints, in the Valley of the Great Salt Lake* (Philadelphia, 1852); Jules Remy and Julius Brenchley, *A Journey to Great Salt Lake* (2 vols., London, 1861); and J. Howard Stansbury, *An Expedition to the Valley of the Great Salt Lake of Utah* (Philadelphia, 1852).

An excellent survey of the relations between Mormons and the federal government is Leland H. Creer, *Utah and the Nation* (Seattle, 1929). Dale L. Morgan, "The State of Deseret," *Utah Historical Quarterly*, VIII (1940), 65–251, is a thorough account of governmental beginnings. Juanita Brooks, *The Mountain Meadows Massacre* (Stanford, 1950), is scholarly and objective, and the atmosphere of those tense days is reflected in John D. Lee, *Mormonism Unveiled; or the Life and Confessions of the Late Mormon Bishop, John D. Lee* (St. Louis, 1877), which contains the confession of the leader of the Mormons in the massacre. No satisfactory book on the "Utah War" exists; E. Cecil McGavin, *U. S. Soldiers Invade Utah* (Boston, 1937), is a jumbled collection of antiquarian jottings.

The California Gold Rush

John W. Caughey, *Gold Is the Cornerstone* (Berkeley, 1948), and Rodman W. Paul, *California Gold: The Beginning of Mining in the Far West* (Cambridge, 1947), are readable and scholarly works. Papers dealing with all aspects of the rush are collected in John W. Caughey (ed.), *Rushing for Gold* (Berkeley, 1949), and another useful survey is Owen C. Coy, *Gold Days* (Los Angeles, 1929). A similar collection of papers describing the first discovery is in *California Gold Discovery: Centennial Papers of the Time, the Site and Artifacts* (San Francisco, 1947). Briefer is the chatty biography of the discoverer, George F. Parsons, *The Life and Adventures of James W. Marshall; the Discoverer of Gold in California* (San Francisco, 1870; repr., San Francisco, 1935). Ralph P. Bieber, "California Gold Mania," *Mississippi Valley Historical Review*, XXV (1948), 3–28, is a valuable account of the spread of the gold fever to the East.

Owen C. Coy, *The Great Trek* (Los Angeles, 1931), describes the rush of the forty-niners, and Archer B. Hulbert, *Forty-Niners* (Boston, 1931), is a synthetic diary that captures the atmosphere successfully. Collections of letters and diaries originating on the overland trails have been assembled in Walker D. Wyman (ed.), *California Emigrant Letters* (New York, 1952), and Valeska Bari (ed.), *The Course of Empire* (New York, 1931). The standard histories of the sea routes to the gold fields are John H. Kemble, *The Panama Route, 1848–1869* (Berkeley, 1943), and Raymond A. Rydell, *Cape Horn to the Pacific: The Rise and Decline of an Ocean Highway* (Berkeley, 1952). A convenient collection of journals kept on these sea voyages is John E. Pomfret (ed.), *California Gold Rush Voyages, 1848–1849: Three Original Narratives* (San Marino, Calif., 1954).

No history of the overland trails has been written, although the introduction to David M. Potter (ed.), *Trail to California: The Overland Journal of Vincent Geiger and Wakeman Bryarly* (New Haven, 1945), is general enough to be of great value. More than one hundred diaries of miners following the Central Route in 1849 have been discovered, and some seventy more for the 1850 migration. Among the fullest of these are J. Goldsborough Bruff, *Gold Rush: The Journals, Drawings, and Other Papers of J. Goldsborough Bruff, Captain, Washington City and California Mining Association, April 2, 1849–July 20, 1851* (2 vols., New York, 1944); William G. Johnston, *Experiences of a Forty-Niner* (Pittsburgh, 1892); and Madison B. Moorman, *The Journal of Madison Berryman Moorman, 1850–1851* (San Francisco, 1948). Documents relating to emigrants who branched from the main trail to enter southern California are collected in LeRoy R. Hafen and Ann W. Hafen (eds.), *Journals of Forty-Niners, Salt Lake to Los Angeles* (*The Far West and the Rockies Historical Series,* II, Glendale, Calif., 1954).

An excellent description of travel over the southern trails is in Ralph P. Bieber (ed.), *Southern Trails to California in 1849* (Southwest Historical Series, V, Glendale, Calif., 1937). The most complete diary of the Santa Fe route is H. M. T. Powell, *The Santa Fé Trail to California, 1848–1852* (San Francisco, 1931); that for the El Paso route, Robert Eccleston, *Overland to California on the Southwestern Trail, 1849* (Berkeley, 1950). This trail is described in Mabelle E. Martin, "California Emigrant Roads through Texas," *Southwestern Historical Quarterly,* XVIII (1925), 287–301, and the trail across Mexico in Glenn S. Dumke, "Across Mexico in '49," *Pacific Historical Review,* XVIII (1949), 33–44. One of the better diaries of the Mexican route is W. B. George Evans, *Mexican Gold Trail: The Journal of a Forty-Niner* (San Marino, Calif., 1945).

Life in the mining districts is popularly described in Joseph H. Jackson, *Anybody's Gold. The Story of California's Mining Towns* (New York, 1941), and in the reminiscences and diaries of numerous miners or travelers. Among the fullest of the diaries are E. Gould Buffum, *Six Months in the Gold Mines* (Philadelphia, 1850); John Steele, *In Camp and Cabin. Mining Life and Adventure in California during 1850 and Later* (Lodi, Wis., 1901; repr., Chicago, 1928); and Daniel B. Woods, *Sixteen Months at the Gold Diggings* (New York, 1851). The fullest travel account is Bayard Taylor, *Eldorado, or, Adventures in the Path of Empire* (2 vols., London, 1850, repr., New York, 1949).

The Miners' Frontier Moves Eastward

The general histories of mining during this period are journalistic and valueless. William J. Trimble, *The Mining Advance into the Inland Empire* (Madison, Wis., 1914), is still the only satisfactory treatment of developments in the Northwest. The Fraser River rush also lacks a historian, although the introduction in Frederick W. Howay (ed.), *The Early History of the Fraser River Mines* (Victoria, B.C., 1926), reveals the possibilities of the subject. Additional information is in Walter N. Sage, *Sir James Douglas and British Columbia* (Toronto, 1930), and Donald Sage, "Gold Rush Days on the Fraser River," *Pacific Northwest Quarterly*, XLIV (1953), 161–165. An older work, William C. Hazlitt, *British Columbia and Vancouver Island* (London, 1858), reproduces some of the documents. The Cariboo rush is described by an observer in William C. Hazlitt, *The Great Gold Fields of Cariboo* (London, 1862).

A brief discussion of Arizona mining is in Rufus K. Wyllys, *Arizona* (Phoenix, 1950), and Clement Eaton, "Frontier Life in Southern Arizona, 1858–1861," *Southwestern Historical Quarterly*, XXXVI (1933), 173–192, describes social conditions. More information can be gleaned from the reminiscences of one of the miners, Sylvester Mowry, *Arizona and Sonora: the Geography, History, and Resources of the Silver Region of North America* (3rd ed., New York, 1864), and from a travel account, J. Ross Browne, *Adventures in the Apache Country; a Tour through Arizona and Sonora* (New York, 1869).

A modern study of Nevada mining is Grant H. Smith, *The History of the Comstock Lode, 1850–1920* (Reno, 1943), while the briefer account in Effie M. Mack, *Nevada. A History of the State from the Earliest Times through the Civil War* (Glendale, Calif., 1936), is scholarly. Early histories valuable for their detail and the documents reproduced are Myron Angel, *History of Nevada* (Oakland, Calif., 1881), and Eliot Lord, *Comstock Mines and Miners* (Washington, 1883). By far the best account by a contemporary is Dan De Quille, *The Big Bonanza: An Authentic Account of the Discovery, History, and Working of the World-Renowned Comstock Lode of Nevada* (San Francisco, 1876; repr., New York, 1947).

The story of Colorado mining is briefly told in LeRoy R. Hafen, (ed.), *Colorado and Its People* (4 vols., New York, 1948), and documents are reproduced in Nolie Mumey (ed.), *History of the Early Settlements of Denver, 1599–1860* (Glendale, Calif., 1942). Jerome C. Smiley, *History of Denver* (Denver, 1901), also reprints many contemporary items. More essential are the collections edited for the Southwest Historical Series by LeRoy

R. Hafen: *Pike's Peak Gold Rush Guidebooks of 1859* (IX, Glendale, Calif., 1941), *Colorado Gold Rush; Contemporary Letters and Reports, 1858–1859* (X, Glendale, Calif., 1941), and *Overland Routes to the Gold Fields, 1859, from Contemporary Diaries* (XI, Glendale, Calif., 1942). Their introductions provide the best history of the rush yet written. In addition to numerous "letters from the mines" printed in historical journals, three travel accounts are especially valuable in describing mining conditions: Henry Villard, *The Past and Present of the Pike's Peak Gold Region* (St. Louis, 1860; repr., Princeton, 1932); Horace Greeley, *An Overland Journey, from New York to San Francisco, in the Summer of 1859* (New York, 1860); and Albert D. Richardson, *Beyond the Mississippi* (Hartford, 1867).

Two excellent articles describing the evolution of mining-camp government are Percy S. Fritz, "The Constitution and Laws of Early Mining Districts— in Boulder County, Colorado," *Colorado University Studies*, XXI (Boulder, 1934), 127–148, and Thomas M. Marshall, "The Miners' Laws of Colorado," *American Historical Review*, XXV (1920), 426–439. Documents from nineteen mining districts are reproduced in Thomas M. Marshall (ed.), *Early Records of Gilpin County, Colorado, 1859–1861* (Boulder, 1920).

The Reuniting of East and West

The only general history of western transportation is Oscar O. Winther, *Via Western Express & Stagecoach* (Stanford 1945), which is popularly written but scholarly. W. Turrentine Jackson, *Wagon Roads West* (Berkeley, 1953), describes road building. Oscar O. Winther admirably describes stagecoaching in California and Oregon in *Express and Stagecoach Days in California* (Stanford, 1936), and *The Old Oregon Country. A History of Frontier Trade, Transportation, and Travel* (Stanford, 1950). Ernest A. Wiltsee, *The Pioneer Miner and Pack Mule Express* (San Francisco, 1931), deals with the origins of the express business in California, and the best of the many studies of the concern that eventually monopolized that business is Edward Hungerford, *Wells Fargo: Advancing the American Frontier* (New York, 1949).

The standard history of freighting is Raymond W. Settle and Mary L. Settle, *Empire on Wheels* (Stanford, 1939), which is actually a history of the firm of Russell, Majors & Waddell. Of the few reminiscences of freighters that have survived, the best is Charles R. Morehead, Jr., "Personal Recollections," in William E. Connelley, *Doniphan's Expedition and the Conquest of New Mexico and California* (Topeka, 1907). Alexander Majors, *Seventy Years on the Frontier* (Chicago, 1893), is disappointingly brief.

LeRoy R. Hafen, *The Overland Mail, 1849–1869* (Cleveland, 1926), is the definitive work on this subject. More detailed is the remarkable history by Roscoe P. Conkling and Margaret B. Conkling, *The Butterfield Overland Mail, 1858–1869* (3 vols., Glendale, Calif., 1947). Two excellent accounts of travel in the Butterfield coaches are Waterman L. Ormsby, *The Butterfield Overland Mail* (San Marino, Calif., 1942), and William Tallack, *The California Overland Express, the Longest Stage-Ride in the World* (Los Angeles, 1935). Both are reprinted in Walter B. Lang (ed.), *The First Overland Mail: Butterfield Trail* (n.p., 1940), which also contains accounts by other passengers. The most usable reminiscences left by travelers are Joseph C. Tucker, *To the Golden Goal and Other Sketches* (San Francisco, 1895), and H. D. Barrow, "A Two Thousand Mile Stage Ride," *Annual Publication of the Historical Society of Southern California, 1896* (Los Angeles, 1897), 40–44.

Mail service over the Central Route is described in scholarly articles by George A. Root and R. K. Hickman, "Pike's Peak Express Companies: Solomon and Republican Routes," *Kansas Historical Quarterly,* XIII (1944), 163–195, 211–242; and "Pike's Peak Express Companies: The Platte Route," *Kansas Historical Quarterly,* XIII (1945), 485–526; XIV (1946), 36–92. The best of the reminiscences of those serving on this route are those of Frank A. Root, in Frank A. Root and William E. Connelley, *The Overland Stage to California* (Topeka, 1901), and of Hiram S. Rumfield, in Archer B. Hulbert (ed.), "Letters of an Overland Mail Agent in Utah," *American Antiquarian Society Proceedings,* n.s., XXXVIII, Pt. 2 (1929), 227–302. Of travelers' accounts of the journey, the classic is Samuel L. Clemens, *Roughing It* (Hartford, 1872). Also of value are Albert D. Richardson, *Beyond the Mississippi* (Hartford, 1867); Horace Greeley, *An Overland Journey, from New York to San Francisco, in the Summer of 1859* (New York, 1860); Richard F. Burton, *The City of the Saints* (New York, 1861); Samuel Bowles, *Across the Continent* (Springfield, Mass., 1865); and Demas Barnes, *From the Atlantic to the Pacific Overland* (New York, 1866).

The only scholarly history of the Pony Express is Raymond W. Settle and Mary L. Settle, *Saddles and Spurs. The Pony Express Saga* (Harrisburg, Pa., 1955). The best of the many popular histories is Arthur Chapman, *The Pony Express: the Record of a Romantic Adventure in Business* (New York, 1932), although William L. Visscher, *A Thrilling and Truthful History of the Pony Express* (Chicago, 1908), reproduces many documents. Anecdotes describing the adventures of riders are collected in Henry Inman and William F. Cody, *The Great Salt Lake Trail* (New York, 1908), and Howard R. Driggs, *The Pony Express Goes Through* (New York, 1935). The standard history of the telegraph is Robert L. Thompson, *Wiring a Continent. The History of the Telegraph Industry in the United States, 1832–1866* (Princeton, 1947). The final phases of stagecoaching are described in J. V. Frederick, *Ben Holladay: The Stagecoach King* (Glendale, Calif., 1940).

Index

Set in Intertype Baskerville
Format by D. F. Bradley
Manufactured by The Haddon Craftsmen, Inc.
Published by HARPER & BROTHERS, *New York*

1.75
55
8 75
8 75 .25
9 5 .25

Date Due

JAN 1 4 '61			
NOV 13 '61			
MAY 1 5 1962			
MAY 29 1962			
NOV. 12			
DEC. 19			
MAY 29			
MAY 4			
MAY 1 8			
DEC 12			
MAY 3			
MAY 2 1			
ℬ	PRINTED	IN U. S. A.	